best *Food* WRITING 2008

best *Food* WRITING
2008

Edited by

HOLLY HUGHES

Da Capo
LIFE
LONG

A Member of the Perseus Books Group

Copyright © 2008 by Holly Hughes

Pages 375–377 constitute an extension of the copyright page.
All rights reserved. No part of this publication may be reproduced, stored in a retrieval system, or transmitted, in any form or by any means, electronic, mechanical, photocopying, recording, or otherwise, without the prior written permission of the publisher. Printed in the United States of America. For information, address Da Capo Press, 11 Cambridge Center, Cambridge, MA 02142.

Cataloging-in-Publication data for this book is available from the Library of Congress.

ISBN: 978-0-7382-1251-7

Published by Da Capo Press
A Member of the Perseus Books Group
www.dacapopress.com

Note: The information in this book is true and complete to the best of our knowledge. This book is intended only as an informative guide for those wishing to know more about health issues. In no way is this book intended to replace, countermand, or conflict with the advice given to you by your own physician. The ultimate decision concerning care should be made between you and your doctor. We strongly recommend you follow his or her advice. Information in this book is general and is offered with no guarantees on the part of the authors or Da Capo Press. The authors and publisher disclaim all liability in connection with the use of this book. The names and identifying details of people associated with events described in this book have been changed. Any similarity to actual persons is coincidental.

Da Capo Press books are available at special discounts for bulk purchases in the U.S. by corporations, institutions, and other organizations. For more information, please contact the Special Markets Department at the Perseus Books Group, 2300 Chestnut Street, Suite 200, Philadelphia, PA, 19103, or call (800) 810-4145, extension 5000, or e-mail special.markets@perseusbooks.com.

10 9 8 7 6 5 4 3 2 1

CONTENTS

TECHNIQUE

STOCKING THE PANTRY

THE MEAT OF THE MATTER

Personal Tastes

INTRODUCTION

by Holly Hughes

Food ought to be the simplest thing in the world. Since when did it become so politicized?

It used to be that being a food person put you into a special little club—a club only the most delightful members could join. This year, all that changed. How often lately have I found myself at a restaurant or at a dinner party gloomily debating how to fix our broken food supply system with people I don't normally consider foodies? Everyone has an opinion; no one seems to have a solution—not yet, at least.

Last year, thanks to Michael Pollan's *The Omnivore's Dilemma*, I'd learned all about how dependent America's food supply is on corn. Even if you don't buy Pollan's conspiracy theories about how the situation evolved, he makes a pretty convincing case for how dangerously hooked on corn our nation is. Then wham bang, Pollan's dire predictions came true, seemingly overnight—the corn apparently vanished, eaten up by ethanol (or so certain pundits claim), and we tipped over into a global food crisis.

I have to admit to being skeptical. How can ethanol use have skyrocketed that much in one year, when so few people I know use it? But it does seem tragically ironic if, by trying to save the planet—by reducing our dependence on petroleum—we've stressed an already precarious global food system to the point where prices have soared for even basic commodities like milk. And that's just in the United States; in countries where starvation is just one bad harvest away, the situation is even bleaker.

It's telling that the language experts at the *New Oxford American Dictionary* named *locavore* their New Word of the Year. Everybody I meet lately claims to be jumping on the "eat locally" bandwagon and erasing their carbon footprint by shopping at farmer's markets.

In practice, however, it may not be so easy to carry out (check out Mark Anderson's experiment on page 36 and Rick Nichol's thoughtful column on page 277). I'm sure I'm not the only person who doesn't remember until 1:30 on Friday afternoon that Friday is the day for our nearest greenmarket. By the time I get there, the best farmers have already packed up and gone. And just when I get primed to buy a share in our local CSA (community supported agriculture), I notice that this week's haul is a bulging bag of rutabagas and turnips, which nobody else in my family would *touch*. Still, I've just discovered a new grocery store that has a whole section of the produce aisle featuring food from local farms. That's got to be good for both farmers and food shoppers. That store will be getting more of my business, I can tell you.

Meanwhile, Michael Pollan's off on a new tangent with this year's book, *In Defense of Food* (page 2), a blanket indictment of all the additives and processing that our food goes through, even when it's supposedly "fortifying" the food or making it healthier. (Sugar-free, fat-free, fiber-added, vitamin-enhanced, you name it.) After reading Pollan's book, a walk through an ordinary grocery store began to feel to me like a visit to a house of horrors. I realized that I'm just as guilty as anybody of falling into the trap of using food as medicine—puritanically obsessing over the health value of what I eat, instead of just enjoying whatever tastes good.

Here in New York City, our mayor has decreed that fast-food restaurants list the calories of the food they serve. In France, of all countries, starting in January 2008, smoking was banned from restaurants. In Chicago, the city council forbid restaurants to serve foie gras on the grounds that force-feeding is cruel to geese (you can just imagine the mocking outcry—including Peter Sagal's satirical blast on page 13–which eventually overturned that measure). It's getting harder and harder to go out for a relaxing meal without the government passing judgment.

Yet somehow, with all this intervention, our food system has never seemed less safe. Last year, it was spinach tainted with *e. coli*; this year, it was tomatoes, which at one point seemed to be causing outbreaks of salmonella poisoning around the country—*spinach and tomatoes,* two of the healthiest foods around. And even though it now seems that jalapeño peppers were the salmonella culprit, that doesn't change the underlying scenario: Things have come to a pretty sad pass when you have to worry about eating fresh produce. See Sona Pai's piece (page 291) about the battle over importing mangoes, Ben Paynter's article on cloned meats (page 25), and Sarah DiGregorio's profile of an artisan salami-maker's battle with regulators (page 16). Policing food sources is getting to be downright schizophrenic.

I've been grossed out for years by accounts of how cattle and poultry are raised in this country, but I hear the dialogue between vegetarians and carnivores getting more strident of late—and not just in my own household. After catering to the no-red-meat demands of two of my kids, I actually wound up with acute anemia for a while this spring (there went my intentions to stop treating food as medicine). With my heightened sensitivity, it seemed every magazine I opened had another defiant article about eating meat. It wasn't just my imagination, there really were an extraordinary number of carnivorous essays, as well as three entire books written in defense of meat-eating. I began to wonder if we shouldn't rename this collection *Best Meat Writing 2008.*

Though I've devoted an entire section to the topic (The Meat of the Matter, page 298–323), you'll also find meat popping up in other sections. There's Elaine Cicora's account of a pig roast (page 111), Guy Saddy's attempt to dry-age his own steaks (page 262), Kathleen Purvis's recipe for pork belly (page 265), Jill Silva's look at heirloom poultry (page 282), and John Kessler's essay on buying humanely-raised beef (page 288). There are even two articles on lapsed vegetarians by Christine Lennon (page 46) and Khyber Oser (page 326). I swear, I'm not stacking the deck; I'd have included pro-vegetarian essays too, if I'd found ones that hit similar heights of wit, intelligence, and passion. This year, though, the carnivores seemed to dominate the zeitgeist.

Along with that came a flood of articles fretting over the economics of the restaurant business. See the reports by Jessica Battliana (page 115), Robb Walsh (page 122), Brett Anderson (page 131), Andrea Weigl (page 146), and Laura Taxel (page 196). It even affects the high-end chefs whom Larrissa MacFarquhar (page 169) and Lolis Eric Elie (page 190) wrote about. Tough times, indeed.

That's when I turn to articles that remind me of the comforting power of food. I know I can always trust writers like Alice Waters (page 233), Scott Peacock (page 241), Bethany Jean Clement (page 87), Molly O'Neill (page 272), Sara Roahen (page 353), and John Thorne (page 336) to reaffirm my faith in why cooking matters. Truth is, we all still believe in it—that's why folks feel so betrayed when politics cast food as The Enemy. The sooner we get that pendulum to swing back, the better.

And now, excuse me, I'm going to go make a soothing pot of stew. With *meat* in it.

Food Fights

In Defense of Food

Michael Pollan

from *In Defense of Food: An Eater's Manifesto*

A fascinating sidebar to Pollan's 2006 best seller *The Omni-vore's Dilemma*, this new book turns a searchlight onto the politics of America's eating habits—and finds them in dire need of revision.

The first time I heard the advice to "just eat food" it was in a speech by Joan Gussow, and it completely baffled me. Of course you should eat food—what else is there to eat? But Gussow, who grows much of her own food on a flood-prone fin-ger of land jutting into the Hudson River, refuses to dignify most of the products for sale in the supermarket with that title. "In the thirty-four years I've been in the field of nutrition," she said in the same speech, "I have watched real food disappear from large areas of the supermarket and from much of the rest of the eating world." Taking food's place on the shelves has been an unending stream of foodlike substitutes, some seventeen thousand new ones every year—"products constructed largely around commerce and hope, supported by frighteningly little actual knowledge." Ordi-nary food is still out there, however, still being grown and even occasionally sold in the supermarket, and this ordinary food is what we should eat.

But given our current state of confusion and given the thou-sands of products calling themselves food, this is more easily said than done. So consider these related rules of thumb. Each proposes a different sort of map to the contemporary food landscape, but all should take you to more or less the same place.

Don't eat anything your great-grandmother wouldn't recognize as food. Why your great-grandmother? Because at this point your mother and possibly even your grandmother is as confused as the rest of us; to be safe we need to go back at least a couple of generations, to a time before the advent of most modern foods. So depending on your age (and your grandmother), you may need to go back to your great- or even great-great-grandmother. Some nutritionists recommend going back even further. John Yudkin, a British nutritionist whose early alarms about the dangers of refined carbohydrates were overlooked in the 1960s and 1970s, once advised, "Just don't eat anything your Neolithic ancestors wouldn't have recognized and you'll be ok."

What would shopping this way mean in the supermarket? Well, imagine your great-grandmother at your side as you roll down the aisles. You're standing together in front of the dairy case. She picks up a package of Go-Gurt Portable Yogurt tubes—and has no idea what this could possibly be. Is it a food or a toothpaste? And how, exactly, do you introduce it into your body? You could tell her it's just yogurt in a squirtable form, yet if she read the ingredients label she would have every reason to doubt that that was in fact the case. Sure, there's some yogurt in there, but there are also a dozen other things that aren't remotely yogurtlike, ingredients she would probably fail to recognize as foods of any kind, including high-fructose corn syrup, modified corn starch, kosher gelatin, carrageenan, tricalcium phosphate, natural and artificial flavors, vitamins, and so forth. (And there's a whole other list of ingredients for the "berry bubblegum bash" flavoring, containing everything but berries or bubblegum.) How did yogurt, which in your great-grandmother's day consisted simply of milk inoculated with a bacterial culture, ever get to be so complicated? Is a product like Go-Gurt Portable Yogurt still a whole food? A food of any kind? Or is it just a food product?

There are in fact hundreds of foodish products in the supermarket that your ancestors simply wouldn't recognize as food: breakfast

cereal bars transected by bright white veins representing, but in reality having nothing to do with, milk; "protein waters" and
"nondairy creamer"; cheeselike food-stuffs equally innocent of any
bovine contribution; cakelike cylinders (with creamlike fillings)
called Twinkies that never grow stale. *Don't eat anything incapable of
rotting* is another personal policy you might consider adopting.

There are many reasons to avoid eating such complicated food
products beyond the various chemical additives and corn and soy
derivatives they contain. One of the problems with the products of
food science is that, as Joan Gussow has pointed out, they lie to
your body; their artificial colors and flavors and synthetic sweeten-
ers and novel fats confound the senses we rely on to assess new
foods and prepare our bodies to deal with them. Foods that lie
leave us with little choice but to eat by the numbers, consulting labels rather than our senses.

It's true that foods have long been processed in order to preserve them, as when we pickle or ferment or smoke, but industrial
processing aims to do much more than extend shelf life. Today
foods are processed in ways specifically designed to sell us more
food by pushing our evolutionary buttons—our inborn preferences for sweetness and fat and salt. These qualities are difficult to
find in nature but cheap and easy for the food scientist to deploy,
with the result that processing induces us to consume much more
of these ecological rarities than is good for us. "Tastes great, less
filling!" could be the motto for most processed foods, which are far
more energy dense than most whole foods: They contain much
less water, fiber, and micronutrients, and generally much more
sugar and fat, making them at the same time, to coin a marketing
slogan, "More fattening, less nutritious!"

The great-grandma rule will help keep many of these products
out of your cart. But not all of them. Because thanks to the FDA's
willingness, post-1973, to let food makers freely alter the identify of
"traditional foods that everyone knows" without having to call them
imitations, your great-grandmother could easily be fooled into
thinking that that loaf of bread or wedge of cheese is in fact a loaf of
bread or a wedge of cheese. This is why we need a slightly more detailed personal policy to capture these imitation foods; to wit:

AVOID FOOD PRODUCTS containing ingredients that are a) unfamiliar, b) unpronounceable, c) more than five in number, or that include d) high-fructose corn syrup. None of these characteristics, not even the last one, is necessarily harmful in and of itself, but all of them are reliable markers for foods that have been highly processed to the point where they may no longer be what they purport to be. They have crossed over from foods to food products.

Consider a loaf of bread, one of the "traditional foods that everyone knows" specifically singled out for protection in the 1938 imitation rule. As your grandmother could tell you, bread is traditionally made using a remarkably small number of familiar ingredients: flour, yeast, water, and a pinch of salt will do it. But industrial bread—even industrial whole grain bread—has become a far more complicated product of modern food science (not to mention commerce and hope). Here's the complete ingredients list for Sara Lee's Soft & Smooth Whole Grain White Bread. (Wait a minute—isn't "Whole Grain White Bread" a contradiction in terms? Evidently not anymore.)

Enriched bleached flour [wheat flour, malted barley flour, niacin, iron, thiamin mononitrate (vitamin B$_1$), riboflavin (vitamin B$_2$), folic acid], water, whole grains [whole wheat flour, brown rice flour (rice flour, rice bran)], high fructose corn syrup [*hello!*], whey, wheat gluten, yeast, cellulose. Contains 2% or less of each of the following: honey, calcium sulfate, vegetable oil (soybean and/or cottonseed oils), salt, butter (cream, salt), dough conditioners (may contain one or more of the following: mono- and diglycerides, ethoxylated mono- and diglycerides, ascorbic acid, enzymes, azodicarbonamide), guar gum, calcium propionate (preservative), distilled vinegar, yeast nutrients (monocalcium phosphate, calcium sulfate, ammonium sulfate), corn starch, natural flavor, betacarotene (color), vitamin D$_3$, soy lecithin, soy flour.

There are many things you could say about this intricate loaf of "bread," but note first that even if it managed to slip by your great-grandmother (because it is a loaf of bread, or at least is called one and strongly resembles one), the product fails every test proposed under rule number two: It's got unfamiliar ingredients (monoglyc-erides I've heard of before, but ethoxylated monoglycerides?); un-pronounceable ingredients (try "azodicarbonamide"); it exceeds the maximum of five ingredients (by roughly thirty-six); and it contains high-fructose corn syrup. Sorry, Sara Lee, but your Soft & Smooth Whole Grain White Bread is not food and if not for the indulgence of the FDA could not even be labeled "bread."

Sara Lee's Soft & Smooth Whole Grain White Bread could serve as a monument to the age of nutritionism. It embodies the latest nutritional wisdom from science and government (which in its most recent food pyramid recommends that at least half our consumption of grain come from whole grains) but leavens that wisdom with the commercial recognition that American eaters (and American children in particular) have come to prefer their wheat highly refined—which is to say, cottony soft, snowy white, and exceptionally sweet on the tongue. In its marketing materials, Sara Lee treats this clash of interests as some sort of Gordian knot—it speaks in terms of an ambitious quest to build a "no compromise" loaf—which only the most sophisticated food sci-ence could possibly cut.

And so it has, with the invention of whole grain white bread. Because the small percentage of whole grains in the bread would render it that much less sweet than, say, all-white Wonder Bread— which scarcely waits to be chewed before transforming itself into glucose—the food scientists have added high-fructose corn syrup and honey to make up the difference; to overcome the problematic heft and toothsomeness of a real whole grain bread, they've deployed "dough conditioners," including guar gum and the afore-mentioned azodicarbonamide, to simulate the texture of super-market white bread. By incorporating certain varieties of albino wheat, they've managed to maintain that deathly but apparently appealing Wonder Bread pallor.

Who would have thought Wonder Bread would ever become an ideal of aesthetic and gustatory perfection to which bakers would actually aspire—Sara Lee's Mona Lisa?

Very often food science's efforts to make traditional foods more nutritious make them much more complicated, but not necessarily any better for you. To make dairy products low fat, it's not enough to remove the fat. You then have to go to great lengths to preserve the body or creamy texture by working in all kinds of food additives. In the case of low fat or skim milk, that usually means adding powdered milk. But powdered milk contains oxidized cholesterol, which scientists believe is much worse for your arteries than ordinary cholesterol, so food makers sometimes compensate by adding antioxidants, further complicating what had been a simple one-ingredient whole food. Also, removing the fat makes it that much harder for your body to absorb the fat-soluble vitamins that are one of the reasons to drink milk in the first place.

All this heroic and occasionally counterproductive food science has been undertaken in the name of our health—so that Sara Lee can add to its plastic wrapper the magic words "good source of whole grain" or a food company can ballyhoo the even more magic words "low fat." Which brings us to a related food policy that may at first sound counterintuitive to a health-conscious eater:

AVOID FOOD PRODUCTS that make health claims. For a food product to make health claims on its package it must first *have* a package, so right off the bat it's more likely to be a processed than a whole food. Generally speaking, it is only the big food companies that have the wherewithal to secure FDA-approved health claims for their products and then trumpet them to the world. Recently, however, some of the tonier fruits and nuts have begun boasting about their health-enhancing properties, and there will surely be more as each crop council scrounges together the money to commission its own scientific study. Because all plants contain antioxidants, all these studies are guaranteed to find *something* on which to base a health-oriented marketing campaign.

But for the most part it is the products of food science that make the boldest health claims, and these are often founded on incomplete and often erroneous science—the dubious fruits of nutritionism. Don't forget that trans-fat-rich margarine, one of the first industrial foods to claim it was healthier than the traditional food it replaced, turned out to give people heart attacks. Since that debacle, the FDA, under tremendous pressure from industry, has made it only easier for food companies to make increasingly doubtful health claims, such as the one Frito-Lay now puts on some of its chips—that eating them is somehow good for your heart. If you bother to read the health claims closely (as food marketers make sure consumers seldom do), you will find that there is often considerably less to them than meets the eye.

Consider a recent "qualified" health claim approved by the FDA for (don't laugh) corn oil. ("Qualified" is a whole new category of health claim, introduced in 2002 at the behest of industry.) Corn oil, you may recall, is particularly high in the omega–6 fatty acids we're already consuming far too many of.

> Very limited and preliminary scientific evidence suggests that eating about one tablespoon (16 grams) of corn oil daily may reduce the risk of heart disease due to the unsaturated fat content in corn oil.

The tablespoon is a particularly rich touch, conjuring images of moms administering medicine, or perhaps cod-liver oil, to their children. But what the FDA gives with one hand, it takes away with the other. Here's the small-print "qualification" of this already notably diffident health claim:

> [The] FDA concludes that there is little scientific evidence supporting this claim.

And then to make matters still more perplexing:

> To achieve this possible benefit, corn oil is to replace a similar amount of saturated fat and not increase the total number of calories you eat in a day.

This little masterpiece of pseudoscientific bureaucratese was extracted from the FDA by the manufacturer of Mazola corn oil. It would appear that "qualified" is an official FDA euphemism for "all but meaningless." Though someone might have let the consumer in on this game: The FDA's own research indicates that consumers have no idea what to make of qualified health claims (how would they?), and its rules allow companies to promote the claims pretty much any way they want—they can use really big type for the claim, for example, and then print the disclaimers in teeny-tiny type. No doubt we can look forward to a qualified health claim for high-fructose corn syrup, a tablespoon of which probably does contribute to your health—as long as it replaces a comparable amount of, say, poison in your diet and doesn't increase the total number of calories you eat in a day.

When corn oil and chips and sugary breakfast cereals can all boast being good for your heart, health claims have become hopelessly corrupt. The American Heart Association currently bestows (for a fee) its heart-healthy seal of approval on Lucky Charms, Cocoa Puffs, and Trix cereals, Yoo-hoo lite chocolate drink, and Healthy Choice's Premium Caramel Swirl Ice Cream Sandwich—this at a time when scientists are coming to recognize that dietary sugar probably plays a more important role in heart disease than dietary fat. Meanwhile, the genuinely heart-healthy whole foods in the produce section, lacking the financial and political clout of the packaged goods a few aisles over, are mute. But don't take the silence of the yams as a sign that they have nothing valuable to say about health.

Bogus health claims and food science have made supermarkets particularly treacherous places to shop for real food, which suggests two further rules:

SHOP THE PERIPHERIES of the supermarket and stay out of the middle. Most supermarkets are laid out the same way: Processed food products dominate the center aisles of the store while the cases of ostensibly fresh food—dairy, produce, meat, and fish—line the walls. If you keep to the edges of the store you'll be that much more likely to wind up with real food in your shopping cart. The strategy is not foolproof, however, because things like high-fructose corn syrup have slipped into the dairy case under cover of Go-Gurt and such. So consider a more radical strategy:

GET OUT OF THE SUPERMARKET whenever possible. You won't find *any* high-fructose corn syrup at the farmers' market. You also won't find any elaborately processed food products, any packages with long lists of unpronounceable ingredients or dubious health claims, nothing microwavable, and, perhaps best of all, no old food from far away. What you *will* find are fresh whole foods picked at the peak of their taste and nutritional quality—precisely the kind your great-grandmother, or even your Neolithic ancestors, would easily have recognized as food.

Indeed, the surest way to escape the Western diet is simply to depart the realms it rules: the supermarket, the convenience store, and the fast-food outlet. It is hard to eat badly from the farmers' market, from a CSA box (community-supported agriculture, an increasingly popular scheme in which you subscribe to a farm and receive a weekly box of produce), or from your garden. The number of farmers' markets has more than doubled in the last ten years, to more than four thousand, making it one of the fastest-growing segments of the food marketplace. It is true that most farmers' markets operate only seasonally, and you won't find everything you need there. But buying as much as you can from the farmers' market, or directly from the farm when that's an option, is a simple act with a host of profound consequences for your health as well as for the health of the food chain you've now joined.

When you eat from the farmers' market, you automatically eat food that is in season, which is usually when it is most nutritious. Eating in season also tends to diversify your diet—because you can't buy strawberries or broccoli or potatoes twelve months of the year, you'll find yourself experimenting with other foods when they come into the market. The CSA box does an even better job of forcing you out of your dietary rut because you'll find things in your weekly allotment that you would never buy on your own. Whether it's a rutabaga or an unfamiliar winter squash, the CSA box's contents invariably send you to your cookbooks to figure out what in the world to do with them. Cooking is one of the most important health consequences of buying food from local farmers; for one thing, when you cook at home you seldom find yourself reaching for the ethoxylated diglycerides or high-fructose corn syrup.

To shop at a farmers' market or sign up with a CSA is to join a short food chain and that has several implications for your health. Local produce is typically picked ripe and is fresher than supermarket produce, and for those reasons it should be tastier and more nutritious. As for supermarket organic produce, it too is likely to have come from far away—from the industrial organic farms of California or, increasingly, China.* And while it's true that the organic label guarantees that no synthetic pesticides or fertilizers have been used to produce the food, many, if not most, of the small farms that supply farmers' markets are organic in everything but name. To survive in the farmers' market or CSA economy, a farm will need to be highly diversified, and a diversified farm usually has little need for pesticides; it's the big monocultures that can't survive without them.**

If you're concerned about chemicals in your produce, you can simply ask the farmer at the market how he or she deals with pests and fertility and begin the sort of conversation between producers and consumers that, in the end, is the best guarantee of quality in your food. So many of the problems of the industrial food chain stem from its length and complexity. A wall of ignorance intervenes between consumers and producers, and that wall fosters a certain carelessness on both sides. Farmers can lose sight of the fact that they're growing food for actual eaters rather than for middlemen, and consumers can easily forget that growing good food takes care and hard work. In a long food chain, the story and identity of the food (Who grew it? Where and how was it grown?) disappear into the undifferentiated stream of commodities, so that the only information communicated between consumers and producers is a price. In a short food chain, eaters can make their needs and desires known to the farmer, and farmers can impress on eaters the distinctions between ordinary and exceptional food, and the many reasons why exceptional food is worth what it costs. Food reclaims its story, and some of its nobility, when the person who grew it hands it to you. So here's a subclause to the get-out-of-the-supermarket rule: *Shake the hand that feeds you.*

---

*One recent study found that the average item of organic produce in the supermarket had actually traveled farther from the farm than the average item of conventional produce.

**Wendell Berry put the problem of monoculture with admirable brevity and clarity in his essay "The Pleasures of Eating": "But as scale increases, diversity declines; as diversity declines, so does health; as health declines, the dependence on drugs and chemicals necessarily increases."

As soon as you do, accountability becomes once again a matter of relationships instead of regulation or labeling or legal liability. Food safety didn't become a national or global problem until the industrialization of the food chain attenuated the relationships between food producers and eaters. That was the story Upton Sinclair told about the Beef Trust in 1906, and it's the story unfolding in China today, where the rapid industrialization of the food system is leading to alarming breakdowns in food safety and integrity. Regulation is an imperfect substitute for the accountability, and trust, built into a market in which food producers meet the gaze of eaters and vice versa. Only when we participate in a short food chain are we reminded every week that we are indeed part of a food chain and dependent for our health on its peoples and soils and integrity—on its health.

"Eating is an agricultural act," Wendell Berry famously wrote, by which he meant that we are not just passive consumers of food but cocreators of the systems that feed us. Depending on how we spend them, our food dollars can either go to support a food industry devoted to quantity and convenience and "value" or they can nourish a food chain organized around *values*—values like quality and health. Yes, shopping this way takes more money and effort, but as soon as you begin to treat that expenditure not just as shopping but also as a kind of vote—a vote for health in the largest sense—food no longer seems like the smartest place to economize.

LET THEM EAT PÂTÉ: NOTES FROM THE FOIE GRAS UNDERGROUND

By Peter Sagal

from *Saveur*

Chicago's much-ballyhooed 2007 citywide ban on foie gras
(which has since been rescinded) stirred up diners nation-
wide, pitting animal rights advocates against epicures. Peter
Sagal, host of NPR's *Wait, Wait . . . Don't Tell Me*, waded into
the fray with his usual sharp wit.

In April 2006, Chicago—not Berkeley, not Santa Fe, not
Northampton, Massachusetts—became the first city in the
United States to ban the sale of foie gras. How, in the name of Upton Sinclair, could that have happened? This is a city that grew up,
and grew rich, by being cheerfully cruel to animals on an industrial scale. This is a city with a vast and varied and hungry immigrant population, meaning they're cutting the heads off live ducks
in Chinatown and doing things to the inside of a pig out in the
Polish butcheries on Archer Avenue that you wouldn't wish on,
well, a pig. But a French delicacy of fattened goose liver or duck
liver? That offends our sensibilities? Makes you want to weep for a
once great city, it does. Why, time was, you couldn't claim to have
thrown a real Chicago shindig if you hadn't force-fed some animal
through a metal tube and then butchered it to harvest its distended
organs. Or, if no goose were handy, we'd do it to the guests. And,
dammit, they liked it.

"Our city is better for taking a stance against the cruelty of foie
gras," said Alderman Joe Moore, the city politician behind the
measure.

"This is the silliest ordinance the City Council has ever passed," said Mayor Richard M. Daley.

"What about my hamburger?" said my wife, Beth, who just wanted her hamburger.

Specifically: the $17 hamburger at Sweets & Savories, on Fullerton Avenue, which the menu describes as "Strube Ranch American Kobe beef with foie gras pâté and truffled mayonnaise and toasted brioche roll" and which, when served with a side of duck-fat fries, is the kind of meal God would cook for houseguests if God were a 12-year-old kid.

Seventeen dollars is a lot to pay for hamburger, especially one that does not come with a toy in the bag, but a couple of things you should know are, first, that it is enormous, the size you remember your first Big Mac's being when you finally convinced your parents that you were old enough to graduate from Mc-Nuggets, and, second, that the heat from the beef melts the pâté, just a little bit, so it seems to absorb the truffle mayo above it and then ineluctably swirls into both the beef and the bread, infecting them with glory, the way Agent Smith converted everybody into himself in those awful *Matrix* sequels. The result inspires guttural grunts of pleasure as you realize you must put the burger down, because if you don't, it will fall apart, but instead you take another bite *mmmph mmmph mmmph.*

As Beth says, "It's yummy."

We went down to Sweets & Savories recently, about half a year after the ban went into effect. The restaurant is a converted storefront run by chef-owner David Richards, who is always visible by the stove in the back, cooking exactly what he wants, and what he wants to cook is foie gras, city of Chicago be damned. Or so we hoped.

"We came for the burger," I said to the waiter, trying to adopt the knowing manner of a gentleman knocking on the door of a speakeasy.

"Of course," he said.

"Is it still, you know . . . *the burger?*"

"It comes with all its . . . accessories," he said. It is possible he laid his index finger along the side of his nose.

He didn't have to be coy. There it is, right there on the menu. Like most chefs in Chicago, Richards thinks the foie gras ban is insane. His method of protest is simply to continue serving it, both on the hamburger and by itself, as "Seared Hudson Valley Foie Gras"—as stark and plain an act of civil disobedience as Gandhi's march to the sea. By contrast, the anti-foie gras protesters' method of protest is to actually protest, right outside the restaurant, with poster-size photos of tormented geese and custom-composed chants.

"It's the Animal Defense League," says Richards. "They showed up on weekends for over a month. Last Friday, my tenant upstairs started throwing water balloons at them. Then I think they decided to take the summer off."

He has not yet suffered the wrath of city hall for defying the ban. A complaint submitted to the city occasions a visit from a health inspector, and the first time she came, Richards says, they ended up having a "spirited discussion of the ban and other interesting political issues" while she poked about the kitchen, looking for contraband liver. One gets the sense that the inspector would rather have spent her time inspecting restaurants for less delicious violations, like rats. But it was one of the few days when there was no foie to be found, so Richards escaped a possible $500 fine.

It is hard not to be sympathetic to the protesters—even compared with the other routine degradations involved in factory farming, force-feeding poultry is pretty harsh. And one wants to feel for the aldermen of Chicago, who, knowing their city is neither the entertainment capital nor the financial capital of the country, hoped to get some headlines by being the City Most Friendly to Poultry. But my feelings, and my allegiance, have been bought by a mere hamburger. Long live the *résistance*! But not, please, the goose.

The Salami Maker
Who Fought the Law

by Sarah DiGregorio

from *Gastronomica*

Anyone who has read Upton Sinclair's *The Jungle* knows why
the meat processing industry should be regulated, but DiGregorio's insightful profile of an artisan of cured pork shows
how regulations can, paradoxically, also hinder food quality.

Before Marc Buzzio became the best charcuterie maker
in the United States, he was just a boy in his father's
shop—fetching coffee, answering the phone, and watching his father, Ugo, turn out old-fashioned Piedmontese and French charcuterie. When Marc was about fourteen, Ugo gave him a soft pine
dowel and a length of string and instructed him to tie knots
around the dowel without making a dent in the wood. Marc tied
the knots as gently as he could. But when his father untied them,
he found tiny impressions in the wood—Marc was not yet deft
enough to tie the delicate and expensive natural casings Ugo used
for his sausages. So Marc kept at it with the string and the dowel
until Ugo let him stuff and tie the larger items—fat sopressata
coated in black pepper and lengths of saucisson sec. Finally, after
years of apprenticeship, Ugo allowed Marc to fashion the tiny cacciatorini, the smallest and most difficult of all. "And that," says
Marc, "is when I knew I had made it."

From the outside, Salumeria Biellese, on 8th Avenue and 29th
Street in Manhattan, looks like any other corner deli. There's a
lunch counter with steam trays of baked ziti and lasagna. In the
morning, a steady stream of hurried customers stops in to order

the ubiquitous Kaiser roll with egg and cheese. But piled in a cooler, next to bottles of Snapple and cola, are hunks of Berkshire prosciutto, aged a full year. Stacks of salame Biellese and saucisson sec are still in their string netting. In another cooler, fresh sausages spill out of bowls—how Italian; chicken, apple, and jalapeño. Salumeria Biellese is the place Thomas Keller and Daniel Boulud call when they need a length of saucisson à l'ail or a hunk of lomo.

Marc Buzzio is short and round, with thinning dark hair and a handlebar mustache. His everyday outfit is a white apron with a meat thermometer sticking out of the pocket. He has a brusquely gregarious way about him, talking with his hands and giving a double-cheek kiss to say hello. "Ciao" is how he says good-bye. Above his desk is a sign that reads, in Italian, "There is no medicine for the stupid." His phone rings off the hook with calls from chefs around New York City. ("I'll send you down some treats. Ciao.") He's like a cartoon of the classic Italian butcher.

Since the early twentieth century, the Buzzio family has been making traditional charcuterie and fresh sausages and selling them out of this unassuming storefront. But in the summer of 2002, disaster struck in the form of new United States Department of Agriculture (USDA) regulations for dry aged, ready-to-eat products. The regulations were written with industrial producers in mind, not mom-and-pop operations, and certainly not this beloved neighborhood store where dry-cured sausages have been made in the same careful way for nearly eighty years. None of that mattered to the USDA, which shut down Salumeria Biellese's production of cured meats. For the first time in its history, the salumeria sold no salami.

The new USDA regulations require producers to prove their products safe and wholesome by showing that they meet lethality standards for *Listeria monocytogenes* and *E. coli*—meaning that at the time of sale, the process of curing the meat has made it impossible for those bacteria to survive.

At first, such standards sound reasonable enough, but "proof" is a surprisingly subjective term. Making cured sausages the same way your father did, the way others have for hundreds of years, doesn't constitute proof. Neither does the fact that no one ever gets sick on your product or that you use only heirloom pork and tend to your salamis like some people tend to their children. It isn't even proof if your product tests negative for bacteria. All the USDA cares about is the process. The traditional method—raw meat transformed into an edible product with nothing but a little salt and a lot of time—makes them very nervous.

So how could Salumeria Biellese prove that their meats were safe? Marc knew that the surefire way to approval was to include a kill step. Cook the product to a certain temperature, irradiate (microwave) it or add preservatives, and the USDA would consider his cured meat safe and wholesome. But for small, traditional producers like Marc who do not want to include a kill step, the situation in 2002 was dire, not to mention confusing. Essentially, they had to come up with a proof that would satisfy the USDA, with very little guidance from the regulators themselves. As Steven Cohen of the USDA's Food Safety and Inspection Services (FSIS) put it: "Processors of these products have to define what makes their product safe."

The FSIS did try to help by conducting numerous workshops across the country to show small producers how to adapt to the new regulation. They also now run a small-plant outreach program, where producers can find sources for scientific information. Even so, the USDA strongly recommends that the processor implement one of the three kill steps. This is essentially coercive legislation. Producers don't have to use a kill step, but if they don't, it's not clear how they will prove that their process is safe.

Because most larger, industrialized producers were already using a kill step, it was easy for them to prove that their products met lethality. But Marc refused to give in. "Here's how we make salami," he told me, throwing his hands in the air, his mustache jumping up and down. "Salami 101: Raw meat, salt, hang it to dry. We use no starter cultures, no lactic acid, no preservatives. If we heat our product, all the delicate layers of flavor produced by the long fermentation, the long aging, is lost. If we complied with USDA, we would ruin the product. I'm not Hormel! How could I compete in that market? Why would I want to? Might as well close the doors."

Closing the doors of Salumeria Biellese would have meant breaking the link between a Manhattan street corner and a small town in the Italian Alps. Ugo Buzzio was born in the United States, but his grandmother took him back to Italy as a child, and he grew up with her in the small town of Curino, near Biella, Piedmont. As a teenager and young adult he apprenticed under the village's charcuterie maker, Mario Fiorio. In that part of Italy, there is little division between French and Piedmontese charcuterie; the two countries are separated only by the Alps. So Ugo learned how to make pâté de campagne, peperoni, saucisson à l'ail, merguez, bresaola, prosciutto, cotto, pancetta, guanciale, mortadella—anything that could be made with salt, spices, and good, rich meat.

When Ugo moved back to the United States, in the 1930s, he got a job at a charcuterie that had opened five years earlier, and it soon came to be known as Salumeria Biellese. Many years passed. In 1962 Ugo got a call from the man under whom he had apprenticed in Italy. His eighteen-year-old son, Piero, wanted to come to America—would Ugo give him a job? Piero ended up working with Ugo at Salumeria Biellese for decades, seven days a week, twelve hours a day, making charcuterie exactly the way it had been made in Curino. Now Piero's son-in-law, Paul, works with Marc at the salumeria and little has changed.

Modernization passed Salumeria Biellese by. When artificial casings came on the market, Ugo wasn't interested. When pneumatic sausage stuffers were all the rage, he kept his slower machine. "I'd say, 'What about a clipping machine? What about this or that?'" says Marc. "And Piero would look at me, smack me on the head, and say '*Ma te mosch?*' Which in Piemontese slang means, 'Are you out of your mind?'" Piero calculated figures with a pencil on a white marble slab that he would wipe clean every day. He had one phone with a rotary dial. When Marc took over more of the business, he finally got a computer, which allowed him to spend Saturdays with his family instead of doing the bookkeeping. But the belief that the dry-cured meats should be made the slow, old-fashioned way had been ingrained in him. "There's a benefit to being stubborn," he says. "Had we kowtowed to modernization, we'd be producing a mediocre product."

Salumeria Biellese's aging room gives new meaning to the words "low tech." In a cramped hallway, with workers in white jackets bustling by, Marc yanks open the door to a refrigerated room, revealing about five hundred sausages and prosciuttos hanging from the ceiling. There are short and fat ones, tiny, bite-size ones, and some that are two feet long—a dense forest of salami, in a room the size of a small walk-in closet. The ventilation system is a fan hung with rope from the ceiling. A dehumidifier hums in a corner. Despite the low-rent trappings, the drying room is immaculate, every item tied in a neat net of string. The smell makes it clear that something amazing is happening here. This is a smell with a presence, one you could scoop up with a spoon. It is deeply savory and musky sweet. There is nothing sour, or off, about the smell, although it has the low funk of aging meat.

"So," says Marc, "how do we judge the aging process? I rely on my senses. I look, feel, touch, taste. I look at every salami individually as it ages. There's no machine for that. It smells sweet in here, right? It's not a sour smell; it smells good. Guess what, it's drying correctly. If it smells like rotting meat, it's not." Marc picks through the rows of hanging sausages and pork legs. He checks that each one is dry on the outside, not tacky or clammy, and that white, powdery Lactobacillus coats the outside of each one. Not only does Lactobacillus inhibit harmful bacteria, it's also desirable for its ability to impart flavor, much in the same way that bacteria impart flavor to cheese. "Now here I see a problem," says Marc, from among the hanging salamis. "See this one, how it has a spot of moisture on the outside?" He removes the offender. "I have to wash this off and let it dry before bringing it back in here with the others. A computer wouldn't have caught that. A computer can't tell you about each individual piece."

Next door, in the salumeria's workroom, a half dozen workers chop onions, rosemary, and apples, while others fill casings for fresh sausages. In the hallway, Paul is rubbing pink and white slabs of pork belly with a blend of salt, sugar, and spices for pancetta. Marc decides to make saucisson à l'ail. He throws handfuls of minced garlic and a gallon of good red wine into an enormous standing mixer filled with ground pork. In goes a spice mixture of nutmeg, mace, and white pepper, which puffs up in an aromatic cloud as it combines with the other ingredients. Marc is swift and practiced, stopping to add more wine when the mash looks too dry. Finally, he turns the mixer off and sticks one big hand into the bowl. It emerges with the meat and spice mixture sticking to his fingers like bread dough. He knows it's ready by touch.

"You know what I'd love to do, but I can't?" Marc asks. "Piedmontese donkey salami. *Das.*" He chortles. "Here." He hands over a piece of lomo, cured pork loin, thinly sliced and translucent as a petal. It was made from a Four Story Hill Farm pig (Marc gets all his pork from there or from Eden Natural). The flavors in that one bite of lomo unfurl slowly, for what seems like ages—delicately porky and redolent of rosemary.

The term *charcuterie* encompasses any preparation designed with the goal of preserving meat: smoking, curing, confiting, and making pâté are among the most common. Before refrigeration, cooks had to come up with inventive ways to keep their food from spoiling. Some of the methods—such as smoking and curing—are as old as humankind itself. French and Italian style charcuterie (salamis, saucisson, pâté, confit, and the like) are perhaps best known in the United States, but any region with a long history is likely to have some charcuterie tradition. Northern Germany has summer sausage, Switzerland has landjager, and Poland has kielbasa. In fact, for centuries charcuterie was used to feed armies because it keeps well and is lightweight and nourishing.

Dry curing, one of the oldest methods of making charcuterie, is the process of preserving meat or fish in salt and hanging it to dry. Cooks most likely discovered through trial and error that dry curing prevented food from going bad. They knew it worked because it tasted good, and no one got sick or died from it. Dry-cured sausages like salamis, sopressata, peperoni, cacciatorini, and saucisson sec are made of seasoned, salted ground meat and fat stuffed into a natural casing and hung to dry. Prosciutto, a cured pork leg; pancetta, cured belly; and guanciale, cured pork jowl, are simply raw meat that has been coated in salt and spices and hung to dry.

Dry-cured meat needs to be aged in a carefully controlled environment, much in the same way that sourdough starter and wine need certain conditions to thrive and age properly. Dry curing is a slowly cascading sequence of events which, when done right, eliminates harmful bacteria. Bacteria generally need three things: protein, moisture, and warmth. Some also need oxygen.

Take away any one of those elements, and you prevent bacterial growth.

Salt, a natural preservative, makes all of this possible by dehydrating both the meat and the microbes themselves (microbes need moisture to thrive). One of the reasons good prosciutto is so expensive is that the producer essentially takes as a loss the enormous amount of water weight lost in the drying process. Botulism, one of the most dangerous anaerobic bacteria, is prevented from growing by the addition of nitrates, or pink salt, which have been used in charcuterie since the 1500s. In a good drying room, especially one that has been in use for a long time, the air is rich in the beneficial bacterium Lactobacillus, which helps to create an acidic environment. Acidity, in turn, prevents the growth of harmful bacteria. It's a balancing act, passed down through generations—a skill that is an important part of a culture's patrimony.

Even with the widespread use of refrigeration, the art of making charcuterie endures. Part of the reason has to do with taste—a great salami has the same complexity and layers of flavor as a well-aged wine or cheese. But it's not only hedonism that explains charcuterie's appeal. Brian Polcyn, the coauthor of *Charcuterie: The Craft of Salting, Smoking, and Curing* and a charcuterie maker himself, says: "The younger generation remembers that their grandparents used to make sausage. And they get into it for the love. It's a love affair. There's nothing like a beautiful sopressata or coppa. It's essential, there's a soul to this food." Polcyn considers Salumeria Biellese the best salumeria in the United States.

But back in 2002 being the best salumeria in the United States wasn't going to cut it with the USDA. It seemed as though Marc and Paul would either have to give up the old way of doing things or abandon salami making altogether. But then they started looking through the USDA literature and identified a scientist cited frequently by the USDA. They called this scientist and commissioned him to do a study that would replicate their recipes and aging processes. And they shelled out one hundred thousand dollars of their own money to pay for it. The scientist followed Salumeria Biellese's process to the letter, with one exception: He injected each product with pure *E. coli* and *L. monocytogenes*, producing much higher levels of bacteria than would normally be found in raw meat. Then he aged the products in the same way that they are aged at the salumeria. When the scientist tested the meats at the end of the aging period, he found that the very high levels of bacteria had been eliminated. Essentially, his study validated what centuries of practice had already demonstrated—that dry aging, when done knowledgeably and with care, makes raw meat safe to eat.

When presented with this study, the USDA conceded that Salumeria Biellese had proved its products to be safe and wholesome. These days, the salumeria simply needs to test each batch of dry-aged meat for bacteria before releasing it for sale. But because the scientist's study contains secret family recipes, its content is confidential, meaning that other small producers are still in the same difficult position as before, bearing the burden of having somehow to prove the safety of their process to the USDA. "We don't want the burden of regulations to make it impossible for people to be in business and make traditional products; that's not the result we want," Cohen emphasizes. But he admits that "it can be challenging for traditional processors to validate their processes."

So the salami maker fought the law—and he won. Both Marc and Paul are quick to say that the USDA representatives were very reasonable once they saw the study. But Marc contends that his victory is only part of a larger story. "We're going to lose the artisanal products of different cultures, because the mom and pops just can't fight this battle. They don't have the resources. The large producers are ecstatic. They have a lobby. They have Congress in their corner. And if they knock out two thousand little guys like us, the competition is gone."

To Marc, the whole dust-up indicates what he sees as a sea change in the way that meat regulation is done in this country—a shift from inspectors who were knowledgeable about meat to a regulating body more concerned about paperwork and litigation than actual food. "They come in and inspect your paperwork, not your meat," Marc says. "The inspectors used to smell, touch, feel. They used to know about meat. Not anymore."

One morning when I was in the shop, Salumeria Biellese's USDA inspector stopped by to tell Marc and Paul that it was his last day on the job—someone else would be taking over for him. The inspector was a slight, jovial man in a hardhat and heavy-duty work jacket. He, Marc, and Paul all slapped each other on the back. "You should come work for me now," Paul joked.

"These are good people," said the inspector to me, gesturing to Marc and Paul. "If you notice something, they take care of it. Their paperwork is in order, second to none."

THE *OTHER* OTHER WHITE MEAT

by Ben Paynter

from *Wired Magazine*

If the idea of eating cloned livestock sends a shiver up your
spine, journalist Paynter's exploration of this futuristic
branch of agribusiness may erase some of its sci-fi creepiness
factor—but it raises a whole other set of questions.

Karyn Schauf sets a frosty glass of milk on the red-checkered tablecloth in front of me; a plate of Oreo knockoffs sits beside it. Two identical cows prance across the glass. In fact, nearly everything in the kitchenette—plates, cookie jars, wallpaper trim—is emblazoned with cows. And why not? We're next door to the Schaufs' 99-cow milking stables, Indianhead Holsteins, in Barron, Wisconsin.

I swirl the glass: A thick lather coats the sides. I sniff: It has a rich, almost buttery aroma. I hate the idea of milk over ice, but the drink is on the rocks because it was squeezed in a steamy, unpasteurized froth just half an hour ago from Mandy2, a 5-foot-tall behemoth with hindquarters as big as truck wheels and a posterior as flat and broad as the tailgate of a pickup. Her massive bone structure supports an udder the size of a beer keg, capable of producing more than 15 gallons of milk a day.

I sip: The milk tastes crisp and creamy, almost velvety—probably because it's fresh and raw. I dunk a cookie, and it gets soggy fast; when I bite into it, it feels like a chocolate milk shake on my palate.

Schauf tips her own glass to her lips, chugs it in two big gulps, and sighs loudly.

"You don't have to drink all that if you don't want to," she says. But I do. Mandy2 has outdone herself. Her milk is delicious. There's no reason it shouldn't be, but I'm surprised.

That's because Mandy2 is a clone. She was conceived in a laboratory seven years ago and purchased last summer from a farmer in Illinois. Because creameries were creeped out by her mad-science heritage, Indianhead was able to pick her up on the cheap for $2,800—about $1,000 less than a nonclone adult cow of the same age (calves cost much more—older animals depreciate like cars).

The Schaufs have owned Indianhead for 26 years. They aren't afraid of science, and they know a bit about cloning. In the mid-'90s, Indianhead was a leader in the Wisconsin dairy industry, relying heavily on a Holstein named Blackrose. She—and her daughters—could churn out huge volumes of milk, rich in protein and butterfat. By 1999, when Blackrose was nearing retirement, the Schaufs had heard about Infigen, a now-defunct cloning company with a too-good-to-be-true sales pitch. Using just a pinky-nail-sized chunk of animal skin and a process called somatic-cell nuclear transfer, Infigen would replicate your favorite cow or pig.

Karyn's husband, Bob, had concerns about playing Creator, but he reconciled them beneath the 8-foot-tall cross affixed to their barn. "God gave man dominion over animals," Bob says. As for Blackrose: "She was getting old and we wanted to keep the factory going. Sometimes you never get one quite as good as the old lady." The Schaufs corralled two more farmers as investors, and in 2001 each received a Blackrose duplicate. Indianhead had a new mascot: Blackrose3.

For several years, the Schaufs sold milk from Blackrose3's offspring—conceived via artificial insemination but having the traditional number of parents, two, and possessed of the same talent for butterfat as the original Blackrose. But in April of this year, the local creamery that processed that milk into cheese for distribution throughout the upper Midwest dropped Indianhead. Another client had complained about the "clone farm."

The problem is that the FDA never actually approved the introduction of meat or milk from clones or their offspring into the human food chain. In 2002 the National Academy of Sciences issued a report saying clone meat was safe, and in December 2006 the FDA called duplicate animals and their offspring "as safe to eat as food from conventionally bred animals." But the agency continued to ask producers to keep clones and their offspring out of the market. You can make 'em and you can milk 'em. You can sell them to other ranchers, and you can even eat 'em, if you want. But the FDA really, really doesn't want them in supermarkets—and typically, the industry does what the FDA wants.

In 2006, Stephen Sundlof, director of the FDA Center for Veterinary Medicine, told the *Washington Post* that approval could come by the end of 2007. But the agency has since backed off that time line. "The FDA is in the process of updating the risk assessment and reviewing the public comments," spokesperson Laura Alvey says. "There is no estimated timeframe on when this will be finished."

Clones were supposed to revolutionize breeding methods, taking the guesswork out of animal husbandry and ushering in a new era of plentiful, delicious steak and bacon. The availability of genetically identical copies of animals would upend the economics of ranching, edging out the old model based on selective breeding and artificial insemination. But consumers can't get past a visceral revulsion at eating clones or the offspring of clones, or even drinking their milk. Part of the FDA's foot-dragging can probably be chalked up to the more than 145,000 public comments the agency has received opposing the sale of clone meat. Meanwhile, health problems continue to plague the clones themselves.

The farmers who bet on that world of wonder-meat have seen their custom-built workforce blacklisted and their financial hopes turn to gristle. Tired of waiting for the future, many are throwing up their hands, grabbing a fork, and eating their profits.

On the day I visit Indianhead, the Schaufs' 17-year-old son, Jacob, is showing a red cow named Rvnge Fire, a granddaughter of Blackrose3, at a local 4-H event in the nearby town of Rice Lake. A win here would add to the dairy's cachet—and to Rvnge Fire's potential price at auction. Born later than some competitors in her class, Rvnge Fire looks small, like a station wagon parked between SUVs. But despite defecating in front of judge Peter Coyne, she wins the first-place blue ribbon. Coyne grabs a microphone, gushing that Rvnge Fire is "extremely angular all the way through," with "strong posturing" and "a good set of feet." "She places well above the rest of the class," he tells the rows of wrinkled farmers lining the bleachers.

After the show, I tell Coyne about Rvnge Fire's pedigree.

"I had no clue who the calf was," he says. He pauses for a moment. "I would say that the uniqueness would add value to it."

But who would buy her if they couldn't sell the milk?

Coyne is a polite man, and etiquette in this part of the world says you don't criticize what someone else does with their own time and money. "I do believe there's beginning to be a shift," he says finally. "But it costs an awful lot to clone cows, and with the moratorium . . . A number of dairymen are still unsure that it makes sense."

DON COOVER WATCHES his assistant toss the last of his clone-offspring T-bones onto the barbecue. We're standing on the sidewalk in front of his semen-shipping business, SEK Genetics, a pitched-roof office building amid a patchwork of fields near Galesburg, Kansas. Coover is dressed in denim and wears a dusty ball cap that says GENETIC HORIZONS!—the original name of his company. He doesn't cook out much: The words "Wash Me" were long ago smeared into the oil on the grill lid and have refilled with dust.

As the steaks pop and spit, Coover explains the sperm business: Ranchers don't care about animals, per se. They care about traits. Lots of meat on the bone, high butterfat content in the milk, resistance to disease—these are all desirable traits. And the way you get more animals with better traits is breeding together the good ones you already have.

Trouble is, cattle are hard to move around. They're heavy and stupid. But genetic material comes in a simple package, and it's reasonably easy to get if you have a strong stomach and own a fake cow vagina or an electric prod sized to fit up a bull's anus.

What's not easy is keeping semen fresh. In the early 20th century, ranchers and businessmen tried everything—they packed it in dry ice and alcohol, they rushed samples to their destinations by tossing them out of airplanes in parachute-equipped boxes.

None of it worked very well. But in the 1950s, the first modern sperm banks arose, and cryopreservation of semen using liquid nitrogen made it transportable. Researchers developed assisted reproductive technologies like artificial insemination, multiple ovulation, and embryo transfer to customize herds in a matter of years, not generations.

The birth of Dolly, the first cloned mammal, in 1996 made all that seem almost quaint. Instead of gambling on the genetic shuffle that happens when you cross two animals, you could just grab a cell from a moneymaker, scoop out the nucleus, and implant that genetic core into an egg from a donor cow. Give the egg a shock to trick it into thinking it's just been fertilized, and bang—you have a twin. By the late 1990s, farmers were banking cell lines, waiting for the right time to resurrect their animals.

Coover, who wears a West Point class ring emblazoned with a caduceus (he's trained as a vet), bought SEK Genetics from a neighbor in 1995. Six years later, Coover found an Oklahoma rancher with a durable, all-black Chianina show bull named Full Flush. In return for $35,000, Coover got part interest in five clones of Full Flush—or, more specifically, exclusive rights to sell their semen. Agriculture students came from as far away as Texas A&M to see the little clone herd that industry magazines called the Dream Team.

When the meat is done cooking, Coover and I each slide a steak onto our paper plates and head into the office to sample it. My inch-thick slab is an unpalatable cadaver-gray. I have to saw gingerly to avoid snapping my plastic utensils. I make two perpendicular incisions in the meat. When it seems loose enough, I pinch a small chunk between my fingers and start twisting in circles to get it loose. I pop a morsel into my mouth and immediately regret it—it tastes spongy and stale. I try not to gag.

Coover moves his plate from the table to his lap for more torque. "I can't even cut this," he grumbles to himself. Prying loose a wedge, he bites into it and winces.

"This is terrible," he says matter-of-factly. He chuckles. "Now I know why they were still in the freezer."

I ask if the taste and texture are functions of the meat being from a clone. He checks a date on the label: The meat was frozen in early 2006.

"It's probably a function of being in the freezer for about three years," he says, exaggerating.

Our meal comes from an offspring of a Full Flush clone. The cow was lame, so Coover, fearing that it would be trampled at auction, butchered it. He now has just four Dream Team progeny left at his ranch (though he still has Dream Team semen on ice). Coover says he shipped the rest of his lot to market.

"Wait. You mean into the food chain?" I ask.

"I never worried much about it," he says. "Unless you tell them it's a clone, no one can tell."

After the National Academy of Sciences report in 2002, Coover started selling his own Full Flush progeny to meatpacking plants and hawking clone sperm to a network of undaunted farmers. He calls the idea that the resulting meat might be unsafe to eat "total bullshit."

"The FDA has never made a decision, but that's because of politics, not science," he says. Besides, keeping clone offspring out of the food chain is "impossible to police."

Other cloners are chafing against the FDA's inaction. Farm-tech company Cyagra sent its clients clone-meat summer sausage as a gift. And two years ago, the company took beef left over from 11 clones created for the FDA's risk assessment study and served it to employees. "If you believe in the technology and you believe it's safe, then there's nothing wrong with eating the meat. Second, it just seemed like a huge waste to have it all destroyed," says Steve Mower, Cyagra's director of marketing.

Like it or not, guys like Don Coover have already turned meat-eaters into a test market for the safety of cloned meat. "It's inevitable that there are large numbers of clone progeny in the food supply," says Blake Russell, vice president of sales and business development at ViaGen, another cloning company. "The likelihood that anyone could credibly say 'Our animals are not descended from clones' is zero."

The reason cloning makes economic sense isn't that ranchers will sell the actual clones for food. The idea is to sell their offspring. Artificial insemination and semen shipping have made breeding for optimum genetics a highly profitable business. The owner of a champion bull can charge top dollar for its breeding services or its descendants. Eventually, of course, that animal will get too old to reproduce. But if you clone it, you can keep that revenue stream open. Clones can be bred just like their progenitors, spreading those popular qualities further into the gene pool. "Part of the value of cloning is that you're buying something with unique genetic potential. It's almost like brand identity," says John Lawrence, an extension livestock economist at Iowa State University. "In many regards it's less risky, because you can say you have a proven animal."

Today, it costs about $1,500 to raise a naturally conceived dairy heifer from conception to breeding age; it costs roughly $17,000 to clone a cow. The figures are about $200 versus $4,000 for hogs. (The price drops if you make multiple copies.) But with natural or assisted reproduction, roughly 5 to 10 percent of all females and 50 percent of all males bred for better genetics don't inherit their parents' best qualities and must be sold at a loss, as "salvage" animals. Cloning, on the other hand, almost guarantees the high-fidelity replication of desirable traits. So the clone of a champion bull has higher downstream breeding potential than, say, that bull's brother. If the original bull was a good breeder, then the clone's semen sells for more and its offspring are worth more. For hogs, the numbers add up fast: Through artificial insemination, one boar can impregnate 400 sows a year, yielding about 4,000 piglets. But if that boar was cloned from a proven superior male, its progeny will be worth about $6 more per piglet in "improved feed conversion, growth rate, survivability, and meat quality," says Russell of ViaGen. "So a $3,000 investment in cloning can create $24,000 in added value per year."

Coover is trying to make the math even more favorable for cattle ranchers by turning cloning into a DIY affair. After lunch, I sit shotgun in his boxy 1994 Chevy pickup as he plows through waist-high prairie grass about 15 miles from his office. The truck has a large, hydrant-shaped feed dispenser mounted on the bed. He doesn't like AC, so our windows are down, filling the cab with hot wind and dust. Coover spots about 25 crossbred Angus cattle grazing beneath a tree on a distant ridge and blares his horn.

He slams on his brakes and whips the truck around. "It's the boss! It's the boss!" he shouts, waving his arms maniacally to get the animals' attention. He checks his rearview mirror—the herd spots the dispenser and makes the connection: Dinner is served! They stampede. Coover accelerates, and we bounce across the field at 5 miles per hour, lurching toward a gated pasture about 200 yards away.

Coover leads the herd into the pasture and pulls up beside a long, narrow feed trough set between a toolshed and a couple of rusted grain bins. Hopping out of the truck, he angles the slide of the dispenser outward, moving fast to avoid being crushed by the cattle. An animal groans, unleashing a loud, steady stream of urine. Coover gets back into the cab, hits a switch on his dashboard, and drives forward slowly as feed pours out of the hopper.

This has been more than just a ranch chore. Coover is looking for some old friends: his last surviving descendants of Full Flush clones. Their bodies are huge, raised high off the ground to support maximum meat yield. It's an obsolete body type—ranchers today want shorter, stockier cows that require less feed. So Coover has repurposed the clone offspring into surrogate moms. He paid $12,000 for 60 embryos cloned from cattle around the country, shipped overnight from Cyagra. He implanted them himself—it helps to be a vet—with the hope of slashing the sticker price of cow copies to about $3,000 a pop. That's right: Coover has implanted clone embryos into the offspring of other clones. It's hard to imagine what the animals' pedigree chart will look like.

Coover reaches out and gruffly pats one of his man-made cows on the muzzle. She munches feed, drooling slightly. Both eyes roll upward to get a good look at him. She has a yellow ear tag for identification, but he doesn't check it. They all look pretty much alike to me, and I ask Coover how he knows he's got the right cow.

"She's just a good cow," he says. "She looks different. She's an individual."

SECOND-GENERATION PIG FARMER Steve Earnhart is convinced that clone-derived meat tastes different only if you know about its heritage. So he's turned my introduction to clone-offspring bacon into a blind taste test.

The timer dings on his microwave. Earnhart pulls out a plate with four strips divided into two courses. On the right side lie two fat ribbons of meat. On the left, two strips that look more charred and have curled up like question marks. One side is cut from the offspring of a clone; the other isn't.

When I pick them up, the strips on the right bend limply, looking like flat, translucent alien fingers. They're obviously undercooked. My first bite squeaks greasily between my teeth with overpowering notes of wax and salt. The curled batch, though, crunches reassuringly, exuding a familiar smoky flavor that grows stronger and heartier the longer I chew.

I point to the alien fingers. "That's the clone."

Earnhart shakes his head. "It was the other one," he says in a clipped drawl. "Only difference you taste is the cut of the meat."

A burly guy in a plaid shirt and Dickies, Earnhart runs Earnhart Hamps, a 150-sow breeding operation in Albion, Indiana. He sends 1,500 hogs—about 270,000 pounds of meat—to market every year. Earnhart is unique among clone-pig farmers simply because he's still in business. Sows can reproduce more than twice as often as cattle, and their litters are 10 times as big, meaning most of the pig farmers who engineered herds at the start of the clone boom had entire proto-farms ready for market in a year and a half—long before anyone wanted to buy them, even if the FDA had approved. Many of those farmers have stopped breeding clones.

Earnhart didn't have the chance to breed unwanted goods. His first foray into cloning was a science fiction disaster. In 1995, his meaty black-and-white Hampshire pig named Mohican sired a boar that sold for $40,000 at the Indiana State Fair. "That gave me money to play with," Earnhart says.

Mohican, named after the action-romance flick *Last of the Mohicans* because he was the only one to survive when his mother accidentally sat on and crushed the rest of his litter, was talented enough for a sequel. In 1998, Earnhart cut off a piece of Mohican's ear and had it frozen. Four years later he called up ViaGen and ordered a four-hog tribe expansion. He didn't tell other farmers, for fear of being seen as some city-boy elitist. "This is not a fancy operation," he says, shrugging. "By no means."

Within weeks of delivery in September 2002, the first piglet got sick and died. Another dropped dead two months later. A few days before Christmas, Earnhart walked into his heated barn at feeding time and spotted his last two piglets belly-up in the straw. The cause of death was apparently their identical, adult-size ulcers. "I felt sick," Earnhart says. "I thought maybe someone was telling us we shouldn't have done this." ViaGen promised to ship replacements, but Earnhart says he was told that two more litters had died at the lab.

The demise of the Mohicans may have resulted from a well-known, poorly understood side effect of somatic-cell nuclear transfer called sudden death syndrome. Genes from adult progenitor animals sometimes manifest themselves too early in their clones; Mohican might have had hereditary ulcers that his piglet doppelgangers developed prematurely. Earnhart won't speculate—the reasons don't really matter to him. "It just nearly killed us," he says.

Problems like sudden death syndrome are why the Humane Society, the Consumer Federation of America, and the Center for Food Safety have asked the FDA to ban cloning or mandate "clone-free" labels at supermarkets. According to the FDA's risk assessment, many animals created with the SCNT process have an "increased risk of adverse health outcomes" over other animals born via assisted reproductive technologies. Clones also suffer from large offspring syndrome, meaning they grow dangerously fast inside their surrogate mothers.

According to Jaydee Hanson, a policy analyst with the Center for Food Safety, those mysterious disorders point to the real question holding clones back: What if? What if clones become ubiquitous and then turn out to be preferentially vulnerable to some emerging disease? And what if eating those clones makes people sick, too? "They need to look at multigenerational studies of these animals to see what happens as they breed," Hanson says.

Konrad Hochedlinger, a biologist at Massachusetts General Hospital's Center for Regenerative Medicine, says the birth defects and early deaths are proof that SCNT is an "inefficient and faulty process." But clone offspring, he says, are conceived naturally. That "resets" the chromosomes of the animal to an age-appropriate mode. "Any abnormalities you see are erased in the next generation," he says. "In terms of food safety, it's not really a problem. The meat is the same." Despite the "ick" factor in the marketplace, that's pretty much the party line at the Biotechnology Industry

Organization, too—Barb Glenn, BIO's managing director of animal biotechnology, says she still thinks the FDA will come through with that approval before 2008. The National Cattlemen's Beef Association, a powerful industry lobbying group, wouldn't mind seeing clones in the food stream—with nary a label. There's no special supermarket shelf for artificial-insemination-derived steaks, says Joe Schuele, the NCBA's spokesperson. "We don't have it because it's not necessary."

The afternoon after our bacon breakfast, Earnhart pulls on his galoshes to show me his clones at work. The day is hot and humid, and flies rise like storm clouds over pens of manure. We plod over to a metal shed to meet a pig: a pregnant sow panting on her side in a thick metal cage. She's a clone, one of 10 copies Earnhart received as compensation from ViaGen in September 2005. Earnhart bows over the sow like an expectant father. He is considering sending the piglets to market, though he might also breed them, just as he has bred the piglets from his other cloned sows. "If we don't send them to market, there's nothing profitable to be done with them."

Well, there's one thing. Earnhart and I head back to his house for an early supper: pork chops with cheesy potatoes, biscuits, and lemonade. My fist-sized chop is glazed in a sugary, thick-as-molasses marinade. It tastes better than anything I've had at a restaurant—moist, succulent, and wonderfully tender.

"When we go out and pick a hog, we usually try to pick out the best one," Earnhart says. He points to the plate. "This is the one we want to eat." Whether it's born of a clone, Earnhart won't say. "If you can tell the difference, it's in your head."

MILES TO GO BEFORE I EAT

by Mark C. Anderson

from *Monterey County Weekly*

The experiment: To eat only food from a 150-mile radius for two weeks. Anderson's wry report shows that it's not as easy as you'd think, even if you do live in the localvore haven of Northern California.

I now boil down seawater for salt, survive off raw brussels sprouts for entire afternoons and never touch tortillas. I suddenly know and admire goat farmers for unexpected reasons. I serve waitstaff pop-geography quizzes and cook at odd hours so I'll lose less weight. I drink Clear Madness Moonshine from Gonzales with fresh-squeezed orange juice from Madera, and drink tap water and local Pinot over Evian and France's best Bordeaux. I am considering erecting a monument to free-range organic bacon from a ranch called Tastes Like Chicken.

Yes, life as a *localvore*, a term the *New Oxford American Dictionary* recently named its New Word of the Year, is a different existence than that I knew before. It can be expensive—to wit, I've dropped $60 on luxury Carmel Valley olive oil alone in the past two weeks. It can be complicated, though my diet has been simplified significantly. And there's this to chew on: Because eating close to home can involve some far-ranging adventures around Monterey County and beyond, the intended consequences of this 15-day, 150-mile diet—to reduce the carbon costs of my eating habits by grazing upon food items that don't have to travel long distances to make cameos on my nonstick pan—has grown a little dubious.

But the auxiliary benefits have proved downright addictive: The original experiment was slated to last a week, but the fact that the foods I've been eating are fresher, healthier and wonderfully unprocessed—and that my habits have kept my food monies within the local family farm circuit—inspired me to stay in localvore lockstep longer than I originally planned. Moreover, as the right-around-here diet demands some strategic planning, especially during an active workweek, I was just getting vaguely proficient by day seven, so the thought of quitting then seemed a little half-cooked.

Meanwhile, the discoveries I continue to make on a daily basis, even through day 14, have gathered a self-perpetuating momentum all their own. Just today, after decades of ignorant abstinence, I discovered San Joaquin Valley persimmons. I ate four in two hours.

There was another factor, however, that helped clinch the continuation: The inherently intriguing stories behind the milk and honey, the bacon and eggs, the apples and onions allow for another layer of flavor I didn't necessarily anticipate. With food playing such a fundamental role in our day-to-day existence and basic social-cultural experience—in a world where we are increasingly isolated from our food by monsoon-proof packaging and intercontinental processing and shipping—it tastes damn good to step outside the industrial food complex and personally know the nexus of my nourishment, especially when that nexus is a goat pasture next to a yurt in the hills outside Watsonville.

Sometimes, it turns out, nourishment can come from a little *too* nearby. At Summer Meadows Farm, well within 150 miles of the *Weekly* office in Seaside, California, but up a steep twisting dirt road outside of Watsonville—past five abandoned cars, several grazing horses and three generally gregarious dogs—Lynn Selness and her family learned that the hard way. They were sitting down to some succulent goat loin in their wood-and-fabric yurt when the kids, who homeschool so they can help with the demands of milking, feeding and grazing their sizable herd of goats, realized Slurpee was the main dish for dinner.

Standing next to her goats' feeding trough while throwing leftover produce and small branches of live oak to her herd, which they grind through with stunning efficacy, Selness says that was the end of goat steaks. "Slurpee [the goat] was one of the kids' favorites—they named him," she says. "From then on it was only ground hamburger. That way they didn't think about what they were eating."

One of the slogans championed by the local food movement goes by any variation of the following: Know your fisherman/farmer/rancher. At Summer Meadows, I get to know the goats. Selness herself knows each little charismatic mammal by name, all 70-plus, including Cinnamon and Chocolate, Flora and Fauna, Morning Star, Lucy and Mary Lou. A contagious smile covers her face as she describes their courtship ritual: Her two breeding bucks (Jacob and Stinky Reuben) get as smelly "as possible by peeing on themselves." The hierarchal class system the females establish, and the ritual they practice when a member of the herd returns after time with another farm, still amaze her. Her eyes well up as she recounts the day the now-deceased matriarch goat Brownie marched an entire pasture full of goats, including many that had long ago bullied past her in rank, to the barn with a simple but particularly poignant "Bleeaah."

"There's a lot more going on with the goats than we know," she says. "We don't know anything."

Back in her yurt, Selness strains some raw goat milk drawn earlier in the day by her daughter, Meadow, into recycled bottles sitting in the kitchen sink. Almost all of it is destined to enhance Live Earth's boxes of community-supported agriculture; I get a quart, the first salvo in an attempt to crack my pasteurized past. But I've come for the cheese. She offers me a taste of her ricotta, then quickly stashes it back in the fridge, as the family's running low. I take chevre instead, a half-pound for an agreed $8 (it's not normally for sale). Instinctively, I up the purchase to a pound. After going more than two days without one of my major food groups—cheese, hot sauce, bacon and beer—I need me some cheese.

They must see the savage orange ache of sausage-withdrawal in my eyes. "Corralitos Market," comes the common chorus. "You have to go." But when I enter the market before visiting the goat ranch, the report from the meat market floor is sobering.

The incomparable cheesy Bavarians, robust Kobasicas and glorious Creole sausages all are expertly treated, seasoned and processed in-house. But the mouthwatering meats themselves hail from as far off as Canada and, yes, Bavaria. Dave Peterson and his savvy Corralitos staff do process local hunters' hogs into sausages, but my closest canine companion is scared of guns and my musket is rusty. To leave with something I can eat, it's all I can do to find some local salmon that's been cured and smoked in-house.

The near local-food shutout seems surprising at a time-honored spot like this, but it's not a unique vision as I look through my 150-mile lens. At the Monterey Sea Harvest's fresh-fish market, less than one-quarter of the 32 different types of seafood offered is local—and according to the attendant, their lemons are from China (fortunately my petrale sole will be splendidly edible with just garlic and honey). Back by Corralitos, Freedom Meat Locker is stuffed with great cuts of devoutly manly red meat, but the attentive butcher I encounter can only offer me a brochure to S/K Cattle Co. in King City when honoring my local focus. On a Tuesday at Whole Foods Market in Monterey, the butterfish from Monterey Fish Co. is the sole fish that formerly swam the bay, despite the fact that there are dozens of different kinds of seafood on display. At many local restaurants (and many bars with underwhelming wine lists), there is nothing offered that doesn't involve several well-traveled ingredients—with some truly heaven-sent exceptions at super-local-savvy places like Stokes Restaurant in downtown Monterey and the Aquarium's Portola Cafe.

The smoked salmon represents a common conundrum. The fish is local, the smoking and seasoning done on the premises. But the label tells me it is cured with salt, sugar, sodium nitrate and sodium phosphate, things not likely found within a remote radius. The fact that I buy it anyway constitutes my first moment of weakness (the others, albeit fleeting, involved gum, multivitamins, a bourbon tasting, two loaded nacho chips and a tiny double-baked soufflé). It also speaks to a crux of this 150-mile odyssey: *How far am I willing to go to stay local?*

Nerve involves asking the waiter at Stokes to swap out the complimentary sparkling water from Europe for some of the stinky tap water from the kitchen. Courage is refusing a birthday-party shot of Crown Royal at a table of 20. And shame means having to ask for a fresh persimmons refund. The farmer at the folding table at the Old Monterey Marketplace looks at me with a fermented blend of disgust and pity the moment I request my money back. When his coworker leans over and asks in Spanish why I don't want the perfectly good persimmons, he flips a dismissive hand toward me and grumbles, "*Ciento cincuenta,*" Spanish for "150."

Such things happen on day two and three of my diet (and continue at points thereafter). I am unfazed, ready to go the distance for this diet—and prepared to be rather ruthless in my self-enforcement of the 150-mile limit. If the food *might* be from farther away, I don't want it. As I bought the persimmons and began to move away, I asked from where the fruit hails, only to find that their farm is east of Fresno, which I quickly and ignorantly calculate to be about 2 ½ to three hours by car, or around 150 miles away. As I'm erring on the side of draconian self-discipline, east of Fresno equals no sale.

With the number 150 all-important, I plan on cutting zero corners—after all, I already had made my peace with the hardest part of the deal: namely, I can eat nothing if it contains wheat. Dory Ford, executive chef at Portola Cafe, whose parent company Bon Appétit toes the 150-mile line whenever possible, broke the news when I called him for strategic insight.

"No pasta, rice, anything that contains flour," he said with a chuckle. "No sauces, unless you make it from scratch—too many ingredients. Watch out for dressing. Where's your oil coming from to make vinaigrette? No beer—you're gonna have to go to wine only. That could get expensive.

"And you can't use pepper, no spices, no salt."

Early on, I encounter little danger to my devotion: I actually stay within just a few miles of my food sources by cooking the treasures I score in my Community Supported Agriculture box from Carmel Valley's Serendipity Farms ($20 a week): sweet bell peppers, rainbow chard, heirloom tomatoes, artichokes, red torpedo onions, dandelion greens, Italian parsley, romaine lettuce and gorgeous ochre, light-brown and pale-green eggs. A bottle of cold-pressed Carmel Valley Extra Virgin Olive Oil ($35) offers crucial help for the initial meal, the first omelet I've made since I was tall enough to reach the stove where cheese isn't involved, and the first in a decade where Tapatío doesn't splash happily upon the perfect fold of yellow egg. Fortunately the earthy heirlooms and torpedo onion, left undiluted, flex mighty flavor. They play with eggs that don't so much taste better than standard food industry offerings as they simply *taste*. So what if I can't wrap the omelet in a warm flour tortilla?

A visit to the Wine Market in Pacific Grove on the way back from the CSA pick-up spot at the mouth of Carmel Valley arms me with an affordable local Chardonnay to go with the omelet. Before I leave the store, owner George Edwards even decides he will take it upon himself to put together a list of local wines at modest price points. He later hits up Trader Joe's to give me more options.

The next day, I add some strawberries, pasilla peppers and honey from the Old Monterey Marketplace on Alvarado Street before I have my run-in with the understandably angry persimmons man. But as snappingly fresh as my staple foodstuffs taste, the novelty wears off rather quickly, and my dishes develop a decidedly Spartan aspect: a romaine salad with heirloom tomatoes, a few hard-boiled eggs, and a handful of artichokes is no way to go through a day. I dream of the time needed to find the ingredients for and to actually make aioli from scratch with some dexterity— as I inwardly debate whether to illicitly reassign an intern from an important story to a homemade mayonnaise mission.

Simultaneously, I experience unprecedented four-minute headaches. My editor, who (like all editors) is a crack expert on everything from anthropology to zoology, summarily declares them "starch headaches."

When the newsroom infantry marches past my desk with pungent deadline-night bacon-chicken-ranch pizza, I feel an internal twitch somewhere near my brain stem. That must be where my self-discipline lives.

The Summer Meadows goat cheese helps me handle life sans bacon pizza. Suddenly, a fat slice of apple with cheese and honey is a luxury. And I have another technique to temper my dietary temperance: When my stomach lining trembles at the specter of the day's 16th and 17th servings of fresh fruit and vegetables, I distract it by accessing memories of the fowl theatrics at Glaum's Organic egg farm.

When $2 bills go into a vending machine there, a gorgeous rack of 21 fresh eggs emerges—and a display case full of small chicken figurines in customized Halloween costumes launch into a cluck-ing "bup-bup-bup-ba" version of "In the Mood." When that dis-traction device reaches its expiration date, a slug from a gallon of the best beverage I know, angelic apple juice from down the road at Watsonville's Gizdich Farms, offers another coping mechanism.

As I'm grinding through the midmorning honey and fruit, local foodstuff wonder welds me to my swivel seat. Jim Dunlop of Tastes Like Chicken Ranch in Watsonville drops off some gloriously gor-geous bacon from free-range organic pigs (who mingle with the free-range chickens), some eggs and some super creamy Claravale Farm raw milk from completely hormone- and chemical-free cows. Then a colleague delivers a serious stash of goods from the Santa Cruz Farmers Market—basil, eggplant, golden potatoes and a big pumpkin-like kombucha squash—and a fifth of the only lo-cal spirit I've been able to locate. Osocalis, an artisanal alambic brandy made from local Colombard, Pinot Noir and other coastal California grapes, reveals a stiff $37.99 sticker but a damn smooth taste.

Thing is, Dunlop had to drive to me and my colleague had to drive to Santa Cruz and back to supply such splendor. The goat cheese, smoked salmon and apple juice round-trip to Watsonville racked up 42 miles. Later in the operation, after I scoop the Pacific into jars at San Carlos Beach, it takes a full hour of high heat to re-duce it to the salt I seek. I can streamline things by visiting Whole Foods and using its "locally grown" labels to track down some very good cheeses and chicken that source within 150 miles—but as *Weekly*-reporter Zachary Stahl pointed out in the first installment of this two-part series, regional and national shipping infrastruc-ture doesn't always guarantee that foodstuffs move in straight lines from the source to the shelf.

James McWilliams understands that these confounding variables are hard to avoid—and are therefore dangerous to the righteous food-milers I aspire to emulate. McWilliams is a fellow at Yale in the agrarian studies program and is writing a book called *Just Food*, which he says will build upon a high-profile op-ed he wrote for the *New York Times*. His op-ed describes the pitfalls of going local one-dimensionally; in the book he plans to provide a pragmatic guide to eating ethically with that in mind.

"People who want to make the right decision for the environment are buying local and thinking, therefore, 'I'm doing my part for the larger issue of the environment,'" he says. "My problem with that is that conveys a certain false satisfaction."

Sautéeing TLC Italian sausage with Gilroy garlic, portabellas from Ariel Mushrooms and Serendipity's torpedo onions is a wonderful way to spend a lunch hour. Watsonville strawberries blend beautifully with Gizdich olallieberry syrup, Straus yogurt from their family-owned Point Reyes ranch, and sage honey from a secret local location. Spaghetti squash "pasta" from Carmel Valley, bathed in roasted heirloom tomato and pearl onion marinara sauce—with pan-fried Petaluma chicken and zucchini on top—is a down-home way to make a houseguest happy. Same goes for goat-cheese-stuffed pasilla peppers and catch-of-the-day petrale sole.

These are just the beginning of the insights I've gleaned since I began my diet 15 days ago. My knowledge has deepened in other ways: Watsonville's Ariel Mushrooms sells some 60,000 pounds of fungi a week; Morganic Hilltop Crops keeps its hive locations clandestine to guard against bee-and-honey heists, and nearly all of my local sources practice progressive sustainability habits.

McWilliams says this is just a beginning, however—eating according to food miles is still a one-dimensional way to evolve dietary habits. "Life-cycle" considerations must take place. This requires calculations that only economists might find appetizing.

"Factor inputs and externalities," McWilliams writes in his *Times* piece, "like water use, harvesting techniques, fertilizer outlays, renewable energy applications, means of transportation (and the kind of fuel used), the amount of carbon dioxide absorbed during photosynthesis, disposal of packaging, storage procedures and dozens of other cultivation inputs."

McWilliams understands that extensive research and arcane math are a lot to digest. He adds that with so many complex food factors out there beyond consumer control, it's as impractical as it is unsavory. "To eat totally ethically," McWilliams says, "would require you to suspend reality.

"At this point, sure, I couldn't do a life cycle assessment of a vegetable I buy in the store, and I'm not suggesting anybody try to do that," he continues. "But thinking in long term, the movement to put food mile labels on products really encourages people to help see down the road. It's in the scientific literature, not as much in the media yet, but it's starting to get a lot more attention."

Until then, even the most modest food-mile-informed actions can net powerful gains, as Barbara Kingsolver, Camille Kingsolver and Steven L. Hopp point out in their seminal food tome *Animal, Vegetable, Miracle: A Year of Food*. "If every U.S. citizen ate just one meal a week (any meal) composed of locally and organically raised meats and produce," Hopp writes, "we would reduce our country's oil consumption by over 1.1 million barrels of oil every week. That's not gallons, but barrels."

Animal, Vegetable, Miracle is not found in the food section at Borders, but in psychology. Fifteen days of local food help me understand why—the half month gone by hasn't been so much about what I gave up, but what I gained: a much broader perspective on what I put in my body.

Better yet, the local community has gained with me. "Eighty-five cents of every food dollar goes to the food industry, the processors, marketers and transporters," Kingsolver and Hopp report. Over the past two weeks, my caloric commerce made a lot more cents for local farmers like Jim Dunlop and Lynn Selness.

Not that the free-range bacon and organic egg odyssey has been all gains. The scale tells me I've lost three pounds.

Serious Withdrawals:
10 Things It Was Hard to Go Without

Behold the power of flour. It gives life to tortillas; it makes it possible to break bread. Alas, most domestic wheat is grown out of state. Best-selling author Barbara Kingsolver, who spent a year eating locally, allowed her family to use grains (they baked their own bread) and oil from outside the area just to help them stay sane. Each family member also was allowed a luxury item; Dad chose coffee, the kids dried fruit and hot chocolate. Here's what would top my luxury list—in order of what I missed most:

1. Tapatío. There's only one Tapatío, and only one supplier of its ingredients—in Mexico.

2. Spices. This was Kingsolver's "luxury" item(s). I get it—garlic is great, but a little curry or Italian herb can really lift a dish.

3. Flour tortillas. Quesadilla, I took you for granted. Burrito, come back to me.

4. Bread. At one point I might've swapped my passport for a good sourdough melt.

5. Rice. So versatile, so easy, so affordable, so long.

6. Beer. English Ales in Marina and microbrews to the north and south do delicious elixirs, but they get their barley and hops from far off.

7. Pepper jack. There are a few local cheeses, but no PJ.

8. Condiments. Making mayo from scratch and styling salad dressings without spices is a lot harder than advertised. And this amount of fruits and vegetables beg for a decent dip.

9. Bananas. Called the Humvee of food miles by some, the banana still holds a place in my heart.

10. Coffee and tea. Ranks at the top for most folks, for obvious reasons.

Why Vegetarians Are Eating Meat

by Christine Lennon
from *Food & Wine*

Decades after vegetarianism became a countercultural
lifestyle choice, Lennon investigates a curious phenomenon:
the number of committed vegetarians who've begun to
reconsider—and why.

To a die-hard meat eater, there's nothing more irritating
than a smug vegetarian. I feel at liberty to say this because I am one (a steak lover) and I married the other (a vegetarian
with a pulpit). For me, "Do you now, or would you ever, eat
meat?" has always been a question on par with "Do you ever want
to get married?" and "Do you want children?" The answer to one
reveals as much about a person's interior life, and our compatibil-
ity, as the response to the others. My husband Andrew's reply to all
of those questions when I asked him three years ago was, "No."

Obviously, we're now married. We had twins earlier this year.
And somewhere in between those two events, the answer to the
third question was also reevaluated, and the vegetarian soapbox
was put to rest, too.

Yes, my husband has started eating meat again after a seven-year
hiatus as an ethically motivated and health-conscious vegetarian.
About a year ago, we arrived at a compromise: I would eat less
meat—choosing mostly beef, pork and poultry produced by local
California ranchers without the use of hormones or antibiotics—
and he would indulge me by sharing a steak on occasion. But arriving at that happy medium wasn't as straightforward as it sounds.

In the three years we've been together, several turns of events have made both of us rethink our choices and decide that eating meat selectively is better for the planet and our own health. And judging by the conversations we've had with friends and acquaintances, we're not the only ones who believe this to be true.

For Andrew and about a dozen people in our circle who have recently converted from vegetarianism, eating sustainable meat purchased from small farmers is a new form of activism—a way of striking a blow against the factory farming of livestock that books like Michael Pollan's *The Omnivore's Dilemma* describe so damningly. Pollan extols the virtues of independent, small-scale food producers who raise pasture-fed livestock in a sustainable and ethical manner. In contrast, he provides a compelling critique of factory farms, which cram thousands of cows, pigs or chickens into rows of cages in warehouses, feed them drugs to plump up their meat and fight off the illnesses caused by these inhumane conditions, and produce innumerable tons of environmentally destructive animal waste.

The terms "grass fed" and "pasture raised"—meaning that an animal was allowed to graze the old-fashioned way instead of being fed an unnatural and difficult-to-digest diet of mostly corn and other grain—have now entered the food-shoppers' lexicon. But Andrew and I didn't fully understand what those phrases meant until we got to know Greg Nauta of Rocky Canyon Farms. Nauta is a small-scale rancher and farmer from Atascadero, California, who grows organic vegetables and raises about 35 animals on pastureland. Since we met him at the Hollywood Farmers' Market a year ago, it has become even clearer to us that supporting guys like him—by seeking out and paying a premium for sustainably raised meat—is the right thing for us to do.

Nauta's cattle graze on 200 leased acres of pasture in central California and are fed the leftover vegetables and fruits he grows that don't sell at the farmers' market, supplemented by locally grown barley grain on occasion. "That's dessert," he says of the barley, "not a main course. That would be like us eating ice cream every day."

Three times a week, Nauta loads his truck full of coolers stocked with cattleman's steaks and handmade pork sausages and drives to the Los Angeles–area farmers' markets. Selling his vegetables and meat directly to conscientious eaters, people to whom he talks weekly about rainfall averages and organic produce, Nauta says, is "the best way small guys like me can compete." In the past several months, Nauta has noticed a handful of curious vegetarians, like Andrew, wandering over to his booth to ask questions. And they're satisfied enough with the answers to give his meat a try—and come back for more.

If preserving small-scale farming isn't a compelling enough reason to eat beef or pork, consider the nutritional advantages grass-fed meat has over the factory-fed kind. "One of the benefits of all-grass-fed beef, or 'beef with benefits,' as we say, is that it's lower in fat than conventionally raised beef," says Kate Clancy, who studies nutrition and sustainable agriculture and was until recently the senior scientist at the nonprofit Union of Concerned Scientists. "The other thing is that the meat and milk from grass-fed cattle will probably have higher amounts of omega–3 fatty acids, which may help reduce the risk of heart disease and strengthen people's immune systems. What's good for the environment, what's good for cattle, is also good for us."

Combine these findings with the questions being raised about meat replacements derived from soy and wheat gluten, and the real thing seems better by the minute. "What we know about soy is that as you process it, you lose a lot of the benefits," says Ashley Koff, a Los Angeles–based registered dietician. "Any soy-based fake meat product is incredibly processed, and you have to use chemicals to get the mock flavor. Any other whole-food diet is going to be a lot better for you." Vegetarians like Andrew—he once brought a tofu sandwich to a famous Texas barbecue restaurant—may now have a harder time justifying their "healthier" dietary choices.

Former vegetarians are some of the most outspoken proponents of eating meat. "I was vegan for 16 years, and I truly believed I was doing the right thing for my health," says the actress and model Mariel Hemingway, who is the author of *Healthy Living from the Inside Out*. "But when I was vegan, I was super-weak. I love animals, and we should not support anything but ethical ranching, but when I eat meat, I feel more grounded. I have more energy."

Even chef Mollie Katzen, author of the vegetarian bible *The Moosewood Cookbook*, is experimenting with meat again. "For about 30 years I didn't eat meat at all, just a bite of fish every once in a while, and always some dairy," she says. "Lately, I've been eating a little meat. People say, 'Ha, ha, Mollie Katzen is eating steak.' But now that cleaner, naturally fed meat is available, it's a great option for anyone who's looking to complete his diet. Somehow, it got ascribed to me that I don't want people to eat meat. I've just wanted to supply possibilities that were low on the food chain."

Recently, when responding to the invitation to her high-school reunion, Katzen had to make a choice between the vegetarian and the conventional meal. She checked the nonvegetarian box. "The people who requested the vegetarian meal got fettuccine Alfredo," she says. "It's a bowl full of flour and butterfat. I'd much rather have vegetables and grains and a few bites of chicken."

For Andrew and many of our ex-vegetarian friends, the ethical reasons for eating meat, combined with the health-related ones, have been impossible to deny. "The way I see it, you've got three opportunities every day to act on your values and have an immediate effect on something you're concerned about," Andrew says. "You're probably worried about Darfur, too, but what can you do about that every single day? Write a letter? It doesn't have the same kind of impact."

Supporting ranchers we believe in, and the stores and restaurants that sell their products, has a very tangible impact that we experience firsthand all the time. But ask most vegetarians if the battle between small, sustainable ranchers and industrial farming is at the top of their list of concerns about eating meat, and you'll probably be met with a blank stare. "For people who are against eating meat because it's wrong or offensive to eat animals, even the cleanest grass-fed beef won't be good enough," Katzen says.

Convincing those people that eating meat can improve the welfare of the entire livestock population is a tough sell. But we'll keep trying. What we've discovered is that you can hover pretty close to the bottom of the food chain and still make a difference, quietly. We've found a healthy balance somewhere between the two extremes—which, come to think of it, is also a good way to approach a marriage.

Dining Around

The Surprise Slice of My Cook's Tour

By Jane Black

from the *Washington Post*

Thanks to Anthony Bourdain, culinary tourism has somehow
turned into an extreme sport, an exercise in one-upmanship.
A staff writer for the *Post*, Black skewers this gonzo phenomenon—
and then proceeds to execute a perfect example of it.

The alarm squawked at 5:30 a.m. It was Sweden in July,
which made it less painful than it might have been. But
still. The sun was already rising high over the Baltic Sea, turning
the puffy clouds pale pink and Creamsicle orange after just four
hours of darkness. I tried to take in the natural beauty. But all I
could do was roll over and curse Tony Bourdain.

It was because of Bourdain, author of *Kitchen Confidential* and a
television culinary adventurer, that I had arranged to be at a small
bakery 20 miles away at 7 a.m. I was on a quest to learn about *spettkaka*, a spit-roasted cake that looks like a cross between a wedding
cake and a bird's nest.

You may never have heard of spettkaka (SPET-eh-KAW-ka), a
specialty of Sweden's Skåne region—or any spit-roasted cake, for
that matter. And that was the point. Spurred on by gastro-explorers
such as Bourdain, I wasn't searching only for good food. I was on
the hunt for an undiscovered culinary gem.

It was Bourdain's fault that I had spent weeks before my trip
scouring the Internet for that wacky something. It was his fault
that our host, Marie, had spent hours phoning around to locate
some picture-perfect, wrinkly old woman who, as a young maid,

had learned to make spettkaka from her grandmother. It was, I thought grumpily, Bourdain's fault that the alarm was sounding at 5:30.

These days, culinary tourism has become an extreme sport. It's not enough just to try the local cheese: Food lovers who want credentials have to seek out the obscure and the exotic. They harvest grapes from the vine and gather their own mushrooms. They eat street food in far-flung parts of the world. And they sigh with envy when they turn on the TV to see Bourdain swallowing roasted sheep testicles in Morocco, the still-beating heart of a cobra in Saigon and a deep-fried Mars bar in Scotland (which, actually, is really very good).

Oh, the pressure! There's chef Todd English on TV learning how to massage Kobe beef. There's Andrew Zimmern crunching whole insects on the Travel Channel. And on PBS, hip *Gourmet* magazine writers skip from New York to Shanghai to smoke pork, salmon, duck, even mushroom ice cream.

Even the simplest things must be off the beaten path: If it's pappa al pomodoro, the simple Tuscan bread and tomato soup, the (stale) bread had better be homemade, and, if possible, the soup should be cooked over a fire made by rubbing two sticks together.

Looking back at what I did on my Swedish summer vacation, it was clear that subliminal pressure had led me to spettkaka. And to taste arctic yellow cloudberries, smoked eel, 10 kinds of pickled herring and a cod roe paste sandwich, a Swedish child's equivalent of peanut butter and jelly.

Some were good; all were better than the spettkaka, which had a powdery texture and one overriding flavor: sweet. (The cake I carefully carried home to my colleagues sat for days on the tasting table and then was thrown out.)

For days, we trekked through the Swedish countryside. By Day Four, even I was exhausted. So we took the morning off, opting for a simple lunch of cheese, bread and salad out in Marie's garden. The sun was surprisingly strong, and after my first helping, I closed my eyes and leaned back to work on my Scandinavian tan. I wondered: What was I missing? The fish was fresh. The apple cake was lovely. But maybe we should have gone somewhere like Bora Bora after all. I sat up and grabbed a third slice of bread from the basket.

Then it hit me. The best thing I had tasted wasn't off the beaten path. It had been right in front of me. Half Irish soda bread, half Bavarian hearth bread, it was moist, not too sweet and studded with seeds, apricots and walnuts. It was breakfast! It was dessert! And it was available at almost every restaurant I went to in Sweden as well as Marie's local bakery.

The feeling was akin to waking up one morning and realizing that all this time you've been in love with your best friend. That it wasn't the dangerous biker (the eel) or the BMW-driving prepster (the spettkaka) who made your heart skip a beat. It was the sweet, loyal guy who had always been there, just waiting for you to come around.

My love was as intense as it was sudden. What was in this bread? How much could I carry home? Or, better, could I make it myself?

That evening, we had dinner at a small seafood restaurant in Simrisham, on Sweden's southern coast. At 7, the sun was still high in the sky. I sat down and impatiently awaited the arrival of the bread basket. The object of my desire was in there, dark and lovely and dotted with cherries. I reached for a slice and asked the waiter if the kitchen might share the recipe. He nodded and promptly returned with a neatly printed sheet.

It was in Swedish, of course, and the ingredients included deciliters of flour, soured milk and mörk sirap, a dark syrup made from sugar beets. I smiled: Let Bourdain eat his pork blood cakes. This was my kind of culinary adventure.

Fruity Swedish Quickbread

When it comes to making this Swedish bread, the culinary adventure begins with a search: Everyday Swedish ingredients, such as graham flour and mörk sirap, aren't widely available here.

We found Bob's Red Mill dark rye flour at some Safeway stores and Hodgson Mill graham flour at Chevy Chase Market. (Both are also available online.) The mörk sirap, a rich chocolaty syrup made from sugar beets, is available at Ikea. It gives the bread a wonderful depth of flavor, but if necessary, you may substitute dark molasses.

Serve for breakfast or tea with a dab of butter, or toasted and plain. To store, wrap in plastic wrap and refrigerate for up to 1 week. Or wrap the bread whole in foil, then in plastic wrap, and freeze for up to 2 months.

Makes two 9-by-5-inch loaves

4 cups buttermilk, preferably not low-fat
2 teaspoons baking soda
1 cup mörk sirap
3 ½ cups whole-wheat flour
2 cups graham flour
1 cup dark rye flour
2 teaspoons salt
1 cup unsalted sunflower kernels
1 cup flaxseed
2 cups mixed dried fruit and nuts, such as apricots, cherries and walnuts

1. Preheat the oven to 350 degrees. Lightly grease two 9-by-5-inch loaf pans. Have ready two clean dish towels.

2. In a 2-quart measuring cup, combine the buttermilk, baking soda and mörk sirap, stirring to combine.

3. In a separate large mixing bowl, combine the flours, salt, sunflower kernels, flaxseed and mix of dried fruit and nuts. Add the buttermilk mixture and blend until just combined; the batter will be loose. Divide evenly between the loaf pans and bake for about 1 ½ hours or until a toothpick inserted in the center comes out clean. Transfer the breads from the pans to the dish towels and wrap loosely. For best slicing results, let the loaves sit for at least five hours before cutting.

Adapted from Maritim, a restaurant in Simrisham, Sweden

THREE CHOPSTICKS

by Calvin Trillin

from the *New Yorker*

Journalist, humorist, and novelist Calvin Trillin—a true triple threat—frequently discourses on his appetites in periodic *New Yorker* articles, as well as collections such as *Alice, Let's Eat, Third Helpings,* and *Feeding a Yen.*

When I think back on the conversations that took place after I told people that I was going to Singapore to eat, I'm reminded of the scene in "Little Red Riding Hood" when the title character first encounters the big bad wolf. I play the wolf:

"Singapore!" Little Red Riding Hood says, in an improbable New York accent. "But Singapore is supposed to be the least exotic place in Asia. There's nothing to see there, unless you're a connoisseur of skyscrapers or container ports or obsessive street-cleaning."

"All the better for guilt-free eating, my dear. Your meals can't be spoiled by remorse over not having conducted a thorough inspection of the second-most-important cathedral."

"And isn't Singapore the place where you can get fined for chewing gum?"

"But, my dear, you can't chew gum while you're eating anyway."

From those conversations, I have concluded that the governmental ban on chewing gum, promulgated in 1992, remains the fact most strongly associated by Americans with Singapore. If Singapore tested a nuclear device tomorrow, the stories in American newspapers would mention the gum ban by the second paragraph. (Three years ago, the government relented a bit, in order to satisfy the requirements of a free-trade agreement: you can now buy nicotine gum by prescription.) There is a collateral awareness of the penalties that Singapore imposes for such malefactions as dropping a candy wrapper on the sidewalk. According to what's listed on a widely sold souvenir T-shirt emblazoned "Singapore— A Fine City," the acts that can bring you a serious fine include not only gum-chewing and littering and smoking and spitting but also carrying a durian on a public conveyance. A durian is an astonishingly odoriferous melon, much prized in Southeast Asia. Having smelled a durian, I must say that the prohibition against carrying one on a public conveyance (for which there is actually no specific fine) strikes me as a very solid piece of legislation. In American terms, it's the equivalent of a law against carrying a cattle feedlot on a public conveyance.

I'd always thought that I wouldn't go much further than that in supporting Singapore's efforts to treat tidiness as the nearly Athenian ideal of government. Still, had I known that it was happening I would have backed the government's scheme in the seventies to bring food venders, called hawkers, off the streets and into centers that have proper sanitation and refrigeration and running water—a scheme that was inspired by a desire for tidy streets, along with public-health considerations and the needs of traffic control and, presumably, the relentless modernization that seems to have a momentum of its own in Singapore. My support would have been based on enlightened self-interest, one of the cornerstones of democracy. For years, as I've walked past food stands in foreign lands, I've struggled to keep in mind that for an American visitor the operational translation for signs that ostensibly say something like "*bhel puri*" or "*tacos de nopales*" is "Delivery System for Unfamiliar Bugs That You Will Bitterly Regret Having Ingested." The temptation to throw caution to the wind has been excruciating, since I may love street food above all other types of food. I have never figured out just why, although I've considered the possibility that, through some rare genetic oddity, my sense of taste is at full strength only when I'm standing up. (The fact that I particularly enjoy whatever I eat while standing in front of the refrigerator could be considered supporting evidence.) For a while, I thought about testing the standup hypothesis at some fancy Manhattan restaurant by springing to my feet halfway through the main course and trying to gauge whether that makes the roasted organic chicken with fricassée of spring vegetables and chanterelle polenta taste as good as those sausage sandwiches you get at Italian street fairs.

Gathering food venders into hawker centers, under the purview of public-health inspectors, meant that a Western visitor not only can have a safe shot at a variety of Singaporean delicacies but can do so in a setting so convenient that his energy is reserved for eating. All over Singapore, there are open-air pavilions where an island of tables and chairs is ringed by eighty or a hundred hawker stands—many of them selling only one item, like just satay or just fish-ball noodles. The government has established hawker centers in the central business district and hawker centers at the beach and hawker centers attached to the high-rise public-housing projects where the vast majority of Singaporeans live. In some of the fancy skyscrapers and department stores, private operators run air-conditioned, upmarket versions of hawker centers called food courts—a term presumably selected by someone who had never tasted what's passed off as food at an American shopping-mall food court. In Singapore, even the establishments called coffee shops are essentially mini hawker centers. They might have started as places that served coffee and the pastries that the British Empire, for reasons of its own, inflicted on unsuspecting colonials throughout the world, but these days the proprietor is likely to operate the drink concession himself and rent out two or three stalls to specialists in, say, fish-head curry or Hainanese chicken rice. It has become possible to eat in Singapore for days at a time without ever entering a conventional restaurant. Since I have never been much taken with the concept of courses—my eating habits are more on the order of a bit of this, a bit of that, and, now that I think of it, a bit of something else—it almost seems as if the Singapore government of forty years ago had arranged its hawker policy with me in mind.

I don't mean that I would check the flights to Heathrow if I heard that some entrepreneur in East Anglia had created a logistically flawless collection of food stands that allowed a diner to switch with ease from, say, bangers and mash to mushy peas to bubble and squeak. Convenience isn't everything. Singapore, though, has always been noted for the quality and variety of its street food and, not coincidentally, for having a citizenry whose interest in eating borders on the obsessive. The population combines migrants from several parts of China with minorities of Indians and Malays and people who look Chinese but are known as Peranakans—a separate ethnic group, long prominent in the government and business life of Singapore, which traces its origins to early Chinese traders who absorbed some of the culture and the genes of the local Malays. The evidence indicates that every one of these groups arrived hungry.

Soon, Hainanese were cooking Peranakan specialties and Indians were frying noodles in the Chinese manner. Old dishes were transmogrified. New dishes were invented. Eventually, Singaporeans were lining up at hawker stands to eat any number of dishes available only in Singapore. Even in New York, a famously polyglot city that has, for example, three restaurants specializing in the food of the Uighur people of the Xinjiang Uighur Autonomous Region, a yearning for Singapore hawker food is surprisingly difficult to satisfy. (Singapore mei fun, a noodle dish often found in Chinatown restaurants, is, it almost goes without saying, unknown in Singapore.) You can find the Malaysian version of some Singaporean dishes—*asam laksa*, a terrific soup with an unlikely sour-fish taste, has some similarity to the Peranakan version of *laksa* served in hawker centers, for instance—and some dishes in Chinatown restaurants are similar to the dishes brought to Singapore from, say, Fujian or Hainan. There are, of course, some upmarket pan-Asian places in Manhattan that do versions of street food, including Singaporean hawker food. Apparently, though, a dish that is reminiscent of what's found in Singapore serves only to make overseas Singaporeans long for the real article. Culinarily, they are among the most homesick people I have ever met.

I commiserated with a number of them this spring, when the Prime Minister's office organized a Singapore Day in Central Park. Singapore Day was supposed to be for expatriate Singaporeans and their guests, but I was among some New York feeders who wormed our way in when we heard that the festivities would include Singaporean dishes prepared by a dozen hawkers flown in for the occasion. Six thousand people stood patiently in line for a go at some food from home—completely ignoring the government exhibitions and the requisite rock band. As they waited, they spoke of the stands they head for when they can manage the eleven-thousand-mile trip to Singapore—the coffee shop in their old neighborhood that has the best *kaya* (a sort of coconut custard, served on toast), the fried-prawn-noodle stand in Marine Parade they always visit the first day back, the place with the best halal version of chicken rice. Nobody I spoke to mentioned any restaurants. Even though the hawkers complained that they couldn't get all of the proper ingredients in New York, the tastes I had of *roti prata* (a sort of Indian crêpe with dipping sauce) and *chwee kueh* (rice cakes topped with bits of fried preserved radish) and *char kway teow* (a dense fried rice-noodle dish that includes, among other ingredients, eggs and Chinese sausages and cockles and chives and fried lard) and *laksa* confirmed the wisdom of my plan to go to Singapore to eat.

The hawkers who came to New York had been handpicked by K. F. Seetoh, a Singaporean of Cantonese descent, whose connection to hawker food is similar, on a smaller scale, to the connection the France family has had with stock-car racing: that is, he managed to recognize a lot of scattered, unexalted activity as a cultural force and figured out how to merchandise it. An energetic, self-assured man in his midforties, with a hint of blond in his hair, Seetoh, as he's known to everybody, began his career as a photographer. But his avocation—which is eating, since he is a lifelong resident of Singapore—eventually became his profession. He started in 1998 by putting together a hawker-food guide called *Makansutra, makan* being the Malay word for "eat" or "food." The guide lists what Seetoh considers the best stands for about a hundred and forty traditional hawker dishes—the best being all that any book would have room for, since Singapore has what Seetoh estimates to be about twelve thousand stands in the government hawker centers alone. The ratings are on a chopstick scale, with the most distinguished stands receiving three pairs of chopsticks. Seetoh's business card now identifies him as the chief executive and "makan guru" of a company that is also called Makansutra. He puts out other Southeast Asian food guides, appears on television, and does consultancies. He even presides over a small collection of hawker stands in the slick marina area that's part of Singapore's modernistic perform-ing-arts center—a building that, because of its shape (though not, presumably, its smell), is sometimes referred to by the locals as the Durian. Seetoh is helped in these endeavors by his wife, Patricia. Although Patricia says that before meeting her husband she ate mostly sandwiches and French fries, she comes from a Peranakan family that had good food as a priority. According to the Seetohs, when Patricia's father was on his deathbed he whispered something that made his family gather closer, thinking that he had some final instructions or blessings to impart. What he was saying turned out to be "*laksa.*" They brought him a bowl of it.

, Seetoh and I had become acquainted when he was in New York for Singapore Day. The next evening, at one of the sophisticated Southeast Asian places that he'd wanted to try, the Seetohs and I sampled some of the Singaporean dishes on the menu and he re-sponded more or less the way you'd expect a barbecue nut from Tennessee to respond to what was advertised as a pulled-pork-shoulder sandwich in, say, Helsinki or Leeds. He was moved to de-scribe the authentic Singaporean *nasi lemak* and the authentic Singaporean chili crab I'd eat when I got to Singapore. Given the fact that I wouldn't have thrown rocks at what we'd just eaten, I could hardly wait to sample the three-chopstick versions. I told Seetoh that I'd be in Singapore as soon as I could arrange it.

In Singapore, it was clear from the moment Seetoh picked me up at my hotel that, as interested as he was in authenticity and quality, pure capacity would also be an issue. He is an enthusiast. For Seetoh, there's always another noodle dish around the corner. He's quite willing to admit that there is plenty of mediocre hawker food in Singapore, but superior hawker fare renders him rhapsodic. The icon chart in *Makansutra* translates two and a half pairs of chopsticks—one notch below the top—as "Divine." Three pairs of chopsticks means "Die, Die Must Try!" which has become a sort of motto for Seetoh and his enterprises. It's a direct translation, he says, of a Cantonese phrase that means, more or less, "to die for." In addition to Cantonese and Mandarin and Malay and Hokkien, Seetoh speaks idiomatic English plus Singlish, a slangy local patois that is spoken only idiomatically. He speaks all of these languages rapidly.

Working mainly from my samplings at Singapore Day and from dishes that had been labeled "Popular Local Favorite" in the 2007 edition of *Makansutra*, I'd come up with a preliminary list of dishes that I considered, well, must try. There were nine: *chwee kueh* (the rice cakes with radish), grilled stingray, *roti prata*, curry puffs (which Seetoh describes as, more or less, a Chinese improvement on an Indian samosa), chili crab (and its cousin, pepper crab), *laksa*, fish-head curry, carrot cake (which would startle someone who'd meant to order the dessert you might get in the sort of restaurant whose waitresses slouch around in sandals: it's fried white radish and flour cake, with garlic and eggs and scallions and other vegetables), and *charkway teow*. Seetoh looked disappointed.

"Wrong list?" I asked.

Not wrong. Insufficient. I had left out Hokkien fried-prawn noodles. I had left out *otah*—fish paste, mixed with chilies, folded into a coconut leaf, and grilled. I had left out *rojak*—a sort of salad that's held together with a sauce the color and consistency of Mexican *mole*, unless you get the Indian rather than the Chinese version, which is totally different and, of course, a must-try item. I hadn't mentioned *mee siam*, a Thai-sounding noodle dish that is not available in Thailand. I hadn't mentioned fish-ball noodles—which is odd, since I am devoted to fish balls. I hadn't even mentioned *bak kut teh*, a simple pork-ribs soup that is, improbably, considered a breakfast treat. (Eventually, Seetoh and I had some *bak kut teh* for breakfast—in a place next to the port that is said to be the busiest in the world—and I can say unequivocally that it beats Cheerios by a mile.) I had left out *popiah*, a Hokkien-style spring roll that includes stewed turnips. By the time we reached the Maxwell Road Hawker Centre—near where Makansutra has an office, in a row of colonial-era three-story buildings known as shop-houses—my list had about twenty items, and for the next few days every hawker center seemed to remind Seetoh of a dish I had to try before I went home. "You can't leave without having it," Seetoh would say, when he instructed me to add another dish to my list. "It'll knock your socks off."

Sampling what Seetoh considers the very best rendition of each dish required some traveling around town—a remarkable chicken rice here, an amazing *chwee kueh* there, a mind-blowing *laksa* somewhere else. At one center, though—the modestly named Old Airport Road Temporary Food Centre, which was serving a public-housing project during some construction that's part of an ambitious, ten-year hawker-center upgrading program that the government launched in 2001—we were in the presence of three venders who had been designated by Seetoh as hawker masters. There, without descending into the realm of the merely divine, you can start with *rojak*, then tear into some chili crab, and then decide whether you might want to end the evening with Hokkien fried-prawn noodles or have the chili-crab specialist do a pepper crab as a change of pace before you end the evening with Hokkien fried-prawn noodles. I had no doubt that I was indeed eating the food of masters. In fact, while eating at the Old Airport Road Temporary Food Centre I realized that it was incorrect to think that my taste buds operated at full strength only when I was standing: we were eating this food while sitting at a table, after all, and it was knocking my socks off. One of the principles of scientific inquiry is that even an elegant hypothesis has to be abandoned if irrefutable evidence to the contrary is encountered.

Seetoh seemed quite confident about his selection of the very best stand for each hawker dish, but, as I had learned from the people I'd met at Singapore Day—people whom Seetoh had described as "deprived and depraved"—a Singaporean devotee of hawker food doesn't have to be the author of a food guide to be absolutely certain that he knows where to find the best version of just about anything. One evening, while we were eating some fish-head curry—a dish that in Singapore includes an entire snapper head staring up through the curry sauce—a friend of Seetoh's named Daniel Wang shook his head sadly when he heard where Seetoh had taken me for *char kway teow*. Wang, who retired in 2004 as Singapore's director general of public health, happened to be the Ministry of the Environment engineer put in charge of building the original hawker centers, in the seventies. At his retirement, he had just presided over a $2.5-million upgrading of a beach venue called the East Coast Lagoon Hawker Centre, which was turned into something so reminiscent of a tropical resort that Seetoh refers to it as "Daniel's Club Med." Wang's contribution to hawker centers can be seen as a monument to enlightened self-interest: given his line of work, he's quite conscious of hygiene, but he happens to be crazy about hawker food, particularly *char kway teow*. As a schoolboy, Wang regularly observed the cooking technique of a particular *char kway teow* hawker, and he remains loyal to that hawker's son—a vender who had learned well from his father, Wang explained, how to cook the noodles in lard to keep them from sticking and how to make his stock from prawns and squid and precisely when to sprinkle on white pepper. Dismissing the suggestion that childhood nostalgia might be making him a less than objective judge, Wang went on to extoll the *popiah* produced by a hawker who had not been among the five *popiah* hawkers listed in *Makansutra*.

Wang was so enthusiastic about the snubbed *popiah* that there was nothing to do but go to the Newton Food Centre and give it a try, as soon as we had polished off the fish-head curry. At the Newton Centre, Seetoh was barely polite about the *popiah* and Wang did not pursue the matter, having become caught up in a discussion of a sort of oyster omelette that we'd picked up from a nearby stall. I assumed that the *popiah* discussion was at an end. The next evening, though, while the Seetohs and I were on the way to the East Coast Lagoon Hawker Centre to have some salted vegetable and duck soup (a dish that has replaced French fries in Patricia Seetoh's pantheon), Seetoh pulled up in front of a shopping mall called the Shaw Centre. While we waited in the car, Patricia ducked in to get some *popiah*, so that I could understand what a divine—or maybe even a die-die-must-try—*popiah* is like. In Singapore, I should have realized, a discussion about the relative merits of various *popiah* stands is never at an end.

The more we ate, the longer my list got. We couldn't seem to stay even. On my last evening, while we consumed some *mee siam* and the Indian version of *rojak* with Daniel Wang and a couple of his friends, Seetoh was still lamenting the dishes I hadn't had—steamboat (a sort of hot pot) and a Malay noodle dish called *mee rebus* and *lontong* (an Indonesian dish of rice cakes with tofu and vegetables simmered in a coconut curry) and *nasi briyani* (a dish of Middle Eastern origin) and a Hakka tofu dish called *yong tau foo* and Indian *mee goring*. One of Wang's guests said that when she gets back to Singapore on the flight that arrives around dawn she stops for *kueh chap* before she even goes home—*kueh chap* being a bowl of broth with sheets of rice-flour noodles served with pig intestines, or what Wang calls "spare parts." Seetoh said, almost apologetically, that he hadn't taken me to a *kueh chap* stand, and I said, "My mother used to say that it's always good to save something for the next trip."

I was, indeed, thinking about the next trip as I studied my list on the plane home. I deeply regretted having had *char kway teow* only once, for instance, and I didn't see how I was going to repair that deficit without returning to Singapore. I was also thinking of how convenient it would be if other cities—New York, for instance—had hawker centers serving the local specialties. New York's current mayor does not disdain tidiness, after all, and New York mayors have thought of street venders as congestion at least since the reign of Fiorello LaGuardia, who gathered some of them in places like the Essex Street Market.

A hawker center could be set up by the next time the Seetohs visited New York. I could imagine us at a place than looks a bit like the East Coast Lagoon Hawker Centre, Daniel's Club Med, although it would overlook the Hudson rather than the Strait of Singapore. There's a stand selling Italian-sausage sandwiches, of course, and a stand selling Vietnamese *banh mi* sandwiches. The Mayor has persuaded the *dosa* man of Washington Square to come into the operation and leave the Washington Square cart in the hands of a trusted cousin. There are stands run by the venders from the Red Hook ball fields—one selling *pupusas* and one selling ceviche and one selling Honduran tacos. A couple of Belgian French-fry venders are there, with fries good enough to make Patricia Seetoh consider reverting to her former eating habits. The Mayor's people have persuaded the legendary Arepa Lady of Jackson Heights to give up the chancy weather of Roosevelt Avenue for the Hudson River Hawker Center. There's a jerk-chicken stand and two competing falafel stands. I've been in nearly constant movement between our table and the venders all evening, bringing back, say, bocconcini or two kinds of fish balls—the plain ones and the ones with meat at the center, familiar from Eldridge Street noodle-soup restaurants like Sheng Wang and the exquisitely named Young City Fish Balls. Seetoh is saying that he's getting a bit full, and reminds me that he and Patricia have to get up early for the long flight back to Singapore. "But you haven't had a calzone yet," I say. "You haven't had a zeppole. We still haven't gotten you a classic New York pastrami sandwich, not to speak of a knish. I'm not talking about one of those nasty commercial knishes that look like vinyl coin purses. I'm talking about an authentic New York potato knish. You can't go home without eating a knish. It'll knock your socks off."

NEW DAY, NEW DEVON

By Raphael Kadushin

from *Bon Appetit*

A frequent *Bon Appetit* contributor, Kadushin—who's also a
senior editor at the University of Wisconsin Press—combines
his wanderlust and his refined palate, globe-hopping in
search of remarkable local food scenes.

Look outside the picture window of the Michael Caines
Restaurant in the Abode Exeter hotel, and you know
exactly where you are. The epic Gothic cathedral, the row of red
brick Georgian houses, and the sweep of lawn are all as quintes-
sentially English as tweeds, high tea, and sticky toffee pudding. But
glance down at the desserts gilding your table, in the airy contemporary dining room in the Devonshire market town of Exeter, and
the British clichés fade fast. Instead of that sticky toffee pudding
Michael Caines Restaurant serves a velvety vanilla crème brulee
paired with walnut nougatine, butterscotch sauce, and pear sorbet.
There are none of the British nursery room sweets with the
squeaky, slapstick names that defy you to take them seriously—no
fat rascal, spotted dick, or meringue roly poly—but there is a very
mature warm fig and orange tartlet with spiced jelly. And while
old Devonshire favorites like Goosey Fair toffee apples won't make
their appearance, an urban mille-feuille of bitter chocolate ganache
with coffee parfait manages to compensate.

Forget the doorstop scones and the overcooked roasts too,
though none of this—along with the decline and fall of the old
boy puddings—should come as a big surprise. The culinary revolution that rocked London in the nineties, and made it a global

dining destination, has long since seeped out into England's regional counties. What is surprising is that the current epicenter of the country's creative cook-off has become twee Devon—a southwestern English shire always known more for its scenery and cozy cream teas than any ambitious cuisine. The fact that it is now home to six Michelin stars and more maverick chefs than the average London borrough is real proof that the British dining renaissance has swept the whole island.

Blame Devonshire's surprise ascendance on Caines himself, a local boy who had a vision when he left home.

"I'm originally from Exeter," Caines says. "And though I trained in London with a lot of great chefs and then cooked in France, coming back to Devon was a true homecoming for me, because I could see what a brilliant larder we had here, and I could be part of a big change. For the first time now we're championing our own farmers and fishermen. And in the process we're creating a local food culture in the same way a rich regional culinary tradition has always existed in France and Spain and Italy."

What makes Caines's larder particularly brilliant is its range. Start with the lamb and the beef that graze on Devon's inland pastures. Caines first did them justice when he took over the kitchen at Gidleigh Park—a country house hotel on the edge of Dartmoor—and won two Michelin stars. The legacy continues in Exeter at his Michael Caines Restaurant, which the chef co-owns (along with the Abode Exeter hotel it helps anchor), and where there is no need to race to the dessert list. Under Caines's mentorship, executive chef Ross Melling is turning out a Devonshire red ruby fillet of beef with roasted shallots and wild mushrooms that is a delicate tumble of flavors. So is his classic local spring lamb napped by onion puree and braised fennel.

But the Devonshire harvest isn't only a meaty one. Just south of Exeter sits Torquay, a seaside resort town formerly patronized as a third-rate Brighton, where your fish wasn't cooked until it came dripping out of the deep fryer. Things change quickly in the West Country though. Chef Simon Hulstone of the Elephant Bar & Restaurant has won a Michelin star two years running for his deft, delicate way with the local catch.

"Our menu can be 70 percent seafood," he says, "because it would be criminal not to use the fantastic fish we have on our doorstep—all the shellfish, the Torbay sole, the turbot. We have one guy who just dives scallops and lobster for us." Making the most of the briny haul are Hulstones' Brixham crab and creamed avocado martini, served with warm crab beignets; a pan-roasted John Dory laid over a parsnip emulsion; and a roast fillet of sea bream coupled with the earthier accent of hog's pudding, a local sausage made from cooked pork and oats.

To get a real sense of what is drawing more diners and chefs to Devon, though, you have to drive into the heart of the shire—the untouched, sprawling, heather-cushioned Dartmoor National Park—and witness the way another regional trademark has been rediscovered, and reimagined. A brilliant larder can only lure travelers if it comes wrapped up in a brilliant showcase, and what made Devon the epitome of the great English country getaway in the nineteenth century were the epic Dartmoor estates that signified a kind of British fantasia: the idyll of glossy scenery, ruddy sports, and the sumptuous feasts that always capped a day of fishing and riding.

Helping fuel Devon's return to opulent form, those mythic estates, many reduced to ruined piles over the years, have recently been resurrected as luxe country house hotels that offer a repackaged, updated version of the Anglo good life, sublime meal included. Among the pioneers and an ongoing model of Devon's revived estate inns is Gidleigh Park, which recently underwent a multimillion dollar renovation. The half-timbered Tudor-style manor, overlooking the North Teign River, now flaunts relaid Devon oak floors, a new wing of sleeker, more contemporary guest rooms, a third dining room, and refitted bathrooms that mix a touch of Deco with urban luxury (think under-floor heating). The hotel's real white heat, though, still blasts out of Caines's kitchen, which has been updated and expanded so that the chef can refocus his uncompromising blend of modern European cuisine and peerless regional ingredients. Among the signature dishes, netted by fishermen rocking in day boats off the southwestern English coast: a fricassee of lobster, roused by a lobster bisque of garlic, white peppercorns, coriander, thyme, plum tomatoes, and cardamom.

Gidleigh's renewed energy infuses the whole moor, and its bor-
derlands. Just south at Bovey Castle, a jazz-age estate framed by an
18-hole championship golf course, dishes like grilled sea trout
bathed in citrus butter get served in a dining room wallpapered
with button-eyed songbirds. A longer drive north to the Devon
harbor town of Ilfracombe brings more intrepid diners to 11 The
Quay, a former Victorian seaside inn transformed, by renegade
British art star Damien Hirst, into an equally cutting-edge restaurant. And due east, overlooking its own ripe tableau of ancient
meadow and forest, is the Elizabethan Combe House Hotel, which
features a fall-out of four-poster beds and ancestral portraits, along
with a walled garden that supplies head chef Hadleigh Barret with
his own in-house larder of jams, Devon honey, chutneys, herbs, and
vegetables.

An easy ride southwest, across the moors, leads to a double culinary attraction. The appetizer is the high Victorian market town of
Tavistock, where the long-running (as in nine hundred years or so)
Tavistock Pannier Market is designed to outfit a West Country
picnic. Among the best of the shops running beside the Market is
Country Cheeses, where the clerks turn poetic over Devon blue
cheeses and "the smooth, mellow Belsone," and where you get a
geography lesson with your wedge of creamy Sharpham, made
with the milk of Jersey cows grazing on pastures overlooking the
river Dart, in South Devon. Hungry yet? The main course is at the
nearby, one-star the Horn of Plenty, which lives up to its name.

"I love riding to work over the Moor and passing the lambs I'm
sourcing," says chef Peter Gorton, who runs cooking classes out of
the ten-room hotel's kitchen, when he isn't plating the kind of
dinner that doesn't believe in understatement or in counting truffles. His seared squid and king prawns come crowned with sweet,
tempura-battered asparagus and a roast breast of wood pigeon is
dressed with sautéed foie gras, though none of the patrician
touches detract from Gorton's own ode to the Devon harvest. "A
local lady rolls our butter in her sink by hand," he smiles. "She has
arms like Popeye."

But if time is tight, the best one-stop foray from Gidleigh is the
drive west to Devon's newest star estate, Hotel Endsleigh, across
the whole raw space of the moors, where passing signs warn of

sheep lying on the roads and where everything looks like an elegant still-life—the Dartmoor ponies and sheep grazing on the hills; the pastures scored by a rolling necklace of high hedgerows; the villages with names that tease the palate. Chipshop, Plummy, Sourton, Cornwood, Appledore, and Rosemary Lane.

"It's like the last open space," Alex Polizzi laughs, shaking her brown curls. "My heart went over my head when I first saw this place. No wonder Devon used to be such a chic playground and why it's Devon's turn again. The English educated themselves abroad and now we're rediscovering the joy of our own countryside and our own food. It's a shock for a city girl like me to find myself in charge of 180 acres but I love it."

Who wouldn't? Polizzi's own version of a country playground is an especially playful one. Designed in the early nineteenth century, for the Duchess of Bedford, as a cottage orne—which means it's as cottagelike as Caesars Palace—the flamboyant Regency showpiece has been updated by Alex's mother, the hotelier and designer Olga Polizzi. (The fact that her recent redo of London's venerable Brown's Hotel directly preceded her acquisition of Endsleigh says something, in itself, about Devon's ascending status.) The result is another sequence of still-lives, though these are exquisitely whimsical ones. A seashell grotto fittingly mixes homey Devon shells and exotic tropical coral. Guestrooms are punctuated with neoclassical busts, architectural prints, and flea market finds. At night the parlor and halls glow with enough votive candles to light up the long nave of Exeter's cathedral.

Chef Shay Cooper's clean, down-to-earth cooking doesn't try too hard (a salmon fillet is framed by cockles and baby leeks) until teatime. Then local tradition suddenly prevails and the gleaming mahogany table in the library fills up with tiers of sandwiches, blocks of shortbread, potted strawberry jam, bowls brimming with clotted cream, and pyramids of scones. This is the textbook Devon cream tea reborn, the clotted cream so thick it cascades in silky layers from the silver serving spoon, the small, biscuity scones so feathery they crumble under the weight of the bone-white cream. Devon etiquette suggests—okay, politely insists—that you spoon your cream on your scone first, and then the jam, and when the sun surfaces you're meant to take your china cups to the side terrace, supported by tree-trunk columns and paved with sheep knuckles, for an ethereal view of the Tamar River Valley.

If that makes for an oddly classic ending to the stylish Devon getaway, maybe the climax is fitting. The best revolutions always come full circle to reclaim their roots. And the fact that coconut rice pudding is a favorite on Endsleigh's dinner menu is a sign that tea may not constitute the only return to form. In fact, it's probably only a matter of time before the schoolboy puddings make a local comeback. But the ones streaming out of Devon's bright new kitchens will be cleaner, grown-up versions, and nothing at all to laugh at.

In a '64 T-Bird, Chasing a Date With a Clam

By David Leite

from the *New York Times*

It's an irresistible combination: Summer, a convertible, and
road food. David Leite, proprietor of the award-winning Web
site leitesculinaria.com, cruised the Northeast in search of a
nostalgic taste from his childhood.

Recapturing a childhood memory is nearly impossible.
Chasing after it in a black 1964 Thunderbird convertible with red interior certainly helps.

The memory: lightly fried clams with big, juicy bellies, like the
kind I munched on nearly every summer weekend growing up in
Swansea, Massachusetts. The car, owned by my friend Bob Pidkameny: a nod to my godfather, a local celebrity and stock car driver,
who would pile my two cousins and me into whatever sleek
beauty he was tinkering with and take us to Macray's in Westport,
Massachusetts. There we sat—three lard slicks—digging into red-
and-white cardboard boxes, while screams from the riders on the
Comet, the wooden roller coaster at a nearby amusement park,
floated across the highway.

Fried clams are to New England what barbecue is to the South.
Like barbecue, the best clams come from small roadside shacks run
in pragmatic mom-and-pop style. Flinty Northerners, like their
porcine-loving counterparts, can be fanatically loyal to their favorite spots. To eat at any place but Macray's was considered famil-
ial treason when I was growing up—it was Macray's or nothing,
until it was shuttered and we were set adrift.

This summer, in search of the clams of my youth, Bob and I covered more than 625 miles, visited 16 shacks and unashamedly basked in the attention the Thunderbird commanded from Branford, Connecticut, to Portland Maine, and back. In between rolls of antacid and scoops of ice cream, the unofficial finish to a fried-clam meal, we found that this summertime classic is even more fleeting than the season of its peak popularity.

Storms, public taste, government warnings about saturated fats, even school vacation schedules conspired to keep the clams of my memory mostly out of reach. But every once in a while, fate jiggered events and passed me a pint or two of the luscious, plump-bellied beauties I remember.

To many New Englanders the humble clam, which stars in chowders, clambakes and clam cakes, reaches its quintessence when coated and fried. And ever since July 3, 1916, when Lawrence Woodman, aka Chubby, the founder of Woodman's in Essex, Massachusetts, fried a clam in lard normally reserved for his famous potato chips, cooks have been trying to create the perfect fried clam.

But unlike pit masters who rabidly guard their secret sauce recipes, fry cooks are an open book. All work with the same four elements: soft-shell clams, a dipping liquid, a coating and oil. According to almost all the cooks and owners I met the liquid is usually evaporated milk, and the coating is nothing more than some combination of flours: regular, corn or pastry. Most places use canola or soybean oil, which are high in unsaturated fats. Only Woodman's and Essex Seafood, in Essex, Massachusetts, still fry clams in pure lard.

So why are the clams I dream of so hit-or-miss?

"I've been doing this for 21 years," said Dave Blaney, owner of the Sea Swirl in Mystic, Connecticut, "and the hardest part is training the new kids." He explained that it takes two weeks to train summer help, usually college students, but it requires almost two months of supervision to turn them into bona fide fry cooks. He warned me about visiting shacks too early in the season (when the students are gearing up) or too late (when the exodus occurs, and deep fryers can be left in the hands of most anyone—the owners' sons or daughters, say, or the cleaning help).

Improperly cooked clams can range from oil-laden to burned. Indeed, the Clam Shack in Kennebunkport, Maine, a favorite place I've been recommending to friends for years, presented Bob and me with a pint of puny dark-brown clams that tasted faintly of burned liver. Champlin's Restaurant in Narragansett, Rhode Island, another well-regarded spot, served clams so overcooked we dumped them after eating only a few. In both places, the kitchen crews looked like a cast from "The Real World" on MTV.

The Sea Swirl's clams, on the other hand, were golden, with a light crunch, and the bellies, while on the smaller side, were plump and filled with ocean flavor. What caught my attention was that the siphons, or "necks," were snipped off. That made for a soft chew, without the rubber-eraser bite common to most fried clams—even, I must admit, those from the hallowed boxes I remember at Macray's.

I asked if this was a customary practice of purveyors. "No, I snip them here," Mr. Blaney said. "Otherwise I'm at the mercy of the supplier, and I can't afford that." Of all the places we visited, only the Sea Swirl offered completely snipped necks; the others sold clams with just the tops nicked off.

This snipping, though, shouldn't be confused with the iconic, and tasteless, clam strips featured on every Howard Johnson menu in New England. These impostors can be as varied as de-bellied steamers—a rarity—and slices cut from the "tongue" of the larger multipurpose Atlantic surf clam. No strip has the oceanic flavor of a true steamer with its belly firmly attached.

It was later that day, after leaving two small Massachusetts shacks empty-handed, that we understood just how much weather influences what we eat, or rather do not eat. As a result of several days of heavy downpours and runoff earlier in the week, the clam flats, the most highly prized of them off the coast of the state's North Shore, specifically Ipswich and Essex, were closed.

The water can take several days to normalize after a big storm, according to Curt Fougere, a great-grandson of Chubby Woodman and the manager of Woodman's. That's why those smaller spots, which don't sell as many clams as Woodman's, had to turn us away. Larger places with purchasing muscle can buy from Cape Cod or even as far away as Maryland and Canada, but none of those clams have the Ipswich richness, a by-product of the nutri-ent-filled mud.

"Cape Cod clams tend to be gritty," Mr. Blaney said, "because they come from sandbars rather than mud flats." Maryland steam-ers, while deliciously large, are too soft, he said, and break apart while cooking. Maine clams are considered the closest to Ipswich clams, and are the most common substitute.

In between shouts from classic car enthusiasts along Route 1, Bob and I theorized about the reasons for the dearth of the big-belly clams. We batted around global warming, pollution, disease, but none seemed likely to have knocked out only the pudgy clams. No, the biggest threat, we discovered, was far more menac-ing: fashion.

"Clams kind of go through cycles," said Terry Cellucci, an owner of J. T. Farnham's, one-third of the famous Essex clam shack trifecta that includes Woodman's and Essex Seafood. For years, she explained, smaller clams have been in vogue. "Right now that's what our customers like, so that's what we buy." The same was true of most every place we visited. The clams at Farnham's fried up dark golden and pleasantly crunchy but were missing that burst of juicy belly brininess.

Two diners at the next table in Farnham's, Janice Shohet of Lynnfield, Massachusetts, and her guest, Stacey Malcolm, of Wichita, Kansas, were of the plump-clam camp. When asked their favorite of the three popular Essex spots, Ms. Shohet tapped the table. "I like it here—it feels like a real seaside place," she said, re-ferring to the deep-blue inlet outside. Then she mentioned the most important clue to my past: "But we love the Clam Box, too. They give you a choice of big or small bellies."

As we pulled up outside the Clam Box, eight miles northwest in Ipswich, Massachusetts, the first thing we noticed—aside from the whimsical roof that looks like (what else?) an opened clam box—was the line snaking out the door. It numbered more than 20 and according to the owner, Marina Aggelakis—known to all as Chickie—had started forming, as always, 30 minutes before opening.

Taking Ms. Shohet's advice, I searched the huge menu above the order window and found the one line of neat, tight printing I was hoping to see: *Big belly clams available on request.* The Clam Box was the only shack on our trip to offer up this critical piece of information unbidden.

When I ordered a pint of the big bellies, the woman behind the counter winced: "Are you sure? They're big."

"I'm positive."

"You'll only get about nine," she said.

"That's fine."

She tried once more to dissuade me, but I resisted. When my number was called, a tray was pushed through the pickup window: on it was a mound of golden clams with bellies so big and soft the coating was chipping off. The necks, though not trimmed like those at the Sea Swirl, had none of the elastic bite I had encountered in many pints along the way. And the bellies dripped sweet, briny clam juice down my chin.

To pull this all off, Ms. Aggelakis uses only Ipswich clams unless bad weather or high demand causes her to turn to Maine suppliers. She also double-dips her clams while cooking. Excess coating stays behind in the first deep-fryer, allowing for cleaner cooking in the second. In addition, she closes the restaurant between lunch and dinner—unheard-of—to change the oil, ensuring a clean taste all day long.

It was an offhand comment, though, that gave me the final piece of the puzzle: darker-fried clams, she said, have a nuttier taste, while the lighter version lets the clam flavor predominate. Bingo. "I like to please my customers," she added. "Some like them big, small, lightly fried, dark—we give them what they want." Funny, the concept of requesting anything special at a clam shack's takeout window had eluded me for 40 years.

Putting together the experience from the trip, I decided to try my hand at customizing my meal at Lenny's Indian Head Inn in Branford, Connecticut. First, I called ahead because we had had two days of steady rain. The clams were frying. When I ordered, I asked the waitress, a bubbly young woman, if the restaurant had big-bellied clams. She wasn't sure, so went to ask the cook.

She returned deeply crestfallen. All he had, she said, was medium-size, "but he'll try to pick out the biggest ones." Equally crestfallen, I agreed and asked for them to be lightly fried.

What was placed in front of me 10 minutes later was a platter with clams nearly as large as those at the Clam Box. They had a light golden almost tempura-like coating. And the bellies? They were briny, sweet and so juicy a lobster bib wouldn't have been out of the question.

I could almost hear the screams from the Comet again.

Cajun Country by Car: A Native Son's Freewheeling Tour

By Thomas O. Ryder

from *Food & Wine*

What does the CEO of *Reader's Digest* do when he retires? Well, if you're a gourmand like Thomas O. Ryder, founder of the Aspen Food & Wine classic during his tenure at American Express, you hit the road looking for great Southern cooking.

Hot Boudin,
Cold Couche-couche,
Come On Tigers,
Push, Push, Push!
—Louisiana State University Football Cheer

Only in food-obsessed Louisiana would the favorite cheer of the favorite college football team reference epicurean delicacies. Well, perhaps "delicacies" is a stretch.

Boudin (a pork and rice sausage) and couche-couche (a kind of fried cornmeal mush) are staples of a Cajun cuisine that thrives in a relatively small area of southern Louisiana and influences menus and food intelligence around the country. It is bold, rough, workingman's food, with French, German, Spanish, Italian, African and West Indian influences, created from the area's abundance of seafood, game, herbs and vegetables.

It is a hard cuisine for outsiders to love and understand. But occasionally, a particularly talented local chef, like Paul Prudhomme, will move to a bigger stage in a prominent city and rekindle a national interest in what may be our best and most unique native food.

Following Prudhomme's example, Donald Link is off to a great start at establishing himself as America's best new Cajun chef. Link is chef and owner of two of New Orleans's best restaurants: Herbsaint, a seven-year-old Southern bistro in the downtown area, and the dazzling new Cochon, a sophisticated, country-casual spot in the Warehouse District that is drawing SRO crowds of food-smart locals and tourists.

Cochon is refreshingly different. It is decidedly Cajun in a city that cherishes its Creole roots; it is surprisingly inexpensive for its level of quality; and, most significant, its menu is filled with beautifully executed and clever reinterpretations of the food Link grew up with in southwestern Louisiana. Cochon is not for those with timid palates or a lack of culinary curiosity. Here are some dishes on offer: hog's head cheese; fried alligator; ham hocks with grits and peppers; fried boudin with pickled peppers; shrimp and deviled-egg gumbo; pork belly with potatoes, carrots and lima beans. Courage is rewarded at Cochon, as this is exuberantly good food.

My brother Robert and I, and our wives, Francie and Darlene, all grew up in Louisiana. Rob and Francie never left. We have spent much of our lives eating less polished versions of Link's food, and we weren't scared off. We were fascinated by the quality of it, and by the very smart riffs on dishes we thought we knew. So we spent a week eating at Cochon and Herbsaint and then tracing the roots of the food back to Cajun country, trying to get inside Donald Link's head.

Link grew up in Lake Charles, just west of Cajun country. His ancestors were Links and Zaunbrechers, among the Germans who settled the prairie that runs along the western edge of Cajun country. He was a restless kid who worked in restaurants from the time he was 15. He studied finance at Louisiana State University but quit after five years "to drink beer and play golf," he says, an endeavor funded by working in the kitchen at Sammy's in Baton Rouge, a local hangout of some note. Wanderlust took Link to San Francisco and several funky restaurants, including the Elite Cafe, where he was asked to introduce his Cajun food to the menu. After a bit he went back to Louisiana to cook with Susan Spicer at Bayona in New Orleans, then back to San Francisco to help Traci

Des Jardins launch Jardiènere. In 2000, he again went "home," this time working with Spicer to open Herbsaint.

On our first day at Cochon, we are given a tour of the kitchen by Link and his partner and co-chef, Stephen Stryjewski. It is a small, busy space in which practically every square foot is employed. There is barely room for the 150-pound (dressed and cleaned) pig that has just arrived. In true Cajun style, virtually every morsel will be used in some dish on the menu, hence the name Cochon (French for "pig"). Over the next few days, we smile as we see parts of our porcine friend show up on the plate.

Link loves boudin, but he serves only a less challenging version. He says he is afraid some tourist will eat the sausage casing and choke to death, inspiring a headline in the local paper, to wit: "Tourist Chokes to Death on Link Sausage." So, only boudin balls are on the menu. These are the inside of the sausage shaped into balls, rolled in flour, dipped in buttermilk, covered in bread crumbs and fried. Most of the diners at Cochon don't have a clue what they are eating, but it is hard to deny the looks of pleasure as they try to figure it out.

I grew up with hog's head cheese. My Uncle Leland (rest his soul) made it and served it with saltines. It was a fiery, gelatinous mess, and it scared the hell out of me. The name alone retarded my willingness to experiment with food, and I have seldom seen hog's head cheese since. But it was on the Cochon menu, and how can you not order something with a name like that?

Wanna know what's in it? Pig snout and pig parts, mostly. They're boiled down until everything falls apart. Then the meat is picked out. The bones and sinew and skin are discarded, the broth is cooked down with spices and green onions, and the meat is added back in. Then it chills and sets. This is a dish that doesn't exactly grace a plate, so it's nice to have a garnish. Link's version has a secret ingredient that gives the cheese a distinctive tang. I silently apologize to Uncle Leland for failing to appreciate his artistry and say to Link, "You put vinegar in it, didn't you?" He just gives me an enigmatic smile.

Over two days we eat all his pork dishes, and we are bigger and better people for it. We love the ham hocks and pork shoulder, but not the grilled ribs. There's rabbit on the menu, too. I think the rabbit stew with German dumplings is inspired, but Darlene has visions of the Easter Bunny and disagrees. What does she know?

Fully half the menu is seafood—oysters, shrimp, crab, catfish, crawfish, alligator and saltwater fish taken from the marshes, swamps, lakes, rivers and farms that run through and around the remarkable Cajun countryside. At Cochon, Link makes brilliant use of this largesse. His oyster roast, for instance, is an appetizer of perfectly fresh oysters drizzled with a sauce of lemon butter, garlic and chile and then barely warmed through in the wood-burning oven. The taste of the sea with a hint of smoke is exhilarating.

Over a long dinner, preceded by a tasting to make sure none of the bourbons on the list have spoiled, I get Link to talk about the restaurants that have most influenced his thinking. He doesn't have to try hard to name six establishments, taking care to emphasize that they are not accomplished restaurants, but places from which he'd learned something important. The next day, after a generous infusion of aspirin and a mannerly and delightful lunch at Herbsaint, we set off with Link's list on what we call "the beer, bourbon and boudin tour."

Boudin is a loose rice sausage made most often with pork, pig liver, onions and spices. The mixture is extruded into casings, tied off into links and kept in steam pots in gas stations, meat markets, general stores and roadside stands all over Cajun country. For some people, like me, eating boudin comes naturally. I simply cut a link apart, put the open end into my mouth and bite down gently while pulling. A delicious surprise is deposited on my tongue. Some use another perfectly acceptable method. They hold the open end of the link in their mouth and use the thumb and forefinger to squeeze the good stuff out. One often sees, but seldom respects, foreigners who extrude the contents onto a plate and take delicate little bites with a fork. Ain't nothing delicate about boudin.

It is said that Cajuns will eat anything that runs, walks, swims, crawls or slithers, and they serve it all with rice. My brother tells the story of a Cajun named Boudreaux who is awakened by his wife in the middle of the night. She tells him something like a flying saucer has landed on the levee behind the house and little green men are getting out of it. Boudreaux looks out and says, "I don't know what that is, no, but I'll take care of 'dis. Hand me my shotgun, you, and cook some rice."

One other caution about boudin: This stuff looks scary. It is long and plump and slightly translucent and deathly gray. Think entrails, the large animal kind.

Boudin for breakfast is bracing. We start at Poche's Market and Restaurant in Breaux Bridge at 10 a.m. I've bought boudin from them by mail, and I know it's good. But at that hour of the morning, it makes my companions queasy. We persist and are rewarded. The stuff is ridiculously good. Deeply porky and richly creamy with liver, it bites the tip of your tongue and the back of your throat with just enough spice to wake you up. Francie, a skeptic, eats about a pound-and-a-half. As we head out, one of the delightful young women behind the counter spots us as enthusiastic eaters and suggests we stick around for the cow-tongue cook-off that weekend. We pass.

After visiting a few other boudin places recommended by locals, we drive to the place Link most wanted us to visit: Mowata (pronounced MO-wata) Store. It's in Mowata, Louisiana, near the community of Link (yes, Link), between Crowley and Eunice, but not on any map known to humankind. You just have to drive by and look for it. The place does a steady business selling boudin and cracklings. We sit at one of the two tables and order some of both. Damn, they're good. The boudin has an intense, swiney flavor with a slight whiff of chitlins and an aggressive spice. It's the spiciest we will taste, but it's missing the unctuous richness of liver. Two of us like it more for that reason, two less. But, hey, let's not quibble. This is inspired food.

I am pretty sure Link's lesson here is about boudin as a symbol. It is about Cajun simplicity and frugality and creativity. As Poche's motto suggests, they cook "everything from the rooter to the tooter." The motto is also about pride and the commitment to excellence displayed by these people, who try every day to make at least one thing better than anyone else in the world—in this case, boudin.

That night, we are genuinely excited as we head to one of the best-known places on Link's list, Pat's Fisherman's Wharf. Pat's sits between Bayou Amy (pronounced ah-ME) and the levee that holds back Henderson Lake, a body of water formed by the Atchafalaya River basin, a vast flood plain that spawns one of the most impenetrable networks of swamps in the world. It is also the source of the best crawfish and catfish in America, a lot of which is processed near Pat's. You can imagine the catfish and crawfish and alligators swimming up to Pat's back door to surrender. Pat's looks perfect.

The food is incredibly bad, but we order a lot. Some is cold, some is greasy, some is just badly conceived. I want to call Link and threaten to knock a wart on his head for inflicting this place on us. We spend the whole drive back to our $49-a-night motel, through ominous rain and lightning, arguing about what he was saying by directing us there. Francie suggests he was trying to show how good Cochon is by contrast.

I wake up during the night and realize what Link had learned from Pat's: "You can't quit trying."

The next night is so good, it almost makes up for the previous one. We go to Hawk's in the town of Rayne. Hawk's is a big corrugated-tin shed plopped down right in the woods. It's open only a few months a year, when crawfish are in season. I'm pretty sure Hawk's makes boiled crawfish better than anyplace in the world. It starts by purging the crawfish, leaving them in running spring water for about 24 hours until the intestines are cleaned out. Hawk's says the fat changes color during the process, and tastes better.

We start with five pounds of crawfish—big ones. A couple of these would scare the hell out of a wimpy lobster. But size is not the secret to Hawk's. Its success is all about absolutely fresh crawfish, boiled until the moment of perfect doneness (my guess is five to seven minutes). Then they are sprayed with spice, hot or regular. These crawfish almost "ping" with freshness when you bite into them—the texture is that flawless—and the taste is sweet and spicy. Five pounds isn't enough.

On the day we visit Hawk's for dinner we also have a wonderful lunch at Frey's Crawfish House in Welsh. It's not much to look at, but it feels good when you walk in the door. Link thinks the owners of Frey's, the Zaunbrechers, may be distantly related to him, but apparently they don't know him and aren't too impressed with the idea of a New Orleans chef, anyway. We order two gumbos, two bisques and two étouffées, this being a light lunch before we go to

Hawk's for dinner. The shrimp and corn bisque turns out to be one of our favorite dishes of the entire Cajun-country trip, and the gumbo rivals the one at Herbsaint as the best we taste. The crawfish étouffée is so infused with flavor, I think it is made with some kind of crawfish espresso. I'm not far off. Shonda Zaunbrecher, the chef at Hawk's, tells us the secret is undercooking the crawfish so that the fat becomes runny and can be poured into the étouffée.

She convinces us to try dessert. We say, "OK, but just a bite." Then daughter Angelica brings us a bread pudding topped with a whiskey sauce that is, hands down, the most delicious I have ever tasted. We eat every last crumb of it. And nap that afternoon.

The best is saved for last. Those who think Disneyland is the happiest place on earth have never been to Café Des Amis in Breaux Bridge at 7:30 on a Saturday morning. We arrive at 6:50 for a table at the zydeco breakfast. By 7:30, when the door opens, people fill most of the block. The room is soon buzzing. We meet travelers from Rhode Island and France and Australia, but most of the customers have Cajun accents that indicate they are locals. We order great beignets and a huge bowl of couche-couche and omelets with tasso (a Cajun ham), plus grits and pork sausage, and, of course, Francie and I get eggs and boudin. We wash it down with rich café au lait and serious Bloody Marys and mimosas and wonder how we got so lucky.

While we are waiting for the music to start, we talk about Link and the amazing job he has done taking lessons from his family and neighbors in Cajun country and reinventing some of the best for use in his New Orleans restaurants. And we know that he has sent us here to emphasize the connection between food and fun and music and life that is a hallmark of the Cajun spirit.

At 8:30 sharp the music starts. People start dancing with "those who brung 'em," but soon, a natural selection takes place. The best dancers find the best dancers, and they fill up the floor, plus the spaces between the tables, and then the dancing extends out into the street. They dance—men and women, adults and children, women and women, men and men, black and white—and it is a rare moment of absolutely perfect joy.

As we leave Breaux Bridge at about 10:30, sated from our breakfast, we see a sign that says, POCHE'S, ONE MILE. Rob and

I look at each other at exactly the same moment, and Rob says, "What the hell, it's only a mile."

A Native Son's Cajun Travel Itinerary

Cochon A sophisticated city spot where star chef Donald Link updates the Cajun home cooking he grew up with—hog's head cheese, boudin, rabbit and dumpling stew. *930 Tchoupitoulas St., New Orleans; 504-588-2123.*

Poche's A restaurant, market and mail-order operation that sells richly creamy, deeply porky boudin. *3015A Main Hwy., Breaux Bridge; 800-3-POCHES.*

Mowata Store Not on any map known to humankind, Mowata is the place to buy aggressively spiced, intensely swiney boudin. *29017 Crowley/Eunice Hwy., Mowata; 337-457-1140.*

Hawk's A big corrugated-tin shed in the middle of the woods open for only a few months a year, when crawfish are in season. The crawfish are exceptionally huge and absolutely fresh, boiled just until the moment of perfect doneness. *416 Hawks Rd., Rayne; 337-788-3266.*

Frey's Crawfish House The shrimp and corn bisque, intensely flavorful crawfish étouffée and bread pudding topped with whiskey sauce are fantastic. *12289 Frey Rd., Welsh; 337-734-2585.*

Café Des Amis Locals and tourists alike line up at dawn for the Saturday breakfasts (which begin at 7:30 a.m.) featuring excellent beignets, omelets with tasso, eggs and boudin, rich café au lait and serious Bloody Marys; everyone dances to the live zydeco music. *140 E. Bridge St., Breaux Bridge; 337-332-5273.*

PIE TIME

By Bethany Jean Clement

from *The Stranger*

Clement's food reviews for this free Seattle alternative weekly
newspaper generally take on a quirky, first-person edge, in
keeping with the paper's hipster persona. They're not just
about the food on the plate but about the whole eating-out
equation.

Baking is said to be a science, a simple exercise in following directions exactly that any fool—any patient,
painstaking fool—can carry out. It's not true. Baking is rife with
mystery, fraught with hazard. I failed right out of the gate at age 8
with a complicated, many-egged Mad Hatter tea cake from a mis-
leadingly cheerful Alice in Wonderland cookbook. The cake
emerged from the oven an unholy, inch-high, inedible sludge; I
was crushed. The same people who say baking is a science say to
persevere, which I have, with mixed results (that mix being of mid-
dling to very poor). Fairly recently, I baked a cake so objectively
terrible that I threw it out a window. I did all right with pie crust
for quite a while. Crust is notoriously difficult: touchy about being
handled too much, involves a rolling pin. One bad crust, and I lost
my nerve. Crust can sense fear. There's no going back.

Luckily I am surrounded by better people than I, Renaissance
people who can do normal things with aplomb and, additionally,
bake like angels in the most important area of all: pie. Pie possesses
the beauty of restraint, of balance, of texture against texture; your
savory pies—potpie, quiche, etc.—satisfy far beyond the sum of

their parts. Pie is the true superfood, good after (or for) dinner, even better at breakfast, restorative, iconic, simple yet awesome.

My mother makes pie with rhubarb from her garden. We don't cotton to strawberries in our rhubarb pie; it's already a sweet-tart experience nonpareil, with the places where the filling bubbles out and caramelizes making life worth living. Also in her repertoire: huckleberry (summer; Priest Lake, Idaho; baked in a wood-fired stove), classic pumpkin (holidays, made from Libby's). My brother inherited the pie-making gene; he makes, among other pie-things, a goat-cheese-and-sweet-onion galette that sometimes shows up on my doorstep, like maybe there is a god. We have e-mail exchanges about minute adjustments to the crust recipe. Another friend makes pie so good and so pretty, it should be launched into space to show aliens the best of humanity.

If you're baking-impaired and your family/friends are far away/hateful/sub par, I'm sorry, but fear not. Store- and even bakery-bought pie has historically been only an approximation, the filling gelatinous, the crust a travesty—generally a rendered-horse-hooves-and-cardboard deal. But with the terrifying juggernaut of consumerism comes a few welcome specific steps in the right direction. Here is one: Shoofly Pie Co. in West Seattle.

Why did Kimmy Hsieh Tomlinson start a pie company?

"I just really enjoy making pies," she says.

(Peripherally, she noticed the sad lack of availability of good, handmade pie. Some people don't mind going to Costco and paying $5 for a giant [gross] pie. She's cool with that. These are not her people.)

Out at Shoofly Pie Co. last Saturday afternoon, an older lady with a tweed-and-leather hat ordered a slice of lemon meringue ($3.75), talking with someone else in line about her mother, who had 14 kids. "Did she make pies?" the someone else inquired. "She made everything—babies, pies." Laughter. (Later, across the room, eating her pie, in answer to a raising of the eyebrows, the older lady smiled and nodded once, emphatically.) Also in line: Two women with blond highlights and one baby, the baby being admired by a man in jogging tights who looked like a cross between Slade Gorton and Larry Craig. ("Let's give the pumpkin [$3.75 slice, $21 whole] a whirl!" he said.) Later: interracial gay couple, repeat customers, "I like cherry [$3.50/$20]. He's hard to please." They looked in the glass case, jammed gloriously full of pies. The hard-to-please one, the cherry-liker guessed, might be pleased by the chocolate tart ($4/$22).

In the back, Tomlinson and a few other people who just really enjoy making pies cut up bricks of butter for the all-butter crust, beat logs of dough with thin rolling pins, pressed star-shaped cutouts onto the tops of pale pies ready for the oven. Some pies get sprinkled with granulated sugar; most get painted with melted butter with a four-inch paintbrush. The back door stood open for fresh air.

Really good pie doesn't bear a lot of description. You know it when you taste it. Shoofly's pies are really good. The crust is fearless, light, with an extra-thick ridge around the outside (known in baking parlance as fluting). Apple ($3.50/$20) is one of the best sellers, all tart Granny Smith, with visible cinnamon, both crust and filling a pleasing uniform golden color, the apple pieces walking the fine line between getting saucy and still remaining firm. The namesake Shoofly pie ($3.50/$20), an exploration of cake-in-crust, has a gooey layer of molasses at the bottom; it's dirty-spicy-sweet instead of sugary-sweet. Quiches ($4.50/$24) are on the eggy-light rather than custardy-thick side. Chicken potpies ($6 mini, $25 whole) are both salty and peppery, with even the lowly cubes of potato tender and delicious.

A sign inside Shoofly Pie Co. says it all: "Pie Fixes Everything."

The Restaurant Biz

Waiterly Conduct

By Jess Thomson

from *Hogwash*

Most restaurant reviewers haul out a thesaurus's-worth of glowing adjectives to describe dining at Chicago's Alinea restaurant. Seattle-based food blogger Jess Thomson, however, comes at it from an entirely different perspective: as a surreal bit of theater.

My first experience with molecular gastronomy was like so many of life's great initiations: by definition, the first time can only happen once. Even before I got to Chicago, my anticipation was matched by a twin disappointment, a lurking acknowledgment that once I had experienced Alinea once, I could never eat like a virgin again.

The difficult thing about Alinea is that for someone like me, someone who's relatively used to judging food, it's a little weird to be dropped into a situation where I can no longer tell whether something looks or smells or tastes right because I have nothing to compare it to. How am I supposed to know if a horseradish-infused cocoa butter ping pong ball has been well executed? When was the last time I or anyone else had a powdered Picholine olive?

Let me say that on one hand, it was thrilling, because it stripped me of all previous assumptions about food; Alinea served foods which in another situation I might not have identified as consumable. I loved the way each course blasted away my expectations and presented intriguing, playful, and architecturally interesting food art. This is not food meant to be cooked at home;

Alinea defines (somewhat too energetically, maybe) why people like me eat out.

On the other hand, I almost felt like they were cheating. How can I compare the food at Alinea to any other restaurant, unless I've been to Moto or El Bulli? And where's the real food? It's like asking a kid about his trip to Disneyland when he's only been to the state fair. Of course it was cool.

Alinea was everything I'd hoped it would be: it was an expansive, expensive experience in avant-garde food theater. To say the food was innovative, creative, and surprising would be a massive understatement. But it was also a few things I hadn't expected: the food was very personal (because each one of us interpreted the food in a different way), sometimes sexy (if not downright sexual), and in a few cases, disgusting. I'd heard walking into Alinea is like entering a private club; still, I felt a little thrill opening the door on the unmarked building. The steely grey entrance corridor reminded me of the Antarctic ice cap—cool, silvery light bounced off the wall's vertical cuts in a way that might have made me feel claustrophobic, had I not read that an almost-invisible door to our left would swish open, admitting us like visitors to some sort of culinary Enterprise.

The experience, in present tense

Grace, Stephanie, Kathy and I are bustled to a quiet upstairs corner and tucked into a deep, plush booth. We sort of stare at each other at first. There are clearly no menus involved so we sit, wondering why they've chosen slick, dark wooden tables that put almost three full feet of distance between the people sitting face to face and why one of the suited servers is obsessively arranging and rearranging four eight-inch rosemary sprigs in stainless steel holders in the center of our table.

The entire waitstaff is beautiful, almost disturbingly sprite, and impeccably well-groomed. They are not waiters, they are model-waiters, and they seem to know it. Model-waiter #1 arrives with a wine list, but as we began to ask normal restaurant questions, his answers make it clear that we are not at a normal restaurant. We've already committed to a $135 twelve-course "tasting menu," the smaller of their two dining options, which includes unlimited pours of Chicago's dubious tap water. But we're all a bit hesitant to spend much more. We're interested in wine, but none of us recognizes anything on the by-the-glass menu.

Model-waiter #1: Can I interest you in a wine-pairing tour?

Kathy: Can you tell us how much it is?

MW #1: That depends.

We're all wondering how difficult a question this is.

Kathy: On what?

MW #1: On what wines you order.

Kathy, looking like she's pulling teeth: I'd like something simple.

MW #1 looks pained: The cost of a wine pairing is equivalent to roughly three-quarters of the cost of your food tour.

Kathy is baffled that this man insists on making her do algebra to earn her wine.

Kathy: I'm not too good at math. How much is that?

MW #1: $95, give or take.

Kathy: Give or take *what*?

It goes on like this until Kathy just asks for a glass of white wine. MW #1 sends the sommelier over, who turns out to be a model also. He recommends a glass of white burgundy.

Kathy: Can you tell us how much of an investment that would be?

Model-sommelier scurries off, and returns with an odd reply: $5 per ounce, ma'am.

We eventually get over the feeling that we've secured a deal in some illicit substance and explain our preferences well enough that he outfits each of us with a glass of something unpronounceable that knocks our respective socks off. (I had a champagne cocktail made with Pineau de Charentes and some good French champagne.) Model-sommelier smiles and tells us about Chicago.

We sit. It occurs to me that this might be the first time I eat at a restaurant without having the slightest idea of what's coming—I didn't bother to look at the menu closely ahead of time, because the sample menus online read like an SNL skit. "CHANTERELLE: carrot, curry, ham."

Then it starts, an exciting, then inspiring, then completely overwhelming fifteen-course tour of food as I know it, presented as I'd never imagined it. Each course baffles me. I try to take notes, but some of the courses are so complicated that I have page after page of words that have been started but never finished. It is an awesome assault.

Each course comes with a verbal instruction manual. The model-waiters detail not only what's in each dish, but whether to play with it first, how to eat it *("Don't use your hands, ladies, just dive in and suck this one up!")*, and where to put the utensils afterward.

Here they are, twelve courses that somehow morphed into fifteen, with my own personal recommendations for course titles, should Alinea need help with future menu descriptions:

ONE: Hot Liquid Tuna Tater Tot

In what we will soon recognize as the tag-team model-waiter swoop, a mini white ceramic pedestal lands in front of each of us simultaneously. It's a croquette, a tiny panko-crusted deep-fried bomb with sorrel, fried capers, candied endive, and caviar on the top. We pick the pedestals up and knock the croquettes back like shots, as instructed. As the crust breaks, hot sour cream soup oozes onto my tongue. It tastes like a liquid tuna fish sandwich, and the outside is crunchy like a tater tot. I love it.

TWO: Octopus Salad

First, we get a shallow round-bottomed glass ramekin; it looks like something I once put a bacteria specimen on in 10th grade chemistry. Next, a model-waiter hands each of us a round-bottomed bowl that we must hold, because it would tip over if we put it on the table. The edge of the bowl is notched, so a fork piled with an exquisitely detailed composed salad can rest half-inside the bowl. Smoky grilled octopus and scallions, avocado, and a microscopic (and undoubtedly tweezer-placed) arrangement of papaya, wasabi shoots, and pink shiso blossoms perches precariously over a warm, shallow bath of mint-infused toasted soy milk, which we obediently drink after nibbling the minisalad off the fork in one small bite. It's herby, smoky, and minty all at once, and the octopus is almost too tender. Perhaps it was octopus, pureed and regelled using agar to resemble octopus? We place the forks on the little ramekins, as instructed.

I've eaten next to nothing, and my brain is already tired. The conversation floats from May Ray to the waiters to our experience at Hog Doug's earlier that day to the other conference attendees at nearby tables.

THREE: Chanterelle-Carrot Surprise

Alinea becomes a study in obsessive-compulsive waiter behavior. Model-waiter #2 brings four square plates. Each has been fitted with linen-covered pillows. He begins to arrange them in the center of the table, nudging and pushing and tapping them around so that they're absolutely perfectly aligned. I wonder for a moment if MW #2 had experience showing jewelry, but I bite my tongue when he starts fiddling with our water glasses and I realize he's just setting the table. We'll be getting both forks and spoons on the little pillows for each course, so we can always choose the implement we prefer. He tells us it's "against the law" to put silverware on the table at Alinea, both because the table is scratchable and because they'd prefer we don't put table germs in our mouths. I obnoxiously wonder out loud why a restaurant would actually install tables not meant to touch silverware. He shoots me a dark look.

Salty, herby rolls come with polished little butter quenelles of goat's milk and cow's milk butter; both spreads have the consistency of regular butter but must somehow be molecularly morphed, because they melt more quickly than usual in my mouth and the deep dairy flavor almost makes me dizzy. Or is it the champagne?

The next course comes in a wide, flat bowl whose rim extends almost all the way back down to the table. In its center sits what appears to be a verrine of six or seven shades of orange and brown, piled into a shot glass with apparent insouciance, like the chef was packing up his miniature culinary leftovers. MW #1 lists the layers: pureed chanterelle mushrooms, sautéed chanterelles, an egg yolk poached perfectly at 165 degrees just to its gelling point, sweet, sticky apricot leather molded around Madras curry, a ball of Dijon sautéed spinach, a wisp of dried proscuitto . . . The whole thing is topped with a flurry of carrot foam. There's so much to write that I'm flying from one detail to the next, trying to zoom out and capture the whole dish in a single frame in my mind, figure out why fruit leather and proscuitto and carrot will work . . . then the model-waiters swoop down and remove the shot glasses, which I now realize are bottomless glass cylinders, and the food collapses together in the bottom of my bowl. I am a little girl and it's Christmas; I want to clap happily because I appreciate the surprise, but it would be so loud and awkward.

It works: silky mushroom puree, chewy apricot, earthy curry, and rich, bold egg yolk collide peacefully in my mouth. We all groan with pleasure.

I want so badly to ask if they do take out, just to see what the model-waiters would say.

FOUR: Passover Ping-Pong Balls

Now it gets weird. Tall, bullet-shaped shot glasses appear to be holding some greenish liquid and a ping pong ball. I realize I have an automatic food identification mechanism that's no longer working.

Model-sommelier looks at us earnestly and gives us instructions that are difficult not to construe as sexual: "Ladies, these balls are bigger than they appear. We suggest you swallow the whole thing in one bite: take all the liquid at once, including the ball, and close your mouth around the ball so that the liquid inside the ball doesn't spurt out everywhere." We avoid each other's eyes and giggle like 14-year-olds. Is he doing this on purpose?

I do as I'm told, and yes, the balls are much bigger than they look. Celery juice goes down first, and right as the ball—really a cocoa-butter shell infused with horseradish—hits my tongue, it shatters, releasing a cold, sweet granny smith apple juice that chases the celery juice, leaving the cocoa butter shell in my mouth, unwanted as an empty candy wrapper and not that different in texture. It's like I'm chewing an apple- and horseradish-flavored pair of those red wax lips. I force myself to swallow, but I can't get rid of the aftertaste fast enough. We all make horrible faces.

"I think Passover just erupted in my mouth," says Kathy.

By our count, we are now a third of the way there, and I'm starting to get nervous. What if it gets worse than this? I'm silently thankful that I'm not meeting anyone for the first time tonight.

FIVE: Monkfish (I think they got this title right)

This course scares me at first, but it tastes right, and looks more like real food than what we've seen so far.

It's monkfish, the fish that poses in texture and flavor as lobster. It's in a wacky cylindrical bowl with an hourglass outline and an oval-shaped opening. Banana and lime puddings are tucked into the cavernous interior, along with monkfish prepared a few different ways: some is poached, some has been ground and fried to a crisp, and yet more has been pureed and formed into a perfectly mousseline quenelle that quivers when I touch it with my (exceptionally clean) spoon. Model-waiter #3, the one who I think might not like us anymore, identifies the brown leaf balanced on the top as "onion paper." He senses us trying to wrap our intellects around what monkfish, lime, and banana might taste like together, and assures us that even though the flavors may seem disparate, they will work if we eat them together, rather than one at a time. We try. They do.

A very pregnant woman walks by and I wonder what her fetus thinks of all this.

The rosemary is beginning to wilt on the table, and I guess that its lifespan is somehow connected with the length of our meal.

SIX: Hush-hush

Model-waiter #3 sticks a long, thin paddle into our conversation. On it, he balances four small cinnamon meringues, which are filled with an ice cold duck product of dubious legality in Chicago. We wonder why Alinea can serve this when Hot Doug's got nailed for it, and the model-sommelier tells us it's not actually a course, but a *gift*. They are not *selling* fois gras, and in Chicago, there is no law against giving it away.

"This is really kind of icky," says Grace. She's right. I think about leaving it after the first tiny bite, but there are no plates and by now I'm afraid to set anything on the table. I force it down.

SEVEN: Underwear Drawer Duck

There is more rearranging, water *here*, plates *there*. One person has both still and sparkling water (*"would you like hard bubbles or soft bubbles?"*), and the waiters seem to disagree about which goes where, so she's constantly guessing which is which and wondering how many minutes it will be before another person touches her water glass(es).

I sense the whole table recoiling when the waiters begin marching over again; it's been almost three hours and we're beginning to fade. But wait, are they reading our minds? They come bearing pillows—big, square pillows covered in crisp white linen—and I'm momentarily convinced it's naptime. As they get closer, an unmistakable lavender aroma envelopes our space, and I think how wonderful it would be if one of these pillows arrived in the middle of a transpacific airline flight, instead of on my dinner table where I think my plate should be.

But there will be no nap. Duck-laden plates land on each pillow, and we're instructed to eat, quick. Each time I cut into the duck (tender breast cured in juniper and spiraled so it looks like a shrimp on the plate; moist, shreddy confited duck legs; searingly salty, crisp duck skin), invisible puffs of lavender air escape from the pillow and season the duck through my sense of smell. I'm delighted—I don't like the tiny turnips braised in red wine, and the stabilized yogurt water seems sort of superfluous next to the rich duck flavor, but this combination of textures and senses makes me want to buy a candle in every food flavor.

Some disagree. "I found the lavender really offensive," says Kathy. "It was like eating my underwear drawer."

EIGHT: Braised Beef with Guinness Pasta

Stephanie begins asking the waiters to repeat the ingredients of each dish slowly, as if the evening is actually making us all deaf. I'm thankful.

Next we each get a gigantic square plate—this is why the tables are so big!—which carries a dish one of the model-waiters describes as "beef and beer." It looks like multiple chunks of brightly-hued baby food sealed under a big transparent sheet of ravioli, and it turns out to be braised Kobe short ribs, soft and tender, with broccoli puree and peanut pudding, sealed under a layer of Guinness beer that magical food science has transformed into a sticky but solid film. I can't help but think of organs when I see how the film is stretched over the different scoops of food, but the broccoli flavor is wonderfully intense, as if each little particle of broccoli has been trained to burrow into my taste buds at the molecular level. Oh wait, maybe it has. The peanut works well with the beef, and the miniature fried broccoli florets add great texture. I agree with what Grace said about feeling like a giant eating miniature food.

NINE: Hot Potato Cold Potato
(This is their name, and again, it works.)

This one is tiny. It's a small ramekin, like something you'd put soy sauce in, filled with what looks like potato soup. (Yay! Positive identification!) The bowl sprouts a miniature stainless steel pin, on which is skewered a small butter cube, a small piece of Parmesan, and finally, a marble-sized white ball with a slice of black truffle balanced on top. Instructions: pull the pin, which deposits the butter, Parmesan, and what turns out to be a hot potato ball with the truffle on top into cold truffled potato soup, then slurp it all down together. It's wonderful; the contrast between the hot mashed potato and the cold soup in my mouth reminds me that we very rarely eat hot and cold things together. I set the tiny bowl down and find it's made of wax, though I'm not sure why.

I play with the pin, which now looks like a medieval medical device. The woman at the next table is performing bread voodoo with her pin, stabbing it into the paprika roll that came paired with the previous course. (Yes, some of these courses have bread "pairings," at no extra charge.)

TEN: Brick Lamb

By this time, we're beginning to get really tired, as I'm sure you are of reading this. Lines are starting to blur. I am almost ready to go home. It seems somewhat dangerous, then, when the model-waiters bring out hot sizzling terra cotta bricks—now, when we're most likely to let our attention lapse and burn ourselves.

Nevertheless, the bricks are here, and the rosemary is finally put to use—the waiters nestle the end of each sprig into a small hole in the brick, so that the heat from the brick forces the rosemary needles to give their scent up and send it to mingle with the three pieces of lamb searing in front of us. The lamb cubes are each decorated with something different, first mastic, the resin of a type of evergreen tree typically used to flavor gums and candy most famously in Greece and the Middle East, then dates and sherry vinegar, then red wine-braised cabbage. After so many courses of squishy food, I'm loving how I have to chew the lamb, but I'm the only one that finishes. One of us leaves the lamb completely untouched. We are overwhelmed. I'd love a salad.

ELEVEN: Bacon in Headgear

Now this, one of Alinea's poster children: a flat piece of applewood-smoked bacon, drizzled with butterscotch and wrapped in some sort of apple leather with a sprig of thyme, is suspended from a wire as if on some sort of trapeze. The wire is connected on both sides to a semicircular metal frame that reminds me of orthodontic headgear. We're instructed to rock it back and forth a bit, and as we do so, the meat slides back and forth. If Calder did bacon, this would have been included in his circus sculptures. Model-waiter #1 tells us it's our culinary bridge between savory and sweet, a sort of introduction to dessert, and he's right, it's delicious, only I'm so sick of meat I have trouble appreciating it.

TWELVE: Creamsicle, Modernized

The first dessert arrives: it's a little napoleon of orange sorbet, olive oil ice cream, and almond tuile, surrounded by alternating piles of chamomile pudding, dehydrated picholine olives, and dehydrated olive oil spiced with vanilla, garnished with olive brine gelee and a basil jelly that must be the essence of all the basil in Italy. I can't even begin to guess how one reduces a liquid fat like olive oil to a powder.

The sorbet/ice cream combo is a little ho-hum after the previous courses; its creamsicle flavor seems so pedestrian compared to, say, dehydrated olives. But I like it. I want to send the rest to NASA—if I want olive oil, I'll pour it, thank you, and even though I love the way it mixes with vanilla, I really don't understand this fascination with solidifying things that are clearly meant to be liquids. How about a simple vanilla–olive oil cake? I make the mistake of trying the chamomile pudding on its own, rather than blended with some of the other ingredients, and I can't shake the thought that it just tastes like bad herbal soap. Combined with the dry, sandy texture of the dehydrated ingredients (you know how much I like dry things), the various garnishes make me physically recoil.

Model-waiter #2 can tell we don't like it, and chastises us. "This dish is typically quite successful," he intones, as if knowing that other people have liked it will change our minds instantaneously. He skulks away with our half-eaten plates, looking wounded.

The model-waiters move the water glasses again, as if playing a game of chess only they know about. Grace gets annoyed and starts moving the little silverware pillow-plates around, nudging them so they're just off-center, and we get all giggly again as one waiter nonchalantly returns and fixes everything.

THIRTEEN: The Hairball

We're over twelve courses, and we're not sure how many we have left. We promise each other we'll fast the next day, baffled by what the caloric content of our meal thus far must be. We're getting giddy, overtired, overstimulated.

Apparently Alinea can sense this. It's their time to have fun with us.

We're almost in lockstep with the table next to us; somehow we've caught up to them and we watch as model-waiter #2 presents them with what he calls The Antenna.

He carries a small, heavy-looking stainless steel disk, which sprouts a foot-long flexible wire. At the end of the wire is what appears to be a giant chocolate hairball about the size of a golf ball; it bobs and weaves on the bending wire as he approaches the table. Everyone's laughing, and I collapse into giggles when I picture my cat producing this exquisitely formed hairball and presenting it to me like this. Apparently I'm the only one who doesn't immediately associate the hairball with pubic hair.

I finally recover and watch the waiter as he turns to face the guest. He sets the disk on the table, tilted toward the guest so that the wire leaves the table at about a 45-degree angle and the hairball is bobbing dangerously (and suggestively) close to the guest's mouth. She sort of has to dodge it to avoid losing an eye.

We're all laughing, my table and the next. MW #1 tells us we're not allowed to use our hands, and we're meant to take it all in one bite. Now we're actually crying because our imaginations are running wild, watching each other perform oral sex on a miniature cake made of frozen licorice puree, orange confit, and anise hyssop and shrouded in spun licorice sugar. I hate licorice, but I don't taste it because I'm still laughing so hard, and trying my best not to think of pubic hair.

One of my friends opts out. One of the other guests eats half, and decides she's done.

MW #2: Are you going to enjoy this?

Guest: I've enjoyed it as much as I'm going to.

More giggles.

What do they serve the men?

FOURTEEN: Overkill

Grace moves the pillows again, and a waiter rearranges them once more. My stomach aches from laughing.

I think someone's kid designed the next course. All the elements are interesting and delicious, but the presentation, which must have been some Picasso-inspired attempt at artful disorganization, is messy and overwhelming. There's a perfect, light, refreshing cube of lemongrass ice, a squiggle of chocolate ganache that reminds me of Bill Cosby and must have come out of a toothpaste tube, a tart, tropical squirt of passion fruit gelee, a perfectly smooth (as in yogurt-textured) rice pudding that I'd gladly eat by the vat, a miniscule dollop of soy sauce gel (yes, soy sauce for dessert), and a baton of sticky soy marshmallow. I try to eat each element alone, but the sheer number of flavors disappoints me. It's at least a month's worth of dessert flavors, and I'm hardly in the mood for one.

FIFTEEN: Caramel Donut Lollipop

Alinea has all of its tableware handcrafted, so each dish/platter/doo-hickey is created specifically for the food it supports. Now we get a beautifully-machined stainless steel and copper disk, on which the model-waiters place something that looks like an upsidedown version of one of those new whisks that are actually multiple metal sticks with balls at the end. Nestled in where the sticks meet the base of the object is a giant ball of tempura-fried caramel studded with preserved Meyer lemon rind. It's been speared with a giant cinnamon stick, so that when I dislodge the fried caramel from its home, a strong cinnamon scent shoots up my nose. Despite the late hour, I'm smitten; I love learning to associate tempura lightness with sweet brown sugar and spice, and the caramel inside is warm and gooey but not so liquidy that it comes dribbling out.

It's funny to see how my notes mirror my energy level—for the first five courses, I catch everything, then the whole experience starts to get blurry, as if my drink has been spiked. Before I know it we're hemorrhaging money and thanking the waiters for take-home menus that have been individualized to reflect our particular Alinea experience. Then we're back in the steely entrance hallway, then out in the night air, and the maitre d' is opening the door to a waiting cab. It's over.

THE MOUTH THAT MATTERS

By Dan Barber

from *Gourmet*

Chef-owner of New York's Blue Hill and Blue Hill at Stone
Barns, Barber has earned his reputation as a star chef honestly, a passionate proponent of eating locally. He's also a
gifted writer, who can deftly sketch a restaurant kitchen's
behind-the-scenes madness.

"Bill Grimes is in the house." I hear it from across the
kitchen, above the whir of the blender, the scream of
the espresso machine, and the clap of stacking plates. There's no
sense in repeating it, but I repeat it anyway. "Bill Grimes. Bill
Grimes is in the house." I'm running now to our famously unflap-
pable general manager, Franco, who's standing by the kitchen
door, pointing through the window. I run to him and we stand
huddled together, like children past their bedtime, to sneak a look
at our surprise dinner guest.

It's a clear view. No one's blocking the 50 feet between the two
of us and the unassuming middle-aged man sitting alone at the bar,
reading the menu. But he feels worlds away, which is how I wish
things were. I'm not ready, not even one bit, to watch the most
powerful restaurant critic in the country decide our fate.

I spin around. The kitchen falls silent. No one moves. "That's
Grimes," I say authoritatively, thinking all the while, *Is it?* In an instant, the line cooks are cleaning and organizing, furiously wiping
down their stations, stashing towels, and sharpening their knives,
preparing for the action just ahead—which is what line cooks do

when there's nothing to do, like on-deck batters and their ritualistic practice swings.

"All busboys change—now!" I scream, looking at Ahmed's wrinkled shirt. "Bathrooms!" I hiss to Juan, the dishwasher, who doesn't understand. "Toilets?" he asks, so instead I run to one bathroom myself, change the toilet paper, wipe the sink, bend down to empty the garbage, and then stop and see myself reflected in the mirror.

I look pale. Not because it's just three weeks after opening night, or because the floors have yet to be stained and the wall sconces have yet to be mounted, or because we haven't hired a prep cook, a reservationist, or even a bathroom porter. None of this is on my mind. I look at my reflection and think: *Exactly what is Grimes doing at Blue Hill?* It seems like a waste of his time as well as a rejection of what we believed ourselves to be—a small, quaint neighborhood restaurant a long way under the radar of the *New York Times*.

Tick, tick, tick, comes the order from the bar: single diner, titled, ominously, "Grimes?" Appetizer: "Bass ceviche." Entrée: "Monkfish with a stew of braised bacon and cabbage." I turn to yell the order as Blake, the fish cook, comes striding out of the walk-in with a whole striped bass under one arm and an entire monkfish under the other.

Out of the corner of my eye, I see Manuel, the meat cook, shake his head and wince. Grabbing at the scraps of what remains of the pork belly—a few shreds impossible to serve at anything other than the staff meal—he makes eye contact with me sorrowfully, like a surgeon having just lost a close one. "Goddamn," I say. "Goddamn, no way," I say, raising my voice, but Manuel stares down at the dried-out pieces and shakes his head. There's nothing more he can do.

I want to cry. Manuel is asking me to tell the only reviewer who really matters that tonight at Blue Hill—where there are six entrées on the menu and about as many customers in the dining room—we're sorry. We're sorry not only that we've run out of the best dish on the menu and one you'd undoubtedly write glowingly about—but, that in addition, we've forgotten "in the rush of things" to let you know it's not available.

Without taking my eyes off Manuel, I say, "Blake, break down the halibut and take two pieces from the belly side, center cut. And Franco"—here he appears out of nowhere, waiting for direction—

"tell him we've run out of the pork belly. Get him to order a special of halibut with saffron."

"Right," Franco says soothingly, as only Australians can do, that perfect mix of "Will do right away" and "Right choice, mate, thinking the same thing meself."

John, the sommelier, runs through the kitchen on his way to the wine room. "Grüner Veltliner," he imparts, with a Jack Nicholson smile, excitement tinged with creepiness. "This guy's legit. He's reading the wine list cover to cover, like a freakin' novel."

Plates chilled, bass sliced, the cooks gather around me. The far ones get near and the near ones get nearer. I carefully plate the fish and kiss it, gently, with the vinaigrette and then, fingers hovering, sprinkle sea salt as if it's particles of gold. *Keep it fresh*, I say to myself. *Plenty of acid, let it speak for itself.* "Manuel, blanch the asparagus, the ones from the market this morning. Pete, get some spring onions sweating and grab a quart of veg stock and reduce it. Hurry. Franco, let me know when he's three minutes from being cleared—we're giving him soup as a midcourse." And before Franco can remind me that the golden rule of restaurant reviewers is to never be recognized, that allowing Grimes to know that we know who he is might greatly jeopardize the review—I put a few words in his mouth. "Apologize for the monkfish and pork, and say, 'Here's a little taste of spring before the halibut.' Not too much, don't overplay it, less is more with this guy, okay?"

"Brilliant, mate," he says, and turns away with the bass. Within minutes, I'm pulsing the bright-green asparagus, the spring onions, the vegetable stock, and a few cloves of garlic confit in the blender. "Worthy of four stars," says Franco, as he straightens his back and takes the soup to the dining room.

"Blake, two pieces of halibut in the pan. Manuel, let's finish the saffron sauce—reduce, reduce, reduce," I say hurriedly, my hands tumbling around each other like a turbine. I plate the nicer of the two pieces of halibut, perfectly seared and firm, and consider adding butter to the sauce before deciding against it. *Was it a mistake to have pushed the halibut?* Looking at it plated, it feels unfinished and unremarkable. The waiter whisks it to the dining room.

And I'm correct: The halibut returns not quite finished, but Franco's just behind the plate, offering reassurances. "He said great, those were his words, he's just full. Wants to have the rice pudding and be on his way."

We've just started cleaning the kitchen when Franco opens the check presenter. An American Express card sits naked on the sleeve: F. M. Holozubiec. "Holozubiec," I say.

"Holozubiec," Franco repeats with a broad smile. "F," he says, pursing his lips. "M," he goes on, slowly, as if to say: What does this guy think—we're idiots?

NINE O'CLOCK, the morning after. I'm in the office reviewing an old fax sent to several New York restaurants from a well-known general manager in midtown. "William Grimes's Current Known Aliases" is handwritten in block letters. The next line, "Managers take note: Green American Express card for all" is followed by a list of three names: Blake, Taylor, and Henry. No Holozubiec. I go to call Franco, to ask if he's checked the list, when the reservation line rings. "Good morning, Blue Hill," I say, grabbing a pen.

"Hi, this is Bill Grimes from *The New York Times*," says the voice on the other end. "No kidding," I reply as the pen falls from my hand and drops to the floor. "No kidding," he agrees. "I was wondering if you would please fax me a menu and wine list."

Two days later, in Friday morning's paper, his Diner's Journal column contains a short, first-impression piece on Blue Hill that acts as a precursor to a formal review. He refers to the asparagus soup, the halibut ("a dish in search of a personality"), and the rice pudding. "Nailed him," says Franco.

During the next five weeks, F. M. Holozubiec makes three reservations. With each visit, we assign our best waiters, giving them only Grimes for the night and backing them up with extra help. We order additional flowers for the dining room, we pay for late-afternoon deliveries of freshly baked bread. We pick out a corner banquette, iron the tablecloth, repolish the glass and the stemware, and hold the table open for the first seating in case he arrives early. One of his reservations is on a rainy Tuesday night, with few guests on the books, so we call friends and family and pack the room full of admirers, instructing them to moan at certain points in their meal and say things like, "Where on earth did this place come from? Blue Hill is my new favorite restaurant."

I ask the waiter, Patrick, for his impressions after Grimes's third visit. "Nice," he says, but he doesn't sound convincing. I call him on his hesitation. "No, no—food and service, flawless. Four stars. It's just that, well, I sort of can't believe he's a food critic. Asked me some crazy-ass questions, like whether Blue Hill Farm was growing the avocados for the trout dish."

I get into bed that night. *Avocados in the Hudson Valley?* It had to be a test, a diversion to throw us off the scent. As I fall asleep, my respect for Grimes, the master of subterfuge, swells.

Eight-thirty on an overbooked Saturday night, and the restaurant is bursting with energetic approval. I gaze out on the happy customers, practically levitating on all the enthusiasm. In walks Grimes, for his fourth reservation. Blue Hill is a different restaurant since his first visit. Smoother service, more controlled cooking; overall, a more polished experience.

I run to the front of the kitchen and retrieve my checklist: "Okay, people," I say. "No mistakes. One more time: Kyle, another sweep of Table 34. No crumbs, right? Bathrooms, Juan. Franco— can someone get Franco? Remind him to tone down the music? It's too loud, way too loud and funky for Grimes. And Michelle, get some new menus, right?" Michelle walks past, nodding calmly, having just retrieved a set of unused menu covers from the Grimes kit we've assembled in the office.

The kitchen works brilliantly—it's focused, efficient, and perfectly in tune with the front of the house. Grimes's first course, a crab lasagne, is plated and served without incident, the line cooks adopting a slightly arrogant "seen this, done this" swagger.

As we prepare to assemble Grimes's main course, Robert Bohr walks into the kitchen. Rob is an early devotee of Blue Hill, and, as a seasoned New York waiter and sommelier (today he's the wine director at Cru restaurant), he's provided us with much helpful advice in our opening weeks. "Can't talk, Rob," I say abruptly. "Grimes is in the house."

"No way! Holy shit, I missed him out there," he says, his voice a mixture of embarrassment and disbelief. He slips into the dining room to investigate and returns just a few minutes later. "Dan," he says. "Table 34? That's not Grimes." I hardly hear him. "Dan," he repeats, louder this time. "That's not Grimes." And now the kitchen comes to a complete halt as I look up. "It's Grimes, Rob, trust me."

Rob comes up very close, with narrowed eyes and a blowtorch smile, and puts his hand on my shoulder. "Dan, I know that's not Grimes like I know that's not my sister."

In a matter of seconds, I'm standing in front of Table 34, extending my hand to our mystery guest. "Good evening," I say. "Mr. Holozubiec?" For the first time, I can see his face clearly. I look into his eyes and I know it immediately. This man is not a food critic. I don't even have to ask, but I do anyway. "You've been so supportive of Blue Hill, Mr. Holozubiec. Are you. . . ." And here I pause, unsure as to how to frame the question. "Are you in the business?"

"In the business?" he repeats. "I'm a commercial litigator, if that's what you mean."

That night I sit alone in the office. It's well past midnight, everyone is already gone for the evening, and I try to concentrate on placing the fish order for the following day. The fax machine suddenly groans, and out comes a memo marked "Urgent." It's from the midtown general manager. Franco had spoken to him just days before, informing him of Grimes's recent visits to Blue Hill and impending review. "All Managers Take Note. Grimes's New Alias: F. M. Holozubiec."

Within two weeks, Grimes—the real Grimes, that is—awards us two stars and a favorable review. I can't help but think that we owe some of that to Mr. Holozubiec. His visits, ridiculously, emboldened us, but they also made us become a better restaurant. Ironed linens, dishes announced at the table, spotless stemware—these restaurant details are the kind that get maintained, but are very rarely improved upon.

Mr. Holozubiec did something else for Blue Hill by being our first regular customer. He recognized what every obscure restaurant desires, what we all desire, which is to have someone take your small and little understood love and treat it with the kind of importance you deem it to have, or know it deserves.

Shakin' the Bacon Tree

By Elaine T. Cicora

from *Cleveland Scene*

For years James-Beard award winner Elaine Cicora was this Cleveland alternative weekly's food editor, parsing the city's restaurant scene through good times and bad. This was one of her last pieces for the *Scene* before leaving in the dust of a merger with the city's other alternative weekly.

Crisp, crackling, and sizzling hot, my soon-to-be-dinner stares up at me from its final resting place on Lolita's stainless-steel counter. It's a thought-provoking moment, actually. On one hand, this beautifully roasted critter, fresh from a field in Wayne County, could be the very Poster Pig for the "farm-to-table" movement. On the other hand, with those fixed blue eyes, tiny hooves, and curly tail still intact, he looks considerably more like Babe than a blue-plate special. But does this mean I won't savor each and every bite? Hah. I am Carnivore; hear me roar.

There's still work to be done though, if this little piggy will be my dinner, as signaled by the approach of a knife-wielding Matt Harlan, Lolita's chef du cuisine. "The first cut is the deepest," he says without irony, grabbing the beast by the snout and letting the blade slip through the neck. Then, with a deft twist of the wrist, he separates the head from the body and places it off to one side.

"Show me the pork cheeks," I ask greedily, and Harlan obliges by peeling back layers of skin and fat until the outline of the jawbone is visible. There, like a small brown nut connecting top jaw to bottom, rests the tiny cheek muscle. Harlan scoops it out with his index finger and hands it over. It melts on my tongue like butter.

This moment might be the high point of my recent Tuesday at Lolita, a day that found me following the progress of the weekly pig roast from tip to tail. Since that day, I've shared snippets of my observations with several acquaintances, including some food-savvy friends. Their response is generally the same: a little shudder, a nervous giggle, a brief averting of the eyes. I take it as a measure of how far removed we've become from the sources of our sustenance. Evidence that pork comes from an actual *pig* is somehow kind of shocking.

But my motivation for observing the event was more than just unnerving my acquaintances. Basically, I wanted to know what chefs know: the heft and hue of a dressed piglet; the secrets of seasoning and slow roasting; the ways the final product is apportioned and presented. Plus, of course, I *really* like pork.

I arrive at 11:30 a.m., a full five and a half hours before the first happy-hour bargain-seeker wanders in. But my arrival has been preceded by that of a free-range, Amish-raised pig. Barely three feet long from snout to corkscrew tail, the cleaned-and-dressed suckling weighs in at around 28 pounds. He cost the restaurant nearly $90.

Once roasted, the animal will yield about 20 eight-ounce servings, Harlan estimates. Paired with appropriate sides, he'll price them at $19 each. The markup reflects not only Lolita's considerable cachet, but the extensive time and labor involved in the process.

Still, Harlan seems upbeat as he hauls the heavy roasting box out of the basement. "I'm so glad Michael decided to do these," Harlan says, referring to his boss, Mike Symon, owner and executive chef of Lolita and her downtown sister, Lola. "It's fun for me, the meat's delicious, and even if we only sell 12 or 15 orders, it's well worth the trouble."

The first step is slicing through the pig's undercarriage with a long serrated knife, so the carcass can be laid open like a book. Because the meat is so intensely marbled, Harlan says, only kosher salt and freshly ground pepper are required for seasoning. The salt, he throws on by the handful; the pepper, he applies by way of a well-worn brass mill that he twists furiously. Then Harlan hoists the pig in his arms and carries it out to the patio behind the restaurant, where the pine-and-stainless-steel roasting box awaits.

In goes the pig, rib-side-up, onto a wire rack; a matching rack is laid on top and secured to the bottom one by three S-hooks. Not only does this arrangement keep the animal lying reasonably flat to promote even cooking, but it makes it possible for Harlan and an assistant to flip the beast over when the time arrives. Then on goes the stainless-steel cover, recessed like a Dutch-oven lid, to hold the requisite 20 pounds of charcoal. After a year of these weekly pig roasts, the cover is appropriately beat-up, so Harlan tosses on a couple of rusty 10-pound weights and a pair of rocks to ensure a tight seal.

By 12:20 p.m., the two stacks of coals are glowing, and Harlan spreads them out with a rake. In the next three and a half hours, he'll add approximately 30 additional pounds of charcoal in 5- to 10-pound increments. That will keep the temperature inside the box steady at around 350 degrees.

We wander off to let the pig and the flames forge their mysterious synergy. Other than giving off the occasional whiff of *l'aire du campfire*, the actual roasting process is kind of a bore. That changes at 4 p.m. though, when Harlan raises the lid and prepares to turn the pig.

Sheets of fragrant steam come rushing out, turning the bleak, gray patio into a slice of pig heaven. Pools of mahogany juices have gathered in the rib cavity, and the skin has been transformed into burnished gold. We stand briefly in mute admiration of this primordial miracle. Then Harlan and his helper flip the pig, and the chef scores the paler back skin into a series of neat diamonds.

An hour more, and it is done. The meat is carried into Lolita's open kitchen and settled on the countertop, where Harlan removes the head and carves the remainder into large portions— ribs, shoulder, loin, and butt—setting aside the head, legs, and miscellaneous scraps for other uses.

"Some of this meat we'll use for the pulled-pork pizza; some of it will end up in the pork ragu, for the gnocchi; and some of the bones, I'll turn into stock for sauces and demiglace," he explains. The best bits, though—a couple of dainty ribs, a morsel of fat-lined skin, and mounds of tender meat—are destined for diners' plates, where tonight they're joined by mascarpone-enriched polenta and a drizzle of salsa verde, a blend of finely diced parsley, garlic, shallots, chile flakes, lemon zest, and EVOO.

On top of my plate, Harlan also adds three golden diamonds of deep-fried skin. He doesn't generally serve the cracklings—"Most people won't eat them," he says with what seems like true regret—but he knows I'm not one of those. Crunchy yet stunningly rich, they pair fabulously with a glass of flowery French Cinsault.

Later in the evening, as the night winds down, Harlan reports he's sold 19 of the 21 portions, with two left over for the staff to nibble on.

"You can always tell when it's been a good one," he says approvingly. And by all measures, *this* little piggy kicked butt.

THE CHECK REPUBLIC

By Jessica Battilana

from 7X7

Associate food and drink editor for this San Francisco
lifestyle magazine, Battilana—who also has a diploma from
La Varenne Ecole de Cuisine—covers San Francisco's
restaurantscape with nervy intelligence and more than a
touch of cynical wit.

Driving across the Bay Bridge one bright Friday morning with Michael Tusk, chef-owner of Quince restaurant, I find myself looking at the dashboard of his beat-up car, ablaze with warning lights, and thinking how unfortunate it would be if we were to break down right here, right now. For one thing, it's starting to rain. Also, we've got a car packed with produce we just picked out at Monterey Market—cases of kishu mandarins, romanesco broccoli, kumquats, oro blanco grapefruits—and, in the backseat, two whole 40-pound lambs, together worth about $400, which we retrieved from Chez Panisse. Loosely wrapped in plastic sheeting, the lambs look like extras from an episode of *The Sopranos*. A breakdown would be, in California parlance, a real bummer.

This round-trip isn't unusual for Tusk: In an ordinary week, he goes to the farmers market—whether in Berkeley, Marin or San Francisco—two or three times. (The lambs hail from Cattail Creek Farm in Oregon and are delivered locally only to Chez Panisse; as a favor to Tusk, the Chez chefs let him piggyback his order onto theirs.) Whereas other chefs are content to phone in orders to their suppliers, Tusk insists on hand-selecting most of the raw material he uses. He'd admit it's not the cheapest or the easiest way to run a kitchen, since every minute at the market is a minute he's not in the kitchen, overseeing the day-to-day operations and acting as "the idea guy," as kitchen manager Morgan Maki calls him. But in the ultra-competitive world of San Francisco restaurants, Tusk's rigorous attention to ingredients has become Quince's calling card.

Quince turned four years old last December, an anniversary that puts this 42-seat restaurant in the minority: National studies suggest more than half of the restaurants that open each year never see their third birthday. And here in San Francisco, it's become more expensive than ever to operate a restaurant. With the recent launch of the city's universal health-care system (a groundbreaking mandate that requires all businesses with more than 20 employees to contribute between $1.17 and $1.76 per hour, per employee, to the city of San Francisco to cover the uninsured—regardless of whether they already offer health benefits), in addition to a high minimum wage (currently set at $9.36 an hour, without allowing, as NYC and L.A. do, tips to be considered as part of a worker's hourly wage) and the longstanding employment tax (a 1.5 percent levy on payroll), small businesses are feeling the squeeze. Michael Dellar, cofounder and president of Lark Creek Restaurant Group, is candid about his displeasure. "People in city government are killing the goose that lays the golden egg,," he says. "[Dining in] this city has been attractive because historically we've offered great value." But restaurants' ability to continue to do so is in jeopardy. As costs rise, so too does the average price a diner is going to pay for a plate of food.

San Franciscans are faced with something of a conundrum. We champion the neighborhood restaurant, love the local organic farm and want every worker to have health care. But diners—especially in the midst of a recession—also bristle at the rising cost of the San Francisco entrée, perhaps not realizing the enormous effort that goes into producing food at some of the city's top restaurants, and perhaps also secretly believing that along the journey from farm to table, someone's getting rich off that $40 entrée. Indeed, the $40 entrée *is* becoming the new norm. There's the astonishing $45 veal porterhouse at Epic Roasthouse, for example, and the ceiling-breaking $46 rack of lamb at Boulevard. *San Francisco Chronicle* critic Michael Bauer noted the upward trend in his "Between Meals" blog in late January: "In the next few months, we're going to continue to see an increase in menu prices, whether the prices are broken out as surcharges or not." We are, in essence, at a tipping point: Can we afford to put our money where our mouths (and ideals) are?

The economic reality of rising costs leaves little in the way of options for restaurateurs: Prices must go up in order to keep the business afloat. Bill Briwa, a chef-instructor at the Culinary Institute of America in St. Helena, teaches menu development to students as part of the Associate Degree curriculum. He describes the relationship between diners and restaurants as "a simple equation: Food (quality and portion size) plus atmosphere and service divided by cost, wait and service equals perceived value. If some part of that equation falls apart, then the perception of value falls apart with it."

For the patrons of Quince, their sense of perceived value is affected by the restaurant's Pac Heights location, its well-appointed dining room and its formal service. The attention lavished on diners here is exceptional, befitting a restaurant that has one Michelin star. Service is choreographed so that dishes are presented to diners at the exact same moment; ask servers the provenance of the watercress on the plate and they'll recite not just the farm's name, but its location and acreage. Still, some customers don't seem to feel the prices are justified. Tusk recounts a recent evening spent catering to a group dining at the chef's table, an intimate eight-person spot set in the center of the kitchen. The group had the seven-course tasting menu, a dedicated server and many special touches. But when the chef ran into one of the customers some days later, her first comment was, "I haven't spent that much on dinner in a long time!"

Eric Rubin, managing partner at Tres Agaves, says people respond to menu prices in a unique way. "They see an $18 entrée and say, 'I could make that at home for $5.' But you'd never say that about a new car or a new sweater. Everyone thinks they're an expert on food and beverage because they cook at home."

Tusk knows other restaurants may offer similar-seeming dishes at lower prices. "Yes," he admits, "there is that question of value. [People] ask me, 'How can that restaurant charge $8.95 for spaghetti with red sauce when you're charging $19?' But do they know that we use a single varietal wheat pasta from Italy that I get trucked here from Brooklyn? Do they know we use handpicked capers and tomato paste from Sicily?"

San Franciscans have come to terms with plenty of other expenses that are part of daily life in this city—from astronomical real estate and gasoline to an 8.5 percent sales tax and pricey organic produce. Yet, judging from diners I've spoken with (and countless others who've been airing their disapproval online), the arrival of the $40 entrée feels less like a restaurant's practical response to a real business problem and more like an affront. "Diners expect more from a $40 entrée—they want the whole experience," says SF restaurant consultant Andrew Freeman. "Restaurants should know that if they're charging $40, every detail will be examined, since not everyone is aware of the driving forces behind those price increases." Even I will admit that, had you asked me two months ago what I thought of Quince, I would have been quick to praise the food—and to warn you it was *expensive*. The burden we place on restaurants to provide value is higher than in almost every other sector—here, pleasure is quantifiable, but also highly subjective. Because restaurants exist in part to cocoon us from the rigors of daily life—to whisk us away from concerns about bad jobs, rocky relationships and recessions—the arrival of a bill at the end, even though we know it's coming, can at times feel a bit jarring. If a meal is successful in transporting us, then a high tariff at the end seems easier to bear. If not, we're left wondering whether the meal was worth it.

In response to the perception that by raising prices he's increased his take, Tusk says, "I feel like calling people and reminding them that we're in the restaurant business. Maybe they should come in and spend a week working here and see how hard it is, how much effort we put in. Then you'd understand why an entrée costs what it does."

Although I can't spend a full week working at Quince, I arrive at the restaurant's kitchen early one Wednesday morning to see firsthand what goes into producing a dish of its food. Tusk, an easygoing 40-something with a ready smile, is on his way back from the market, and I kill an hour trailing Maki while I await his return. In one corner, a cook turns out pencil-thin breadsticks and petite rolls—he'll do this all morning in order to prepare enough for dinner service. He's joined by the pasta maker, who will log a full eight-hour shift making tortellini and agnolotti. When he leaves, a second pasta guy takes over: In total, some 16 man-hours a day are spent making fresh pasta. The menu changes daily, meaning things are perpetually in a state of flux. When Tusk arrives, he shows me a cheat sheet he's produced for his cooks, who have begun to take over some of the ordering. It's two pages, organized by day of the week and written in chef shorthand: "DG rabbits," for example, refers to rabbits from Devil's Gulch Ranch.

Rather than ordering from a national distributor such as Sysco, which would deliver everything from mayonnaise to onions to T-bone steaks, Quince uses a dizzyingly complicated network of suppliers. "OK, it's Wednesday, so we'll pick up the pigs at Chez Panisse. The wild mushrooms should be coming in; I'll go to the market for eggs; we've got half a calf from Sonoma on its way. The fish is coming in from Maine—stone crabs, but they didn't have any sea urchin—and I'll pick up some of those Guru Ram Das blood oranges at the market." It would be easier (and probably less expensive) to order everything from a single source, but doing so would be antithetical to the guiding philosophy behind the restaurant. "I don't think I'm better than anyone else," Tusk says. "I just wouldn't want to do this if I had to cut corners."

The white asparagus that is debuting on tonight's menu, for example, Tusk picked up earlier in the day, at the Greyhound station on Fremont Street. It comes from Fairview Gardens in Goleta: Founded in 1895, the 12-acre plot west of Santa Barbara is one of the country's oldest organic farms, and one of a few in California that grow white asparagus; it's shipped to San Francisco in the luggage compartment of a bus.

That asparagus costs Tusk $11 a pound wholesale—and that's before shipping, which runs another $65 for 10 pounds. It's in the chef's best interest to make the most of the product, so his plans for the spears are grand: He's creating four distinct tastes, which he'll plate together. It'll be, in his own words, "a blowout." He's thinking he'll do a *sformato* (blanched, puréed white asparagus, béchamel and local Crescenza cheese); a soup served in a tiny shot glass; asparagus "tagliatelle" (paired with Maine lobster and fava beans from Freewheelin' Farm in Santa Cruz); and a warm composition of tender peeled stalks (topped with the yolk from a poached farm egg that has been breaded, fried and drizzled with brown butter). Tusk figures his cooks will spend some four hours working on the various components. To the labor and food cost, add the time he spends running around picking up ingredients, as well as all of his overhead costs: the lot across the street, which he rents for the valet parking, for example, or the air conditioning he installed last year, or the antique tableware. When you consider that a side dish of jumbo green asparagus, steamed and dressed with hollandaise, goes for $10.75 at Morton's steak house, the Tusk creation seems more than worth his estimated asking price (were it offered à la carte and not, as it is, as part of a tasting menu) of $16. "I'm putting white asparagus on the menu because it's exciting. If I don't provide special things, things that other restaurants don't have, then I'm in trouble."

Bill Briwa, who owned a cafe up in St. Helena in the late '80s, sums up the trouble local restaurants are facing. "Many struggle to keep their doors open," he says. "Rents are high, minimum wage is high and now there's the health-insurance thing to contend with. Restaurants are faced with this ugly dynamic: They've got to raise their prices, but they're loath to do so for fear it'll impact their business."

Some restaurateurs, in the interest of transparency, have decided to explain the increases to their customers—Delfina, Luna Park and Delessio's have all instituted surcharges, from a $1.25 *coperto* at Delfina to a 5 percent tariff on all receipts at Delessio's—hoping that informing diners of the reason for these additional charges will help assuage the effects of increases. Other restaurateurs, such as Lark Creek Restaurant Group's Dellar, admit they'll be raising prices "as modestly as possible to get by" but don't plan to go the surcharge route. "We shouldn't air our dirty laundry to our customers or burden them with our business decisions," Dellar says. Tusk says he understands the impulse to slap a surcharge on the menu, but you won't see one at Quince anytime soon. Rather, he's hoping his loyal customer base, many of whom dine there weekly, understand the lengths he goes to in order to make a meal memorable, and will continue to patronize his restaurant even as prices increase.

There's no doubt dining in San Francisco can be an expensive proposition, and in a tough economy, the prices we pay for things—and how often we can afford to enjoy them—are bound to be affected. Yet our standards show no signs of lowering—if anything, the demand for special, locally sourced ingredients and flawless service has increased in the past decade, as diners in San Francisco become ever more savvy. But it's time we realize the things we hold dear have real costs—for the farmers, for the restaurateurs and for us, the dining public—and decide, once and for all, whether we're willing to pay them. Because, after all, there's no such thing as a free lunch.

Guess Who's Making
Your Dinner

By Robb Walsh

from *Houston Press*

There's very little about food in Texas that Robb Walsh hasn't
explored, either for the *Houston Press* alternative weekly,
Natural History magazine, NPR's *Weekend Edition*, or books
ranging from *Legends of Texas Barbecue* to *The Texas Cowboy
Cookbook*.

My tablemate dipped her doughnut into the cup of hot
chocolate and purred while she chewed. "Is this the
best thing you ever ate, or what?" she said. We were splitting an order of *churros* and hot chocolate, which the waiter recommended
as the best dessert on the menu at Hugo's, the popular upscale
Mexican restaurant on Westheimer.

A churro is a Mexican doughnut made by extruding dough
through a nozzle into a deep fryer. The nozzle gives the long stick-
shaped doughnut pronounced ridges, which trap the cinnamon and
sugar topping. At Hugo's the kitchen doesn't fry the churros until
they're ordered, so they're served piping hot. Hugo's also cuts them
in three pieces, fills the inside with the caramel syrup called *dulce de
leche* and serves them on a plate with a dainty scoop of mocha ice
cream.

There are hundreds of Tex-Mex cantinas, authentic Mexican
restaurants, *taquerías, carnicerías, panaderías* and taco trucks in Houston.
But ever since it opened in 2002, Hugo's has been the best Mexican
restaurant in the city. In the 2003 "Best of Houston" issue, the *Houston Press* named Hugo's Houston's "Best Restaurant," period.

The restaurant roasts its own cocoa beans and grinds them by hand in an old-fashioned stone mill imported from Oaxaca. The fresh-ground cocoa powder is used to make its signature mole poblano, as well as the cup of hot chocolate that comes with the doughnuts.

The churros and hot chocolate at Hugo's are sensational. Churros are a common street food snack in Mexico City, which is fitting since Hugo Ortega, the owner and head chef, grew up in one of Mexico City's worst slums. Ortega entered the United States illegally, and like an enormous number of Mexican immigrants, he found work in the restaurant industry.

The restaurant industry is the nation's largest employer of immigrants, according to the National Restaurant Association, which estimates that 1.4 million restaurant workers in the United States are foreign-born immigrants. Seventy percent of them work in the lowest-paying jobs, as dishwashers, busboys, prep cooks and cleaning help.

The National Restaurant Association lobbies on behalf of restaurant owners, and predictably, it's one of the loudest proponents of immigration reform. "While the government claims stepped-up enforcement . . . will discourage future illegal immigration across our nation's borders," the NRA Web site says, "in reality, all they are doing is eliminating a sizeable portion of the workforce without providing any legal avenue to hire foreign-born workers to do jobs that Americans are no longer taking."

Meanwhile, anti-immigration groups such as U.S. Border Watch, which intimidates day laborers as they wait for employers to pick them up, remain active. "It makes me sad," Ortega says about a recent confrontation in northwest Harris County. "If immigrants are selling drugs or committing crimes, then put them in jail or send them back to Mexico. But please judge immigrants as individuals and for their contributions to society."

"You only hear one side of the immigration debate, because the people who really know what's going on can't say anything," one Houston restaurant owner told me. "If you own a restaurant and you speak out about immigration, you make your business a target."

There's a weird disconnect between perception and reality for those who work in the business. Thanks to media demagogues like

Lou Dobbs, much of the American public is ready to "send 'em back to Mexico." Meanwhile, Spanish is what you're most likely to hear in a restaurant kitchen.

Author and TV star Anthony Bourdain is one of the few chefs who's been willing to speak frankly on the issue. He says the American restaurant industry would be in big trouble if all the illegal immigrants in this country were rounded up and deported. "The bald fact is that the entire restaurant industry in America would close down overnight, would never recover, if current immigration laws were enforced quickly and thoroughly across the board," Bourdain told me. "Everyone in the industry knows this. It is undeniable. . . . I know very few chefs who've even heard of a U.S.-born citizen coming in the door to ask for a dishwasher, night clean-up or kitchen prep job. Until that happens, let's at least try to be honest when discussing this issue."

THE TWO ROASTED POBLANOS were stuffed with shredded pork shoulder that had been slowly braised with pears, peaches and raisins, and spices. I ate some of the filling with the spiciest part of the chile, the thick flesh around the stem. There was so much going on—the sweetness of the pork, the kick of the fiery green chile and the creaminess of the thick walnut sauce, sparked with the intense tartness of pomegranate seeds that burst as I chewed—it was a baroque fugue of flavors.

"I learned the secret of the walnut sauce from a lady in Puebla," Hugo says. The secret is to buy walnuts in September when they're still white inside and then soak them in milk until the bitter skins slip off easily.

Hugo's serves chiles *en nogada* through the fall or as long they can get fresh pomegranates. In the summer, the menu switches over to dishes made with squash blossoms. The restaurant also serves such exotica as *huitlacoche* (corn fungus) and sautéed *chapulines* (grasshoppers) when they're available.

The chiles en nogada at Hugo's are the best I have ever eaten—even better than the supposedly definitive version I once sampled at Osteria San Domingo in Mexico City.

The dish is associated with Mexican patriotism. The green chiles, white walnut sauce and red dots of pomegranate garnish are traditionally arranged in the order of the colors of the Mexican flag. Chiles en nogada were created by the nuns of the Santa Monica convent of Puebla in 1821 to commemorate the arrival of Agustín de Iturbide, architect of Mexican independence. Iturbide's celebrity was short-lived; he was crowned emperor in 1822, deposed in 1823 and executed in 1824. So maybe the fiery chiles en nogada should also be considered symbolic of the cruel fate that befalls so many Mexicans.

It's hard to picture the soft-spoken, slender and genteel-in-his-chef's-whites Ortega climbing over a barbed-wire fence with the Border Patrol in pursuit. Like so many others, he crossed the border for little more than the promise of washing dishes and busing tables.

"My teen years were pretty awful," he says, remembering his struggle to take care of seven brothers and sisters and his decision to cross the border. "My dad was beating my mom and me. He hardly ever came home. When I was 15, I quit school and started working for Procter & Gamble in Mexico City loading boxes of soap into cartons on an assembly line. My family was going hungry. I was buying rice and beans, but that was it. There was never enough. Then my mom had twins and got sick. I was raising the kids and working. It was a bad deal."

Ortega couldn't earn enough to live, no matter how hard he was willing to work. Hope arrived in the form of a letter from a cousin named Pedro (not his real name) who had made it to Houston.

Pedro wrote about the terrible journey. The van he was riding in blew up. He had to walk across the desert with nothing but a couple of tacos to eat. But he made it. He was living in a shotgun shack between Taft and Montrose. "He said he was making $200 a week," Hugo remembers. That sounded like a lot of money.

"I was young. I wanted to do something with my life. And I wanted to help my mom and my family," he says. "What would you do?"

In April of 1983, at the age of 17, Ortega decided to go to the United States. "My mom was very sad and very concerned when I left. When I quit my job at Procter & Gamble, I got 200 pesos in back pay, which was less than $20. I bought a bus ticket to Juárez with the money."

Ortega arrived in Juárez along with an older cousin, who was 23, and three other friends. A coyote met them as soon as they got off the bus and asked if they were going across. "You have to give him a phone number of somebody in the U.S. If you don't have a phone number, they won't cross you. My cousin and I gave him Pedro's number in Houston. Pedro had to agree to pay $500 for each for us. He really stepped up to the plate."

For five days, Hugo and his group stayed in a junkyard in Juárez, sleeping in wrecked cars and eating potatoes and eggs. On the fifth day, they attempted to cross the border.

"We had to inflate a plastic boat by blowing into it. There were 35 people including little kids and fat ladies who could barely walk. We took turns going across in the boat. I was scared to death because I couldn't swim. The mosquitoes [helicopters] came with their lights, and we tried to hide in the bushes. The coyote cut a barbed wire fence, and we ran. We got to a road. It was perfectly smooth, with no potholes. I thought, 'Wow, what an amazing country.' We got caught by the Border Patrol. They tied up our hands and put us in a van, took us to the bridge and sent us back across the border. We crossed again three more times, but we kept getting caught."

"The fifth time, we all split up, and the young guys who could run fast went by themselves. We crossed two fences and got to the railroad tracks where we were supposed to wait. Someone opened the door of a railroad car and then they locked us and two coyotes in there. The coyotes told us if we coughed or made a noise, they would kill us. I believed them."

"They had a special seal so that the customs people wouldn't open the rail car. We were in there for three hours before the train moved. After awhile, we could barely breathe. We took turns putting our faces up to a crack in the floor to get air."

"When we got close to San Antonio, the coyotes had to hack through the railcar's wooden wall with a pickax so they could get the door open. One of the coyotes cut his hand open, so there was blood everywhere. We had to jump out while the train was still moving. Finally we got to a house in San Antonio. People were talking, and it was half English and half Spanish. That was the first time I ever heard English.

"They had taken the seats out of a green Impala and put blocks on the shocks. They crammed 13 people into that car. I was one of five guys in the trunk. We drove to Houston and stayed in a house until Pedro came to get us. We were so dirty and skinny, he didn't recognize us.

"I hated Houston at first. It seemed like a ghost town after Mexico City. There was nothing going on in the streets, no music, no soccer, nothing," Ortega remembers.

He took a job cleaning offices. When his cousins decided to try their luck in California, he stayed in Houston so he could keep his job. But the company he was working for relocated, and Hugo found himself unemployed and homeless. "I was broke and sleeping outside on Dunlavy Street behind where the Fiesta is now. I was really depressed."

Ortega's culinary career began by chance. Some fellow immigrants he met playing soccer offered to take him to Backstreet Café off Shepherd where they worked so he could apply for a job. Owner Tracy Vaught was impressed with Hugo's attitude and industriousness from the first day. At Backstreet, Hugo slowly worked his way up from busboy to prep cook to line cook.

Ortega says the restaurant didn't know he was illegal. "I gave them a Social Security number," he says.

Soon after they arrive, illegal immigrants buy fake IDs and Social Security cards at flea markets or on the street. As a result, of course, they're paying income tax and Social Security—and never see income tax refunds or Social Security benefits.

But Ortega says this didn't bother him. "I didn't care," he says. "I was just happy to be able to work."

THE DARK BROWN SAUCE that cloaked the chicken leg quarter was dotted with sesame seeds. The version of mole poblano served at Hugo's was velvet on the tongue. The incredibly smooth texture married the rich taste of dried chiles, fresh-ground cocoa powder, toasted sesame seeds, aromatic almonds and other nutty flavors. But there was a deeper wave of flavor in this version of mole poblano, a wonderfully complex fruitiness and a shining high note of tartness that I'd never encountered before.

"Very few restaurants in Puebla serve mole poblano," Hugo Ortega says. "Because everybody's grandmother makes it better."

Ortega's mole has unusual fruit flavors. "That's the raisins and
the plantains you're tasting," Hugo says. I have made a lot of moles
from recipes in Mexican cookbooks, but I have never seen a mole
poblano recipe that called for plantains.

American foodies make the mistake of thinking that reading
Diana Kennedy or Rick Bayless's cookbooks is all it takes to master Mexican cuisine. Cookbooks only skim the surface. Native
chefs like Ortega are a reminder of how deep Mexico's culinary
traditions really go.

The Ortega family has mole in their blood. A relative of Hugo's
makes the mole at the restaurant. "She learned from her mother,
who learned from her mother and so on. [Her] mole poblano is
fourth-generation. You should taste the mole that my grandmother
makes back in Puebla," Hugo says with a grin.

Hugo Ortega's favorite childhood memories are of his days in
Progreso in the state of Puebla. His family moved back to their ancestral village when his father became too sick to work. This period came before his father began abusing his family. Hugo was
nine years old when he arrived in Progreso. He was sent to the
mountains with a herd of goats to tend.

"I was scared to death at first," he remembers. But he learned
how to herd goats and was happy in the country. In Puebla, he
learned about Mexican cooking traditions from his grandmother.
Some days he would help his aunt, who was the village baker.
Other times he would assist his uncle, who lived in the mountains
and made cheese.

But Ortega's childhood in the country came to an end when
his father recovered and moved the family back to the slums of
Mexico City.

Hugo's maternal grandmother remained in Progreso. There,
she's the member of an informal club, a group of around a dozen
women who travel around the countryside cooking dishes like
mole poblano for weddings and other celebrations.

Hugo recently returned to Progreso to attend a family wedding.
He was shocked by what he saw. "There's only women and children left in the village. All the men and boys are in the United

States. It's like that all over Mexico. Things are different. The younger generation isn't picking up the old traditions. Where are the women who will go from village to village cooking mole for weddings after my grandmother and her friends are gone? I am afraid that Mexico's culinary culture is going to disappear."

ON MY MOST RECENT VISIT TO HUGO'S, I sampled one of the nightly specials, a mesquite-grilled black Angus tenderloin. The steak was medium-rare and nicely charred around the edges. It sat in a luscious puddle of *guajillo* sauce. The rich dried-chile flavor was rounded off with butter and garlic. On the side, two mole tamales and some grilled asparagus spears sat on a bed of sautéed spinach leaves.

To go with my steak, the waiter recommended a glass of 2005 Tikal "Patriota" wine, a Malbec-Bonarda blend from Argentina. It was a big, bold red that stood up brilliantly to the dried chile sauce.

My dining companion tried another entrée from the list of specials, a thick salmon steak cooked rare in the middle and balanced on a bed of mashed Peruvian purple potatoes. The fish was garnished with mussels, and a disk of corn pudding was served on the side.

This isn't traditional regional Mexican cuisine, and it isn't supposed to be. This is modern American cuisine with a Latino spin, and it speaks well of Hugo Ortega's culinary training. "The dinner specials are different, more innovative," he says. "I learned French techniques in cooking school, and I apply them to Mexican cooking."

Hugo Ortega was issued a Temporary Resident (green) card in April of 1988 under the "Reagan Amnesty." With the help of Tracy Vaught, he enrolled in the culinary arts program at Houston Community College. He graduated in 1992 and worked as chef and executive chef at Backstreet Café and Prego before opening Hugo's in 2002. He has made two guest chef appearances at the James Beard House in New York City.

And there are a lot more Hugo Ortegas on the way, thanks to philanthropists like Kit Goldsbury, heir to the Pace Picante Sauce fortune. Last year, Goldsbury contributed $35 million to a small San Antonio cooking school called the Center for Foods of the

Americas. His goal was to create a top-rank culinary academy specifically for young Latinos.

The nation's foremost culinary school, the Culinary Institute of America, became a partner in the project. The San Antonio cooking school is now known as the Culinary Institute of America's Center for Foods of the Americas. It will offer extensive financial aid to struggling Hispanic students and, for the most talented, a chance to transfer to the CIA's prestigious main campus in Hyde Park, New York.

Hugo Ortega and Tracy Vaught were married in 1994, and in February 1997 they had their first child, Sophia Elizabeth. Ortega became a naturalized American citizen in 1996. As a citizen, Hugo was entitled to bring members of his family to the United States. "I think I am more patriotic than most Americans," he says. "I love this country like my mother. When I hear the national anthem of the United States, it sometimes makes me cry."

His mother and father live in South Houston, and all of his siblings have joined Hugo here as well. Alma works for Mary Kay selling cosmetics. (One day she hopes to own a pink Cadillac.) Ruben is a pastry chef at Backstreet Café and Hugo's. Sandra works as an administrative assistant during the day and at a local restaurant at night. Rene, a graduate of Reagan High School, works as a mechanic for Admiral Linen Company. Twins Gloriela and Veronica now sell real estate in the Heights. And Jose Luis, who worked in the kitchen with Hugo, recently moved from Houston to Belize to become the chef at The Victoria House.

Hugo's nephew Antonio will graduate from South Houston High School in May of 2008. Tony has received scholarship offers from Harvard, Yale and Rice, among others. It's a difficult decision. But because he doesn't want to be too far away from his family, he's leaning toward Rice.

Hugo is working on a cookbook that will combine old family recipes from Mexico and innovative dishes he created in Texas.

Rebuilding Mandina's

By Brett Anderson

from the *Times-Picayune*

The New Orleans restaurant beat was still fairly new to Brett
Anderson when Hurricane Katrina ravaged the city in 2005.
Since then, his mission has become clear—to chronicle every
step this great food capital takes on its road to revival.

On October 11, 2005, Cindy Mandina put a hip to the
side door of Mandina's restaurant and stepped into her
new world of disorder.

The tableau brought to mind a Salvador Dali painting. The
asphyxiating aroma suggested the inside of a garbage bin.

Cindy, 35, was joined by Martial Voitier, Mandina's bleach-
blond manager and a 20-year employee. Both had visited the
flooded-out restaurant, yet fresh astonishment still registered for
them inside a building Cindy referred to as "maggot heaven."

Evidence of the rise and fall of Mid-City floodwaters was etched
onto the walls of the Mandina family's 75-year-old restaurant, now
striped by several brown-yellow flood lines, the highest measuring
5 to 6 feet off the ground. The bar along which generations of regulars rested many an old-fashioned had been lifted from its foundation and set down at a slight angle, like a boat washed ashore.

Chairs were stacked atop tables anchored by heavy metal bases.
Because the restaurant's foundation sits slightly above street level,
the water stopped just below the tops of the tables, some of which
still were set with glass sugar dispensers and bottles of Crystal and
Tabasco hot sauce, just as Cindy had left them on August 27, 2005,
a Saturday, the final evening of service at the old Mandina's. The

flood's most striking visual impression was left on the tabletops themselves, a few of which had warped dramatically, their sharp corners curling downward in perfect symmetry.

"Oh, look at my menus," Cindy moaned, fingering an unblemished paper insert detailing Mandina's regular Sunday specials: shrimp Creole, fried chicken, trout amandine, Italian sausage with spaghetti and vegetables. "All ready for the next day."

Waterlogged boxes of unbroken Abita Amber and Barq's bottles littered the hallway leading from the bar past another dining room and into the kitchen, which felt creepily subterranean. The few rays of light that sliced through the darkness revealed a mass of heavy equipment corroded almost beyond recognition.

Voitier had to raise his voice to be heard over the hard buzz of insects and running water. "It's been dripping for at least two weeks," he said of the dishwasher.

Cindy and Voitier were awaiting the arrival of John Montgomery, an architect whom the Mandinas had hired to guide the restaurant's rebuilding. Cindy was upstairs, in the living quarters where her father Tommy was raised, when she paused to discuss the task ahead.

The office where father and daughter worked side-by-side at folding tables was in disarray, the victim of looters and the wind and rain that had entered through smashed windows. Time cards were strewn about the floor, where a copy of the August 28, 2005, edition of The Times-Picayune—headline: "Katrina Takes Aim"—lay encased in its plastic delivery bag.

"We want to knock the building down," said Cindy, her New Orleans-seasoned accent the type most Americans guess is Brooklyn-bred. "But money is going to dictate what we do."

Cindy walked back downstairs to join Voitier and Montgomery, who upon arrival began preaching the importance of cataloging every lost item, including ashtrays, for the insurance claim.

"There might be a walk-in refrigerator or a stove worth thousands of dollars that you haven't remembered," he said to Voitier. "We need to get all of this on the claim. . . . "

By the following week, Tommy was calling Montgomery "the lead dog" at a six-person meeting of the preliminary players enlisted to determine Mandina's future. The pink clapboard restaurant was too hot to occupy, so the group met in front of it, below the awning and its snuffed-out, multicolored neon trim.

Tommy wore sunglasses atop his bald forehead, which he rubbed repeatedly as he tried to glean from the assembled professionals what, if anything, could be salvaged of a family business that began at the turn of the last century, when his grandfather, the Sicilian immigrant Sebastian Mandina, opened a grocery inside the building behind him.

"It's easier to get up-front construction money than business interruption money," advised Dwaine Foster, president of American Construction Management Services.

"I'm hoping we can come to the conclusion that we're going to tear it down," Montgomery said. "Then we can start to plan."

"It's going to take a couple of meetings," Tommy warned. "I talk things to death."

A tear-down appeared to be a foregone conclusion—two contractors at the meeting were demolition experts—until Montgomery mentioned that preservationists could cause problems. Tommy, a thorny personality even when he's in good humor, answered, "What are they going to do? Put me in jail? There is no jail! . . ."

"This is going to be a little more emotional for him," Cindy said of her father, who had disappeared inside the restaurant following the meeting. "This is where he grew up."

Tommy seemed winded when he emerged. It was hot. He was resting his hands on his knees when a man approached and asked, "When you guys going to have turtle soup?"

Tommy straightened his back and told the man what he told everyone who passed by that October morning: "Give me a year."

MANDINA'S WAS RIPE FOR RENOVATION, perhaps even demolition, long before it flooded. The restaurant's layout involved nothing in the way of what an interior decorator would call flow. The floors sloped. The bar facing the front dining room backed up to another dining room of limited functionality. Narrow and illogically placed, it was a wellspring of congestion, with one door leading to a hallway near the kitchen that was hardly big enough for two people to pass. Another opening led to the back of the bar, a passage used with greater frequency the more crowded the restaurant became, as barkeeps streamed through to keep their bins filled with ice from Mandina's only ice machine, which was next door in an old Creole cottage used for storage. On balance, there were more bad tables than good.

Mandina's expanded into what is still called "the new building," a former barbershop, in the early 1990s. The building, at least a century old, contained video poker machines, bathrooms and extra dining rooms to help with overflow but lacked the energy found in the original sections. A customer could, of course, opt to wait for a table in the location of his choosing, provided he was equipped with the fortitude to endure the often hot and occasionally unpleasantly fragrant experience of waiting for a table on the cracked sidewalk along Cortez Street.

And those were just a few of the flaws that endeared Mandina's to its regulars.

"I've seen this, where you change the physical structure of a business and the business disappears. People don't come back," Montgomery said. "In New Orleans, people don't like change, good or bad."

Six years ago, Cindy Mandina boarded an American Airlines plane for Maui and opened up the in-flight magazine to a profile of Harry Connick Jr. She was stunned to read her family's name. "Mandina's has crab fingers in this butter sauce and some of the best po-boys in town," the magazine quoted Connick as saying. "They also have grilled pork chops and string beans, and stuff you can get anywhere. It just tastes better there."

"Holy Moly!" she remembers thinking. "He mentioned us!"

Cindy had worked at Mandina's periodically throughout her life, including while completing her Masters in Business Administration from Loyola University. Her path to graduate school passed through a kitchen where deep-fryers and no air-conditioning could have conspired to make days behind a desk look like a dream come true. She joined the family business anyway, even though in her mind it was always "just a joint."

The story on Connick changed her outlook. In Cindy's reading, the article suggested that Mandina's was viewed by its customers as something more than an aging restaurant where one could enjoy a reasonably-priced plate of trout amandine with a cold beer. For scores of customers, it channeled the spirit of New Orleans itself.

"I always thought of Mandina's as just a neighborhood restaurant," Cindy said. "Dad went to work. Mom was home raising the kids. Dad came home. That was it. Who knew?"

If Cindy is guilty of having undervalued her inheritance, it could be because she represents the first generation of Mandinas to grow up farther than a flight of stairs away from it.

She and her sister, Valerie Larmeu, were raised in Metairie. Their mother Judy Mandina, who is divorced from Cindy's father, never worked in the restaurant.

Tommy, like his father and uncle before him, was raised in the apartment above Mandina's—a residence he maintained, on a part-time basis, until August 28, 2005. The most time Cindy spent in that apartment was when she went there with her sister and parents to seek shelter during hurricanes.

"Mid-City didn't flood," Valerie quipped, paraphrasing the conventional wisdom her family once followed.

Cindy was a toddler when her father took over Mandina's from his father Anthony, who died in 1975. She started busing tables at 8 and writing checks to vendors such as the P&J Oyster Company when she was 11, in Tommy's view the ideal age to break someone into his business.

"When I get them when they're 15 or 16, they're a pain in the ass," he said. "Get them when they're 12, by the time they're 15, they can run the place. It's not rocket science."

Cindy's involvement in the rebuilding of the family business—which included the opening of a Baton Rouge location in February 2006 and a Mandeville location eight months after that—ensured that Mandina's would continue under the guidance of a Mandina for a fourth generation.

Were it not for her dogged determination, Mandina's might never have reopened. In September 2005, Tommy, who is semi-retired, saw little reason to attempt returning to life as he knew it.

"He was devastated," said Cindy, who had taken over day-to-day operations of the restaurant just before the storm. "This is the building he grew up in. This was his whole life. To see it destroyed, like everyone else in New Orleans, he said, 'I'm done. This is going to be too hard and take too long.' I said, 'I want to do it.'

"I said, 'What's the worst possible thing that could happen, dad? We walk away with our heads held high. If we fail, we fail. Who's going to rebuild the city if it's not the people in their 20s, 30s and 40s? I wasn't born to be a quitter.'"

Cindy continued, "Plus, he had everyone saying to him, 'Are you going to come back, Tommy? You have to come back. [Mandina's] is an institution. It wouldn't be New Orleans without it.'"

Cindy's father characterizes his change of heart more succinctly: "My daughter said we were going to come back, and she's my inspiration. . . ."

SEBASTIAN MANDINA CAME to New Orleans from Salaparuta, Sicily, by way of New York, one of the scores of Sicilians who found a new home in south Louisiana in the late 1800s and early 1900s. Around the turn of the century, he purchased a house at the corner of Canal and Cortez streets, moved it to the back of the lot, and built a two-story structure in its place. He made his home in an apartment on the second floor. He opened Mandina's downstairs.

Sebastian was a farmer-cum-entrepreneur for whom the term restaurateur had little meaning. He did, however, understand that people need to eat, drink and be in, if not always enjoy, one another's company. The business that rose from this notion was typical of those operated by many of his fellow Italian-speaking immigrants: a small neighborhood grocery, barroom and sandwich shop where regulars tended to linger, often over beers or, during Prohibition, bootleg hooch.

Sebastian's wife died while giving birth to their second child, Frank, whom the father raised, along with brother Anthony, in the apartment above his store. When Sebastian died in 1932, Mandina's fell to Frank and Anthony, who together with Anthony's wife Hilda transformed the grocery and barroom into a full-service restaurant: Mandina Bros.

"When my daddy took it over, that's when (he) started doing the cooking and adding dishes like red beans on Monday, the beef stew on Tuesday," Tommy Mandina said.

Frank worked behind the bar. The kitchen belonged to Anthony, who, with the help of a long line of mostly African-American and black Creole chefs, developed what would become an archetypal New Orleans neighborhood restaurant menu: a mash-up of Creole, soul food and red sauce Italian cuisine, with a few incongruous oddities, such as corned beef and cabbage, thrown in for good measure.

"Ms. Lola, who worked for us for years, was an absolutely wonderful cook," Tommy remembered. "Her redfish courtbouillon was to die for."

In those early days, an oyster bar ran along the far wall of the main dining room, perpendicular to the stool-less liquor bar where customers stood, a foot propped on the brass boot rail fixed to the bar's base. In-the-know regulars bet on horses and sports events—"there might have been a little gambling, a little bookmaking in the place at the time," said Tommy—and a board on the wall posted scores of Pelican baseball games. By the '50s, pinball machines and a jukebox added to the rattle and hum.

"One of the secrets of Mandina's was always the drinks," said Noel Cassanova, a lifelong friend of Tommy's who has been dining in Mandina's for 60 years. "In my lifetime, I don't recall them ever measuring a drink. They don't have a jigger in the house. They pour."

No one came to Mandina's for the brothers' warm embrace. "Short, physically and temperamentally," is how Tommy described his father and uncle, who didn't shy from hiring employees of similar dispositions.

The Mandinas' loving recollections of past staff members—the late Henry Braden, a waiter who expressed his displeasure with one customer's tip by throwing it in their face, and "Nubby," the one-armed bartender—suggest an institutional tendency toward antagonism has been an aspect of the restaurant's charm from the get-go.

"My Uncle Frank scared me," Cindy said flatly.

Ms. Hilda was another matter. "She had a personality," Tommy said. "She worked the crowd." When Anthony and Frank went overseas to fight in World War II, Hilda ran the restaurant on her own. Everyone resumed their usual roles when the brothers returned.

Tommy was Anthony and Hilda's only child, and he started peeling potatoes in the restaurant's kitchen when he was 8 years old. "There was never a time in my life when I didn't do something at the restaurant," Tommy said. "I've worked behind the bar since I was 12."

The Mid-City of Tommy's childhood proved an ideal incubator for his family's restaurant. "Everyone lived in the city. There was no Lower 9th Ward. No New Orleans East," he said. "Mid-City was a good neighborhood. Streetcars ran on Canal Street."

"At the bar, you had the bookmaker standing next to the district attorney standing next to the guy who runs the hospital," Cassanova said. "Later on at night, you'd have a couple of police captains in there. It was unbelievable."

The thick reduction of swashbuckling personalities was in part a function of the menu, which crossed class lines by featuring roast beef po-boys and red gravy-simmered meatballs alongside tony French-Creole fair such as shrimp remoulade and trout meuniere.

"A lot of his ideas would come from Galatoire's," Cassanova said of Anthony. "He and Hilda ate there every week."

Isadore Pilart drew in a deep, chest-heaving breath. "You can smell a restaurant going on in here," he announced through a grin that revealed two gold teeth.

It was the morning of February 6, and the chef stood before three 50-gallon pots at the rear of Mandina's kitchen. Steam rose from the contents of each: maroon-red spaghetti gravy, burnished-brown turtle soup and the clear bubbling water he was preparing to turn into seafood gumbo.

A 15-gallon pot of tomato-based Creole sauce simmered nearby. The chef stirred it, coaxing several halved lemons to the surface. At 62, Pilart moves fluidly from stove to oven to freezer, exhibiting an ease of motion manifested outside the kitchen in a well-tailored look that recalls a laid-back Jelly Roll Morton.

Pilart, Mandina's head chef for 26 years, radiates calm, a quality that would prove useful in the days ahead. When he stuck a fork into the beef butts he'd started roasting an hour and a half prior, it was 10:30 a.m. Customers would start lining up in 24 hours.

It had been nearly a year and a half since food was served to customers from the kitchen of the original Mandina's. . . . The new kitchen is twice the size of the one it replaced, extending behind the restaurant onto a lot made available by the demolition of a neighboring house previously used for storage.

Every single piece of equipment, from the 4-foot-long paddle Pilart plunges into large batches of soup to the 10-burner Imperial stove, is new. In a restaurant where the tools lost to the storm were thought to impart flavor from decades of seasoning, the vision of unblemished steel was a touch unsettling.

"We're going to have to burn the pots to get it all tasting right," joked manager Martial Voitier.

Chefs well-versed in Mandina's culinary folkways spent much of reopening day eve bringing fresh hires up to speed. Pilart trained Carl Smith, a Mandina's rookie, how to clean crabs, season meatballs and shovel a mountain of seafood dressing from pan to foil-lined storage container with a plate.

A half-dozen new chefs gathered around Percy Stalls to hear his tutorial on the sundry items that pass through the restaurant's three deep fryers.

"You tell the waitstaff to give 15 to 20 minutes on the fried chicken. We don't pre-fry" Stalls said, dusting a wing, breast, leg and thigh in Zatarain's seasoned flour. "All fried chicken comes with fries—except on Sundays. On Sundays it comes with creamed potatoes."

Stalls started working at Mandina's just prior to Katrina. In terms of years served, he has nothing on colleagues such as Pilart and Terry Hayes, 46, who started at the restaurant when he was 19. But the 26-year-old cut his teeth at the Acme Oyster House as a teenager. "The best fry man in the city" is how Cindy Mandina refers to Stalls today.

Stalls wore the brim of his bright red baseball hat tilted a few degrees to the side as he dipped trout fillets in egg wash. A batch of onion rings, which he triple batters for maximum crispness, were just about brown. Stalls plucked each ring from the oil as it finished frying, carefully stacking them on a plate in a high single column.

"I go on up with them," Stalls said, admiring his own handiwork. "Your presentation is your decision."

IT ULTIMATELY COST NEARLY $2 MILLION to resuscitate Mandina's, its owners say.

The price covered the demolition of two neighboring houses on Cortez Street, which cleared the way for the expansion of the kitchen and parking lot, and a re-imagined restaurant whose atmosphere partially closes the gap between its ramshackle former self and the trout meuniere on the higher end of its steeped-in-New Orleans menu.

Acid-stained concrete replaced the terrazzo floor in the main dining room, which swelled, having usurped the narrow room that once sat between it and the kitchen. Cypress-wrapped columns extend to a high ceiling liberated by the demolition.

Randy Purpura, a Mandina's bartender, built the pine tabletops, an au naturale improvement on the old Formica, as well as the bar—also dark-stained pine—and the ornate shelving holding bottles of bourbon behind it.

The bathrooms boast shiny granite and automatic flush toilets, the expanded overflow dining rooms carpeted floors that don't bow when you cross them. The spaces where the window units growled above the front windows are back to being simply transoms.

At a quick glance, the pink clapboard exterior appears unchanged. The neon window signs still advertise air-conditioning. The old "Mandina Bros." tiles are still fixed to a stair leading to nowhere on the corner. And in February, floodlines still stained the front windows' metal storm shutters.

The one place the restaurant was inarguably scarred by the renovation is found on the second floor, where the three generations of Mandinas before Cindy spent most of their lives. The former living quarters are now unlivable, having been taken over by the machinery necessary to bring the restaurant into the current century.

"My daddy doesn't come up here," Cindy said on the day before the restaurant reopened, standing in a former bedroom overrun with air-conditioning and fire prevention apparatus. "I think to him it's like a death. He remembers it like it was when he was a child. Now it's all sprinkler equipment."

WHEN CINDY MANDINA ARRIVED at the restaurant at 8:30 a.m. on reopening day, the Fire Department already had come and gone. A city inspector followed with what seemed like dreadful news: You can't open.

"He said he didn't have any paperwork from the Fire Department," Tommy explained. Tommy was able to iron out the mix up. He even had a back-up plan for the inspector in the event he had failed.

"I would have just locked him in the freezer," Tommy said.

Cindy wore a black Saints baseball cap and an oversized T-shirt over jeans when she took her position at the front of the kitchen.

Separating her from the front line of fry and sauté cooks was an expanse of steam trays filled with a glossary of New Orleans comfort food: stuffed bell peppers, macaroni and cheese, meatballs with red sauce, beef daube, shrimp Creole, roast pork, boiled potatoes, lima beans, green peas, string beans, yams, white rice, oyster-artichoke soup, two bins of turtle soup and two bins of seafood gumbo.

Ronald Seymour, a newly hired cook, reached over to stir a pan of meuniere sauce, which was nearly as brown as the bin of roast beef and gravy next to it.

"How 'bout that fried chicken!" Cindy shouted in Seymour's direction. "I need three bowls of turtle!"

Pilart worked the more serene back line, his chefs' whites still neatly pressed and unstained. Around noon, John Blancher, owner of the Mid-City Lanes Rock 'n' Bowl and Ye Olde College Inn, walked back to explain why he wasn't going to stay for lunch.

"Tommy came by the bowling alley Saturday night and told me he was trying to open today," Blancher said. "He said I should come by, but this is just crazy. There are people around the block. . . ."

The first customers who walked into Mandina's on February 7 at 11 a.m. were greeted with the flash of bartender Randy Purpura's camera. They responded with cheers.

"You're back!" shouted one man. He disappeared quickly into the throng, out of which another man reached over the bar with both arms to clasp owner Tommy Mandina's hand.

Someone cried: "Beautiful!"

Another: "It's a new era!"

By 11:15, every table was filled. The new restaurant can accommodate 145 to 150 patrons, up from 100 to 115 pre-Katrina. People who arrived at 11:30 were informed they'd wait an hour and a half to be seated.

A TV camera filmed a table of women dining near a front window.

"I'm 65. I've been coming here for 30 years," said Roy Piazza, who grabbed a position near the bend in the bar. Asked what he has been doing during Mandina's hiatus, he responded, "Struggling, like everyone else."

Piazza slapped down a $100 bill and explained that he'd passed by Mandina's countless times in the previous 17 months. He never looked inside.

"I didn't want to spoil it," he said.

Piazza ordered a Bloody Mary. John "J. P." Porter bellied up next to him.

"I'm 59," Porter said. "I've been coming in here since I was 15 with my parents."

Tommy hugged a customer nearby. "No more fist fights!" he said to the man, laughing wildly as he cautioned him off past behavior.

Porter answered his cell phone by shouting into it: "You coming over here?"

The door to the new Mandina's opens, as did the old one, directly next to the long end of the bar. By noon, the area was as crowded as the gate to a Saints game just before kick-off.

The customers who made it inside were greeted to a paradoxical experience peculiar to post-Katrina New Orleans. The building has been subjected to architectural logic and modernity, and the change is shocking. But like so many of post-Katrina New Orleans' rebuilt buildings, it adheres closely enough to its former self to play tricks on the mind.

Once Mandina's fills with New Orleanians, it becomes difficult to remember how exactly it is different than it was.

Connie Comiskey likes to claim herself as a prenatal customer on the grounds that her mother, another regular, ate at Mandina's frequently while pregnant. She was in the company of diners who'd arrived for lunch and stayed through dinner when she cast her eyes over the dining room to offer her perspective on the rebirth.

"They kept the decor, brought it up and made it nicer," Comiskey said. "But it's still Mandina's."

Out front, Paul Marciante—proprietor of Marciante's Gourmet Sausage, a Mandina vendor—reminisced with JoAnn Cuccio about the last time they were at Mandina's, the Saturday before Katrina.

"JoAnn and I are here," Marciante said, patting the edge of the bar. "We are looking at the TV saying, 'Isn't it a shame Pensacola's going to get hit with another storm?'"

In a far corner of the dining room, former state representative Leo A. Watermeier treated his mother Cree to lunch. He had a stuffed bell pepper, a Wednesday special; she had shrimp remoulade and gumbo. They were served by Kenneth Julian Sr., who has worked at the restaurant on-and-off for three decades. Like all the waitstaff, male and female, he was dressed in a tuxedo shirt and bow tie.

Cree has lived in the yellow house across the street from Mandina's since 1959.

"We knew Miss Hilda," she said, referring to Tommy's mother, who died in 1979. "She made a special salad."

"We've been waiting for Mandina's to open since the beginning," Leo said. "At night, the neighborhood is still pretty dark."

A roar of cheers and applause abruptly drowned out the Watermeiers. Tommy had entered the dining room through the kitchen. He was obscured by the crowd that engulfed him as he accepted a standing ovation, his raised fist briefly visible above a mass of appreciative customers.

Mandina's business has been good since the restaurant reopened. But it hasn't been easy.

Not all of the reopening day staff made it to summer. One new cook was arrested during his shift and taken away by police. A busboy who had worked at the restaurant for a decade was caught on video stealing a customer's purse.

Some long-tenured waitstaff fell prey to more stringent codes of conduct. Soliciting large tips through the dispersal of free food and drink, for example, no longer is tolerated.

"That's the old way of doing business," Cindy explained. "I've got too much debt for that now."

"We get a lot of gripes from our customers at the bar that the prices are too high," Martial Voitier said. "But the prices are high everywhere. You drink four Crown Royals and get a bill for $5 and tip the bartender $10, well, it's not like that anymore."

The fallout has included an increase in complaints from old-time customers who can't understand why the waiter who had served them for decades has been replaced by someone they don't recognize. "They're just not used to dealing with new people," Voitier said.

Mark Damico came on as a new manager prior to reopening. He works behind the bar at night, where he said he fields more compliments than complaints. Miss Beverly Cowart, a 50-year Mandina's fixture whose husband built the old brass bar rail at Avondale Shipyards, even brought him a birthday present.

"People ask me all the time, 'What Mandina are you?'" he said.

A former manager at the Fairmount Hotel and of Muriel's on Jackson Square, Damico has helped the Mandinas and Martial confront a forbidding economic climate.

The payroll is twice as much today as it was before the storm, Voitier said. Energy is no better.

"We just got our bill," Cindy reported earlier this summer. "It was like $6,800 for the month of May. Pre-Katrina, my highest bill would be $5,000, and that's in August, when you're running all of your air conditioners. And now I'm all insulated, central air and heat, new wire, new electrical."

Insurance is more expensive, too, as are the debt payments. The Mandinas have filed a lawsuit against Lloyd's of London in an attempt to receive the full amount of their wind and business interruption policies. Cindy doesn't expect the matter to be settled until the end of the year.

That said, the restaurateur is careful not to whine. The Baton Rouge Mandina's closed in June, but the Mandeville location continues to thrive. Earlier this year, Cindy received a call from Little Rock, Arkansas. It was Louise Williams, a beloved employee for 30 years who had gone missing after being trapped on her roof by floodwater.

"She was in such a state when she called," Cindy said. "I was like, 'Everyone thought you were dead!'"

Mandina's is more popular than ever. People recognize Cindy when she shops. Last spring, she became pregnant with her second child.

"I was just someplace buying clothes for my kid," Cindy said last week. "The lady next to me was like, 'I'm glad you guys are back.'"

Cindy enjoys the attention and gratitude, but she draws her motivation from a deeper well.

On opening day she paused briefly to accept a bouquet of flowers delivered by Jeff Weiland, a 15-year Mandina's regular, before promptly returning her attention to a plate of chicken parmesan.

"I need more red gravy!" she shouted. "That's not enough red gravy!"

Starlu Goes Dark

By Andrea Weigl

from the *News & Observer* of Raleigh

Delving into the demise of one restaurant in Durham, North
Carolina, award-winning reporter Andrea Weigl—who writes
on politics and business as well as food—shrewdly captures
the woes of the restaurant industry in microcosm.

On November 28, a few minutes before 2 p.m., Durham
chef Sam Poley sent the e-mail he never wanted to
write—the one announcing the closing of his restaurant, Starlu.

Starlu would close December 22, he told his customers. He invited them to come for a last meal and to say goodbye. "We want
to go out with the same grace with which we entered," he wrote.
"We do not want to be the place that suddenly went dark with no
explanation."

The reason he offered: not enough routine business. The explanation that went unsaid: location.

Poley, 38, is one of those rare chefs who is a master in both the
front and back of the house. He's an inspired chef but also a
charming presence in the dining room. In his white chef's jacket,
khaki cargo shorts, black clogs and brightly colored socks, he
knows how to make diners feel welcome. He calls many of his customers friends.

Starlu was Poley's first restaurant. After a decade of working in
other people's kitchens, Poley decided he had to open his own. He
says he invested $50,000 of his own money and estimates roughly
$950,000 from a private investor. By the end of November, Poley's

wife, Stephanie, tapped the last of the company's savings to make payroll.

The death of Poley's dream illustrates a crucial truth about the eat local movement: In a community where farmers' markets thrive and restaurant menus list that the Camembert came from Chapel Hill Creamery and the pork belly came from Cane Creek Farm, a commitment to eating local has to include dining local, or the restaurants that support those farmers will fail.

In this age of Food Network stars, it seems everyone harbors a dream of running a restaurant. The reality is restaurants are risky ventures. The average profit margin for a full-service restaurant is 4 percent, according to the National Restaurant Association. The failure rate, though not the often-cited 90 percent in the first year hovers at about 60 percent after three years, according to academic research. It is a daunting undertaking to open a restaurant and make it a continued success.

"There is something incredibly immature about opening a restaurant," Poley says, "and something terrifyingly mature about closing it."

A Career Change

Poley ended up in the Triangle for the same reason so many others did: IBM. Poley's father, an engineer, moved the family to Cary when Poley was in high school. Poley was drawn to Durham, a postindustrial town like Kingston, New York, where he grew up. After graduating from Appalachian State University, Poley worked for a prominent public relations firm in Kentucky. He hated it. He moved to Durham and found jobs in public relations and advertising sales. By 25, he wanted a career change. "I essentially crumpled up my degree and got busy," Poley says.

He juggled four jobs, including selling men's clothing and working as a prep cook at Parizade in Durham. He moved from there to Pop's trattoria. He soon decided food was his calling. For many years, Poley was content to work in a kitchen and learn how to cook. He did not want his own restaurant.

"I didn't want the stress of it. I didn't want the hassle. I didn't want the potential to fail," Poley says.

He went on to work as the chef at Squids in Chapel Hill and later at The Weathervane at A Southern Season.

But if you work in kitchens long enough, you start thinking about what you would do differently if the place were yours. That's what happened to Poley. He had to open his own place. Poley concluded he was a risk taker. He wrote a business plan, started looking for financing and scouting locations.

Poley found an investor who made the restaurant's location a condition of support. The space was on the first floor of a six-story office building at the intersection of Shannon Road and University Drive, known largely by the upper-floor tenants, first EMD Pharmaceuticals, then Wachovia. The restaurant's entrance was around back, unseen by passing motorists. Despite the $14,000 sign declaring Restaurant Starlu's presence in 24-inch letters, 30 feet up on the side of the building, first-time visitors would still wonder whether they were in the right place.

The investor agreed to pay for the renovations. Although the location wasn't ideal, Poley agreed. He reasoned that proximity to Durham's most affluent neighborhoods, Duke Forest, Hope Valley and Forest Hills, would help.

Poley kept the copper-topped bar and changed almost everything else. His restaurant was a bright space with clean lines, an open-air kitchen and space to move between tables. The name, Starlu, is a reference to his wife, Stephanie, and their dogs, Arthur and Lu. The restaurant's motto, "It's all about the good stuff," refers to them.

The dining room sat 100. The patio could seat 40 more. And the banquet room could serve 100. At 9,000 square feet, Starlu was an ambitious space for a first-time restaurateur.

After eight months of renovations, Starlu opened in November 2004.

Three months later, Poley received a phone call from Greg Cox, the *News & Observer*'s restaurant reviewer, who was fact-checking his upcoming review.

The 10 days before the review came out were nerve-racking. Poley and his bar manager were at the newspaper racks at 4:30 a.m. They bought six copies for themselves and the others waiting at a nearby apartment. They agreed to read the review together, and not before. They all sat on the dining room floor and opened the paper at the same time.

The review started, "I have just enjoyed, over the brief span of 10 days in January, the two most memorable meals I've had in at least a year." Cox went on to call Poley a "prodigy when it comes to understanding and respecting ingredients, too, and in terms of execution, he rarely falters." Starlu earned 3 out of 4 possible stars.

Before the review was published, Starlu had 12 people booked for dinner that Friday night and 23 for Saturday. Afterward, the restaurant had 83 reservations for Friday night and 123 for Saturday night. That didn't include walk-in customers. Business only got better, Poley says, going from an average of 60 diners on a Saturday night to 250, essentially overnight.

Economy Turns

Business boomed throughout the spring of 2005. But, as the restaurant business goes, it was a slow, lean summer. The first weekend after school started in the fall, Poley says, the dining room was packed. During the Saturday night dinner rush, he recalls exchanging a look with his wife: "They remember us. They like us. We're going to be OK."

But then Hurricane Katrina hit. After that, inexplicably, business slowed. Poley theorizes that although his restaurant benefited from the nearby affluence, those same residents tightened their belts as the economy soured.

Sam and Stephanie Poley say they tried a number of things to revive the business: a lounge area called "Porter's Parlor," named after their 16-month-old son, wine tastings, wine dinners, cooking classes, a chef's table, catering events for Playmakers Repertory Company in Chapel Hill. They even expanded their "Bottles of Change" program, which donated 50 cents for every glass of wine and $2 for every bottle sold to a local charity. Once a month, they donated a cut of a Tuesday night's sales to charity. In three years, the restaurant raised more than $43,000 for needy causes.

Nothing could turn the restaurant around.

The Sign Comes Down

On December 21, Poley stood outside the office building watching workers remove the Restaurant Starlu sign from the side of the building. At 9 a.m., the temperature hovered at 40 degrees with a brisk wind making it seem colder.

With a cup of coffee in his hands, Poley chatted with those who work in the office building or were headed to workout at the first-floor gym. The conversations were all about the restaurant closing.

One man drove up and stopped to talk. "Are you going to re-open anywhere else?" he asked Poley.

"I'd like to," Poley said.

"Location. Location. Location," the man replied.

"I'm going to try to do something with a little more visibility next time," Poley told him.

Saying Good-bye

Funny thing is, Poley's closing e-mail filled the dining room. The upswing led one waitress to quip: "They didn't come to the hospital. They came for the funeral."

For Starlu's last supper, the kitchen stores were spare: four salads, no desserts, a little wine, bottled beer and some liquor. Poley decided to serve the restaurant's former late night menu of fancy hot dogs on buttered, toasted buns. One hot dog is topped with foie gras and maple syrup. Another is wrapped in bacon, deep-fried and served with chopped red onion, mayonnaise and peanut butter.

Twenty-four people were booked for dinner. One loyal customer brought ribs so Poley wouldn't have to cook something to feed the staff at the end of the night.

The mood in the dining room recalled a wake, as if it might be offensive to laugh too loud. An occasional shout filled the air, followed by an exchange of hugs as former employees walked through the door. Some customers left when they learned hot dogs were the only things on the menu. Loyal customers scattered at tables reminisced about Poley's onion rings, and about how welcome they felt even when dining alone at Starlu.

At dinner's end, Poley and his wife started removing items from the walls. Down came artwork, the portraits of their dogs, the framed copy of Cox's review, the sanitation score, the occupancy permits.

By 9:15 p.m., it was time to take down Petunia.

The iron work sculpture of a flying pig was a gift from the contractor when the restaurant opened. Petunia hung above the open-air kitchen, witness to Poley making thousands of meals. Her nickname was Mistress of the Dining Room.

With his hands on his hips, Poley strode up to the pig. He gazed up at her. He paused and turned to look at his wife. His face cracked with emotion. He whispered, "I don't want to take her down."

Poley walked to a back hallway. He crouched down for a private moment, his wife beside him. A few minutes later, Sam came back, wiping away tears.

This time, without hesitation, he walked over and took down Petunia. As he wiped dust off the pig's wings, a couple got up to leave. Putting on their coats, they called out: "Good-bye, Sam. Good-bye, Starlu."

Epilogue: Poley is thinking about getting a tattoo of the Starlu logo. He has lined up a couple of interviews for food industry jobs. Will he open another restaurant? He says he's not sure; maybe as an employee for someone else, maybe on his own. About Starlu, Poley says that ending the dinner service was the easy part. The hard part is now dealing with the lawyers and accountants working to close the business.

Someone's in the Kitchen

Someone's in the Kitchen with Daniel

By Amy Rosen

from *enRoute*

Though her style is sassy and irreverent, Toronto-based food
and travel writer Amy Rosen has enough Cordon Bleu training
to penetrate the culinary mysteries of Manhattan star chef
Daniel Boulud.

Here's why Daniel Boulud's burger is better than yours:
Ordering the original DB Burger served at the chef's
Manhattan restaurant, DB Bistro Moderne, buys you ground sirloin
stuffed with succulent braised short ribs, foie gras and preserved
black truffle, made to order on a freshly baked Parmesan bun. The
accompanying pommes frites, served in a parchment-lined silver
cone, taste more potatoey than any fries I've had before.

Momentarily lost in the reverie that is love at first bite, meat
juice dripping clear past my watchband, I realize too late that I'm
actually meant to use a fork and knife to eat the thing, like the
businessmen surrounding me who also wisely removed their suit
jackets in anticipation. "Yes, that is what most people do," volun-
teers my waiter as I lick my elbows clean.

Bottom line: Daniel Boulud is an evil genius—and if this burger
were single and Jewish, I would marry it. In what must be a culinary first, the superthick stuffed patty sees the shredded short ribs
actually cutting the fattiness of the foie and sirloin. What's more,
the short rib stuffing involves numerous steps, the most impressive
being pouring three bottles of dry red wine into a saucepan and

then setting it aflame. Boulud has taken an essential yet basic piece of Americana and spirited it into a technique-driven masterpiece.

Boulud's pantry is stocked, like most in his culinary bracket, with the cream of the seasonal crop, a legacy perhaps of being raised on the family farm in Lyon. But it's the way the chef handles his raw materials with a neurosurgeon-like attention to detail that must be the secret ingredient. This becomes clear after witnessing him at work during a private cooking lesson, post-burger. I'm here to learn how he transforms something even more pedestrian than the humble beef patty. I mean, it's one thing to make an easy crowd-pleaser like his oft-copied haute burger, but it's another thing altogether to make a potato and leek soup into, well, soupe.

I meet him in the small catering kitchen of Daniel, his flagship restaurant, just down the hall from the gleaming service kitchen. Boulud arrives wearing a pristine chef's jacket, a perfect suntan and a Cheshire grin. I instantly deem him charming, creative and meticulous. In short, he's a French chef. (And no offence to the burger, but if he were single and Jewish, I'd marry him too.)

We set to work on a cold potage Parisien purée with sorrel. "First, you make a soup with potato and leeks and good chicken stock. And then, separately, you blanch Boston lettuce and sorrel in salted water." He squeezes out the water. "Then you boil a little bit of cream. Et voilà." Boulud pours it all into an industrial-grade blender and sticks his spoon into the running blender, which ranks as the second most dangerous thing I've ever witnessed. He adds salt and pepper—"always be seasoning"—a little more stock for that bull's eye consistency, and then he sticks his finger into the moving blender for a taste, which is, hands down, the most dangerous thing I've ever witnessed. After the chartreuse-coloured soup is strained and cooled, he dollops a fluffy cloud of whipped cream atop the bowl, explaining that the quality of the ingredients, the seasonality and the technique make even a simple dish sublime.

But he's not done yet. "And now we have some caviar floating on the cream," he says (of course we do), at which point he starts spoon-feeding me his own line of Caspian osetra straight from the tin. Then the chef employs such gravitas while meticulously arranging fresh sorrel leaves and wee homemade melba rounds around the bowl's outsize rim that I'm just waiting for him to pull out a ruler and calipers. Meanwhile, the cream and caviar gently loll atop the soup before slowly creeping over it like delicious sea foam. "Et voilà!" We both sneak a spoonful. Mmmm.

Sensing the caviar boosts the bottom line and recalling the price of my lunchtime burger ($32), I ask the chef how much he would charge for this lovely potage if it were on the menu. And with that, he laughs the laugh of a man who'd charge $90 for a bowl of soup.

I'm capping off my day in Bouludland on the other side of the kitchen door. The look of Daniel is that of a typical Park Avenue building built in the 1920s: columns and pilasters, velvet settees in the lounge and well-spaced tables in the dining room. It's like entering a fancy restaurant scene in a big-budget movie, and, before long, I start to feel like Marie Antoinette as a stable of liveried servers refolds napkins, refills champagne flutes and presents us with a three-tiered silver tray of amuse-bouches to start. I half expect them to slip off my boots and start fitting me with bespoke Parisian footwear.

Following a remarkable dinner and the chariot des fromages, a series of desserts is upon us, including a *vacherin à la violette, canneberges et litchis* that is almost too beautiful for words. Dressed in a pastel-coloured frock of teardrop meringues, it is delicate, sweet and crunchy. . . By my count, it incorporates no fewer than seven textures, three temperatures and a dozen delightful flavour components, including, I suspect, marshmallow.

Just as I'm marvelling at the artistry of the thing, Daniel Boulud, who's been working the room in his chef's whites, approaches the table, still sporting that Cheshire grin. All I can think is, this is one happy man. He's using an impeccable foundation of technique and inherent talent to turn meringue into magic and burgers into bliss. Something like that would make me happy, too.

Especially if I could charge 90 bucks for a bowl of soup.

Mr. Wizard

By Jason Sheehan

from *WestWord*

Sheehan's restaurant reviews for Denver's alternative weekly
WestWord are already adventures in creative nonfiction;
turning him loose in the kitchen with a whacked-out molecular gastronome like Ian Kleinman just kicks up the surreality
one notch further.

I t begins with a cheese plate.
    One large cube of Point Reyes blue cheese, well mar-
bled with veins of blue-green mold, nicely cut. A small bunch of
grapes. A single breadstick dusted with sea salt and black Tasman-
ian pepper. A little balsamic vinegar. The elements are laid out in
a line on an austere, square white plate: first the cheese, then the
grapes, then the vin. No garnish, no wrap. But the balsamic vinegar
has been caramelized—whipped up into a stiff, peaked foam and
given five seconds of love from the Bernz-o-matic blowtorch on
the line. Each grape has been individually wrapped in a soft jacket
of peanut butter. There's a thin doodle of Alsatian grape syrup
sketched across the plate and then a tiny pile of caviar on top of
the Point Reyes made of that same syrup plus a little algenate, a little calcium chloride.

Still, it is recognizably a cheese plate, that most easy of first
courses on any menu—except this one. With its several culinary
impossibilities (or at least improbabilities), its magical elf powders
and industrial chemicals and artful trickery, this plate took about
fifteen years to create and cost tens of thousands of dollars. It required the obsessive, after-hours work of dozens of stone-crazy

chefs scattered around the globe with the kind of minds that think of things like caramelizing a liquid or wrapping a grape in peanut butter when most normal chefs are concerned only with finding new ways to make soft things crispy—the simplest and most basic description of what a chef does for a living, every day of his working life.

Sitting in the main dining room of O's Steak & Seafood at the Westin Westminster (easily the least likely location I can imagine for a transformative culinary epiphany), I stab a shrimp fork through one corner of the cheese, use the edge of my thumb to add a few beads of glistening grape juice caviar, spear a peanut butter grape and drag the whole bite through the cloud of balsamic foam that has the consistency of a ridiculously light and airy mousse. The smells are powerful: astringent vinegar, funky cheese, the blood of grapes. I put the fork in my mouth and the balsamic foam collapses instantly, flooding my mouth and coating my tongue with its thick sharpness. I bite and the grape explodes, mixing with peanut butter, carrying the Alsace sweetness on its back. Then I reach the cheese—earthy and sour, smooth, delicious.

Tasting all of this is one of the strangest, most amazing sensations I've experienced. Never mind that I've spent the last three hours in the kitchen with Ian Kleinman, O's chef de cuisine and the mad scientist responsible for this plate (among other, even weirder things). Never mind that I've followed every step in its construction, been in on the testing and tasting, watched him make caviar out of grape slurry and turn vinegar into a cloud. Knowing all that, I also know that I will never be able to fully describe this single bite—and that I will never, ever forget it. It will be with me for the rest of my life, because this is the moment when everything changes for me.

This is the moment when it all makes sense.

Like the cheese plate, I've spent many years and unconscionable sums of money to get me to this point. I've read books, lots of books, on molecular gastronomy, the clunky, catch-all name given to the intensely science-driven reimagining of cuisine that covers everything from the use of immersion blenders and thermal circulators to an atoms-up revising of the chemical laws of cookery. I've consulted with chefs over the phone and over many beers. I've flown to Chicago to meet Hervé This—the guy who literally wrote the book on molecular gastronomy, called *Molecular Gastronomy*—and ask him just one very important question: Why?

Even getting to O's to see Ian in action was a long road. It took months for him to get the menu ready for launch—time spent ordering crazily and broadly from Le Sanctuaire (basically getting one of everything from this boutique Santa Monica food company that exists to feed the jones of rich gourmets and chemical enthusiasts everywhere), then experimenting to see what would happen if he mixed this with that, if he overheated carrageenan (it causes cancer) or froze a glass full of olive oil with liquid nitrogen (it explodes). He and I traded e-mails filled with gossip and experimental data and speculation about *Iron Chef*, and then news of Ian's pure genius move: a miso soup that called for taking a big bowl of broth, adding capsules full of freeze-dried or dehydrated ingredients, then injecting noodles into the broth from a fat syringe, with the combination of crème fraîche, togarishi and a high-gelling methocellulose forming up and solidifying as it came into contact with the hot soup. Essentially, Ian had made food pills—that old-fashioned sci-fi conceit that, like the flying car or personal jetpack, had never come true.

Until now.

That encapsulated miso was on the first tasting menu he finally rolled out this month, along with a tableside sorbet of Colorado peaches made with liquid nitrogen, frozen crème anglaise with mango and truffled popcorn, and halibut encased in chicken skin. It took a few more weeks to find a day when I could watch Ian in action, and in that time, he acquired enough tricks to change up his menu weekly. The second week's tasting included smoked blueberries and yellow tomato gazpacho spheres melting over an heirloom tomato tart. I showed up on a Monday: launch day for menu number three. "Three o'clock," Ian told me that morning. "Three, three-thirty. You can come play, help me do some prep. We're gonna have some fun."

I agreed. Fun, and then dinner. It had been exactly one thousand nine hundred and thirty-two days, three hours and a few minutes since I'd last worked in a professional kitchen.

But some habits die hard. Without thinking, I showed up early—twenty minutes early, same as I would've for any shift back in the day, when five minutes early meant fifteen minutes late. I sat down in the O Room, which could've been any bar in any nice hotel anywhere in the world. Long oak, lots of polish, TVs on the walls and bottles in the wells. A conference was letting out for the day in one of the Westin's many ballrooms (uncomfortable *Fear and Loathing in Las Vegas* moment: It was the National Conference on Drugs and Crime), and the bar was starting to fill with top cops and drug counselors from across the country who'd spent the day talking about the dangers of coke and methamphetamine and now wanted to kick back with steak sandwiches and highball glasses full of Jack Daniel's.

Ian came out to take me back to the kitchen. "Learn anything interesting?" he asked.

"Yeah, apparently drugs are bad."

"Really?"

I shrugged. "Who knew?"

He laughed. "Come on back. Let's get you dressed."

Ian's hands are a mess. His fingertips are mauled and swollen, nails anxiety-short, fingers discolored, the backs of his hands and wrists crisscrossed with snaking pink scars that disappear up into the sleeves of his white chef's coat. They are the hands of someone who works for a living. Also, the hands of someone who is absolutely fearless. I watched as he manipulated the syringe filled with algenate-spiked Alsatian grape syrup, warming the syringe, rolling it between those scarred palms, holding it over a plastic cup filled with water and calcium chloride and squeezing out his grape caviar, one teeny drop at a time. As the resplendent purple goo hit the chemical-jacked water, it seemed to recoil, shivering at contact with some catalyst it wasn't expecting. Each drop rolled itself into a perfect, glittering sphere no bigger than the head of a pin and spiraled down to sit at the bottom of the cup, followed by the next one. And the next.

"When I did Aspen Food & Wine, I had to fill three of these," Ian said, stopping the process for a second and, with his wrecked hands, describing a vessel roughly the size of a 7-Eleven Big Gulp. "It took me for-fucking-ever." He picked up the syringe again, hunched himself over the cup of calcium chloride water, let another drop go. "We won't need that much tonight, though." Five minutes passed: drip, drip, drip. Eventually, he straightened up, got a plastic container and a sieve from the shelf above him, set the sieve atop the container and poured—catching the "sphericalization-process faux fruit caviar" in the sieve, emptying the sieve into a third container, adding a shot of the original syrup and swirling them together. Then, taking a spoon, he scooped up about ten minutes' worth of his work and offered it to me.

It tasted like grapes, like very expensive, very powerful gourmet-store jam, but almost carbonated; it was the caviar of a breed of wild grape jelly jars swimming through the deep ocean, stuffed with roe.

"So that's the Alsatian caviar," he said. "That'll go on the cheese plate tonight, I think." He stopped, walked to the edge of his work table, and picked up a sheaf of papers covered with almost completely indecipherable scribbles and hieroglyphic drawings of plate designs. He found the cheese-plate page, ran his finger down it. "Yeah. Cheese plate."

Those papers were the rough draft of the night's menu, still coming together in Ian's head, still being constructed by his hands. He flipped through them as we walked back toward the chef's office and he ran down what had been done, what he still needed to do: *grape cav, whipped bals, nitro, olive dust, clean office.* He put the papers back on his desk, by the computer and the pictures of Ian holding his daughter, Ian grinning maniacally from behind the Lexan shield of what looked like a cop's riot helmet. Most of his work space was taken up by a sheet tray covered with baggies and envelopes and plastic pouches filled with a wizard's array of powders and goops and freeze-dried this-and-that. His Le Sanctuaire order. The only thing I recognized was the dried spearmint.

Ian started talking about marshmallows. The night before, he'd made a marshmallow out of yuzu, pomegranate and Versawhip. But he'd been incautious in his measurements, and it'd blown up to the size of a loaf of bread, then a sheet cake. Ian had wrapped the marshmallow in plastic and tucked it in the cooler, where it had settled, shrunk, taken on the consistency of a sticky steak. "I should've left it out at room temperature," he said. But there's no rule book for this kind of thing, no handbook of best practices. Everything is trial and error. "Want to taste?"

Of course I did. We made our way through the kitchen, passing cooks doing more workaday cook things: chopping romaine, stripping beef bones, making guacamole, slicing tomatoes. From every side, I was assailed by visions of a life I'd abandoned long ago—the crowded shelves of bulk spices, spill of ice melting into a floor drain, rhythmic *tock tock tock* of knives against wood-block cutting boards, the patois of shouted Spanish, English, French and galley slang, and the indescribable smell of a working kitchen that, like the drugs, I don't miss at all except for every day. In the walk-in, the cold, refrigerated air chilled me even through my borrowed jacket as Ian delved into some back corner for his magical marshmallow loaf. He had all his back stock and finished prep for the night's tasting menu stacked on sheet trays in an old baker's proofing box, and it made me happy to see that, xanthan gum, vacuum-sealers and carbonation guns aside, a lot of today's molecular cooking looks just like cooking did for me.

Ian held out a small wedge of sticky pink-and-white fluff. It tasted like a marshmallow made of oranges and lemons and melons, only without the marshmallow. The texture was a little off, but that's what experimenting is for—to get everything right, to make sure that the yuzu tastes like yuzu and the pomegranate tastes like pomegranate and that the magic marshmallow doesn't taste like a marshmallow at all, only looks like one, feels like one. I asked Ian how many of his experiments actually make it onto a menu, rather than, say, getting shoved into a forgotten corner of one of the dozen walk-ins at O's. "Ten percent," he said without even thinking. "Ten percent, maybe. And that's pretty good."

We kept tasting, stopping at one shelf for a spoon, another for a mixing bowl, raiding the baker's station for a silpat and the office for a blowtorch. He showed me a blender hollandaise that had been gelatinized so that, when exposed to heat, it would caramelize and spread into a sheet and then, when cooled, would hold its shape and solid texture. Only it didn't. Not yet. "Just a matter of finding the right chemical," Ian said, "the right temperature."

We moved into the machine room, where a delivery guy was bringing a new tank of liquid nitrogen taller than I am and as heavy as three of me, at least. When Ian moved to unhook the dispensing nozzle from the kicked tank, the delivery guy moved back nervously, bumping into me in his haste to get clear of the cold billows of sublimating nitrogen that filled the cage and shrouded Ian in clouds of smoke. "When my guys have to do this, they wear the mask," Ian said, pointing to the face shield I'd seen in that picture. "The gloves, aprons. But I don't care. I'm not afraid of it."

In the smoke, he looked like a stage devil in chef's whites, a grinning, mad-eyed magician playing with stuff that could kill you if handled wrong (which is to say, handled just the way he was handling it). When it cleared, he hooked up his new tank, screwed in the hose, grabbed a plain metal coffee carafe from a shelf and filled it with liquid nitrogen that he carried, bare-handed, back into the kitchen. The delivery guy was long gone.

"Check this shit out, man," he said, and the two of us got right back to playing. He flash-froze crème anglaise around a single plump blackberry and handed it to me. It tasted like an impossible ice cream bonbon with a whole, fresh and blood-warm berry nestled in the center. He froze olive oil in a tempered glass cup and scooped it out with a spoon. "Eat it," he said, and when I hesitated, just nodded his head as if to say, *Yeah, it's only liquid nitrogen. What's the worst that could happen?*

Liquid nitrogen has a taste, a vaguely chemically, plasticky sort of vaporous flavor that is actually the trapped nitrogen turning to gas inside your mouth at the barest touch of your body heat. My spoonful of olive oil dust tasted like olive oil and nitrogen—tasted like the future of more things than I can count—and turned instantly from a sandy grit to oil again the moment it touched my tongue. To chase it, Ian made me a flash-frozen strawberry sorbet with more olive-oil dust on top, then froze a ball of Captain Morgan spiced rum, plunging his bare hands straight into a mixing bowl full of liquid nitrogen to toss the ball around and freeze it evenly.

"This is the part that hurts," he said, only half-joking as the smoke billowed and he winced at the bite of touching liquid held at negative 346 degrees Fahrenheit. He looked over and laughed. "You want to get some scars, too, Sheehan?" he asked, and nudged the carafe of liquid nitrogen closer with his elbow.

Later, he'll tell me about having recently gone to his doctor to have some tests done, and how the doc had came back in a panic. "I had a white-cell count of like, zero," he'll explain, and all sorts of other problems. "Doctor thought I had hepatitis, all this stuff. He asked me, do you work in a factory? Do you do this? Finally, he asks if I work around any industrial chemicals, and I told him about the menu. That was it. Had to not touch any chemicals for a week, went on a fast . . . "

But even a week away was too much.

Ian told me to hold on for a second while he grabbed something from dry stock, and while he was gone, I looked at the mixing bowl, the smoke. I touched the back of one knuckle to the frosted side of the bowl, and the steel was cold enough that my skin stuck. I looked at the liquid merrily boiling away, the plume of steam that rose when I blew on it.

Fuck it. I reached in. It hurt like a motherfucker.

It would take two days for the feeling to come back to my fingertips, but it was worth it. I was proud of the scars I'd once earned as a cook, as proud as Ian is of his now. And now I'd gotten to touch the future of cooking, too, even if only for a second.

And it felt good.

Before it was time for dinner, Ian and I had tasted our way through most of the menu prep and some of Ian's more unusual experiments. Then we took a break outside the main doors of the Westin, smoking cigarettes and trading stories.

"Gum paste," he said, dreaming aloud of making his own chewing gum to hand out to diners at the conclusion of their meals. He's thinking beet gum would be nice.

"I'm one chemical away from making my own Twinkies," he added, as if this was a good thing, and then he convinced me that it was. Because once he knows how to make Twinkies, he can make better Twinkies than you get at the grocery store.

When I was chasing after Hervé This in Chicago, he said that what makes molecular gastronomy a valid cuisine is that those who practice it well and smartly are chefs who already know how to cook the other cuisines. It's not like Ferran Adria started out making caramel snow globes full of crème brûlée powder or noodles made out of cheese. He started out making chicken, rice, fried squid, whatever. If you use good ingredients, good technique and wisely institute the principles of the new science, there's no reason to assume that the result will be anything less than food. Grilling doesn't make a steak less than a steak—so why would it be less of a steak if it was instantly marinated under extraordinary pressure in a vacuum sealer or turned into a nutritive base and used to impregnate edible paper with a picture of a steak printed on it?

Ian has a slightly different take. He is French-trained. He can bone out a chicken, grill a steak, reduce a demi, make a hollandaise blindfolded, with one hand tied behind his back. He's the son of a chef, did C-school, has fifteen years of cooking behind him in restaurants where he did both well and poorly. Now when he goes to cooking schools, he instructs the instructors on the basic tenets of molecular gastronomy. How to make caviar out of grape juice. "You control the food," he tells them. "The food doesn't control you."

At least, not entirely. After two cigarettes, I followed him back into the kitchen. I watched him assemble four tasting plates for the floor staff and cooks so they could see how each was supposed to look and know how they tasted, laying out squares of gelée off the tip of a knife, spooning out clouds of balsamic vinegar fluffed with Versawhip and piped carbonated cantaloupe jelly.

And each time his hands got close to the plate, they shook.

I taste the cheese, eating that which I, for once and again, was at least tangentially involved in making.

Back in civilian attire, I'm sitting in the dining room. It's beautiful in the setting sun, looking out over a broad courtyard, artistic pillars and a man-made lake on whose far shore buzzes the gaudy red neon of a Rock Bottom Brewery. The waitstaff is young, mostly female, decent to a point but somewhat clumsy in their attempts to sell the tasting menu to other tables; most diners go for more standard fare.

The second tasting course is a single scoop of liquid-nitrogen sorbet—a palate cleanser, pomegranate, agave nectar and roasted tomato with black-olive dust—served in a hand sculpted out of ice. It's Ian's hand. The imagery is not lost on me. It's prepared tableside, and Ian himself wheels out the cart. "How are you finding dinner tonight, sir?" he mugs. "Feeling all right?"

Third course: sous-vide Alaskan king crab that is really double-sous-vide crab because the crabs were boiled whole, sectioned, the meat removed, then re-vacuum-bagged and slow-cooked again for eight hours at some ridiculously low temperature along with some frozen beurre blanc, a sprig of thyme. The plate is the same white plate used for the cheese course, the linear arrangement of elements no less beautiful. The crab is set atop warm, piped parmesan mayonnaise, dotted with green peas, shiitake mushrooms and thyme. On one end, there's a single dot of brilliant red sriracha, in the middle a puddle of carbonated cantaloupe jelly (which I hadn't liked during the tasting and don't like any better now) and on the other end, two squares of roasted melon and spearmint leaves, robbed of their most vital juices, turned into a clear amber gelée and stacked like breath mints.

After three bites of the crab/thyme/mayo/pea/shiitake combination, I have to call for Ian. He sits down next to me on the banquette, beaming because he can see the flush in my cheeks, the tears standing out in my eyes.

"I know, man," he says. "I know."

It is the best crab I have had in my life, the best English peas, the best shiitake mushrooms *ever*. It is an absolute wonder of science and cuisine, of processes I barely understand, of chemicals whose names I can't remember. The crab melts on my tongue like butter, only butter made of crab. The peas have been marinated under pressure, or maybe marinated while frozen. The shiitakes are merely roasted, but roasted to the ideal state of chewy-tender, dry and concentrated doneness. Perfect. I try to tell this to Ian. He just nods, says thank you and slips away, back into the kitchen, his lab, his playground of the future.

After the crab, anything else would be a letdown. I think a blow job and a salad made of hundred-dollar bills would be a letdown. Unfortunately, I don't get to test this theory, but instead move on to the dessert course: a beet meringue topped with almond yogurt turned into ice cream, bits of seared quince and a bed of pine caramel made from tufts clipped from the branches of a pine tree growing right outside the dining room—terroir in extreme. I follow that with a glass of Robert Hall port and a good cigar while I sit beside the fire on the patio.

After a while, Ian huffs down in a chair beside me, and we talk. He tells me that he's tired, that his wife is pissed at him because he isn't home enough and because, working twelve or fourteen hours a day, he isn't getting to see his little girl at all. He says he's going to take a vacation, starting tomorrow. He's taken pictures of all his plates, left prep instructions for his cooks. Tomorrow, they'll be the ones freezing their fingertips, sculpting the gelée, making the caviar—but only if people order the tasting menu, which is never a sure thing.

Last week, Ian sold just seventeen tasting menus. The week before, twelve. There are nights when he and his crew turn 350 in the dining room and not a single person goes for anything overtly molecularly gastronomical—except for the flashy tableside sorbet, which has always been a solid seller.

But even without ordering the tasting menu, the diners at O's still experience molecular gastronomy. Bits of it are scattered all through the menu—asparagus served with the same nitrous-fired parmesan mayonnaise he uses on the crab plate, short ribs done sous-vide—even if Ian doesn't call attention to them. Which is the way to do it, he insists. Have one, freaky, intimidating and bizarre menu full of crazy Mr. Wizard shit available for the adventurous, then take the best things from that menu and incorporate them into the regular board. That's how this new cuisine is going to become acceptable, he insists, how it's going to work. You can't give the people meat paper or fruit caviar until they've gotten hip to sous-vide; you can't get them hip to sous-vide until they've come to accept slow-poaching and immersion blenders. As with anything, there's a process, and though Ian has always been something of a rebel (serving seawater gelée and wasabi popcorn that turned everyone's mouths blue at Indigo; trying to start his own soup company by carrying around samples in a black briefcase and showing them to chefs in parking lots, laying the case on the hoods of cars like some kind of weight coke dealer and asking if they had a microwave he could use), he's growing up a little, thinking more, planning for the future even though, in his kitchen, the future is already here.

"You know how it is," he says. "Being a chef, it's all about the tricks you know. It's all about being the guy who knows more, who does something first. Well, now I've got a whole new bunch of new tricks I know. When I want to cook something, I can just cook it." No longer is cooking about grilling this, searing that. It's about instant freezing and chemicals that have been the tools solely of the food processors for too long. It's about reimagining absolutely everything. "There are no rules, you know? We can do anything."

CHEF ON THE EDGE

By Larissa MacFarquhar

from the *New Yorker*

Known for her insightful in-depth *New Yorker* profiles, Mac-
Farquhar caused many ripples in the food blogosphere with
this long, profanity-peppered piece on iconoclastic chef-of-
the-moment David Chang.

"So Pete, let's just fucking bang out these recipes,"
Chang said.

"We'll get fish in tomorrow and start playing around," Serpico
said.

"Fish is easy. I know you don't want to, but you can use the
buttermilk with the stabilizer and whip it so it's like yogurt."

"I'm thinking a spicy buttermilk. Maybe we'll make it the consistency of the tofu."

"Doesn't Jean Georges have that fluke with a buttermilk dressing and champagne grapes?" Chang said. "It's fucking badass, over
fluke."

David Chang and Peter Serpico were sitting in the basement
office of Momofuku Ssäm Bar, going over what they had to get
done before the opening of Ko. The stoves were in, and the gas
was ready to be turned on, but they couldn't cook there yet, because the fire-extinguishing system wasn't installed. Ssäm Bar was
Chang's second restaurant; Ko was his third.

Chang is only thirty, but in the past couple of years he has un-
expectedly and, in his mind, accidentally and probably fraudu-
lently, become one of the most celebrated chefs in the country. He
is way too neurotic to handle this, however, so he compensates by

representing himself as a bumbling idiot. He is five feet ten, built like a beer mug, and feels that most food tastes better with pork.

Serpico is Ko's chef. He has worked with Chang for a couple of years, after a job at Bouley. He and Chang both raze their hair to buzz cuts, but while Chang's makes his head look rounder and more babylike, Serpico's makes him look sharper, wirier, ready to flee.

"O.K., the one thing we don't have down and standardized is scallops, which we're gonna do right now."

They'd been working on the scallop dish for weeks. It was a thing of beauty: a smear of black nori purée on the bottom of the bowl; then a layer of sea scallops and chanterelles and possibly clams; and then, spooned on top in front of the customer, a soft heap of foaming dashi (kelp and dried-bonito broth), made intentionally unstable with just a little methylcellulose, so that in front of the customer's eyes the bubbles would burst and dissipate into a fishy liquid, at exactly the speed that foam from a wave dissipates onto sand. It looked like the sea and tasted like the sea, and Chang was extremely proud of it. The only thing he was worried about was the word "foam," which, owing to its trendiness in the nineties, had become a symbol of everything pretentious and unnatural about nineties cuisine. In Chang's mind, he was making fun of foam, but of course some people were not going to get that and were going to think he was just another leftover foam slave. "It's gonna piss people off," he said happily.

Serpico noticed a giant eggshell next to Chang's computer.

"Is that the ostrich egg you cooked up the other day?" he asked. "How was it?"

"It was awful," Chang said. "I wanted it over easy, you know—I wanted to pretend I was Fred Flintstone. So I got a big rondeau, put like two inches of oil, and I was gonna deep-fry the motherfucker, but there was so much water content in the white that it just sort of dispersed. It looked like cottage cheese."

"Eww."

"The egg yolk, though—the egg yolk was massive. Equivalent to twenty-four chicken eggs."

"Wow."

"We're gonna be ready to roll next week," Chang said. "If not, I'm gonna chop Hiro's pinkie off." Hiro was Ko's architect.

"I can't wait," Serpico said. "I'm fucking killing myself, man. I've got nothing to do. I guess I could look for an apartment."

Serpico had to be out of his apartment in less than a month but had not yet found another place to live. He has not historically paid much attention to his living arrangements. He is twenty-six and inherited his first bed a year ago. Until then, he hadn't even owned a mattress—he just slept on the floor. He still doesn't have a closet: he drops his clothes at the laundry, then just takes stuff as he needs it right out of the bag. He has cooked at home once in six years. If he isn't eating at the restaurant, he usually gets McDonald's or KFC.

Serpico's habits are not unusual among the cooks at Momofuku. Chang never cooks at home, either—he orders Chinese or pizza. He had a bed in his old apartment, but only because it had been left behind by the previous tenant. Recently, he bought a place, but he had no furniture, so one day he braced himself and went to Crate & Barrel. He had only an hour to shop, though, so he picked out one of the mockup rooms and told a salesperson he wanted to buy everything in it, just as it was. The consequence of this, he realized when the furniture arrived, was that his apartment looked like a hotel room, but at least there was stuff on the floor.

"You're freaking out," Chang said. "Let's go cook, dude."

"This is awesome!" Chang cried to Serpico, running his hands along the countertop. For the first time, Ko was starting to look like a restaurant. It was filthy, it was tiny, it was constructed almost entirely of plywood—walls, doors, counter, cabinets—but it was a restaurant, and soon they would cook there.

"Telepan saw this last night," Chang said. Bill Telepan runs the restaurant Telepan, on the Upper West Side. "He laughed his ass off. He's like, 'This is the smallest fucking place I've ever gotten into.' You're a dumb man, Serpico. Nobody in their right mind would do something like this."

Chang was hoping that the opening of Ko would be marginally less disastrous than the opening of his first two restaurants, but he was expecting the worst. Already they'd saved themselves from several ideas that, in retrospect, seemed to them so incredibly stupid it was hard to believe they'd had them in the first place. The idea that the cooks would wash all the dishes themselves during service, for instance. That had been a kind of principled thing for Chang—he felt that no one who worked for Momofuku should be too proud to help out with the grossest tasks in the kitchen—but it was still a really bad idea. They were sticking to the concept that there would be no servers, because Chang wanted the cooks to get all the tips. ("Servers are such greedy bastards," he says. A server at Ssäm Bar could bring in seventeen hundred dollars in a week working thirty-two hours; a cook working the same hours would earn three hundred and fifty.) On the other hand, most cooks were not fully domesticated, and it was already expecting kind of a lot to have them do their job two feet from normal people who were paying to have a pleasant evening. (Ko is set up like a sushi bar, with all the customers at a counter facing the stoves.) Asking them to act like waiters as well might be one step too far.

It was unbelievable how many decisions had to be made before they opened. Just figuring out how to pour the miso soup into bowls in front of the customer had taken a whole discussion with Cory Lane. (Cory Lane manages the front of the house—servers, setup, beverages—at all three restaurants. He went to cooking school, decided that he wasn't a very good cook, and became a wine expert instead.)

"What would be easier is maybe a small pot, like something ghetto, and then just pour it in," Chang had said.

"No, you're leaning over and you pour it from the pan," Serpico said.

"It's gonna get all over the place!" Chang said. "You wanna spoon it or ladle it. Like a teapot, dude."

"With those sake carafes, you can do them ahead of time and they hold hot for a little while," Lane suggested.

"I don't know, man. You reach over and you pour it right in their bowl," Serpico said, pouring the liquid from a tiny saucepan into a bowl over the back of a spoon, so that it flowed smoothly and didn't splash.

"That I like, pouring it over the back of the spoon like that," Lane said approvingly. "I mean, you can go anywhere and have a soup poured tableside out of a fucking pitcher. I like that."

In the beginning, Chang's whole goal was to open a noodle bar. He didn't really give much thought to what he would do with it once he did. When he thinks back on the ridiculous way he went about starting his first restaurant, four years ago, and the way it succeeded so wildly, despite his complete ignorance of the business and all the mistakes he made as a consequence, and led to another restaurant, and then another, and all the chef's prizes he's received since, it all seems to him like an impossible fairy tale, and he becomes convinced that it could vanish at any moment. "I feel like I didn't deserve any of this," he says. "I blame my parents for my guilty conscience. Growing up, no one ever told me, 'Dave, you're smart, you're fast, you're witty'—it was quite the opposite. I'm still so insecure, I feel like I'm Forrest Gump—I'm mildly retarded, and people are, like, 'Look how far this guy has come!'"

Chang's parents emigrated from Korea as adults in the nineteen-sixties, he from North Korea, she from South. His father, Joe, had fifty dollars when he arrived. He started out working as a dishwasher in New York, and later moved to a suburb of Washington, D.C., and opened a couple of delis. He began making real money when David was a teenager (David is the youngest of four), with a golf-supplies business. David became a junior golf champion but quit when he was thirteen.

Chang was miserable in school and claims to have failed everything. "I never even made the high-school golf team," he says. "I was too much of a head case. Remember that scene in *The Royal Tenenbaums* when Luke Wilson's playing tennis and crying and he throws his shoe? That's what I was like." He went to Trinity College, in Connecticut, but says he only got in because he was Asian; he smoked pot almost every day. But one thing that interested him was religion—his parents and his sister were very involved with a Korean Presbyterian church, and he had turned against that—so he became a religion major and wrote a thesis on Thoreau. Something about the mindful ordinariness of "Walden" appealed to him—the elevation of daily repetitions into an honorable way of life. "Even menial tasks such as domestic chores were a pleasant pastime," Chang wrote. "He enjoyed these duties because he completed them with painstaking diligence."

After college, he spent six months at the French Culinary Institute; at the same time, he worked the dinner shift at Mercer Kitchen and, on his days off, answered phones at Craft until he got a job as a cook. Meanwhile, for years he'd been obsessed with ramen ("momofuku" means "lucky peach," but it is also the name of the man who invented packaged ramen noodles), and he knew he wanted to apprentice in a Japanese noodle shop. Finally, an opportunity presented itself: his aunt was friends with Reverend Paul Hwang, a Korean businessman who had turned a building he owned in Tokyo into a combination church and men's homeless shelter, with a ramen shop on the first floor. Reverend Hwang said that Chang could live in the homeless shelter and work in the ramen shop. As it turned out, Reverend Hwang's ramen shop was one of the few really bad ramen shops in Tokyo, so Chang didn't stay there for long, but his true apprenticeship came from eating around the city and realizing what it meant to live in a food culture where even the smallest, cheapest place served food more delicious than you could get in half the restaurants in Manhattan.

When he got back to New York, he got a job at Café Boulud, a three-star restaurant on the Upper East Side then being run by Andrew Carmellini. He worked six or seven days a week, fifteen-hour days (though only because he felt he had to get there two hours early to keep up). It was brutal. "Café Boulud was intentionally difficult," he says. "It was chip-on-your-shoulder cooking, like, all these other restaurants have twice as many cooks, all this new equipment, and we're gonna fucking outcook them with nothing but our sheer will and technique." But it wasn't just machismo—it was also beautiful. "Andrew knows how things should taste," Chang says. "It's crystal clear in his mind. There were so many instances when he was, like, 'It's missing something, do this,' and it's fucking perfect." Chang felt lucky to be working in such a kitchen, but he was preoccupied with trouble at home—fights between his father and his oldest brother over the family business, then his mother being diagnosed with cancer— and he could feel that he was starting to freak out. His hands were shaking so much that he couldn't sauce plates. Finally, he had an epiphany. "Why can't I cook something simple?" he said to himself. "I'm not an awesome cook—I just want to make noodles." He quit Café Boulud and moved home for a while to help take care of his mother. Then he put together a business plan, asked his father for just shy of two hundred thousand dollars in seed money, and started looking for a place to open a noodle bar.

He signed a lease on a six-hundred-square-foot storefront at First Avenue and Tenth Street in early 2004. He asked some of his friends to come in on it with him, but nobody wanted to leave a job for a venture that was certain to fail. Fine, he thought, I'll do it all myself. But just before the restaurant was due to open he found another cook, a guy named Joaquin Baca, who responded to an ad he'd placed on monster.com. Baca had worked in restaurants in Santa Fe but since moving to New York had been offered only insultingly bad entry-level jobs. He figured he had nothing to lose, and signed up.

At first, it was just Chang and Baca, seven days a week. The menu was very simple: ramen noodles with shredded pork, seven dollars; Momofuku ramen with pork and a poached egg, twelve dollars; steamed rice noodles; pork buns; cash only. Chang was living in a horrible little apartment across the street. He would arrive at the restaurant at seven, prep all the food, take deliveries, and cook the lunch service by himself. He left around four, took a two-hour nap, then came back to help Baca with dinner. They had practically no customers. The Japanese place across the street, which was terrible in his opinion, was always packed. They started hiring people—dishwashers, cooks, servers—but nobody could meet Chang's standards, so he fired them all. Those he didn't fire quit. Finally, Chang and Baca decided that if they were going to go broke they might as well do it in style, and they started cooking what they felt like—stranger, more adventurous dishes with better ingredients. And then it all began to happen.

Just as Ko was finally coming together, at the end of February, Chang stopped by Noodle Bar one day and saw so much sloppiness in the kitchen that he flew into one of his rages. Most chefs yell, but Chang is on a different level. "No one gets angry like I get angry," he says unhappily. "I just turn into a complete maniac. My brain feels like it's gonna explode. It takes me a day to recover—I have to lie down and put ice on my head."

At Noodle Bar, a junior line cook had been cooking chicken for family meal—lunch for the staff—and although he had to cook something like seventy-five chicken pieces and the stoves were mostly empty, he'd been cooking them in only two pans, which meant that he was wasting time he could have spent helping to prep for dinner. Also, he was cooking with tongs, which was bad technique, it ripped the food apart, it was how you cooked at T.G.I. Friday's—he should have been using a spoon or a spatula. Cooking with tongs showed disrespect for the chicken, disrespect for family meal, and, by extension, disrespect for the entire restaurant. But the guy cooking family meal was just the beginning of it. Walking down the line, Chang had spotted another cook cutting fish cake into slices that were totally uneven and looked like hell. Someone else was handling ice-cream cones with her bare hands, touching the end that wasn't covered in paper. None of these mistakes was egregious in itself, but all of them together made Chang feel that Noodle Bar's kitchen was degenerating into decadence and anarchy. He had screamed and yelled until a friend showed up and dragged him out of the restaurant, and his head still hurt nearly twenty-four hours later.

The following afternoon, Chang called an emergency meeting for the staff. Something was rotten in Noodle Bar, and he meant to cut it out and destroy it before it was too late.

"I haven't been spending that much time in this restaurant because of all the shit that's been going on," he began, "but the past two days I've had aneurisms because I've been so upset at the kitchen. On the cooks' end, I question your integrity. Are you willing to fucking sacrifice yourself for the food? Yesterday, we had an incident with fish cakes: they weren't properly cut. Does it really matter in the bowl of ramen? No. But for personal integrity as a cook, this is what we do, and I don't think you guys fucking care enough. It takes those little things, the properly cut scallions, to set us apart from Uno's and McDonald's. If we don't step up our game, we're headed toward the middle, and I don't want to fucking work there.

"We're not the best cooks, we're not the best restaurant—if you were a really good cook you wouldn't be working here, because really good cooks are assholes. But we're gonna try our best, and that's as a team. Recently, over at Ssäm Bar, a sous-chef closed improperly, there were a lot of mistakes, and I was livid and I let this guy have it. About a week later, I found out that it wasn't him, he wasn't even at the restaurant that night. But what he said was 'I'm sorry, it will never happen again.' And you know what? I felt like an asshole for yelling at him, but, more important, I felt like, Wow, this is what we want to build our company around: guys that have this level of integrity. Just because we're not Per Se, just because we're not Daniel, just because we're not a four-star restaurant, why can't we have the same fucking standards? If we start being accountable not only for our own actions but for everyone else's actions, we're gonna do some awesome shit."

Although Chang decided early on that he wasn't going to be doing fine dining in his own career, its titans are still the inspiration for everything he does. A few weeks ago, he took his girlfriend for her birthday to Per Se, a restaurant in Columbus Circle founded by Thomas Keller and now run by Jonathan Benno, who was a sous-chef at Craft when Chang worked there. The meal at Per Se took six hours, and it was flawless. Chang was so overcome by the dazzling perfection of the food, and so drunk from all the paired wines, that he cried.

Chang reveres chefs like Benno and Keller and Wylie Dufresne for bringing adventurous cooking to America, but his idol is the Spanish chef Ferran Adrià. Adrià calls his food "deconstructivist"; few of his dishes are what they appear to be. He was the originator of the foam craze, but that was a long time ago. He continues to contrive ever more rococo and outlandish preparations in his laboratory in Barcelona: slivers of sea urchin enclosed in a transparent raviolo of kombu seaweed, which look like goldfish swimming in water; balls of puréed hazelnut, formed by dropping the purée from a syringe into liquid nitrogen; a two-meter-long spaghetto made of liquid Parmesan jelled in a PVC tube. In Chang's view, two hundred years from now Adrià is the only chef, besides Escoffier, whom people will still be studying and talking about. "He's trying to rethink food," Chang says. "He was the first guy to say, 'Food can be poetic, it can be abstract.'"

Adrià's aberrant fantasies are not, to be sure, daily reference points for Chang's cooking, but the idea of Noodle Bar from the start was to take the humblest meal—a bowl of noodles, a pork bun—and, with a combination of obsessive devotion and four-star technique, turn it into something amazing. Take the chicken wings, for instance. All you knew when you were eating them was that they tasted really good. What you didn't know was that they'd been brined in a salt-and-sugar solution for a whole day (but not longer, or they'd be too salty), then dried out and cold-smoked over mesquite for forty-five minutes, then poached in a vat of pork fat for an hour and a half, then browned on the flattop, then glazed in a chicken-infused soy sauce combined with mirin, garlic, and pickled chili peppers. Each step, executed perfectly, was vital to the dish. This was what the cooks at Noodle Bar had to understand.

"You guys have to ask yourself as cooks, how bad do you want this?" Chang declared at the meeting, warming up to his finale. "Life and death is what it means to me. And next time I see something that is not up to my standards I'm gonna let you fucking go. What we want are people with high character that are gonna look each other in the eye and be like, I gave you my best effort today. We want the person who fucked up not to be able to sleep at night because he's so embarrassed, and the next day to be like, I'm gonna get better, I'm gonna get better.

"In four years, we've gone from that small-ass Noodle Bar to this fucking big restaurant, when the whole goal in the beginning was, let's serve better food than that place across the street. I know we've won awards, all this stuff, but it's not because we're doing something special—I believe it's really because we care more than the next guy. So the next time you're at your station and you see someone going down in flames—and every night someone goes down in flames—you gotta ask yourself, Do I have this person's back? Because when the kitchen's really humming, you know what? Getting into the weeds is a lot of fucking fun."

"This is looking sharp, chef!" Chang said, running his hands over Ko's newly shiny ovens. Serpico had been scrubbing for hours.

"Yeah, I tried to clean the shit out of the floor yesterday but it's still, I don't know," Serpico said.

"Let's put this table back in."

"No, I want to clean the floor one more time. I'm weird about some shit, all right? The floor's fucking disgusting." The floor looked pretty clean, but not clean enough for Serpico. Every cook had something he was weird about. For Chang, it was badly folded towels. For Sam Gelman, it was spoons and aprons. (Gelman, Ko's sous-chef, was twenty-six. He was from Iowa and liked to fish.)

They were making progress. The wine fridge had arrived. The glasses had been taken care of—Ravenscroft had donated them. Christina Tosi, the dessert cook, had come up with an awe-inspiring dish: panna cotta made from cornflakes milk, served on a smear of avocado. A middle-aged man in a black leather jacket came in. It was Pedro, the rep from Cascade Linen Supply.

"O.K., so you guys have nice napkins, serviettes?" Pedro asked.

"Can you bring me a sample?" Serpico said. "White. Do you have nicer chef coats?"

"The ones that you have are the standard," Pedro said. "You want something nice, it's gonna be more expensive. I don't know if you want to go into Bragard chef coats."

"They're not the real Bragards," Chang told him. "They're made in China. They suck."

"Do you have the bib aprons that are longer?" Serpico asked. "I noticed that all your bib aprons now come down to the knee."

"One blue apron for chef," Chang said.

"I'm not wearing a blue apron, dude."

One of the few things that make Chang happy in life is setting up his friends in restaurants of their own, and the fact that Serpico was going to be in charge of Ko made him feel very good. But there were always more friends, and the thought of opening up new restaurants was always alluring. He's been talking to some people about opening a huge Momofuku in Las Vegas, with a several-thousand-square-foot kitchen and top-of-the-line equipment. His mind boggles thinking about what he could do with that kind of kitchen—no more worrying about whether a dish could be cooked quickly on a tiny *plancha* with three guys bumping into one another. Some other people recently offered to help him start a place in Dubai, and he flew out to take a look. He was dazzled—the speed of it, the wild energy, the gigantic buildings going up every day, the indoor ski slope, and everyone seemed to be happy there, even migrant workers seemed to him to have a pretty good deal. He came back feeling as if he'd visited the future and America had no more juice. To be part of something like that—how could he resist?

He knows he wants to open more restaurants, but the question is what kind. The obvious thing would be to open a temple of fine dining that would declare his ascension into the chef firmament, preferably an eponymous temple that would secure his immortality in the public mind, but the idea made him sick. "Why would you name a restaurant after yourself?" he says. "I can't imagine opening a restaurant called David Chang's—I'd fucking off myself. I just want to make sure that I don't become a total asshole." Expansion, like most things in life, seemed to him to offer choices any of which would make him feel that he'd screwed things up forever and lost whatever scrap of honor he once possessed. If he did expand, he'd feel like a whore and an egomaniac, selling his chefly virtue for cash; if he didn't expand, he'd feel like a pretentious artiste throwing away an opportunity that could help his friends because he was so in love with his precious integrity. He'd always liked the idea of starting a fast-food chain—he and Tosi have talked about opening a Momofuku Milk Bar, with soft-serve ice cream, like Dairy Queen. The great thing about fast food was that you could sell out without worrying about it, because fast food was unpretentious and selling out was the nature of the business. Or something like that.

It was always possible, of course, that he would drop dead before he had a chance to do any of this. Some time ago, his doctor told him he had high blood pressure and had to take a vacation, so he went to Costa Rica by himself and sat on the beach and read and felt better. But then last summer was very stressful, what with trying to get Noodle Bar open in a new location, and one day he came into work feeling as if he were dying, and his left cheek went numb. He went to the emergency room, but they couldn't figure out what was wrong. A couple of days later, he couldn't get out of bed because of a terrible pain in his back, so he went to a chiropractor, but the chiropractor didn't know what was wrong, either. The next day, he lost his hearing in his left ear and had a terrible pain in his jaw. Then his face became covered in spots that hurt, so he went to a dermatologist, who told him that he had shingles, and that it meant he was dangerously tense. He told him to take a vacation immediately, somewhere cold and dark where his face could heal, so Chang went to Montreal. He sat in his hotel and went to dinner by himself every night. It was awful. When he got back, he realized that he needed to make some changes in his life, which was why, these days, he was trying to stay out of the kitchen. The trouble was, although not being in the kitchen removed one cause of stress, it replaced it with another. "I'm not cooking every day anymore, and that's the biggest withdrawal," he says. "Cooking is honest work. Now I don't know how to measure myself."

He never set out to become a famous person. He just wanted to see if he could open a noodle bar. Now he finds that he's a public figure, criticized and praised—but mostly praised—by people he's never met. "Getting these awards freaks me out—the last thing I want is a Michelin star—because I know I'm not the best," he says. When he thinks about the cooks he worked with at Craft and Café Boulud and how they were so much more skilled than he, and had put in more years than he had, and yet here he was getting all these prizes and all this attention, he feels himself starting to panic. Sometimes he tries to comfort himself thinking about all the bands he loves that made great music even though they were terrible musicians, but somehow it's not the same. "I feel like I'm losing my ability to understand reality," he says, "like when someone loses their hearing, they can still speak English, but their speech eventually becomes distorted because they can't hear themselves. I don't want to be this crazy. It's tiring. I just want some mental clarity. But I don't like that I'm becoming more self-aware of all my problems. It doesn't make me feel better—I just feel unease almost all the time. I'm a total head case right now, I cannot keep this up. All I want to do is fucking move to Idaho and ski and fish and read books. All I want to do is run away and stop."

There are several mother figures in his life who worry about his health and try to persuade him to run away and stop: Ruth Reichl, the editor of *Gourmet*; Dana Cowin, the editor of *Food & Wine*; Alice Waters, the founder of Chez Panisse. "I never thought that I'd be able to be, like, friends with Alice Waters," he says. "And for her to actually care about me—that is so weird. I think Ruth told her that I had shingles, and that's when Alice had an intervention at lunch. She was like, 'You're not doing anything more, no more, no more!'" Then, there are the older-brother chef figures who know he's not going to stop but who tell him to calm down. Andrew Carmellini bought him yoga lessons. "It was just when Momofuku started to really roll," Carmellini says, "and I was, like, 'Dude, I'm telling you from personal experience, you need to chill out.'" Mario Batali, who has opened seven restaurants in New York, three in Las Vegas, and two in L.A., while hosting two programs on the Food Network and appearing regularly on "Iron Chef," comes into Noodle Bar a fair amount and gives Chang counsel. "Mario's big thing to me is 'Dave, would you fucking be happy?'" Chang says. "He loves it. He loves life. I want to love life as much as Mario loves life." He sighs. "It's not that I'm not happy; I'm just fearful for the future," he says. "I'm fearful that everything's gonna be taken away. Fear is a driving force for most of the things that I do. I don't know if that's healthy."

Sometimes he imagines a way out that wouldn't be just skiing and reading. He could start up some kind of project in New York like Alice Waters's Edible Schoolyard, where kids learn to grow their own crops and work in a garden. Growing vegetables, keeping animals, teaching people about food—he would love that. Recently, he picked out a piglet at a small farm in Jeffersonville, New York—the runt of the litter, to go with the Momofuku underdog mentality—named it Squint, and made arrangements with the farmer to slaughter it himself when it got big enough. He wanted to see if he could kill an animal that he had come to know, that was as smart as a dog, in order to understand better where the hundreds of pounds of pork that he cooked every week were coming from. But then he thinks about all the people working for him, and relying on him, and how they could get rich if he gets rich and then could do whatever they wanted, and the farm thing seems kind of small.

"I'm so sick and tired of how awesome it is to work at Google or fucking Apple or one of those tech companies," he says. "Why can't it be awesome to work for a food company? Why can't we create an environment where people are trying to push each other to do great things, and we're not trying to steal from anybody, we're trying to be good to our farmers and run an honorable business, if there is such a thing anymore? I feel that it would be cowardly and selfish to say, "You know what, screw this." He is trying to make Momofuku a good place to work: he is sharing ownership with his chefs, and he is buying good health-care plans for his permanent staff and sponsoring English lessons for the prep cooks. "If it was solely about money, I could have sold out a long time ago," he says, "but I wouldn't feel good about it, because I'd let everyone down. I don't know. I'm slowly realizing that I'm a highly complex individual."

Even assuming that he can take on more restaurants and not end up in five years dead or in a straitjacket, there are downsides to expansion. "I'm finally dating somebody that I don't hate her guts," he says. "We had dinner yesterday and I was like, I don't hate you at all! You know?" His girlfriend is also Korean-American, and was also raised to be brilliant at something—where he played golf, she played the violin. She now works in the advertising department of Microsoft. She seems to tolerate him amazingly well. "I am the worst boyfriend ever," he says. "I'm high maintenance. I mean, you have no idea how high maintenance." All of this, combined with the fact that he knows his parents want nothing more than for him to marry a girl of pure Korean blood and provide them with grandchildren (none of his siblings seem likely to oblige), has made him think differently about the future.

In Europe, he knows, there are great chefs who open just one restaurant and are happy with that. They have families, they take vacations, they see their friends. On a recent trip to France for a food conference, he and Tosi had an epic meal in Paris at Pascal Barbot's restaurant, L'Astrance. The kitchen was tiny, and the restaurant had only twenty-five seats. It was open Tuesday through Saturday. It closed in August. And it had three Michelin stars. That was integrity, Chang felt; that was dignity. But in America, somehow, a career like Barbot's just didn't seem possible.

After all the waiting, the delays, the mess, the cleaning, the decisions, the ordering, the planning, and the cooking, opening day had come. Ko was scrubbed, Ko was stocked, Ko was ready. It would open officially that evening at five-thirty, and at six o'clock its first two customers would walk through the door, sit down at the counter, and be fed dinner. Of course, they wouldn't be real customers tonight—just cooks from the other restaurants, plus a couple of girlfriends. Chang was nervous, and not just because he was always nervous: something weird was going on. In the past week, four inspectors had shown up at Ko—State Liquor, Workers' Comp., the Fire Department, and the Buildings Department. That was more inspectors than had shown up at either of the other restaurants in a year. It couldn't be a coincidence. Was somebody out to get them?

Chang grabbed some plates and bowls and started lining them up along the counter in order to figure out what the various courses should be served in. Anxiety was making him manic. He couldn't sit still.

"Egg dish in here," he said, putting down a bowl. "Short rib here." He stared at the eight bowls and plates in front of him. "It's a lot of fucking courses, man. Super V.I.P."

Serpico moved around the kitchen slowly and deliberately. He was keeping very calm. "I'm so scared," he sang under his breath. Cory Lane squatted down at the expediting station to stock the chef's mini-fridge with Budweiser and Coke, then leaped up to grab a pile of napkins.

"Eugene!" he called to one of the new cooks.

"His name is *not* Eugene," Serpico said sharply. "His name is James Mark."

"Chang said his name was Eugene," Lane said.

"Dave comes up with the worst nicknames for people, have you noticed that?" Serpico said. He paced up and down behind the counter, checking his *mise en place*, muttering to himself.

"Lychees, I have. Nori. Rice sticks." He looked down at a checklist he had written out. "Buttermilk. Eggs. Caviar. Scallops. Kimchi."

Chang seized a towel and started maniacally wiping down the counter. James Mark was scrubbing the flattop and the *plancha* while Serpico sprayed and polished the front surfaces of the ovens. A man showed up at the door, asking for a job as a dishwasher. Chang picked up his BlackBerry and checked his messages.

"Call Tien Ho," he yelled to Cory Lane. Tien Ho is the chef at Ssäm Bar. "Ask him if he has a spare bo ssäm." Bo ssäm is Ssäm Bar's most famous dish—a whole pork butt, plus kimchi and a dozen oysters, designed to be eaten wrapped in Bibb lettuce. It serves eight or nine, costs two hundred dollars, and usually requires ordering several days in advance.

"Who wants it?" Lane asked.

"Jamie Oliver's coming in to Ssäm Bar tonight."

"The naked chef?" Serpico asked.

"That guy."

At quarter to five, Serpico began filling up his *mise en place* with garnishes. He told James Mark to go to Noodle Bar and bring back one quart of turnips, one quart of carrots, and one quart of celery. Chang sat at the counter, thinking about all the things that were going to go wrong.

"Dude, did you add water to that consommé?" he asked Serpico. "It was fucking strong."

"I got it, I got it." Serpico was going down his checklist again. Chang stewed for a moment.

"Hey, you wanna add squid ink to the nori powder to make it blacker? It looks like dirt."

"I don't know. Maybe."

"Do we have mustard seeds?"

"Yes."

Chang looked at his watch. "Thirty minutes!"

Serpico leaned back against the stove and closed his eyes, his forearm against his forehead, for one second, and then snapped to attention again. Chang went to inspect the bathroom and discovered that the toilet-paper spindle was loose. Cory Lane began setting up for service: a cork at each place to rest chopsticks on, then a folded napkin, then a menu tucked inside the napkin, then a water glass. He measured to make sure that each napkin was exactly one thumblength from the edge of the counter. Then he crouched down at the end of the row and squinted to check that everything was lined up.

"Five-thirty!" Chang called. "We're open!".

"Gelman, you got the short-rib sauce?" Serpico asked his sous-chef.

"Working, chef," Gelman said.

Chang sat down at the counter and started proofreading the menu. "The 'Ko' is overlapping the peach, man," he told Gelman, who had laid out the menu on his computer. The orange peach was the symbol of the Momofuku brand. "And there's a double space before 'Riesling.' Hey, are we clarifying the smoked solution?" he asked Serpico, who was still fiddling with his garnishes. "Because it's turning the eggs brown." He wanted the soft-cooked hen egg—served with caviar, fines herbes, soubise, and homemade miniature potato chips—to taste smoky, but the smoked solution was turning the outside of the egg the color of putty. It looked weird. Maybe even a little gross. White would be better.

He leaned over the counter to inspect Serpico's *mise en place*. "Why don't you have the fish over here?" he asked.

"I didn't want to turn my back on customers while I'm working," Serpico explained. "I think it's kind of shady."

"But you're a shady guy, dude."

"I gotta take a piss. I may not be back."

Gelman was suddenly overcome with the significance of the moment. He whooped and grabbed Chang in a big hug.

"It's the dream, dude!" Chang cried. "The dream kitchen!"

"I love you, dude!" Gelman yelled, still hugging.

"Hey, can we open a bottle of champagne?" Chang called to Cory Lane. "This is a celebration!"

But just then the first customer—Justin, a cook at Ssäm Bar—walked in the door.

"Hey!" Serpico said to Gelman and Chang. "We have a customer in the house."

"Justin, we're going to start you off with a pork skin." Chang placed it before him, perched on a slate slab, and watched intently as he picked it up. The deep-fried skin looked like a chrysalis, its surface all shiny little bubbles, curved around itself. Justin's teeth closed on the bubbles and broke them.

"Crunch!" Chang exulted. "That's awesome!"

Tex, another cook from Ssäm Bar, arrived, and sat down in the next seat. Serpico bent low over two dishes of raw *madai*, the first course on the tasting menu, carefully sprinkling them with poppy seeds and chives.

"You know what'll suck, Pete?" Chang said. "If someone doesn't like a dish."

"Yeah."

"Can I take these for you?" Serpico asked as he removed the plates.

"What a gentleman," Chang said.

"Is it fucked up to take a plate and then dump it in a plastic bus tray?" Serpico asked.

"What's fucked up is if you finish their food in front of them."

"James, you got my consommé for two?" Serpico called.

"Hey, Pete, that's a fucking good-looking dish," Chang commented. "Soubise getting hot? Scallops getting ready? You got the dashi?" He paused. "This is why I can't work here, dude. I'm gonna drive everyone insane."

Tex finished his third course, the hen egg with caviar. There was nothing left on the plate.

"You see, that makes me wonder, Why didn't you finish the consommé?" Chang asked him. Kimchi-infused consommé, poured over an oyster, a slice of pork belly, and a cabbage leaf, had been the second course. Tex smiled weakly.

"I just didn't know how to eat it," he said.

Serpico and Chang were already preparing course number four, the scallop dish with the foaming dashi.

"We need more color on this plate, dude," Chang said. "We need those chanterelles."

"I think it looks fucking sexy," Serpico said. "What do you want, julienne of red pepper?" It was a chef joke. Justin and Tex ate the scallop dish.

"How was it, guys?" Chang asked.

Tex paused. "You have to really like nori," he said.

"You didn't like it?"

Tex paused.

"Hey, with all of you guys, if you think something sucks, you'd better fucking say so," Serpico said.

"You think it sucked?" Chang asked.

"No!" Tex protested. "It's just . . . "

"Get out," Chang said. And then smiled. "So here we have some gelée of Riesling, some pine-nut brittle, and some shaved foie gras."

This foie dish was something else that Chang and Serpico had been experimenting with for a while. Chang had remembered that when Liz Chapman was the sous-chef at Casa Mono she used to freeze pimentón butter and shave it onto summer corn. He figured he should be able to make foie flakes in the same way, since foie gras had the texture of butter—he just didn't know whether anyone else had done it already, so he called around. He discovered that some cook had played with it in the kitchen of Café Boulud, but no one seemed to have actually put it on a menu, so he figured he could claim to be first. (Originality was always a concern: Chang had spent weeks puréeing tofu and mixing it with meat glue, as he'd seen Wylie Dufresne do in the kitchen of WD–50. He then steamed it into a ball and inserted a raw quail egg in the middle, thinking that the faux egg would make a perfect amuse, but at the last minute he'd seen a chef on a food blog doing the same egg thing with cauliflower purée, so he'd abandoned it.) He placed the foie on the counter and looked up at Tex and Justin.

"You guys are really uncomfortable, aren't you?" he said. "You think I'm going to yell at you?"

Tex giggled. He tried the foie gras.

"How's that?" Chang asked.

"Slammin', man!" Tex said enthusiastically.

"See, I knew it, you didn't like the consommé."

It was six-forty-five. Justin and Tex had been eating only for forty minutes but they'd already finished six courses, if you included the pork-skin amuse-bouche. Any faster and it would be KFC.

"Shit," Chang said. "We've got to make everything bigger, man." He watched as Tex ate his short-rib course and laid his knife—an exceptionally sharp Japanese steak knife that Serpico had been very psyched about when they bought it—on the edge of his plate.

"That's dangerous, dude," Chang said nervously, eyeing the knife. "I don't like it. I mean, he turns to the side, customer walks by, they're dead. I'm just saying."

Chang saw James Mark shaving foie gras inelegantly, and he leaped over to stop him. "I can't be back here," he said to Serpico. "I'm gonna lose my shit." He walked out of the chef's area, sat down at the counter next to Tex, and started to make a list of everything that had gone wrong so far. Suddenly Gelman spotted two customers about to eat the oysters and pork bellies in their bowls, not realizing that they were supposed to wait for Serpico to pour consommé on top.

"Hey, hold it!" Gelman shouted at them. "Don't eat that yet!"

"You gonna yell at the customers, man?" Chang asked him.

"Yeah!" Gelman said. "Hey, don't eat that, asshole!" he barked.

"Can you imagine if we did à la carte?" Chang said. They had been going to offer à la carte until about two days ago. "What a fucking disaster."

Serpico was cleaning up his station when two last customers he'd forgotten about, a cook from Ssäm Bar and his girlfriend, walked in.

"Oh fuck, man, two more," he said loudly.

Chang couldn't stop laughing. "Great greeting, dude," he said. "What a bad idea this restaurant is. We're gonna be serving steak and cheese in about five weeks."

When the last customers were on their way to finishing, Chang sent Cory Lane to Noodle Bar for some bourbon to lubricate the postmortem. Serpico squatted in a corner behind the counter.

"It's been a long time since I went down that bad," he said.

"That's not true," Chang told him. "When we opened Noodle Bar, you got smoked *so* bad. You got fucking hosed."

"That's when you threw me a fun-sized Almond Joy."

"Pete, we'll get it right because we can see where all the problems are," Chang said. Serpico nodded. He knew it was so. He stood up and stretched. Chang clapped him on the shoulder. "And it's the first fucking day, dude."

STANDING STRONG

By Lolis Eric Elie

from *Food Arts*

The heartfelt story of New Orlean's post-Katrina resurrection
has a whole corps of narrators, including *Times-Picayune*
columnist Lolis Eric Elie, who's also a widely published food
writer, musician, and author of *Smokestack Lightning*, a fascinating cultural history of barbecue.

I n those first weeks after the federal levees gave way and
Hurricane Katrina's floodwaters inundated New Orleans,
conversations with John Besh revolved around two themes: self-
reliance and faith in his city.

Most New Orleanians felt abandoned by a government that
seemed unwilling or unable to locate Louisiana on the map. Many
Americans questioned whether the birthplace of jazz was worth
saving. Besh would neither blame the feds nor surrender the city.
Then, as now, he dedicated himself to proving that American inge-
nuity and Creole cuisine are sufficiently powerful forces for rebuilding this city and the culture for which it stands.

Having won the Best Chef Southeast award from The James
Beard Foundation in 2006, and having defeated Mario Batali on
Iron Chef America, he has the bona fides to be taken seriously.
What's more, in the two years since the storm, the Besh family of
restaurants has grown from two eateries to four. Restaurant August, the six-year-old flagship, and Besh Steak at Harrah's Casino
have been joined by Lüke, a downtown brasserie, and La Provence,
a Creole-inflected Provençal restaurant across Lake Ponchartrain

from the city. Now Besh has twice as many plates on which to present his case.

At August, he makes his point with a soft shell crab "BLT" served on pain perdu. At the steakhouse, aged beef shares the menu with shrimp rémoulade and fried oysters bordelaise. At La Provence, house-raised baby lamb is roasted and served with local onions, fava beans, and morels; and at Lüke, the Monday brasserie fare includes red beans and rice. But whether diners realize it or not, everything they eat at Besh's restaurants these days goes back in part to the vats of red beans and rice the marine-turned-chef cooked in the days after Hurricane Katrina.

"Monday afternoon, the day that the city flooded, one of the senators in Lafayette asked for people to come in with boats. Wednesday morning, we showed up at 4 a.m.; probably 250 people left Lafayette with boats to come help out. I came in with a lot of those fellows," recalls Blake LeMaire.

LeMaire and Besh met in the marine reserves while both were studying at Louisiana State University. During Operation Desert Storm in 1991, they were deployed in separate units, but they kept in touch and have been friends ever since. While doing rescue work in the city, LeMaire called Besh to tell him that Restaurant August had been spared the brunt of the flooding and the looting. Besh, whose wife and sons had evacuated to North Carolina before the storm, suggested that LeMaire help him gather provisions and cook for the relief workers who were arriving in the city. "With the help of some of my former marine buddies and text messaging, we were able to put together about four 55-gallon drums of gasoline and 100 gallons of diesel fuel and six crawfish pots, along with burners, about a ton of rice, and 700 pounds of red beans," says Besh, who was born across Lake Ponchartrain from New Orleans. They served soldiers, relief workers, and whoever showed up, from a Wal-Mart parking lot.

That good deed brought Besh good luck. As the situation in New Orleans stabilized, some of the folks he'd fed for free hired him to provide catered meals for the oil company workers repairing pipelines, the firefighters, the government relief workers, and the odd television crew. When August reopened, a month after the storm, there were few customers in the city. The profits from the catering jobs subsidized the restaurant's operations.

The experience of the storm proved formative. Besh had seen the plight of New Orleanians waiting for assistance from distant Washington. He had seen how government regulation and bureaucracy had thwarted the efforts of many of the private citizens who wanted to come in with boats or provisions to assist storm victims. And he had seen the smiles that real New Orleans food brought to the faces of the people he served in the days after the storm. He resolved then to narrow the circle of people and institutions on which he relies to run his restaurants. And he resolved to plant his own cooking even more firmly in the bedrock of Creole cuisine and the European foods that had influenced it.

"It made me think twice about the role of government in our lives and the role of insurance and these safety nets that we take for granted," he says. "I need to make decisions in my life, as best I can, that will put me in a situation where I will be less dependent.

"Strength comes from individuals working with each other on a community level versus with people far removed. The more self-sufficient I am, the less I rely on Sysco or the big national companies, and the less affected I am when some of these purveyors don't deliver or can't deliver," he continues. "So that made me dig even deeper to find my fishmonger in Slidell, Brian Cappy, who uses only Lake Ponchartrain crabs, and my oyster man, Sal Sunseri from P&J Oyster Company."

It has also meant that quintessential New Orleans dishes like gumbo and red beans and rice showed up on the fine dining menu of August. "Before, I wouldn't have had gumbo on my menu. This is something else that brought me full circle to the reason why I stayed and the reason I settled here to begin with. It's taken Katrina to shake us all up, to say, 'This is what I love.' You ask, culinarily speaking, what I dig about New Orleans? That's it. It's the tradition. All these crazy bloodlines came in and created this culture here, and it is through that that we are able to really create one of the most interesting, heartfelt, soulful menus that you just really couldn't replicate anywhere else in the country. They have great food all over the place. But is it 'their' food?"

Besh approaches the New Orleans tradition from a broad perspective. A graduate of The Culinary Institute of America at Hyde Park, New York, he'd intended to further his training in kitchens in France and England, but he couldn't get a work permit in those countries. He could, however, get one in Germany and found himself cooking under chef Karl Josef Fuchs in the hills of the Black Forest at Romantik Hotel Spielweg, a popular vacation spot.

"It worked out perfectly because it came at a later time and shaped my entire career. The chefs in that little region would only serve what came from their area, known as the Muenster Valley. That idea of regionalism was something that I knew existed at one time in this country, but we had strayed so far from it."

Besh has collected a set of ideals from his Louisiana upbringing, from his time in Germany, from his experiences after Hurricane Katrina. Had it not been for a pair of post-Katrina strokes of good fortune, though, those ideals might never have reached their full expression. After the storm, Hotel Monaco sold its New Orleans hotel to a company that rebranded it as a Hilton and set out to find a new chef to run its kitchen. In January 2006, five months after the storm, they contacted Besh. He and his business partner, Octavio Mantilla, agreed to take over the kitchen and then began the work of transforming what had been Cobalt Restaurant into what would become Lüke. Before they could get started on that project, Besh got a call from Chris Kerageorgiou, his mentor and the chef/owner of La Provence. Though his name was Greek, Kerageorgiou was French. For three and a half decades he had brought Provençal cuisine to Lacombe, Louisiana, a small city near where Besh grew up. Kerageorgiou, as it happened, was critically ill. He wanted desperately for his protégé to buy the restaurant and keep his vision alive. He wanted the deal done before his pending surgery. Besh and Mantilla thus ended up scrambling to open not one but two new places. In addition, Besh Steak at Harrah's Casino reopened in February 2006.

In order to assure that quality remains consistent across their four restaurants, Mantilla and Besh make partners of the general managers and executive chefs at each location. Steve McHugh, the executive chef at La Provence, had been the chef de cuisine at August for years. Drew Mire, the general manager at the restaurant, had been the manager at Artesia, the first restaurant at which Besh was executive chef. For Lüke, Besh tapped Jared Tees, the former executive chef at Bourbon House, to be his partner in the kitchen, while LeMaire serves as managing partner.

"The business model that John and I have developed acknowledges that you can't be everywhere all the time," Mantilla says. "If we're going to build more restaurants, we have to bring in great chefs, great managers, and give them part of the business."

Though the acquisition of La Provence was hectic, it came with a huge bonus: four acres of farmland behind the restaurant. On those acres, Besh raises Berkshire pigs, goats, sheep, chickens, salad greens, and some other vegetables. A few miles away, he raises Charolais cows, from which he gets beef for all the restaurants except the steakhouse.

"We make our beer in Covington. The pigs are fed the spent barley that comes from the beer, so it doesn't cost us a dime extra," he explains. "This Berkshire pig would cost us up to $20 a pound bringing it in from Iowa, from Niman ranch. But now we've started our own hog operations, and I've got a cousin who agreed to run our breeding program for us. He's in Alabama breeding the pigs, and he sends them down to us when they are about 50 pounds. The things that are high in beta carotene—the carrot trimmings, the beet trimmings—all go in, along with ground-up crawfish shells, to the chickens, so we have nice orange egg yolks."

Using whole animals could be a disadvantage: there are only so many pork chops on a pig. But Besh's dishes often contain two or three cuts of meat: the beef short ribs at Lüke are accompanied by tripe; veal cheeks at La Provence share the plate with sweetbreads; the lamb at August might include braised shoulder as well as a lamb chop. By composing dishes in this way, Besh cooks contrary to the fine dining convention of serving only the choicest cuts of meat cooked medium-rare. By slow cooking large cuts, he's able to make the choice cuts go further and also bring an appealing rusticity to white tablecloth dining.

The theme of local ingredients runs through all four Besh restaurants, but his having four places also allows the chef to focus on different aspects of New Orleans culinary heritage. In studying old menus, Besh discovered that downtown New Orleans restaurants in the 1960s and '70s, like Kolb's and Gluck's, reflected the German-Jewish character of the clientele and the owners. At Lüke, Besh's German training revives a forgotten New Orleans tradition. The menu features such Creole classics as shrimp farci and trout meunière, but it also offers choucroute and house-made sausages.

The menu at La Provence mirrors what you might see on those of restaurants along the French Mediterranean, with offerings such as tuna niçoise, paella negra, and fritto misto. The Creole touches are visible less in the preparations than in the inclusion of such local ingredients as crawfish and Louisiana black fish.

At August there are no strict rules. "When people dine at August, they are more or less subjecting themselves to the whim of the chef. They trust that the chef understands what he's doing. They're dining with a different mentality," Besh says, sipping Champagne at La Provence. "I can get away with a lot more at August than I can anywhere else. If I put any of the August food on this *carte*, I'd be out of business."

Whereas much of New Orleans was damaged beyond repair by post-Katrina flooding, Besh has emerged perhaps stronger. Not only has he doubled the number of restaurants he owns, he may also have hit his culinary stride. Four months before the hurricane struck, Besh and Mantilla bought August from its owner. August is certainly the chef's flagship and standard-bearer. As it goes, so goes the growing Besh empire.

"I think the restaurant has improved. Before, it was a restaurant we had bought," Mantilla said. "Since the storm, it has been our restaurant. It has more soul, more heart than it did before."

Welcome to Dante's Inferno

By Laura Faye Taxel

from *Cleveland Magazine*

In this insightful profile of a local chef, veteran Cleveland
food writer Laura Taxel—who seems to contribute regularly to
every publication in town—digs up enough human interest
angles to make a novel.

The stoves are fired up, the sauté pans are smoking, and it's
hot as hell. But Dante Boccuzzi is in heaven.

This Saturday night, orders are rolling in one after another
without pause at Lockkeepers, the Valley View restaurant he purchased in March. Cooks hustle to keep pace, ladling garlic soup
into bowls, braising fistfuls of endive and throwing steaks on the
grill.

Boccuzzi's directing the action, positioned opposite the stoves
on the far side of a 20-foot stainless steel prep area outfitted with
counters, cooler drawers and a window where finished dishes
await pickup. He reads the tickets as they come rolling out of the
printer and issues instructions to the guys at the hot and cold stations, using a shorthand they all understand.

"Fire a skate."

"I need a wedge."

His voice is commanding, pitched low with a sandpaper edge.
Swigging Pellegrino straight from the bottle, he continues to call
out orders for the next three hours.

"Hold the lamb."

"Where's my tuna?"

"One rav, one chicken. Now."

Every plate comes to him for inspection before servers bring it out to the dining room. Each gets a split second of his full and undivided attention. He cleans the edges, rearranges pinches of microgreens, moves a tiny cup of sauce an eighth of an inch to the left. Anything that doesn't measure up to his exacting standards is sent back. A charcuterie board fails to please him. He grimaces in annoyance, growls a deep throaty rumble and carries it over to the cook who assembled it. "I don't like how the meat's cut. It's too rough. Do it again."

But after spending the past 16 years in fast-paced kitchens around the world, including time as a personal chef to Robert De Niro and a five-year run as executive chef at Aureole, Charlie Palmer's famed New York City restaurant, the 35-year-old with the Michelin-star résumé has earned the right to be critical.

Besides, he owns the place. For the first time in his life, Boccuzzi's the boss. And the stakes are high. This is Lockkeepers after all, one of Northeast Ohio's most revered fine-dining establishments. And it's only going to get tougher. This month he's closing down for a week, and will reopen as Dante on September 29. Then it won't be just his restaurant, it'll be his name above the door.

Dante Boccuzzi has a boyish Mephisto-meets-monk look. Impishly cute with thick black hair, bushy eyebrows and a soul patch pointed like a tail in the center of his chin, he's also beginning to bald. From behind, it appears he's shaved the crown of his head into a monastic tonsure. The imagery is apt. A smooth-running kitchen needs both devil and angel, he says.

The opposing forces tug at him.

Boccuzzi was born and raised in Parma [Ohio]. He still has family in Cleveland, and the chance for his wife and three children to live close to them was a big part of why he decided to return.

In high school, Boccuzzi worked at Stancato's Italian Restaurant on State Road. But it wasn't food that first drew him to the kitchen. "I remember, we catered a party in a VIP room somewhere in the Flats," he recalls. "Being part of the staff gave me a special pass to be there with all these wealthy, beautiful people. I didn't know what else to do with my life, so I decided to enroll in culinary school."

It was his ticket to explore a world he never even knew existed.

He went to the Culinary Institute of America in Hyde Park. Michael Symon was in the class ahead of him. He'd never even heard of truffles or sweetbreads until he arrived there. "I was clueless, a small-town kid with a small-town mentality," he says.

After graduating, he moved to New York and landed an entry-level spot at Aureole. At the time, it was Charlie Palmer's only restaurant (he now has eight with four more on the way). Palmer was in the kitchen every day. "I was terrified and quickly realized how much I didn't know," Boccuzzi recalls. "So I kept my mouth shut for the first four months and just did what I was told."

It was an incredible opportunity to learn from a master. Palmer was still cooking then and Boccuzzi worked at his side. "I got to be on the line next to him, watching how he did things, learning his techniques."

But the lessons came with a price. "The atmosphere in the kitchen was very macho and aggressive," he recalls. "You'd get belittled for every mistake. The sous chef would throw food at you if you pissed him off. Charlie once hit me in the chest with an overcooked steak. Whatever you messed up there you ended up wearing."

Yet, Boccuzzi quickly became Palmer's chosen one, working his way up at Aureole over the next two years. "I look for drive and passion along with talent," Palmer says. "Dante had all three. He was serious and committed, pushed himself, took on more than he had to. Good enough was never good enough for him."

Walking through the dining room, Boccuzzi promises that Dante will be nothing like its predecessor. He points out where the couches and the 16-foot communal table will be. The staid arts-and-crafts space will be replaced with something "sleek, modern and cool," he says.

There will be some familiar things on the menu such as pizza and pasta, but he plans to concentrate on the edgier, push-the-envelope preparations for which he's known. His style, which has earned him two James Beard Rising Star of the Year nominations, one of the industry's highest honors, fuses elements of Asian and Italian cuisine with classic French technique. Expect port-glazed foie gras and tuna terrine (he calls this his first signature dish), cantaloupe carpaccio, and 5-spice roasted langoustines with pickled watermelon.

His winning ways with pork bellies and truffles have earned rave reviews, so before he even caramelized an onion in this town, Boccuzzi generated a fair amount of enthusiastic and anticipatory buzz just by showing up. He knows that's good for business, but doesn't buy into the hype about himself, which is surprising for a guy who's going to christen his restaurant with his name, whose face is on its postcards.

"I'm really a nobody," he says, as if succumbing to his Parma roots or some Midwestern shyness. "I get it that people are impressed with what I've done. I went to New York. I got some recognition. So what?

"Sure, it's cool to have people make a fuss over me," he admits. "But really, I'm not saving lives. At the end of the day, it's just food. Yeah, I cooked for Robert De Niro," he adds, almost reluctantly. "But it's not like I am Robert De Niro."

In fact, the story of how he came to cook for the Hollywood luminary has nothing to do with his talent or his reputation. Boccuzzi was just a last-minute replacement for a Fourth of July celebration held at the actor's country home in upstate New York. As it turns out, one of Boccuzzi's friends was a chef for the family, but was about to have hip surgery and couldn't work the party. "So I filled in," Boccuzzi says. It involved preparing a day's worth of meals for about 15 guests.

After that, the De Niros started ordering takeout from Aureole, where Boccuzzi was in charge of the kitchen, and they'd call him to lend a hand whenever they were between chefs. "There was a week where I went to their apartment to make breakfast every morning," he says. "It had to be ready at 7 a.m., when Bob, as he liked to be called, got done working out with his trainer." Starstruck at first, Boccuzzi quickly got over it. "De Niro is a quiet guy, not much of a conversationalist."

In this era when chefs can become as famous as movie stars, Boccuzzi insists he has no interest in being a celebrity himself. Still, he plans to leverage his accomplishments for all their worth. He's dreaming about turning himself into a brand, launching other restaurant concepts, publishing the cookbook he's almost finished writing, trademarking and manufacturing some innovative tableware he's designed, and doing a TV cooking show for kids—an idea he's been developing with De Niro's wife.

Like the Hollywood actress who needs to prove she's a singer, Boccuzzi is a chef who would love to be a rock star. He says his life has a hard-driving sound track, and he likes to be photographed with his guitar. He's even recorded two CDs. In an attempt to link his two pursuits, he plans to include a guitar pick, imprinted with the Dante logo, along with every check.

At Palmer's urging, the fledgling chef went to Europe, interning at restaurants in France, England and Italy for the next three years, usually for little or no pay. He lived hand to mouth, sleeping wherever he could find a couch and maxing out more than one credit card.

"At L'Escargot in London, we worked from 8 a.m. to midnight, six days a week. There was no staff meal. You'd end up stuffing handfuls of your own *mise en place* [prepped ingredients] into your mouth or eating french fry sandwiches. It was brutal, miserable. The chefs were abusive maniacs. If you fell behind, they'd humiliate you rather than help you. Guys would say they were going out for a cigarette and never come back."

But some good came of it too. He met his wife-to-be, Monica, in England. She was Italian, there to perfect her English. They married after a four-year romance, much of it long distance. She and her mother introduced him to the pleasures of authentic Italian homestyle cooking.

In 1997, with Palmer's endorsement, he took over the operation of Silks at the Mandarin Oriental Hotel in San Francisco. It was a stretch, he admits. "I was definitely in over my head, but I knew I could get help from Charlie," he says. "I called him every day. Sometimes more than once a day."

He did stages in Hong Kong and Taiwan, and then, once again as a result of his association with Palmer, was asked to open and run Armani/Nobu in Milan, Italy. He honed his managerial skills there but the menu was set and there was no room for culinary invention. So he channeled his creative energy into music. Ever since he was a teenager and won a karaoke contest, Boccuzzi has nurtured fantasies of being a rock 'n' roller. He bought his first electric guitar, taught himself to play, and started writing song lyrics when he went to Europe. He even did some recording. In San Francisco he played with the Back Burner Blues Band—a bunch of chefs who got together for a meals-on-wheels benefit and then kept on jamming. But it was when he returned to Milan that he got serious, taking lessons, performing in clubs, and making another, much better CD titled "Parmatown."

At Nobu, he rubbed shoulders with some musical icons, including his idol Eric Clapton, who came in for an after-concert party. "I walked right up to him, introduced myself. That was the first time it really hit me: the power of being 'The Chef,'" he recalls. Other celebrities regularly visited too—George Clooney, Brad Pitt, Jennifer Aniston and De Niro. "I sat down with Phil Collins there too. I was nervous. What was I gonna say, 'I have all your albums?' But all he wanted to talk about was food."

In 2002, Boccuzzi returned to Aureole as executive chef. He wasn't sure he was up to the challenge, but was willing to risk it. "I had lots of reasons to be confident. I knew the restaurant, knew Charlie, his cooking style, and what he expected," he says. "I'm not the type to take chances unless the odds are in my favor."

Palmer says he tapped Boccuzzi for the job because he saw a born leader with a knack for handling people and problems. "If you're in charge, you have to be the cool, level-headed one. When you get crazy so does everybody else. Boccuzzi had the ability to stay calm and focused, to be laid back but step it up and get tough when he had to."

Boccuzzi is convinced that separating from his mentor was a necessary move. "Charlie was a second father to me. And there comes a moment in every kid's life when he has to break away. He and I weren't seeing eye-to-eye on everything anymore. I needed to leave before that hurt our relationship." The fundamental issue, according to Boccuzzi, was simple. Despite the fact that he was there 12 hours a day, it was Palmer's opinion that counted and Palmer who got the final word. "I respect his vision. But I wanted to follow my own."

His old boss calls it a natural progression. "He's continued to develop as a chef and manager. It makes sense that he wanted his own restaurant. He's earned it, put in his time. I think he's ready for this."

Boccuzzi arrives at 10:30 a.m. on a Tuesday, requests his usual espresso (or two) and heads for the office. Not much bigger than a walk-in closet just off the kitchen, it has barely enough space to turn around between the two desks, file cabinet, and a pair of bookcases. One holds his large collection of cookbooks, but an entire shelf is filled with a dozen numbered loose-leaf binders. Each one contains more than 200 recipes. There are no duplicates, and all are his, a map of his cheffing life, and his prized possession.

He started keeping these detailed logs of every dish and tasting menu he created while at Silks. Drawings show exactly how food should be arranged on the plate. He'd copy them for his cooks so they'd know exactly what he wanted. Yet, these are not recipes in the ordinary sense. With no step-by-step instructions and little information about quantities, they are blueprints meant for professionals who understand how to sweat sweet pea sprouts or prepare candied rhubarb shavings.

Over time the renderings have become more polished, the recipes more intricate, and they document a developing enthusiasm for infusing classical preparations with whimsy and fun, his penchant for preparing a single ingredient multiple ways. Some pages are typed but most are neatly handwritten. Every one is spotless inside its plastic sleeve. "Here's an early heirloom tomato salad with goat cheese," he says, then flips to another recipe. "Later, I took the same idea and added a bright red tomato sorbet and a Parmesan crisp."

Visibly excited and at his most animated when talking about his culinary creations, he turns to a third page and describes the elements of the next incarnation, a four-part variation on a theme. "There's a tomato tart tatin with a caramel balsamic, chilled yellow tomato soup with melon foam, a cherry tomato salad with summer truffles, shaved fennel, and sorbet, and another salad that has cockles covered with yellow tomato gazpacho jelly. This is the kind of thing we'll do at Dante."

Natalie Cox, director of private dining, sticks her head in the door to discuss the menu for an upcoming party. A few minutes later David Eselgroth, sommelier and second in command, comes in. He and Boccuzzi need to talk about what went wrong Saturday night and how to make sure it doesn't happen again. (A server got bogged down, failed to ask for help, and orders got backed up big-time. Three tables had to wait so long for their dinners that the meals were on the house.)

Cox and Eselgroth, who are a couple, left Auroele, along with Jared Bergen, a cook, to follow Boccuzzi here. He also inherited an experienced bunch of cooks, including Ky-wai Wong, who was executive chef prior to his arrival. But everybody has to learn to do things the Boccuzzi way.

"My wife asked me if I'm going to be happy living life away from the stove," he says. Silence follows, the question hanging in the air, heavy and charged, while he considers his answer. "I hope so."

Donning a freshly laundered chef coat and a long apron, he takes his place at the center of the hot line, one of three cooks handling lunch. He's juggling three, four, then five orders simultaneously, never hurrying but always occupied. If he's frazzled it doesn't show. He dusts fish filets with flour and drops them in the fryer basket; tosses calamari with dressing, mounding coleslaw neatly on one plate and spicy housemade potato chips on another, popping a few in his mouth. Pivoting back to the stove, he flips a smoked salmon panini and pulls his pot of mussels off the heat. Anyone else would dump them out, but not Boccuzzi. He doesn't believe in shortcuts. He carefully spoons the mussels into waiting bowls, a few at a time.

Whenever he notices burners on but unused, he turns them off. That's his money going up in flames.

All the while he's got his eye on the rest of the kitchen. The minute he spots an empty container or dirty utensil, he whisks it away, keeping counters clear and uncluttered. When he sees a less than perfect plate make it to the serving window, he snatches it back and reassembles it. During a brief pause, he puts squeeze bottles of oil and sauce back in their places, organized and ready for the next round.

He finishes with his whites as immaculate as when he began and his work area almost gleaming. A fanatic about cleanliness, a stickler for order, efficiency and precision, Boccuzzi is relentless in pursuit of flawlessness. He bundles all these ideas together under the heading "finesse."

There are protocols, mantras and philosophies, all aimed at achieving that artful skill and refinement: "You cook how you look. If you're sloppy so are your plates." "Operate like a professional. Take pride in what you do." "You are only as good as your last plate."

"It's good to let them see that I've still got what it takes to do their job," says Boccuzzi, "and do it better and faster." He expects to cook alongside his staff whenever a new dish is added to the menu, and jump in any time they're shorthanded.

But it's not his primary role. As the reopening date approaches there are a million details to attend to, and nothing happens without his approval. "I lie awake at night, going over long mental checklists, wondering what I've forgotten."

The endless decision-making gets to him sometimes. "There are days it feels like everybody needs an answer from me. But then it hits me: I'm in charge. I don't have to report to anybody. It means every screw-up is mine. But every success is too."

But will Boccuzzi the chef stay fired up being Boccuzzi the owner and entrepreneur?

"This restaurant, the cookbook, the TV pilots, everything is my way of searching for that same kind of adrenaline rush that I used to get on the line. Without that kick, it's just a job."

DAN DAN NOODLES!

By Fuchsia Dunlop

from *Shark's Fin and Sichuan Pepper: A Sweet-Sour Memoir of Eating in China*

English cookbook writer Fuchsia Dunlop, author of *The Revolutionary Chinese Cookbook*, reveals just how she came to be so obsessed with Chinese cuisine in this vivid cross-cultural memoir of her travels throughout China.

"*Sa zi mian?* What noodles d'you want?" Xie Laoban gave me his usual surly look as he glanced up from the conversation he was having with one of his regulars.

"Two *liang* of sea-flavour noodles, one *liang* of Dan Dan noodles," I replied, dumping my schoolbag on the ground and perching on an unsteady stool, just inches from the stream of passing bicycles. There was no need to look at the blackboard, chalked up with the names of a dozen or so noodle dishes, because I knew it by heart, having eaten at Xie Laoban's almost every day since I had arrived in Chengdu. Xie Laoban yelled my order out to his staff of three or four young blokes, who were scurrying around inside the noodle shop behind the coal-burning stove. A glass cabinet held bowls of seasonings: darkly fragrant chilli oil, ground roasted Sichuan pepper, sliced green onions, soy sauce and vinegar, salt and pepper. Nearby, potfuls of stocks and stews simmered away on an electric cooker, and skeins of freshly made noodles lay snakily in deep trays of woven bamboo. At the front of the shop, in full view of the street, steam drifted up from two enormous wokfuls of boiling water.

Resuming his conversation, Xie Laoban slumped back in his bamboo chair, smoking a cigarette as he recounted some grimly amusing tale. There was always an embittered look about his face, an edge of hostility and suspicion, and if he smiled at his acquaintances, his smile was tinged with a sneer of sarcasm. In his forties, he had a face pitted with the legacy of acne, sun-darkened yet wan and drawn. He seemed world-weary and cynical, though my foreign student friends and I never knew why. He fascinated us, but while we speculated incessantly about his life, wondering where he lived and with whom, what he did in the evenings, and whether he had ever been happy, in the end it was hard to imagine Xie Laoban being anywhere else but in that bamboo chair in the backstreets around the university, taking orders for noodles and barking at his staff. The bolder among us—Sasha and Pasha from Vladivostock, Parisian Davide—greeted him heartily, trying to engage him in conversation or cracking jokes in a vain attempt to raise the glimmer of a smile. But he remained stony-faced and deadpan, simply asking, as he always did, "*Sa zi mian?*"

I could see the young men assembling my lunch, trickling spices and oils into the tiny bowl for my Dan Dan noodles, sprinkling a little salt and pepper into the larger bowl for the sea-flavour noodles. The appropriate weight of noodles (one *liang* is about fifty grammes) were flung into the wok to cook, and before long steaming bowls were brought to my table. The sea-flavour noodles were, as always, richly comforting in their seafood broth, with a topping of stewed pork and bamboo shoots, mushrooms, dried shrimps and mussels. And the Dan Dan noodles—well, they were undoubtedly the best in town, the best anyone had ever tasted. They looked quite plain: a small bowlful of noodles topped with a spoonful of dark, crisp minced beef. But as soon as you stirred them with your chopsticks, you awakened the flavours in the slick of spicy seasonings at the base of the bowl, and coated each strand of pasta in a mix of soy sauce, chilli oil, sesame paste and Sichuan pepper. The effect was electrifying. Within seconds, your mouth was on fire, your lips quivering under the onslaught of the pepper, and your whole body radiant with heat. (On a warm day, you might even break out into a sweat.)

Xie Laoban's Dan Dan noodles were a potent pick-me-up, a cure for hangover or heartache, and the perfect antidote to the grey humidity of the Chengdu climate. As students, we were slavishly addicted to them. Many, like me, ordered a gentler meal of soup noodles with fried egg and tomatoes or sea-flavour stew, with a small shot of fiery Dan Dan noodles as a chaser, while the fast-living, hard-drinking Russians and Poles invariably ordered a full three *liang* of "*dan danr*". We devoured them at one of the wobbly tables in the street, brushed by bicycles, assaulted by the honk of taxis and their sour aftermath of exhaust fumes. When we had finished, we asked Xie Laoban for the bill, and he would add up the paltry sums, take our crumpled notes, and rootle around in the little half-open wooden drawer for some change.

DAN DAN NOODLES are the archetypal Chengdu street snack. Their name comes from the bamboo shoulderpole that street vendors traditionally use to transport their wares: the verb "*dan*" means to carry on a shoulderpole. Elderly residents of the city still remember the days when the cries of the noodle sellers—"*Dan dan mian! Dan dan mian!*"—rang out in all the old lanes. The vendors would lay down their shoulderpoles wherever they found custom, and unpack their stoves, cooking pots, serving bowls, chopsticks and jars of seasonings. Servants would hear their call and rush out to the gateways of the old wooden houses to order noodles for their masters. Mah Jong players, clattering their tiles in a teahouse, would interrupt their game for a bowlful. Passers-by would slurp them in the street. The noodles were served in tiny bowls, a *liang* at a time, just enough to take the edge off your hunger, and so cheap that almost anyone could afford them.

The noodle sellers weren't the only traders on the move; they were part of a thriving and colourful street life for which Chengdu was renowned. At the end of the Qing Dynasty, in the early twentieth century, a guide to the city by Fu Chongju included descriptions and illustrations of some of its many street traders, including itinerant barbers and pedicurists, water-carriers and flower-sellers, menders of parasols and fans, vendors of chicken-feather dusters, knife sharpeners, and snack makers. The old city was a maze of alleys lined with timber-framed houses, their walls made of panels of woven bamboo that were packed with mud and straw, then white-washed. Stone lions stood on pedestals at either side of imposing wooden gateways. There was a teahouse on almost every street, where waiters with kettles of boiling water scurried around, refilling china bowls of jasmine-scented tea. And amidst the cacophony of the markets and the bustling streets, no sound was more welcome than the cry of a snack-seller, advertising the arrival of some delicious *xiao chi*, or "small eat."

The late nineteenth and early twentieth centuries are remembered as the heyday of Chengdu snacks. Street vendors lived or died by the quality of their cooking, so the secrets of their methods were jealously guarded. In an atmosphere of fevered competition, individual traders devised new recipes, some of which still bear their names. One man, Zhong Xiesen, invented the divine "Zhong boiled dumpling" (*zhong shui jiao*), a tender pork-filled crescent bathed in spiced, sweetened soy sauce and chilli oil, and finished off with a smattering of garlic paste. Another, Lai Yuanxin, left to posterity his squidgy glutinous rice balls (*lai tang yuan*), stuffed with a paste of toasted black sesame seeds and sugar. A married couple who roamed the streets with their cooking equipment had a relationship so famously harmonious that their specialty—slices of beef offal tossed with celery and roasted nuts in a fiery dressing of spiced broth, chilli oil and Sichuan pepper—is still known as "Man-and-wife lung slices" (*fu qi fei pian*). The more successful traders often went on to open their own restaurants, usually named after their most celebrated snack.

The eyes of the older generation tended to mist over when they recalled the street food of their childhoods. One elderly man I met in a teahouse sat with me for an hour, writing out in meticulous detail a list of dozens of kinds of dumplings, categorised according to their cooking method and main ingredients. A portly and jovial chef in his fifties smiled wistfully as he reminisced: "Oh, they were all out there on the streets, sold from the shoulderpole, Dan Dan noodles, 'Flower' beancurd and toffee." And he sang for me a long-remembered street vendor's chant: "I got sweet ones, crispy ones, sugared dough twists!"

During the Cultural Revolution, any kind of private enterprise was banned. The teahouses of Chengdu were forced to close, and snack-sellers were banished from the streets. Yet soon after the end of China's "Decade of Chaos," the old street-food culture heaved itself back into life. Its resurgence was partly a symptom of the "smashing of the iron ricebowl"—the post-Mao dismantling of the old socialist system that had guaranteed jobs and incomes for life. Middle-aged workers suddenly found themselves "laid-off" on subsistence wages, and were forced to find other ways to make money. So some of them would fry up a basketful of *ma hua* (dough twists) in the mornings, or put together some *zong zi* (glutinous rice wrapped in bamboo leaves), which they took out into the streets to sell. And there were peasants making a bit on the side in the slack farming season.

IN THE MID-NINETIES, Chengdu was still a labyrinth of lanes, some of them bordered by grey brick walls punctuated by wooden gateways, others lined with two-storied dwellings built of wood and bamboo. The grand old houses had been divided up into more humble living quarters, plastic signs had been hoisted up above the open shopfronts, and the stone lions had disappeared from their pedestals. But if you closed your eyes to these signs of change, you could imagine yourself walking through a more distant Chinese past.

The old streets of the city were endlessly fascinating, and I spent much of my time exploring them. In shady corners, barbers hung mirrors on tree trunks or the walls of convenient buildings, and set up bamboo chairs for their clients, who lay back to be frothed and shaved with cut-throat razors in full view of the street. Knife sharpeners wandered past in dirty aprons, carrying their wooden stools and long, grey whetstones, ready to bring a keen edge to anyone's cleaver. There were mobile haberdasheries, carried on bicycles that were pegged all over with zips, buttons and reels of cotton. Some pedlars sold their own handiwork— colanders woven from strands of bamboo, or black cotton shoes with padded white soles.

In March, when the spring winds whipped up, there was a kite vendor on every thoroughfare, displaying colourfully painted birds and insects made from bamboo and tissue-thin paper (the whole wide sky was full of them, too, like a swarm). When it rained, sellers of foldaway waterproofs appeared as if by magic; in the soupy summer heat, old men laid out rows of fans on the pavement. I even saw, once, a bicycle stacked with hundreds of tiny cages woven from thin strips of bamboo. Each one contained a live cricket, a potential pet; together, they hummed like a small orchestra.

In the alleys there were wine shops, with strong grain spirits sold from enormous clay vats. Some of the wine was stepped with medicinal wolfberries, some—for the gentlemen, of course—with assorted animal penises. Flute-sellers wandered among the crowds with bamboo pipes slung all over their bodies, playing a melody as they went. And it was hard to go more than a few yards without being tempted to eat. I might be waylaid by an old man selling sesame balls; distracted by someone selling glutinous rice dumplings wrapped in tangerine leaves from a steamer on the back of a bicycle; or arrested by the scent of eggy pancakes stuffed with jam, fresh from the griddle.

The notes *ding ding dang, ding ding dang,* beaten out on two ends of a piece of metal, signified the arrival of the Ding Ding toffee man, selling his pale, malt-sugar sweetmeat, which melted stickily in your hand if you didn't eat it quickly. Best of all was the shouted *"Dou huar! Dou huar!"* of the Flower beancurd vendor. I would rush to catch up with him, and he would put down his shoulderpole and the two red-and-black wooden barrels suspended from either end, and set about making me up a bowl of beancurd. It was still warm from the stove, as soft and tender as crème caramel, with a zesty topping of soy sauce, chilli oil, ground Sichuan pepper and morsels of preserved mustard tuber.

I never saw street vendors selling Dan Dan noodles. Like the famous Zhong dumplings and Mr. Lai's glutinous riceballs, they had disappeared from their original habitat, and were served instead in specialist snack canteens, or as a kind of *amuse-bouche* in more glamorous restaurants. On the streets, they'd been replaced by newly fashionable tidbits: Shanghai fried chicken, Xinjiang potatoes or barbecue skewers. Every few months a new street-eating craze arrived, and a rash of identical stalls would jostle for position with the dispensers of more established fare.

ALTHOUGH THE NAME Dan Dan noodles refers only to the way in which the snack was sold from a shoulderpole, over time it has become associated with a particular recipe, in which the noodles are topped with minced meat and *ya cai*, a famous vegetable preserve whose dark crinkly leaves add salt and savour. Every restaurant serving traditional Sichuanese food has Dan Dan noodles on its menu, and you can now buy Dan Dan noodle sauces in the super-markets that have sprung up since I first lived in Chengdu. I've lost count of the different versions of the recipe I've tried over the years. Yet in all my wanderings, I have never come across Dan Dan noodles as delicious as those made by Xie Laoban in his modest noodle shop near Sichuan University.

Of course I tried to persuade him to give me his recipe, but he would never divulge it in its entirety: instead, he tantalised me with fragments. On one occasion, he grudgingly let me watch his staff assemble the seasonings in the bowls; another time he let me taste his oils and sauces; finally, he told me the ingredients of his *niu rou shao zi*, the marvellous minced-beef topping. Eventually, with a great sense of relief and achievement, I managed to put together the pieces of the puzzle, and to reproduce his recipe at home.

For years afterwards, whenever my Sichuan University class-mates and I returned to Chengdu from Paris, London, Munich, Verona or Krakow, we would go to Xie Laoban's for a nostalgic bowl of Dan Dan noodles. And whatever ends of the earth we had come from, and however many hundreds or even thousands of bowls of noodles we had eaten in his shop in the past, he would look at us without a smile or the merest flicker of recognition, and simply ask in the same deadpan Sichuan dialect, "*Sa zi mian?*" If we were lucky, he might give us a perfunctory nod as we left, bidding him goodbye for another year or so. It became a bittersweet joke among us, this refusal to acknowledge who we were.

It was like that until my final visit to his shop, sometime in 2001. This was during the architectural reign of terror of city mayor Li Chuncheng (or Li Chaiqiang—"Demolition Li"—as he was popularly known). Li was a man determined to make his mark on the era by demolishing the old city in its entirety, and replacing it with a modern grid of wide roads lined with concrete high-rises. Great swathes of Chengdu were cleared under his command, not only the more ramshackle dwellings, but opera theatres and grand courtyard houses, famous restaurants and teahouses, and whole avenues of wutong trees. Chengdu hadn't known such ruin and destruction since the Cultural Revolution, when Red Guards dynamited Chengdu's own "Forbidden City," a complex of court-yards and buildings dating back to the Ming Dynasty (a statue of a waving Mao Zedong now stands in its place).

The lanes around Xie Laoban's noodle shop lay in ruins, bony cadavers of wood and bamboo, and his restaurant clung to one or two other little shops in a precarious island amongst them. When I wandered up for a lunchtime bowl of noodles, Xie Laoban gave me a sunny look and, to my amazement, almost smiled. And as he took orders, settled bills and chatted with his regulars, he seemed mellower and less spiky in his movements. By his own standards, he was radiant with bonhomie. What was behind this miraculous transformation? Had he fallen in love, or won a fortune at Mah Jong? Or had the obliteration of the city, and the impending destruction of his business, just filled him with a sense of the lightness of being? I shall never know. I sat there and ate my noodles, which were as fabulous as ever, and then it was time to go. I never saw Xie Laoban again. Later that year, I went to look for him. I wanted to tell him that I had described him and his shop in my Sichuanese cookery book, and published his recipe for Dan Dan noodles, which was now being read and perhaps cooked by a network of Sichuanese food fans all over the world. But the place where his noodle shop had stood was a moonscape of debris, a great plain of rubble, scattered here and there with shattered pickle jars and rice-bowls. And none of the passersby knew where I could find him.

Technique

THE POWER OF TOUCH

By Daniel Patterson

from *Food & Wine*

Chef and owner of the acclaimed San Francisco restaurant Coi
(pronounced "kwa"), Daniel Patterson has earned raves for
his globally inspired cuisine. If his cooking is as meticulous
and vivid as his writing, it deserves all the praise it has won.

Recently, I was sitting in a friend's kitchen, watching her
toss a salad with a pair of restaurant-issue metal tongs. I
had picked the wild greens just hours before, lovingly washed and
dried them, and now was horrified to see her crushing the delicate
leaves between the tongs and bowl. I asked her why she didn't use
her hands to gently toss the lettuces with the vinaigrette. After all,
fingers are much more effective at this task than tongs. My friend
made a face:"I don't want to get my hands dirty."

At first I thought she was in the minority, until I called Maria
Helm Sinskey, a chef and cookbook author who has plenty of in-
teraction with home cooks. "Oh, yes," she laughed. "It's true. No
one wants to touch their food. You should see people trying to cut
up a raw chicken with a knife in one hand and a fork in the other."

It could be that restaurants bear some responsibility for this sad
state of affairs. When open kitchens became ubiquitous, cooks
seemed to use tongs for just about everything. There was always
some guy wielding them like a prosthetic limb, casually flipping a
steak here and grabbing a piece of fish there, using the tongs to stir
his sauces and then guide the food from sauté pan to plate. This
was ostensibly more hygienic than using hands—except for the
small fact that the cooks generally wiped off the tongs with a

greasy towel, twirled them a few times like a six-shooter and then jammed them into the back pocket of their dirty chef's pants. But it looked pretty cool. So people watched—and then they went out and bought some tongs of their own.

Of course, other factors are more to blame for the hands-free approach to cooking. Consider the rise of equipment like bread machines. And pasta machines. And food processors. Just pour in the ingredients and poof!—instant gratification. Things that once required hands could now be done by machine. This was compounded by the problem that somewhere along the way, people lost their connection to real food. In the 1950s, processed foods soared in popularity, and supermarkets began to sell meat and fish as disembodied, plastic-shrouded parts. "In the '60s and '70s," reminisces cookbook author Paula Wolfert, "the only people close to food were hippies and vegetarians."

But slowly, our food culture has been evolving back toward the primacy of ingredients. As interest in farmers' markets and natural foods has exploded, the way chefs handle those ingredients has changed as well. Tongs, for example, are nowhere to be found in today's best kitchens. "A turning point for me," says chef Graham Elliot Bowles of Avenues in Chicago, "was when I was flipping meat on the grill with a pair of tongs while working at Charlie Trotter's, and the chef de cuisine grabbed the tongs out of my hands and threw them across the room." Many other chefs have similar stories to tell. They now use hands, spoons or a thin, flexible metal spatula, all of which damage the ingredients as little as possible and allow the closest connection to the food.

When you think about it, Americans' aversion to touching their food is an aberration compared with much of the rest of the world. In countries like Morocco, India and Ethiopia, people eat with their hands, not just with utensils. Southeast Asian cooks pound ingredients by hand with a mortar and pestle to make the chile pastes and purees that form the basis of their cuisine.

Perhaps no other food culture is more famously linked to the sense of touch than Japan's. "Hands are like a cooking tool in our cuisine," says Ryuta Sakamoto, co-chef and co-owner of Medicine restaurant in San Francisco. "With touch we can actually tell not only freshness and condition, but the taste of a fish." I know this sounds absolutely crazy, but it's a function of repetition and paying attention: Chefs can touch a piece of fish, then taste it and remember the connection between the two. The next day they'll do it again, and then repeat ad infinitum until they have built up an extremely accurate sensory database that informs them of what a fish will taste like simply by its feel.

I often tell my cooks that the onion on their cutting board is a specific onion, not a generic representation. If the layer underneath the skin feels leathery, they need to peel it off and throw it away—it will never soften no matter how they cook it. The same is true for meat. Before cutting it, cooks will often run a hand lengthwise along the surface. They're feeling the grain, the tightness of the fibers, and seeing where the natural separations of the muscles are, which is especially important when trimming larger cuts such as leg of lamb. How a piece of meat feels can make a big difference in determining the best way to cook it: A softer, looser texture might mean more tenderness, so perhaps a shorter cooking time is in order, while a tighter, denser feel might suggest slow roasting or a braise. And pulling meats gently apart makes it easier to see where to cut, as with that ever-tricky joint between a chicken's drumstick and thigh.

When I first started dating my wife, she would test the doneness of a piece of meat by taking a knife and making a jagged cut halfway through its center. If the meat was undercooked, back it went into the pan, leaking juices that spattered everywhere. A few minutes later she would remove the meat and subject it to a second mauling, at which point it began to resemble an outtake from a low-budget horror flick. I never said anything to her, but eventually she began to watch me feel meat with my fingers when I cooked, and then feel it herself, until she learned how to judge doneness by touch. If you don't happen to live with a chef, a good rule of thumb is to feel your earlobe—that's rare. The tip of your nose resembles medium, and your chin is well-done.

Alain Passard of L'Arpège restaurant in Paris goes so far as to have his cooks prepare whole chickens entirely on the stovetop, in a large pan with butter. They constantly turn the birds by hand for an hour-and-a-half or so, the movement and modulated temperature keeping the butter golden brown without burning, creating a supremely succulent result. His cooks don't just prod the surface of the chicken as they move it around—they're feeling the muscles underneath and the way the proteins are slowly setting, which will tell them when it is fully cooked. I should mention the obvious, however: Cooks have skin like lizards and a high tolerance for pain. It's probably not the wisest technique for a home cook.

The same can be said for a lot of new cooking methods floating around restaurants these days, used to create things like warm jellies, foams and savory sorbets, often requiring highly specialized equipment. But unlike in home kitchens, the machines that chefs rely on supplement, but don't supplant, their sense of touch. Dan Barber of Blue Hill at Stone Barns in Pocantico Hills, New York, cooks pork belly sous-vide, slowly poaching it inside a vacuum-sealed bag in a warm-water bath, then finishes it on the stovetop, using the back of his hand to press the meat into the pan so that it crisps evenly. (This technique also works well for fish cooked with the skin on: Pressing gently on the top of the fillet prevents the skin from curling up at the edges.) Johnny Iuzzini, the famously innovative pastry chef at Jean Georges in Manhattan, says, "Touch is important on so many levels, beginning with the ingredients. We constantly have our hands in mixes to check the springiness of gels, or to feel the development of egg whites in meringues. When combining fragile ingredients, I'd rather do it by hand than use a machine, which might deflate the delicate mixture."

Ironically, as chefs' understanding of complex cooking processes has deepened, the care and sensitivity with which they handle their ingredients has brought them closer to traditional home cooking, or at least the way home cooking used to be. I had an extremely fine, elegant version of hand-rolled couscous recently at Aziza restaurant in San Francisco, where the chef, Mourad Lahlou, told me a story about his Moroccan grandmother, from whom he learned his technique: "She was blind, and she rolled the best couscous. She would throw it up in the air when it was formed, and feel it as it landed on her hands. If she felt jagged edges, that meant that it was too dry, and if it stuck, then it was too wet. Other family members started to close their eyes when they made couscous to try and replicate the results."

I remember vividly watching my own grandmother's hands as she rolled out dough, peeled apples and crimped piecrusts when I was young. I have a feeling that she would be baffled by many of the dishes being served in top restaurants these days, but she would understand the chefs' primal desire to connect with their food. The resurgence of handmade food is ultimately about a movement toward a more intimate connection with what we eat and where it comes from, what Paula Wolfert calls "the essential taste" of food. As she told me, "Without taste, smell—and feel—nobody can cook well."

Chasing Perfection

By Francis Lam
from *Gourmet*

Another gifted chef-writer, Francis Lam has all the classical
training he needs to analyze what he's doing in the kitchen.
But more than that, he's got a philosopher's yearning to find
the deeper meaning of every culinary endeavor.

I hit it once, just once, but it was beautiful. It was exam time
and I was nervous, waiting for my turn. I had the proper
fire. The heat felt right. I made smooth, swirling passes with my
spatula, and when I rolled my pan over the plate, I knew it. Chef
took a look at my omelet and squinted at me. He poked at it,
pinched it, and then he knew, too. He called out to the class,
"When you show me yours, I want it to look like this." He set the
plate in the window for the rest of the school to see, then turned
around and gave me a quick wink.

Before Chef Skibitcky got ahold of my brain, I, like every other
rational person, thought an omelet was something anyone can
make. You throw eggs in a pan, stir them around, fold them in half,
and put them on a plate. Done. No-brainer. It only gets interesting
when you start tossing in other things—ham, some cheese, maybe
a sautéed mushroom or two. Once, there was an omelet contest in
my college cafeteria. The winner had it all wrapped up the minute
he pulled an avocado and a wedge of Brie out of his bag. Young
girls screamed and old men yelled. I stood and watched quietly, respecting him.

But there I was, years later, waking up at 2 a.m. for a class called
A.M. Pantry. Still half asleep, I listened to Chef Skibitcky talk

about French omelets, about how Escoffier himself used to test his prospective cooks by watching them make one. I perked up. I'd heard of roasting a chicken as a litmus test for cooks before, but an omelet? Really? What did they put in it?

Three eggs, salt, pepper, and a little butter. That's all Chef had in front of him when he began his demonstration. I was skeptical. He started to swirl the liquid in the pan, his hands moving slowly at first, deliberately. He curled his wrist and snapped into a sweeping motion, gathering all the eggs back together with his spatula. He shook the handle gently, his movements getting gradually faster. There was something going on here. I saw how careful he was to watch and respond to the eggs, even if I didn't know exactly what he was watching. He gave the pan a good whack with his fist and rolled it over a plate. The omelet slid out, tucking itself into a tidy cigar shape.

We passed it around to taste, and I couldn't believe what I was eating. It was fantastically tender, almost slippery with creaminess. Not quite scrambled and not quite custard, it hit my mouth and dissolved in a cloud of butter and egg. I raised my fork for a third bite, but the other students started looking at me funny. Reluctantly, I passed the plate along.

I wanted more. It wasn't just that it was delicious; it was that I realized that at that moment I was seeing for the first time something I thought I'd known my whole life. Like how, if you grew up with tomato-shaped rocks from supermarkets, your first explosive bite into a tomato off the vine in August shows you what a tomato really is.

Chef made another one, talking us through what he was seeing. It's a precarious balancing act—you want the pan hot enough so the eggs don't stick, but not so hot that they cook unevenly. You want to beat the eggs so that they're fully blended, but not so much that they get foamy and dry out in the pan. You want to cook them gently so that they're smooth and creamy, but not so soft that they weep. We weren't even at the good part yet, and this was really starting to not seem like something anyone can make.

Quickly now, Chef shook and stirred until the very last drops of liquid egg hit the bottom of the pan at the exact same moment, cooking together to form a thin sheet that, when rolled, wrapped around the moist curd inside. "You want baby skin," he kept saying. "Not elephant skin." In other words, you have to set the skin just enough so that it can hold the omelet together, but not so much that it gets wrinkled and rubbery. And then you have to make sure that you cook it long enough so that it develops a little flavor, but not so long that it browns and loses its delicacy.

It was astounding how something so commonplace, so elemental, could have so many variables. You just have to learn to see all those variables, to recognize what effect every moment of heat, every motion of the hands has. To get back to that thing I tasted, I would have to know exactly what to look for and nail it every step of the way.

Three eggs, salt, pepper, and a little butter. That's all there is in a classic French omelet, but it's enough to keep reteaching me this vital lesson: Things are only simple when you've stopped asking the right questions of them, when you've stopped finding new ways to see them. Because what you find, when you learn how to find it, is that even simple things can be wonderfully, frustratingly, world-openingly complex.

It's been half a decade since Chef taught me that lesson, since that morning when I went home and rolled out omelet after awful omelet until my roommate woke up to find plates covering every level surface in our kitchen. Eventually, I let my obsession revert to a healthy level of interest, until a couple of months ago, when I went out to breakfast with a friend. She thought the place was sketchy but ordered anyway, saying to me, "I figured, 'How badly can you screw up an omelet?'"

It was time, I decided right then and there, to get back in touch with my inner egg philosopher. Not long after, I invited some friends over for brunch. Twenty of them.

My guests trickled in, some still groggy and wielding bottles of cheap sparkling wine because nothing cures a hangover like the thing that caused it. As they mingled and mixed Mimosas, I put together my station at the stove. I picked up my pan and held it to my face to check the heat, a weird little habit I picked up somewhere along the way. It was time.

I put a ladle into my clarified butter, grabbed hold of my spatula, took a meditative breath, and promptly mangled my first omelet. It was brutal. The pan was way too hot, the eggs fried instantly, and the skin wasn't elephant skin, it was geriatric-elephant skin. It flopped out like a pancake when I tried to roll it onto the plate.

I gave it to the drunkest guy in the house.

My next two were similarly disgraceful, and I was running out of drunk guests. But soon things began to pick up. The heat was getting intense in my little kitchen; I was sweating through a film of butter. I was starting to feel like a cook again, and somewhere around my 13th try, there were a few that were pretty good. If an omelet can be art, can teach me a new way to see the world, it's funny that I had to feel like a laborer before I could make it.

Still, by the end of the morning, perfection was a long way away. If the beauty of the omelet is its seeming simplicity, that simplicity is unforgiving. Either you nail it and it's transcendent, or it's, well, just eggs. I needed a brush-up on my technique, but Chef Skibitcky had moved across the country. I called in a ringer.

Daniel Boulud is perhaps the finest French chef in America. He is certainly one of the most classically trained, winning national recognition when he was an apprentice in Lyon, where he had to knock out 30 omelets in a row for a staff meal. Today, though, he is a restaurant magnate with a presidential smile, a refined air, a team of beautiful assistants—far removed from his days as a cook, even further from his days as an apprentice.

So, despite his credentials, I didn't expect him to come out firing when I visited him in his restaurant on the Upper East Side of Manhattan. But he was on it before he even took his seat. "To understand the omelet, you have to understand what the omelet represents," he said as he walked in. "You have to understand what the omelet means." Wait a minute, I think we're on the same page.

He started talking about his technique, how he likes to stir finely diced butter into the raw egg so that it melts on the heat, insulating the eggs and controlling how they curdle. He talked about using forks to work the pan because they break up the curds as they form, keeping them tender and creamy, rather than a spatula that just lifts and slaps around big sheets of egg. He talked about finishing the omelet with a touch of butter and a tiny kiss of high heat. He referred to this as "toasting" the eggs but then took it back. He tried "sear" but decided against that, too. He used these words gingerly, knowing that he didn't really mean them. For a man so articulate with the language of food, it's interesting that he struggled for the exact words here. Maybe our high-heat, ass-kicking cooking culture is so invested in brawny terms for powerhouse techniques that we lack words for an effect as subtle as the one he was describing.

As he talked, he motioned with his hands, illustrating his points with miming gestures the way I see only cooks do. I noticed a few burns and scars on his knuckles. They looked fresh.

He asked me about the pan I use, the type and the size, then paused thoughtfully. A second later, he held his thumb and forefinger maybe a centimeter apart. "So you have this much egg in your pan?" I nodded yes, but to be honest, I had no idea. It could be that much, it could be twice that much—I had never noticed. And yet, with just the information I gave him, he thought through the ratios of diameter and volume and could visualize what the beginnings of my omelet looked like. (He was right, by the way.) "Your Teflon pan gives a little magic ease," he said. "Black steel is more capricious." My pan would do, but a well-seasoned black steel pan would be better; it would let me use metal forks, and its angled corners would give the omelet a lip to roll out more evenly.

I scribbled furiously in my notebook, giddy with the sensation of having my mind blown and suppressing the urge to yell, "Yes! Yes! Of course!" When I sat down with Boulud, I thought that I had the theory of the omelet down, that I might just ask him for something like a little tip on how to shake the pan, or how to tell if the heat was right. Instead, our conversation revealed how much deeper he had thought about this than I ever had. The more you learn about something, the more you find out there's more to learn, and I was swimming in new questions.

We talked for almost an hour, causing one of his beautiful assistants to remind him that he was well late to his next meeting. He waved off the warning, pulling down an enormous book on the history of French cuisine to see what it had to say about omelets. In that moment, this Chef, this magnate, looked like an eager young cook again. A cook aiming for the top, because even though we were talking about eggs, we knew what we were really talking about was perfection, about giving the idea of perfection a physical form.

I left and immediately got myself a black steel pan. I've been scouring it with salt and oil to season it ever since, understanding that I'm deeper in a hole, further away from making my ideal omelet than I realized. The other day, as I was scrubbing on my pan again, trying to make new metal old, a friend found me. Gently, but sort of pityingly, she asked, "What . . . are you doing?"

Okay, so maybe it's a little much, this obsession of mine. But tell me: How many places in your life do you know, really know, what perfection looks like? How many ways do you know to chase after perfection?

For me, the first step is to figure out how to keep my pan from rusting.

Omelet

1. Break three large, superfresh, room-temperature eggs into a bowl and beat them lovingly with a little salt and pepper until they are perfectly combined, but be careful not to froth them. Stir in a teaspoon of butter that you've cut into tiny dice, making sure it's evenly distributed. If the butter can't be from Brittany, make sure it's at least chilled, okay?

2. Now take your eight-inch black steel pan that has been well seasoned for 20 years, and that you reserve exclusively for eggs. Heat one tablespoon of clarified butter over a medium-high flame. Get the pan hot enough so that the eggs will start cooking right when you pour them in, but not so hot that they bubble violently and start frying.

3. Use the back of two forks to stir the eggs in silver-dollar-size circular motions at slow speed (120 revolutions per minute), revolving them around the pan. When the eggs have become a thickened liquid containing small curds, gently shake the pan and increase speed to medium (140 rpm). When they're all wet curds, shake more vigorously and speed up to fast (160 rpm).

4. While the eggs are all cooked but still tender and slippery curds, let the pan sit untouched on the heat and count to seven to form the skin. Lift the pan and, with your free

hand, give the handle a couple of good whacks to shake the omelet loose and get it to slide up the top edge. Set the pan down and change your grip so that your palm faces up and the handle is perpendicular to your wrist.

5. Roll the omelet onto a warmed plate by flipping the pan handle-first so that your palm faces down again. Don't be afraid—you just have to commit to it and go. If it doesn't come out, it wasn't meant to be.

6. Now examine your omelet: the tight cigar shape, the rich yellow color, the smoothness, the thinness of the skin. Curse yourself for all the ways it's not perfect, insist that this is a personal failing, and start over.

The Saucier's Apprentice

By Bob Spitz

from *The Saucier's Apprentice*

Like many talented amateurs, Spitz—best known for his biog-
raphies of the Beatles and Bob Dylan—yearned to hone his
skills in a European cooking school. Restlessly sampling a
dozen or so different courses across the Continent, he
learned more than he'd bargained for.

I had no business being in the kitchen of the Meurice. A
friend had persuaded its executive chef to take me under
his wing for a day, but I could tell from the moment I entered what
a mistake had been made. The place hummed with precision; it was
a citadel of culinary perfection, with standards of discipline right
out of the Koran. It reminded me of a bottling plant, if you've ever
been to one, except that it was two rooms instead of one. Besides, it
was Le Meurice, the chilliest joint in Paris—all Brioni suits,
Chopard jewelry, and a lobby with the coziness quotient of Ver-
sailles. On the way in, I'd already passed Warren Christopher, Sting,
the entire ministry of an emerging African nation, and that ladies'-
apparel big-shot from Long Island, you know, the one who stays at
all the five-star hotels and regards them as if they were discos. There
was a stiff unerring orthodoxy to the Meurice that I could appreciate from afar, but as far as cooking there went, it intimidated the
hell out of me.

The real reason, though, for putting myself through such an or-
deal was that the chef, Yannick Alléno, had the reputation for being the most talented cook in Paris. You couldn't walk into a
serious restaurant that season without hearing his name. When he

took over the kitchen in the summer of 2003, *Le Figaro* pro-
claimed it "the gastronomic event of the year." I happened to have
dinner there the night of his début, and it was the kind of mouthwatering experience that surpassed the hype. The food was just
brilliant. The most jaded pickle-faced epicureans twitched like
marionettes in their seats as one dish after another appeared like
the highlight at Sotheby's spring auction. I overheard someone at
a nearby table say Alléno's menu charted the crossroads of French
gastronomy, but if so it was the kind of crossroads Robert Johnson
sang about. Waiters served wine duck in a crust of Indian spices
nesting on a plump roasted peach half. Mounds of puffed potatoes
studded with *girolles* had been sweetened with dried apricot. Alléno presented a sea-bass fillet with aromatic herbs, sweet-pepper
fondue, and sardine cream. If you were lucky, there was room for
one of his signature desserts. I did hand-to-hand combat with
crème brûlée, ice cream swaddled in an orange-flavored biscuit and
decorated with the wild strawberries that someone had shipped
from Andalusia.

Alléno bagged his first star faster than a hooker on Hollywood
Boulevard. By the time I walked through the door again, he'd received a precious second, with rumors of the third being withheld
simply to stabilize his ascent. (He has since hit the trifecta.) Some
said the Michilen judges were influenced by reports of fiery
tantrums, which were legendary. In any case, the starriest object in
the Meurice was Alléno himself, a ridiculously handsome character, so suave and utterly French, with an ever-ready smile that was
more like a fixture than a warm embrace.

He charmed me from the get-go, which was his manner, and I
was duly taken in. It took a certain style to run such a fabulous es-
tablishment, and he had it in spades. He knew how to set a room
in motion just by walking into it. There was something commanding about him. It had nothing to do with the way he cooked or his
exquisite suit of the fine bones of his face. It was the aura, the star
power he radiated that made people react so spiritedly.

He gave me the first-class tour, including a peek at the process he
used for "a new creation" that involved alternating slices of grilled
eggplant, cèpe, boudin noir, and Granny Smith apple in an apple-
basil vinaigrette.

I was beginning, though, to feel like a politician on a fact-finding tour. I'd met the mastermind, seen the kitchen, and glimpsed the *creative process*. Now, if I guessed correctly, we'd probably go play golf.

Next best thing: Alléno turned up his smile, patted me on the head, and stashed me at an out-of-the-way station to clean a tubful of cèpes. This was his lame device for letting an outsider feel like part of the kitchen crew. It almost felt as if he were making fun of my pursuit. Well, I'd be damned if I would give him the pleasure of seeing my abject disappointment. Not a flinch or a hesitation showed on my face. Smile frozen in place, I slipped into an apron, cursing my luck, and wishing I had gone somewhere more sensitive, more willing to play. I was serving a purpose, and even a worthwhile one, but I resented it.

It is amazing how many shapes and idiosyncrasies you can attribute to a cèpe. After an hour brushing those babies, I'd identified half the animal kingdom; in the third hour, I discovered one in the image of the Virgin Mary. If I called the tabloids, it occurred to me, vengeance would be mine.

I wasted the whole day doing KP at the Meurice. Around six, during dinner prep, I spotted my friend Claudia talking to a waiter and waved her over.

"You're getting very special treatment," she said, without a trace of irony. "Few mortals ever spend an entire day with Yannick."

"I can only imagine," I mumbled, wiping the cèpe doo off my hands. "Most, if I've guessed correctly, die of boredom. Am I right?"

Somehow I managed to convey my frustration and begged her to intercede with Yannick on my behalf.

"I need to learn something constructive," I pleaded. "Anything—a recipe or a preparation. But, please—no more scut work. I don't iron, clean blinds, vacuum carpets, or *clean fucking cèpes!*"

It worked. A half-hour later, Yannick walked over with that smile fixed on his face.

"So I hear you want to learn how to cook. Okay," he said, steering me toward the stove, "let's see you make an omelet."

I must have stared at him, blank-faced, for an impudent length of time. Finally, I muttered: "You son of a bitch."

It was a trick, and his delighted laugh told me I had caught him red-handed. Making an omelet was a litmus test in practically every good kitchen in France; it determined whether or not a chef got hired. Stories abounded about seasoned cooks who bungled once-in-a-lifetime opportunities, scraping omelets off a cast-iron pan while a stone-faced chef harrumphed in disgust.

"If you have the skills to make an omelet, it means you have decent hands," my friend Sandy once told me. "A cook has to make his hands do what his mind wants them to do, without thinking about it. That's what makes a cook so valuable working the line. When you're under huge pressure like that, you need to have skills that you aren't thinking about. Chefs are always saying to each other, 'I'll send you this guy—he's got good hands.' It means that he is a real craftsman. Everyone is always talking about the *art* of food. Well, if you can't be a craftsman, you'll never be an artist."

An omelet took skill; it was an accomplishment, a work of art. At my best, I turned out a Greek diner special.

As if to prove a point, I whipped out a fluffy three-egg specimen that never failed to satisfy my daughter. Yannick sat behind me in a chair, with one leg crossed over the other. I could feel his smug grin burning into my back.

"What's this?" he asked with mock disdain when I presented my omelet.

I stared at him, refusing to answer.

"I thought you were going to make an omelet. So?"

The weight of the pan felt good in my hand. I could kill him with one well-placed blow.

I clapped a hand to my heart. "I suppose I don't get the job."

"You wouldn't get the job in a brasserie. But you're in luck." He stood up and took off his jacket. "I am going to teach you how to make an omelet."

Big fucking deal, I thought. You get to show off and put me in my place at the same time. At least I had the sense to keep this to myself.

A transformation came over Yannick as he collected a few utensils for the demo. I watched him with bemusement as he combed the fringes of the room, picking up this and that—a whisk, a metal bowl, a fork, a dozen eggs. He was no longer the debonair two-star impresario but a journeyman cook, eyes hard and focused, all business, with a steady, sure touch. He clutched a scratched-up non-stick pan, not a pretty thing, but well seasoned. With all the instinctive moves, he poured a little straw-colored oil in the bottom and swirled it around. I stepped back to allow him more room.

"Let's start with the base," he said, breaking the eggs into a small metal bowl. He beat them with gusto, dipping a fork deep into the bowl and lifting the egg high in the air. "You have to get underneath it, getting a good amount of air into eggs, beating until the mixture forms a mousse." A fine spray of bubbles frothed along the surface. He sprinkled a pinch of salt into the bowl, followed by a grind of white pepper. When the oil began to sizzle, he turned up the flame.

"It has to be very hot. You wait for a moment until the oil separates in the pan." After a few seconds, he dropped a half-tablespoon of butter into the pan and immediately poured in the eggs. "Now watch carefully. Everything happens very fast."

The process reminded me of a choreographed dance routine. His whole body moved with fluency as he swirled the egg around the pan, hands, shoulders, hips, back, tilting the pan this way and that, bent over the stove like an evangelist. There was a flow and authority in the way he worked. Order reigned. Standing before his steamy pulpit, he conveyed the impression that the stove's heat was his heat, and if the burners ceased to function, he would conduct the body heat he generated to finish the job.

"It's all in the wrist," he said, transferring the pan to his left hand and using his right to run the flat end of the fork back and forth across the bottom, slurrying the egg, as it firmed, toward the center. "Now we change," he said, gripping the handle in his right hand and tilting the pan away from him. The omelet began to slide a bit, just an inch or two toward the edge. He changed hands once more, holding the handle with his left and hitting his wrist three times—"Boom! Boom! Boom!" he intoned—causing the omelet to roll gently his way in three neat folds. Grabbing a plate, he took the pan handle in his right hand, tilting the pan at a forty-five degree angle so that the omelet simply rolled over itself onto the plate.

"Voilà!" he said, as if it were the most natural outcome.

As far as omelets went, it was a masterpiece. There was nothing to it but egg and expertise. It had a beautiful, unblemished texture, glistening with a faint perspiration of butter on its brow. It was everything an omelet should be—downy, creamy, with a slight spring, almost like pastry in your mouth. After my first delicious bite, Yannick grabbed the plate from me and slid the omelet into the trash.

"Now you make one," he said.

I nodded brightly and took up the metal bowl. I tried to seem confident, a little cocksure perhaps, especially when it came to breaking the eggs, which I did one-handed like a pro. Even the mousse produced an approving nod from Yannick.

"Okay, here you go . . . ," he said, winging a chunk of butter into the pan.

He stood over my left shoulder, gently barking out directions. "Good, good," he said encouragingly, when I scrambled the egg on the bottom of the pan. "Now, begin to roll. No . . . *no!* Change hands. *No*—hold the pan differently. Okay, good. Now, hit your wrist—*Boom! Boom! Boom!"*

I didn't know omelets were alive. Mine jumped out of the pan and landed on the counter. He picked it up with a thumb and forefinger, holding it to the light. My cheek flushed under the discipline.

"Okay," he said flatly, "now we do another one."

The second, third, and fourth weren't bad. I was particularly fond of the ninth one, which seemed to scroll at will. From the eleventh omelet on, Yannick took over the *Boom! Boom! Boom!*—pounding me on the wrist with an open fist. After the sixteenth, a red strawberry formed on my forearm where his knuckles made contact. Finally, the eighteenth was perfect. I gazed up at him with pride, handing over the sweetest, purest, smoothest omelet that I had ever seen.

He studied it expressionlessly, his pedagogic spirit spent, and, after a moment, he nodded: "Now let's make an acceptable one."

Once we edged into the twenties, I was like any other torture victim lapsing into delirium. Nothing of consequence mattered anymore. I would even tell him where Jimmy Hoffa was buried.

"Boom! Boom! Boom!"

"Beneath the visitor's goalpost at Giants Stadium . . . the Secaucus toll booth on the New Jersey Turnpike . . . the pilings under the Verrazano Bridge . . . "

"*Boom! Boom! Boom!*"

Wasn't this covered under the Geneva Convention, I wondered, as omelet number twenty-three hit the pan with a splash.

"Ah . . . ," he sounded impassive. "*Voilà!*"

"What do you mean—*voilà?*"

"You understand French. It is an omelet, as I have taught you."

"You're kidding, right? What about doing another one? What about *Boom! Boom! Boom!*"

My pleas blew coolly on Yannick's face as he took the plate from me and decorated it with chervil and a few slices of fruit. With the flick of a hand, he signaled a cook's assistant.

"Where are you going with that?" I snapped at him, slightly louder than I had intended. Lowering my voice, I said, "That's my omelet," in the way a parent says, *my baby . . . my first born!*

"One omelet," Yannick said scornfully, taking a small slip of paper from his shirt pocket, "Room 609. We are sending it up." He put the paper on the plate and handed it to the assistant.

With Yannick's firm, dismissing nod, the omelet disappeared on a tray down the hall. Jarred by the speed with which it was gone, I wanted to race after it.

Suddenly, Yannick began to chuckle in a soft, sly, satisfied way and draped a brotherly arm over my shoulder. Like Louie and Rick after Elsa's quick departure, we walked off, shoulder to shoulder, in the direction of the freezers.

"Now," he said, "let's see what you do with sweetbreads."

SLOW COOKING

By Alice Waters

from *The Art of Simple Food*

It's no exaggeration to say that Alice Waters and her restaurant, Chez Panisse, in Berkeley, California, launched a culinary revolution over a quarter-century ago. With her new
back-to-basics cookbook, Waters carries on her passionate
defense of fresh food honestly served.

Nothing creates a sense of well-being like a barely simmering braise or stew cooking quietly on the stove or
in the oven. The warm aromas wafting in the air are deeply comforting. Dinner is cooking. A simple and economical cut of meat is
slowly altering in moist heat, gradually reaching a state of falling-
off-the-bone tenderness, surrounded by a rich and tasty sauce. I
love the ease and economy of cooking this way, which involves
neither the ostentation of an expensive roast nor the flash-in-the-
pan excitement of a last-minute sauté. Once assembled, a stew or
braise cooks in a single pot, largely unwatched. It can be made
ahead and reheated the next day, without a worry, and it will be
even tastier.

Braising and Stewing Meat

Braising and stewing meat is a long, slow, gentle process of cooking
with moist heat in a small amount of liquid in a covered pot. A
braise is typically made from larger pieces of meat, frequently still
on the bone, while a stew is made from smaller pieces of meat cut
into even-size chunks and cooked in a bit more liquid than a
braise, almost enough to cover. (Fish and vegetables may be cooked

in a similar manner, but being more delicate they do not cook for nearly as long.) The basic components of a braise or stew are meat, aromatic vegetables, flavorings such as herbs and spices, and liquid.

Inexpensive cuts of meat are best for slow cooking as their tough connective tissues melt while cooking, producing a silky texture with lots of flavor. Lean meat, or meat that is mostly muscle, contracts and squeezes out all its moisture as it cooks, leaving it dry like a wrung-out towel. Tougher cuts such as shoulders, shanks, legs, and tails (the parts that do the most work) are full of tendons and ligaments made of collagen; that collagen turns to gelatin when cooked in liquid over time. The surrounding lean, dry muscle fibers absorb this flavorful gelatinous liquid and become deliciously tender. The gelatin enriches and adds body to the sauce as well.

Onions, celery, carrots, fennel, and leeks are called aromatic vegetables. They can withstand long cooking and add flavor and texture to a braise or stew. The vegetables can be removed at the end of cooking or left in the dish. Add them raw, slightly cooked, or even cooked until brown. Raw or lightly cooked vegetables make a lighter, fresher sauce. In general, the more color on the vegetables, the deeper the flavor and color of the sauce. If they are too browned, however, they will become bitter.

Add branches and sprigs of fresh herbs either loose or bundled together into a bouquet tied with cotton string. A bouquet is easier to remove, but if the sauce is going to be strained or if the dish is quite rustic, I usually don't bother to tie the herbs together. When removing a bouquet from the pot, press it well to extract all the tasty juices it holds. Dried herbs are very pungent and can easily take over a dish, so add them judiciously, taste the sauce after 30 minutes of cooking, and add more if necessary. Spices are better added whole, particularly black pepper. Wrap them in a piece of cheesecloth if you don't want them floating around in the sauce.

Wine, stock, and water are the liquids most commonly used in a braise or stew. Wine contributes both acidity and fruit. Before being added it is sometimes reduced (boiled down) to concentrate its flavors. Tomatoes, or a splash of vinegar, can be used instead. Stock will add a depth of flavor and richness that water cannot. Chicken stock works well with any meat and even with some fish. Otherwise, use beef stock with beef, lamb stock with lamb, and so forth.

Whether they are made of earthenware, enameled cast iron, or metal, the best pots to use for braising and stewing are heavy, because they allow for slow, even cooking. Choose a pot just big enough to comfortably hold the meat you are cooking. A larger pot requires more liquid, diluting the flavors of the sauce; a smaller one may crowd the meat too tightly for proper cooking and there may not be enough sauce for all the meat. A comfortable but close environment is best for keeping the liquid at a steady low simmer. A tight-fitting lid is desirable; but a loose one can be augmented, or a missing one replaced, by foil. The pot should be deep enough to accommodate the meat and its liquid, but not so deep that there's a lot of airspace between the underside of the lid and the meat, in which case too much liquid may evaporate and the meat may dry out. If you have to use a pot that's too deep, cut a piece of parchment paper to fit the pot's inside dimensions and lay it over the meat before covering.

To prepare a braise or stew, first season the meat with salt and pepper. For better flavor, do this a day in advance. The meat is usually seared or browned before it is added to the pot, which makes it look more appetizing and adds flavor and color to the sauce. Use the pot the dish will be cooked in if it's suitable for browning meat; otherwise use a heavy pan such as cast iron. Heat the pan well, then add the fat and then the meat, as for sautéing. Don't crowd the pieces or they will start to sweat and will color only with difficulty. Take time to brown them well on all sides, in as many batches as it takes. Remove the meat, turn off the heat, pour off the fat, and while the pan is still quite hot, add the wine or some other liquid. As the liquid bubbles, scrape up all the crusty brown bits stuck to the bottom of the pan; they add loads of flavor. This step is called deglazing the pan. Really scrape up these bits; they won't add much flavor to the sauce if they are left stuck to the bottom of the pan, even if the dish cooks for hours.

If the vegetables are to be cooked, pour the deglazing juices over the browned meat and wipe out the pan. Heat a bit of oil in it and add the vegetables, cooking them as directed. Transfer the vegetables, the meat, and its deglazing juices into the pot they will cook in and pour in the stock or water. For a braise the liquid should come about halfway up the meat; for a stew it should almost cover the meat, but not completely submerge it. Bring the liquid to a boil, reduce the heat, and cook at the gentlest simmer until tender, either on top of the stove or in a 300°F oven. Check occasionally to make sure that it is not cooking too fast and that the level of liquid has not fallen. Top it up if it has.

Some recipes call for various additional elements, such as vegetables and pieces of bacon, to be cooked apart in different ways and added to the finished braise or stew. This preserves the freshness and integrity of the vegetables. For example, roasted small potatoes and steamed turnips can add complexity to a beef stew; or first-of-the-season peas and fava beans can enliven a braise of spring lamb. Glazed little onions, sautéed mushrooms, and browned bacon are always added to coq au vin, the classic French dish of chicken braised in red wine. Scattering chopped tender herbs over any finished stew or braise gives a bright fresh touch, as does a zingy confetti of chopped parsley mixed with finely chopped garlic (and possible grated lemon zest) sprinkled over at the last minute.

To soak up all the tasty juices, serve a braise or stew with fresh pasta or egg noodles, mashed or steamed potatoes, rice pilaf, polenta, or a grilled or toasted piece of bread rubbed with garlic.

Making Stew

Good choices for stew meat are oxtails, shanks, beef chuck, short ribs, pork shoulder, beef cheeks, lamb shoulder, and lamb neck. These cuts all have lots of connective tissue and fat to make them tender and full of flavor. For stew, the meat is cut into smaller pieces. Have your butcher cut bony cuts such as short ribs and lamb shanks into 2-inch lengths. Cut boneless meat such as chuck or shoulder into 1½-inch cubes. The pieces may be cut larger for a more rustic stew, but cut any smaller they tend to fall apart when cooked. If you are buying beef that has already been cut up for stew, ask what cut it is from. Most meat counters use top and bottom round, which I find too lean to make a good stew; they cook up dry. Ask the butcher to cut some chuck into stew meat for you instead, or buy a large piece and cut it at home.

Season the meat with salt and pepper. If you have the time, season it a day ahead. If you make a marinade, stir the meat now and then while it is marinating; this will help the marinade flavor the meat evenly. Any vegetables in the marinade I first cook slightly in a bit of oil, for more flavor. Let them cook before adding to the meat.

Brown the meat well in a fair amount of oil, lard, or fat. Don't crowd the pieces; brown them in as many batches as necessary. You can use the same oil for each batch as long as the pan does not burn. If it does, wipe out the pan and continue with fresh oil. When the meat is browned, drain the fat from the pan and deglaze the pan with wine, tomatoes, broth, or water. Short ribs and oxtails are some of my favorite stewing cuts, because they make such a flavorful sauce. These cuts can be browned in the oven: Preheat the oven to 450°F; lay the meat out on a rack in a shallow pan; and cook until the meat is brown and the fat is rendered. With this method there is no pan to deglaze, but it is quicker and easier than browning on the stovetop.

If the aromatic vegetables are to be left in the stew, cut them into even, medium-size pieces. If they are to be discarded at the end, leave them in large chunks, for easy removal. Put the vegetables, meat, and deglazing liquid into a pot. Choose a pot large enough to accommodate the meat in two, or possibly three, layers. If the meat is piled higher than this, the bottom layer will cook and fall apart before the upper layers are done. Stirring doesn't really help this much, and the chance of sticking and burning is much greater. Add broth or water, as the recipe asks, almost to the top of the meat, but do not submerge it. When I am using a marinade that is mostly wine, I like to reduce it (boil it down) by half or more before adding it to the pot. This removes the raw taste of the wine and allows room for more broth, which makes a richer sauce.

Bring the liquid to a boil, then turn the heat down to a bare simmer, and cover the pot. Use a flame tamer if necessary to keep the stew from boiling. Or cook the stew in a preheated 325°F oven. If the stew boils hard there's a good chance the meat will fall apart and the sauce emulsify (the fat and the liquid bind together, which makes the sauce murky). Check the pot now and then to monitor the cooking and the level of the liquid; add more broth or water if needed.

Cook until the meat is very tender. This will take anywhere from 2 to 4 hours depending on what cut is being used. There should be very little or no resistance when the meat is poked with a small knife or skewer. When the meat is done, skim the sauce well, removing as much of the fat as you can. This is much easier to do after the simmering has stopped and the liquid has had a chance to settle. The sauce may be strained, but do so carefully: the meat is very delicate now and can fall apart. If the stew is being served another day, the fat can be simply lifted off after chilling in the refrigerator.

Thicken a thin or watery sauce with a mixture of one part flour stirred together with one part soft butter. Whisk this into the boiling sauce bit by bit, cooking each addition to the sauce for a minute before going on to the next; you want just enough to give the sauce a little body. I prefer this method to sprinkling flour over the meat as it is browning.

Heat the stew, taste it for salt, and add any vegetables that were cooked separately. The stew is ready! Serve sprinkled with herbs (or not), and be sure to serve something to soak up all the great sauce.

Beef Stew

4 SERVINGS

Season generously, a day ahead if possible:
3 pounds grass-fed beef chuck, cut into 1½-inch cubes with
Salt and fresh-ground black pepper
Heat, in a heavy-bottomed pan over medium-high heat:
2 tablespoons oil
Add:
3 slices bacon, cut into ½-inch pieces
Cook until rendered and lightly brown but not crisp. Remove the bacon and add the meat, browning well on all sides, in as many batches as necessary. Put the browned meat into a heavy pot or braising dish. Pour off most of the fat, lower the heat, and add:
2 onions, peeled and cut into quarters
2 cloves (stick them into onion quarters)

2 carrots, peeled and cut into 2-inch chunks
2 sprigs each of thyme, savory, and parsley
1 bay leaf
A few peppercorns

Cook until slightly browned and add to the beef in the pot. Return the pan to the stove and raise the heat. Pour in:

3 tablespoons brandy (optional)

This may flame up, so be careful. Then add:

1¾ cups red wine

Cook until reduced by two thirds, scraping up all the brown bits from the bottom of the pan. Pour this over the beef and vegetables. Add:

3 diced tomatoes, fresh or canned
1 small head of garlic, separated into cloves, peeled, and coarsely chopped
1 thin strip of orange zest
2 cups beef stock (or chicken broth)

Check the level of the liquid; it should be at least three-quarters of the way up the cubes of beef. Add more if needed. Cover the pot tightly and cook at a bare simmer on the stovetop, or in a 325°F oven, for 2 to 3 hours. Check the stew occasionally to be sure that it is not boiling and that there is enough liquid. When the meat is tender, turn off the heat, and let the stew settle for a few minutes. Skim off all the fat. Discard the bay leaf, cloves, and peppercorns. Taste for salt and adjust as needed.

Serve sprinkled with a mixture of:

1 tablespoon chopped parsley
1 or 2 garlic cloves, chopped fine

VARIATIONS

- Stir in ½ cup small black olives with their pits 30 minutes before the stew is finished cooking. If using pitted olives, add them after the stew has finished cooking.
- Use ¾ cup white wine instead of red wine. Only reduce by half.
- To make pot roast, keep the meat whole instead of cutting it into cubes. Bottom round or brisket can be used

as well as chuck. The liquid should come only halfway up the roast. Increase the cooking time by 1 hour.

• Soak ¼ cup dried porcini mushrooms in ½ cup hot water for 10 minutes. Drain, chop coarse, and add to the stew along with 2 ½ tablespoons tomato paste instead of tomatoes. If the mushroom liquid is not too sandy, substitute it for some of the broth. Omit the orange zest.

THE ART OF THE BISCUIT

By Scott Peacock

from the *Atlanta Journal-Constitution*

Alabama-born Scott Peacock (currently chef at Watershed in
Decatur, Georgia) may be too young to be called a dean of
Southern cooking, but he treads in the footsteps of one, the
late Edna Lewis, with whom he wrote the classic cookbook *The
Gift of Southern Cooking.*

Biscuits are the stuff of legend. The mere mention of
them conjures images of hearth and home, kindly
grandmothers and good-smelling kitchens. A particularly well-
made biscuit has been known to inspire proposals of marriage.

People love eating biscuits. They love talking about biscuits. But
when it comes to making them, the sad truth is that many people,
even Southerners, are often too afraid to try.

Why is this? Why are so many otherwise stalwart souls intimidated by a little piece of bread? I decided to consult an expert: my
mother, a former biscuit-phobe herself.

While bad biscuits didn't singlehandedly end my parents' marriage, they surely didn't help. My father, a true biscuit lover—"they
just have a taste that fits me," he says—was raised by a mother who,
twice daily and without measuring, produced exceptionally fine
biscuits from a wood-burning stove. As a young boy, I remember
that he was less than complimentary of my mother's fledgling efforts to duplicate those skills. "These look and taste just like the
Himalayan Mountains. Hard as them, too!" he used to say.

My mother hasn't forgotten this, either. "He made so much fun
of my biscuits," she told me, "that I finally got too embarrassed to

keep trying and I just quit." She added, a little sheepishly: "I must admit they were pretty bad. Inedible, really. And heavy as lead. You could've put one in a slingshot and killed a bird with it. Maybe a squirrel."

So the biscuit maker in our family was a little doughy man in a white chef's hat named Pop N. Fresh. Talk about a sad state of affairs, especially since making an infinitely superior biscuit from scratch takes little more time than rapping that refrigerated can against the counter (though I admit I did get a certain thrill out of those exploding tubes of dough).

Lacking a role model at home, it wasn't until I was in my early 20s, working as the chef at a small hunting plantation in South Georgia, that I was able to cobble together enough know-how to make a decent batch of biscuits. Under the gun, through reading and experimentation, I overcame the tendencies of overkneading and underbaking that so often stand in the way of success.

At the Governor's Mansion, I refined my biscuit skills and built confidence. But it wasn't until I met and began cooking with the late, great Southern writer and chef Edna Lewis—an exquisite maker of biscuits if ever there was one—that I really learned to love biscuit making and discovered some of the finer points of the craft. Together, we mixed, kneaded, rolled and baked thousands of biscuits.

Experience has taught me that, in the end, a good biscuit really boils down to a few basics: mainly a hot oven, cold fat and a gentle but knowing hand.

But it's the details that make a great biscuit, and simple as they are, they are important and should be followed closely.

The Golden Ideal

To my taste, a biscuit should be crusty and golden brown on the top—and even lightly browned on the bottom—with an interior that is soft, light and tender but not too fluffy. It should be slightly moist, but not so moist that it becomes gummy when you eat it, and dry enough to absorb a pat of good butter as it melts. It should be flavorful and well seasoned, with a slight buttermilk tang, pleasing on its own but an excellent vehicle for other flavors as well.

Ratio of crusty exterior to soft interior is important, and I'm no fan of those big, Hollywood-pumped-up-on-steroids-looking biscuits. I prefer a biscuit no larger than three inches or so in diameter and not much more than an inch in height.

My favorite way to enjoy a biscuit is split, warm from the oven, slathered with excellent, room temperature butter and a drizzle of honey or spread with homemade blackberry or strawberry preserves.

But I would have just as hard a time turning down one with sweet butter and a few shards of country ham tucked inside. Or lightly sweetened and baked into a shortcake filled with berries and softly whipped cream. Or topped with sautéed asparagus and mushrooms and a runny poached egg. Or dipped into a pool of sorghum or cane syrup.

Here are the steps that will take you to your own biscuit nirvana:

First: Use the Good Stuff

Biscuits are a simple affair made with just a few humble ingredients, so each one counts.

Flour: Biscuits are traditionally made with a soft-wheat Southern flour such as White Lily, which is lower in protein than most all-purpose flours and therefore makes an exceptionally light and tender biscuit. However, a very fine biscuit can be made by using any good quality all-purpose flour. (In fact, Miss Lewis preferred unbleached flour—King Arthur—for making biscuits, and hers were some of the best I've ever tasted.) Unbleached flour contains more protein than bleached varieties, so it is stronger and yields a slightly more sturdier product. If using unbleached flour, you will need to use slightly more fat than with regular flour and possibly a bit more liquid—more about that later. No matter which type of flour, you should avoid self-rising varieties. They are loaded with commercial baking powder and salt and to me have a very unpleasant taste.

Leavening: I strongly advocate making your own baking powder, a much simpler task than it sounds. Commercial baking powder contains chemicals and aluminum salts that impart an unpleasant metallic flavor and burning sensation on the tongue. Make your own baking powder by measuring and sifting together, three times, two parts cream of tartar and one part baking soda. Put in a clean, dry container with a tight-fitting lid and store in a cool place away from sunlight. Because it is additive-free, homemade baking powder can settle and clump over time, so you might need to sift again before using. Trust me, the little bit of extra effort is worth it. Homemade baking powder lasts for about four weeks. So make in small batches and use while fresh.

Salt: I prefer kosher or fine sea salt for baking. Both are pure and free of anticaking agents or other additives. Because of its fineness, sea salt measures differently than kosher, so if using sea salt where a measurement for kosher is given, reduce the amount by nearly half.

Fat: All I am saying is give lard a chance! Lard is my preferred fat for making biscuits. It has a very high melting point, so it stays solid longer in the oven, which promotes flakiness and tenderness—much better than tasteless, additive-ridden vegetable shortening, a passable substitute at best. Good lard has a clean, subtle flavor. Lard is usually found in the meat section of your market, or possibly on the shortening aisle. Try to find brands that aren't loaded with preservatives and give it a quick sniff before buying to make sure it hasn't gone rancid. Unsalted butter is another option and it makes a richly flavored biscuit. Whichever you choose, just be sure it is of the best quality and very cold before using. Also, butter and lard absorb flavors and odors easily, so be sure to store well wrapped in the refrigerator.

Liquid: Buttermilk biscuits are my favorite, but you can also make biscuits using regular milk, clabbered milk, heavy cream or half-and-half. Sadly, true buttermilk, the natural by-product of churning cultured butter, is very rarely found these days. The vast majority of what you will find in your market is either skim or whole milk that has had a culture added to it. Either is fine, though obviously, whole buttermilk will make for a slightly richer biscuit. Try different brands and find one with a taste you like, and avoid those that have been artificially flavored or thickened. Buttermilk is typically seasoned with salt, and some are saltier than others. If you find yourself using an especially briny brand, you might want to cut back a little on the salt in the recipe. If you're hankering for some biscuits but don't have any buttermilk on hand, despair not. You can clabber regular milk with a tablespoon of cider vinegar or lemon juice (I like a blend of the two) for every cup. Just stir it in and let it sit for 10 minutes or so to curdle. Because it is thinner than buttermilk, you might need to use a little bit less since it will be absorbed more easily into the flour.

Equipment

Baking pans should be of a good weight that will conduct heat well and bake evenly.

Biscuit cutters should be straight-sided and open on both ends. Size is a matter of preference, but for biscuits to be served as part of a meal, I recommend a cutter that is 2 to 3 inches in diameter. Many recipes suggest a juice glass as an option for stamping out biscuits, but I advise against this. The vacuum created by the glass can compress the biscuit and make it less light.

The type of **rolling pin** you use is up to you, but I prefer the handle-free variety, also known as a "french" rolling pin. If your rolling pin is made of wood, do not wash it. Water will cause the wood grain to swell and open, which will make your pin more likely to stick to your dough. To clean, use your biscuit cutter to scrape off any bits of dough that might be stuck to the pin and wipe well with a clean dry cloth.

Handle with Care

It's true that you need a light hand when making biscuits, but underworking can cause almost as many problems as overworking. While overworking can lead to tough, dry and heavy biscuits, underworking can result in ones that are crumbly and leaden. To get it just right, consider:

- When mixing the dough, stir with a purpose and mix just until the batter is well moistened and begins to come together.

- When kneading, knead gently but quickly, just until the dough forms a cohesive ball. Avoid pressing the dough too firmly and you will be rewarded with lighter biscuits.

- Gently flatten the kneaded dough and use a rolling pin to roll from the center out to the edges. Avoid rolling back and forth as this can overwork the dough.

- Stamp out biscuits as close together as possible to get the maximum yield. Resist the urge to twist the cutter when cutting out the dough. Twisting seals the sides and inhibits rising, a biscuit's most important duty.

- To reroll or not to reroll the scraps: That's a personal decision, but I opt not to. In fact, I very much like the odd bits and pieces of leftover dough baked right alongside the biscuits.

Before You Bake

- Pricking the dough with a fork before baking allows steam to be released during cooking and helps the biscuits rise more evenly. It's also traditional, and tradition counts with me.

- Arrange biscuits on the baking sheet so they almost touch. This will keep the sides from setting too quickly in the hot, hot oven and, as a result, the biscuits are able to rise higher and lighter.

- Bake biscuits in the top third of the oven—the hottest part. They'll bake faster and lighter and develop a better crust.

Serve Them Hot

One of the first stories Miss Lewis told me was of a gentleman from the North who came south to experience Southern cooking—biscuits in particular. When he returned home and was asked how the biscuits were, he sadly replied: "I don't know, I never got to eat one. Every time someone started to bring them to the table, they'd check them and say, "Oops, sorry, they're not hot enough—and disappear back into the kitchen."

While it's true that biscuits are best eaten warm, don't worry if you can't always time them to come straight from the oven. Biscuits can be baked up to a few hours in advance and reheated, uncovered, in a 375-degree oven for three to five minutes until hot.

Be Fearless

Like a dog, biscuit dough can smell fear. But as far as I know, there are no documented cases of a biscuit ever attacking someone. So what if your first batch or two don't turn out like your father's memory of his grandmother's biscuits, or there aren't angels singing when you take your first bite? Practice makes progress, and that's really what it's all about—the satisfaction and enjoyment of learning as you go.

Just ask my mother, who, after 30 years and a little encouragement from her loving son and second and third husbands, now turns out biscuits anyone would be proud to serve.

And even if she should have a bad biscuit day, she can always save the duds for slingshot season.

Scott Peacock's
Hot, Crusty Buttermilk Biscuits

Makes 15 (2½-inch) biscuits
Hands on: 10 minutes
Total time: 20–22 minutes

5 cups sifted White Lily flour (measured after sifting)
1 tablespoon plus 1 ¼ teaspoons homemade baking powder
  (recipe follows)
1 tablespoon kosher salt
¼ cup packed lard, chilled
1 ¾ cups chilled buttermilk, plus a few tablespoons more if
  needed
3 tablespoons unsalted butter, melted

1. Preheat over to 500 degrees. Put the flour, homemade baking powder and salt in a mixing bowl. Whisk well to thoroughly blend. Add the lard and, working quickly, coat in flour and rub between your fingertips until about half the lard is coarsely blended and the other half remains in large pieces about ½ inch in size.

2. Make a well in the flour mixture and pour in the buttermilk. Stir quickly, just until the dough is blended and

begins to mass. The dough should be soft and a bit sticky and there should not be large amounts of unincorporated flour in the bowl. If dough is too dry, add a few tablespoons more buttermilk.

3. Turn the dough immediately onto a generously floured surface, and with floured hands knead briskly 8 to 10 times until a cohesive dough is formed.

4. Gently flatten the dough with your hands so it is of an even thickness. Then, using a floured rolling pin, roll it out to a uniform thickness of ½ inch. (If the dough begins to stick to your rolling pin, dust the pin—not the dough—with flour. Flouring the dough at this point will result in dusty-looking biscuits.) With a dinner fork dipped in flour, pierce the dough completely through at ½-inch intervals.

5. Lightly flour a 2½- or 3-inch biscuit cutter and stamp out rounds. (Do not twist the cutter when stamping out biscuits.) Cut the biscuits from the dough as close together as you can for a maximum yield. Arrange cut biscuits on a heavy, ungreased or parchment-lined baking sheet so that they almost touch. Do not reroll the scraps. Just bake as is and enjoy as a treat.

6. Bake in upper third of the oven for 8 to 12 minutes until crusty golden brown. (Check about 6 minutes into baking and rotate the pan if needed to ensure even cooking.) Remove from the oven and brush with melted butter. Serve hot.

Homemade Baking Powder

Sift together three times ¼ cup cream of tartar and 2 tablespoons baking soda. Transfer to a clean, dry, tight-sealing jar. Store at room temperature, away from direct sunlight, for up to four weeks. Use in any recipe calling for commercial baking powder.

VARIATIONS

- To make biscuits using unbleached all-purpose flour: Increase lard by 2 tablespoons and, if needed, a little extra buttermilk to make a moist and sticky dough.

- To make Cream Biscuits: Increase salt by ½ teaspoon. Instead of lard, substitute an equal amount (½ cup) of cold butter cut into ½-inch pieces. Work in the butter just as you would the lard. Substitute 1 cup heavy cream and 1 cup half-and-half for the buttermilk. Reduce oven heat to 450 degrees. Because they are richer, cream biscuits brown more quickly but also take a little longer to cook through. To be sure they are fully cooked, test one of the biscuits from the center of the tray by gently pulling apart.
- To make Sweet Cream Biscuits: A sweet version of cream biscuits—delicious with tea or as a base for shortcake—can be made by adding 2 to 3 tablespoons granulated or turbinado sugar to the dry ingredients. If desired, a little additional sugar or coarsely crushed sugar cubes can be sprinkled on top of the biscuits before baking. The crushed sugar cubes add an especially interesting appearance and crunch.
- (Note: Because they are so rich, cream biscuits, whether savory or sweet, should always be warmed briefly in the oven before eating.)
- For a perfect Easter brunch splurge: Split and butter a warm biscuit. Top with sliced mushrooms sautéed in butter with a little garlic, a few spears of steamed or blanched asparagus and a soft poached egg. A thin slice of ham can make a nice addition. And if you really want to get fancy, spoon on some hollandaise sauce.

SUMMER EXPRESS: 101 SIMPLE MEALS READY IN 10 MINUTES OR LESS

By Mark Bittman

from the *New York Times*

Simplicity is also the mantra of Mark Bittman, whose best-selling cookbook *How To Cook Everything* is a bible for many home cooks. In his *Times* column The Minimalist, Bittman makes elegant cooking seem downright easy.

The pleasures of cooking are sometimes obscured by summer haze and heat, which can cause many of us to turn instead to bad restaurants and worse takeout. But the cook with a little bit of experience has a wealth of quick and easy alternatives at hand. The trouble is that when it's too hot, even the most resourceful cook has a hard time remembering all the options. So here are 101 substantial main courses, all of which get you in and out of the kitchen in 10 minutes or less. (I'm not counting the time it takes to bring water to a boil, but you can stay out of the kitchen for that.) These suggestions are not formal recipes; rather, they provide a general outline. With a little imagination and some swift moves—and maybe a salad and a loaf of bread—you can turn any dish on this list into a meal that not only will be better than takeout, but won't heat you out of the house.

1. Make six-minute eggs: simmer gently, run under cold water until cool, then peel. Serve over steamed asparagus.

2. Toss a cup of chopped mixed herbs with a few tablespoons of olive oil in a hot pan. Serve over angel-hair pasta, diluting the sauce if necessary with pasta cooking water.

3. Cut eight sea scallops into four horizontal slices each. Arrange on plates. Sprinkle with lime juice, salt and crushed chilies; serve after five minutes.

4. Open a can of white beans and combine with olive oil, salt, small or chopped shrimp, minced garlic and thyme leaves in a pan. Cook, stirring, until the shrimp are done; garnish with more olive oil.

5. Put three pounds of washed mussels in a pot with half a cup of white wine, garlic cloves, basil leaves and chopped tomatoes. Steam until mussels open. Serve with bread.

6. Heat a quarter-inch of olive oil in a skillet. Dredge flounder or sole fillets in flour and fry until crisp, about two minutes a side. Serve on sliced bread with tartar sauce.

7. Make pesto: put a couple of cups of basil leaves, a garlic clove, salt, pepper and olive oil as necessary in a blender (walnuts and Parmesan are optional). Serve over pasta (dilute with oil or water as necessary) or grilled fish or meat.

8. Put a few dozen washed littlenecks in a large, hot skillet with olive oil. When clams begin to open, add a tablespoon or two of chopped garlic. When most or all are opened, add parsley. Serve alone, with bread or over angel-hair pasta.

9. Pan-grill a skirt steak for three or four minutes a side. Sprinkle with salt and pepper, slice and serve over romaine or any other green salad, drizzled with olive oil and lemon.

10. Smear mackerel fillets with mustard, then sprinkle with chopped herbs (fresh tarragon is good), salt, pepper and bread crumbs. Bake in a 425-degree oven for about eight minutes.

11. Warm olive oil in a skillet with at least three cloves sliced garlic. When the garlic colors, add at least a teaspoon each of cumin and pimentón. A minute later, add a dozen or so shrimp, salt and pepper. Garnish with parsley, serve with lemon and bread.

12. Boil a lobster. Serve with lemon or melted butter.

13. Gazpacho: Combine one pound tomatoes cut into chunks, a cucumber peeled and cut into chunks, two or three slices stale

bread torn into pieces, a quarter-cup olive oil, two tablespoons sherry vinegar and a clove of garlic in a blender with one cup water and a couple of ice cubes. Process until smooth, adding water if necessary. Season with salt and pepper, then serve or refrigerate, garnished with anchovies if you like, and a little more olive oil.

14. Put a few slices of chopped prosciutto in a skillet with olive oil, a couple of cloves of crushed garlic and a bit of butter; a minute later, toss in about half a cup bread crumbs and red chili flakes to taste. Serve over pasta with chopped parsley.

15. Call it panini: Grilled cheese with prosciutto, tomatoes, thyme or basil leaves.

16. Slice or chop salami, corned beef or kielbasa and warm in a little oil; stir in eggs and scramble. Serve with mustard and rye bread.

17. Soak couscous in boiling water to cover until tender; top with sardines, tomatoes, parsley, olive oil and black pepper.

18. Stir-fry a pound or so of ground meat or chopped fish mixed with chopped onions and seasoned with cumin or chili powder. Pile into taco shells or soft tacos, along with tomato, lettuce, canned beans, onion, cilantro and sour cream.

19. Chinese tomato and eggs: Cook minced garlic in peanut oil until blond; add chopped tomatoes then, a minute later, beaten eggs, along with salt and pepper. Scramble with a little soy sauce.

20. Cut eggplant into half-inch slices. Broil with lots of olive oil, turning once, until tender and browned. Top with crumbled goat or feta cheese and broil another 20 seconds.

21. While pasta cooks, combine a couple cups chopped tomatoes, a teaspoon or more minced garlic, olive oil and 20 to 30 basil leaves. Toss with pasta, salt, pepper and Parmesan.

22. Make wraps of tuna, warm white beans, a drizzle of olive oil and lettuce and tomato.

23. The New York supper: Bagels, cream cheese, smoked salmon. Serve with tomatoes, watercress or arugula, and sliced red onion or shallot.

24. Dredge thinly sliced chicken breasts in flour or cornmeal; cook about two minutes a side in hot olive oil. Place on bread with lettuce, tomato and mayonnaise.

25. Upscale tuna salad: good canned tuna (packed in olive oil), capers, dill or parsley, lemon juice but no mayo. Use to stuff a tomato or two.

26. Cut Italian sausage into chunks and brown in a little olive oil; chop onions and bell peppers and add them to the pan. Cook until sausage is browned and peppers and onions tender. Serve in sandwiches.

27. Egg in a hole, glorified: Tear a hole in a piece of bread and fry in butter. Crack an egg into the hole. Deglaze pan with a little sherry vinegar mixed with water, and more butter; pour over egg.

28. New Joe's Special, from San Francisco: Brown ground meat with minced garlic and chopped onion. When just about cooked, add chopped spinach and cook, stirring, until wilted. At the last minute, stir in two eggs, along with grated Parmesan and salt and pepper.

29. Chop prosciutto and crisp it in a skillet with olive oil; add chopped not-too-ripe figs. Serve over greens dressed with oil and vinegar; top all with crumbled blue cheese.

30. Quesadilla: Use a combination of cheeses, like Fontina mixed with grated pecorino. Put on half of a large flour tortilla with pickled jalapenos, chopped onion, shallot or scallion, chopped tomatoes and grated radish. Fold tortilla over and brown on both sides in butter or oil, until cheese is melted.

31. Fast chile rellenos: Drain canned whole green chilies. Make a slit in each and insert a piece of cheese. Dredge in flour and fry in a skillet, slit side up, until cheese melts.

32. Cobb-ish salad: Chop bacon and begin to brown it; cut boneless chicken into strips and cook it with bacon. Toss romaine and watercress or arugula with chopped tomatoes, avocado, onion and crumbled blue cheese. Add bacon and chicken. Dress with oil and vinegar.

33. Sauté 10 whole peeled garlic cloves in olive oil. Meanwhile, grate Pecorino, grind lots of black pepper, chop parsley and cook pasta. Toss all together, along with crushed dried chili flakes and salt.

34. Niçoise salad: Lightly steam haricot verts, green beans or asparagus. Arrange on a plate with chickpeas, good canned tuna,

hard-cooked eggs, a green salad, sliced cucumber and tomato. Dress with oil and vinegar.

35. Cold soba with dipping sauce: Cook soba noodles, then rinse in cold water until cool. Serve with a sauce of soy sauce and minced ginger diluted with mirin and/or dry sake.

36. Fried egg "saltimbocca": Lay slices of prosciutto or ham in a buttered skillet. Fry eggs on top of ham; top with grated Parmesan.

37. Frisée aux lardons: Cook chunks of bacon in a skillet. Meanwhile, make six-minute or poached eggs and a frisée salad. Put eggs on top of salad along with bacon; deglaze pan with sherry vinegar and pour pan juices over all.

38. Fried rice: Soften vegetables with oil in a skillet. Add cold takeout rice, chopped onion, garlic, ginger, peas and two beaten eggs. Toss until hot and cooked through. Season with soy sauce and sesame oil.

39. Taco salad: Toss together greens, chopped tomato, chopped red onion, sliced avocado, a small can of black beans and kernels from a couple of ears of corn. Toss with crumbled tortilla chips and grated cheese. Dress with olive oil, lime and chopped cilantro leaves.

40. Put a large can of chickpeas and their liquid in a medium saucepan. Add some sherry, along with olive oil, plenty of minced garlic, smoked pimentón and chopped Spanish chorizo. Heat through.

41. Raita to the rescue: Broil any fish. Serve with a sauce of drained yogurt mixed with chopped cucumber, minced onion and cayenne.

42. Season boneless lamb steaks cut from the leg with sweet curry powder. Sear on both sides. Serve over greens, with lemon wedges.

43. *Migas*, with egg: Sauté chopped stale bread with olive oil, mushrooms, onions and spinach. Stir in a couple of eggs.

44. *Migas*, without egg: Sauté chopped stale bread with chopped Spanish chorizo, plenty of garlic and lots of olive oil. Finish with chopped parsley.

45. Sauté shredded zucchini in olive oil, adding garlic and chopped herbs. Serve over pasta.

46. Broil a few slices prosciutto until crisp; crumble and toss with parsley, Parmesan, olive oil and pasta.

47. Not exactly *banh mi*, but . . . Make sandwiches on crisp bread with liverwurst, ham, sliced half-sours, shredded carrots, cilantro sprigs and Vietnamese chili-garlic paste.

48. Not takeout: Stir-fry onions with cut-up broccoli. Add cubed tofu, chicken or shrimp, or sliced beef or pork, along with a tablespoon each minced garlic and ginger. When almost done, add half cup of water, two tablespoons soy sauce and plenty of black pepper. Heat through and serve over fresh Chinese noodles.

49. Sprinkle sole fillets with chopped parsley, garlic, salt and pepper; roll up, dip in flour, then beaten egg, then bread crumbs; cook in hot olive oil about three minutes a side. Serve with lemon wedges.

50. The Waldorf: Toast a handful of walnuts in a skillet. Chop an apple or pear; toss with greens, walnuts and a dressing made with olive oil, sherry vinegar, Dijon mustard and shallot. Top, if you like, with crumbled goat or blue cheese.

51. Put a stick of butter and a handful of pine nuts in a skillet. Cook over medium heat until both are brown. Toss with cooked pasta, grated Parmesan and black pepper.

52. Grill or sauté Italian sausage and serve over store-bought hummus, with lemon wedges.

53. Put a tablespoon of cream and a slice of tomato in each of several small ramekins. Top with an egg, then salt, pepper and grated Parmesan. Bake at 350 degrees until the eggs set. Serve with toast.

54. Brown small pork (or hot dog) chunks in a skillet. Add white beans, garlic, thyme and olive oil. Or add white beans and ketchup.

55. Dredge skate or flounder in flour and brown quickly in butter or oil. Deglaze pan with a couple of spoonfuls of capers and a lot of lemon juice or a little vinegar.

56. Make a fast tomato sauce of olive oil, chopped tomatoes and garlic. Poach eggs in the sauce, then top with Parmesan.

57. Dip pork cutlets in egg, then dredge heavily in panko; brown quickly on both sides. Serve over lettuce, with fresh lemon, or bottled Japanese curry sauce.

58. Cook chicken livers in butter or oil with garlic; do not over-cook. Finish with parsley, lemon juice and coarse salt; serve over toast.

59. Brown bratwursts with cut-up apples. Serve with coleslaw.

60. Peel and thinly slice raw beets; cook in butter until soft. Take out of pan and quickly cook some shrimp in same pan. Deglaze pan with sherry vinegar, adding sauce to beets and shrimp. Garnish with dill.

61. Poach shrimp and plunge into ice water. Serve with cocktail sauce: one cup ketchup, one tablespoon vinegar, three tablespoons melted butter and lots of horseradish.

62. Southeast Asia steak salad: Pan- or oven-grill skirt or flank steak. Slice and serve on a pile of greens with a sauce of one table-spoon each of *nam pla* and lime juice, black pepper, a teaspoon each of sugar and garlic, crushed red chili flakes and Thai basil.

63. Miso steak: Coat beef tenderloin steaks (filet mignon) with a blend of miso and chili paste thinned with sake or white wine. Grill or broil about five minutes.

64. Pasta with fresh tomatoes: Cook chopped fresh tomatoes in butter or oil with garlic until tender, while pasta cooks. Combine and serve with grated Parmesan.

65. Sauté squid rings and tentacles in olive oil with salt and pep-per and garlic; add chopped tomatoes. Cook until the tomatoes break down. Serve over pasta.

66. Salmon (or just about anything else) teriyaki: Sear salmon steaks on both sides for a couple of minutes; remove. To skillet, add a splash of water, sake, a little sugar and soy sauce; when mixture is thick, return steaks to pan and turn in sauce until done. Serve hot or at room temperature.

67. Rich vegetable soup: Cook asparagus tips and peeled stalks or most any other green vegetable in chicken stock with a little tarragon until tender; reserve a few tips and purée the rest with a little butter (cream or yogurt, too, if you like) adding enough stock to thin the purée. Garnish with the reserved tips. Serve hot or cold.

68. Brush portobello caps with olive oil; sprinkle with salt and pepper and broil until tender. Briefly sweat chopped onions, then scramble eggs with them. Put eggs in mushrooms.

69. Buy good blintzes. Brown them on both sides in butter. Serve with sour cream, apple sauce or both.

70. Sauté squid rings and tentacles in olive oil with salt and pepper. Make a sauce of minced garlic, smoked pimentón, mayo, lots of lemon juice and fresh parsley. Serve with a chopped salad of cucumber, tomato, lettuce, grated carrot and scallion, lightly dressed.

71. Press a lot of coarsely ground black pepper onto both sides of filet mignon or other steaks or chopped meat patties. Brown in butter in a skillet for two minutes a side. Remove steaks and add a splash of red wine, chopped shallots and a bit of tarragon to skillet. Reduce, then return steaks to pan, turning in the sauce for a minute or two.

72. World's leading sandwich: prosciutto, tomato, butter or olive oil and a baguette.

73. Near instant mezze: Combine hummus on a plate with yogurt laced with chopped cucumbers and a bit of garlic, plus tomato, feta, white beans with olive oil and pita bread.

74. Canned sardines packed in olive oil on Triscuits, with mustard and Tabasco.

75. Boil-and-eat shrimp, cooked in water with Old Bay seasoning or a mixture of thyme, garlic, paprika, chopped onion, celery, chili, salt and pepper.

76. Make a thin plain omelet with two or three eggs. Sauté cubes of bacon or pancetta or strips of prosciutto until crisp. Cut up the omelet and use it and the meat to garnish a green salad dressed with olive oil and balsamic vinegar.

77. Sear corn kernels in olive oil with minced jalapeños and chopped onions; toss with cilantro, black beans, chopped tomatoes, chopped bell pepper and lime.

78. Cook shrimp in a skillet slowly (five minutes or so) to preserve their juices, with plenty of garlic and olive oil, until done; pour over watercress or arugula, with lemon, pepper and salt.

79. Liverwurst on good sourdough rye with scallions, tomato and whole grain mustard.

80. Not-quite *merguez*: Ground lamb burgers seasoned with cumin, garlic, onion, salt and cayenne. Serve with couscous and green salad, along with bottled *harissa*.

81. Combine crabmeat with mayo, Dijon mustard, chives and tarragon. Serve in a sandwich, with potato chips.

82. Combine canned tuna in olive oil, halved grape tomatoes, black olives, mint, lemon zest and red pepper flakes. Serve with pasta, thinning with olive oil or pasta cooking water as needed.

83. Pit and chop a cup or more of mixed olives. Combine with olive oil, a little minced garlic, red pepper flakes and chopped basil or parsley. Serve over pasta.

84. Cook chopped tomatillos with a little water or stock, cilantro and a little minced fresh chili; serve over grilled, broiled or sautéed chicken breasts, with corn tortillas.

85. A winning sandwich: bresaola or prosciutto, arugula, Parmesan, marinated artichoke hearts, tomato.

86. Smoked trout fillets served with lightly toasted almonds, shredded fennel, a drizzle of olive oil and a sprinkle of lemon.

87. Grated carrots topped with six-minute eggs (run under cold water until cool before peeling), olive oil and lemon juice.

88. Cut the top off four big tomatoes; scoop out the interiors and mix them with toasted stale baguette or pita, olive oil, salt, pepper and herbs (basil, tarragon, and/or parsley). Stuff into tomatoes and serve with salad.

89. Pasta frittata: Turn cooked pasta and a little garlic into an oiled or buttered skillet. Brown, pressing to create a cake. Flip, then top with three or four beaten eggs and loads of Parmesan. Brown other side and serve.

90. Thai-style beef: Thinly slice one and a half pounds of flank steak, pork shoulder or boneless chicken; heat peanut oil in a skillet, add meat and stir. A minute later, add a tablespoon minced garlic and some red chili flakes. Add 30 clean basil leaves, a quarter cup of water and a tablespoon or two of soy sauce or *nam pla*. Serve with lime juice and more chili flakes, over rice or salad.

91. Dredge calf's liver in flour. Sear in olive oil or butter or a combination until crisp on both sides, adding salt and pepper as it cooks; it should be medium-rare. Garnish with parsley and lemon juice.

92. Rub not-too-thick pork or lamb chops with olive oil; sprinkle with salt and pepper plus sage or thyme. Broil about three minutes a side and drizzle with good balsamic vinegar.

93. Cut up Italian sausage into chunks and brown in a little olive oil until just about done. Dump in a lot of seedless grapes and, if you like, a little slivered garlic and chopped rosemary. Cook, stirring, until the grapes are hot. Serve with bread.

94. Ketchup-braised tofu: Dredge large tofu cubes in flour. Brown in oil; remove from skillet and wipe skillet clean. Add a little more oil, then a tablespoon of minced garlic; 30 seconds later, add one and a half cups ketchup and the tofu. Cook until sauce bubbles and tofu is hot.

95. Veggie burger: Drain and pour a 14-ounce can of beans into a food processor with an onion, half a cup rolled oats, a tablespoon chili powder or other spice mix, an egg, salt and pepper. Process until mushy, then shape into burgers, adding a little liquid or oats as necessary. Cook in oil about three minutes a side and serve.

96. A Roman classic: In lots of olive oil, lightly cook lots of slivered garlic, with six or so anchovy fillets and a dried hot chili or two. Dress pasta with this.

97. So-called Fettuccine Alfredo: Heat several tablespoons of butter and about half a cup of cream in a large skillet just until the cream starts to simmer. Add slightly undercooked fresh pasta to the skillet, along with plenty of grated Parmesan. Cook over low heat, tossing, until pasta is tender and hot.

98. Rub flank steak or chuck with curry or chili powder before broiling or grilling, then slice thin across the grain.

99. Cook a couple of pounds of shrimp, shell on or off, in oil, with lots of chopped garlic. When they turn pink, remove; deglaze the pan with a half-cup or so of beer, along with a splash of Worcestershire sauce, cayenne, rosemary and a lump of butter. Serve with bread.

100. Cook red lentils in water with a little cumin and chopped bacon until soft. Top with poached or six-minute eggs (run under cold water until cool before peeling) and a little sherry vinegar.

101. Hot dogs on buns—with beans!

Stocking the Pantry

Dead Meat

By Guy Saddy

from *enRoute*

Based in Vancouver, Guy Saddy is an incredibly prolific free-lancer who reports on everything from movies to music to lifestyles to, of course, food.

Considering the setting, it was hardly an auspicious occasion. I was in downtown Los Angeles, dining in a converted railway car open 24 hours a day. Expectations: way low. Since the Pacific Dining Car was ostensibly a steak house, I ordered a rib steak. It arrived in classic steak house fashion, on a plate as naked as a newborn. I took a bite. And then, something quite unexpected happened. Clouds parted; a chorus of angels mooed. My steak was amazing: nutty, overwhelmingly beefy. It was an epiphany, the Holy Grail of saturated fat. It was the most exquisite piece of beef I'd ever encountered.

The reason? It was dry-aged, a process of aging beef that, after falling out of practice for decades, is on the rise again. Although not uncommon in New York City's fabled steak joints, elsewhere dry-aged beef has been—pardon the pun—rare. But increasingly, specialty butchers and select restaurants are rediscovering a technique, and a taste, that harkens to a time when great care went into the preparation of all worthwhile things—long before family packs of stringy sirloin changed the very idea of how meat should taste.

All beef needs to be aged. Steak fresh off the cow tastes like boiled shoe and is about as chewy. As meat ages, enzymes break down the muscle fibres, making it tender. The longer beef ages, the more tender it becomes (until about a month, beyond which only minute changes occur). Until the 1960s, there was really only one way to age beef—dry-aging, in which whole or partial carcasses are hung in a temperature-controlled freezer until ready for sale. Problem: Through dehydration and spoilage, almost one percent of the weight is lost for every day aged. To counter this, about 40 years ago producers began vacuum-sealing beef in bags, which aged beef in its own blood. The advantage? Much less shrinkage, waste and moisture loss. In other words, it was much more cost-effective, allowing butchers to maximize profits while still offering customers comparably tender cuts. But in this great march forward, something important was lost.

Although I am hardly Proust, steak is my madeleine, triggering dusty remembrances from childhood. In the late 1960s, after my father started to earn well, our family would frequent the Steak Loft, one of Edmonton's first high-end steak houses. The dimly lit room was a clichéd mix of red and black, a colour scheme that, perhaps not coincidentally, evoked the image of a charred, rare filet. The Steak Loft's beef was amazing, but back in the days before cholesterol, steak meant more than just good food. Eating steak regularly was an ostentatious symbol of how far you'd come, like owning a gold Rolex or a winter place in Palm Springs.

Over the years, however, as incomes rose and more boats floated, steak became accessible, an everyday meal. Demand went up; competition, intensified by the miracle of wet-aging, drove prices down. Steak became available to all, a triumph of free-market forces. But production efficiencies do not always make better products. Unlike wet-aged beef, dry-aged beef develops a highly concentrated flavour as it ages, a side effect of its moisture loss. This intensity of taste is what I had fallen for and, perhaps, vaguely recalled from years ago. And it's what's sadly lacking in bland, supermarket products that, through their ubiquity, have come to define what a steak should be.

This, of course, is simple gospel to those at the forefront of the dry-age revival (see sidebar) and to their acolytes, like the zealots who try do-it-yourself dry-aging at home, which can be done, but not easily. (Refrigerator temperature must hover just above freezing, with a constant humidity of 80 to 85 percent and a steady air movement of around five kilometres an hour. Plus, you cannot age individual steaks—just very large, fatty cuts.) Clearly, home-aging is strictly for those who want a little danger with their dinner.

Since my DIY ambitions are more modest (buy steak, grill steak, eat steak), I head to Sebastian & Co. in West Vancouver, where owner Sebastian Cortez removes a large rib from his freezer and places it on a butcher block. After 40 days, the rock-hard purplish-black surface is the texture of a mummified corpse, and I remember that dry-aging is basically "controlled rotting." But underneath the outer crust is a beautiful burgundy-coloured rib steak, which Cortez cuts 1¼ inches thick. After trimming, there's still a mouldy rind on the fat. "Go ahead, smell it," he says. I lean in and inhale. "Blue cheese, right?" I say excitedly. Cortez nods. "And underneath," I exclaim, "a hint of Bordeaux!" Cortez is too polite to roll his eyes. For comparison purposes, I ask for another steak from another rib, aged just 18 days. I leave carrying two kilograms of meat.

At home, I brush the steaks with olive oil, apply kosher salt and freshly ground pepper. Sear, then finish with indirect heat. About fifteen minutes later, et voilà. The 18-day aged steak is excellent. But the 40-day-old steak is unbelievable—ridiculously flavourful, a steak with gravitas, a Proustian piece of meat that transports me back to an era when the very idea of vacuum-bagged beef would have been anathema to all right-thinking persons. A few bites in, and something else strikes me. More salient than what I taste is what I do not. With dry-aged steaks, you don't taste blood. Today, it's the taste of blood that we know as meat.

I was looking for something to sum that up. Coincidentally, Proust came through:"The only paradise is paradise lost." Smart guy.

The Belly of the Beast

By Kathleen Purvis

from the *Charlotte Observer*

The presiding spirit behind this large North Carolina daily's esteemed weekly food section, Kathleen Purvis has a frank, friendly style that makes readers trust her expertise, whether she's judging barbecue, making the perfect piecrust, or rating trendy new restaurants.

M eat in the middle. Soul on the edge.

Pork belly inspires thoughts like that for me. Maybe it's just the fat rushing to my brain.

But when I introduce someone to pork belly—to soft meat surrounded by fat that is meltingly tender on the inside and crisp on the outside—what I usually hear (through the moans) is, "that is to die for."

"Yes," I reply cheerfully. "And with that in your arteries, it won't be long."

Pork belly, of all things, has become a food world darling. "It's bacon, something you already know and love, just in a different form," says Joseph Bonaparte, the culinary dean at the Art Institute of Charlotte.

Before you blame me, blame Bonaparte, my pork belly enabler. He's the one who gave me my first bite. At a Taste of the Nation event three years ago, Bonaparte and chef-instructor Mark Martin served a blue cheese–walnut cracker topped with a dab of strawberry-rhubarb jam and a slice of braised, seared pork belly. One bite, and my world stood still for a minute.

The meat was both crispy and meltingly soft, sort of like foie gras when it's seared just right. Set off by the savory cracker and the sweet jam, it was pork, but better. It was bacon, but better.

In New York right now, you can cross the city on a pork belly high. At the sleek bistro Tailor in Soho, it's cut into tender slices and tiled across a salty-sweet sauce of butterscotch and miso. At Szechuan Gourmet on West 39th, it's cut thin and double-cooked, like chewy slices of country ham, in a stir-fry of leeks in hot chili sauce. At David Chang's so-hot-they're-cool Momofuku restaurants, it's tucked into soft-steamed buns with hoisin and scallions.

It's in Charlotte, too. At Ratcliffe on the Green, chef-owner Mark Hibbs is serving slices of pork belly with tiny puy lentils, a decadent midwinter riff on pork and beans. At Table, chef Gene Briggs likes to use pork belly to cure his own bacon for a striped bass dish and for salads. He's also used braised belly as an appetizer or in a main dish. "One of our favorite things to do is pair it with scallops. Scallops and bacon, it's just classic. It works really, really well."

For chefs, pork belly is part of the movement toward rediscovering old cuts. "It's like oxtail or shank or shoulder," says Bonaparte. "It's taking the underutilized stuff, the cuts that require more knowledge and skills. You're seeing a lot of educated cooks with good techniques, and they're looking for more than just searing a beef tenderloin. They really want to feature their skills."

In other words, it's more challenge—and more fun—to take trash and make treasure.

"The greatest pleasure is taking the underutilized cuts and making people say, 'Wow—that was good.' Delighting and surprising the guest—that's what every chef wants to do."

THAT'S THE THING ABOUT PORK BELLY. Eat it a couple of times, and you want to play with it.

Facing a week off in February with nothing to do but hang out at home, I took the plunge. I called Bucky Frick, the meat manager at Reid's Fine Foods in 7th Street Station, and ordered 5 pounds. I also left a message at Grateful Growers Farm in Denver, North Carolina, wondering whether they had any pork belly from their old-breed, pastured-raised pigs.

The next morning at the Matthews Community Farmers Market, I stopped by the Grateful Growers stand. Co-owner Natalie Veres opened a cooler and hefted out a large plastic bag. "We didn't know how much you wanted, so we brought you a whole one."

A whole one? It was 11 1/2 pounds of pork belly, rolled up like a summer camp mattress of pink meat and white fat. Combined with my Reid's order, I suddenly had 16 pounds of pork belly.

I cut it all down into 3-pound sections and got to work. To re-create Bonaparte's seared pork belly, I rubbed one section with a mixture of salt, sugar, pepper, ginger, garlic and herbs and refrigerated it for three days. Then I braised it for four hours and chilled it under a weight.

While I waited for that, I turned to Emeril Lagasse, the pork fat king. His recipe for slow-cooked pork belly with a tangerine glaze became my Fat Tuesday dinner, paired with seared mustard greens and sweet potatoes. Leftovers got sliced and fried for breakfast on one memorable winter morning. At Park Road Books, Frazer Dobson helped me track down a recipe for curing bacon from *The River Cafe Meat Book*. Michael Ruhlman's book *Charcuterie* led to a maple-cured version.

By the end of the week, my family was begging for a rest.

If there's a nutritional upside to pork belly, it's this: You can only eat a little at a time. Maybe that's why bacon is sliced so thin.

After I finished all my experiments, I did something bold. I made my own version of Bonaparte's original dish, this time served on cheddar mustard crackers with strawberry jam. Then I packed it up and drove over to the school, to feed the chef his own dish.

We sat in the empty dining room, sampling his version and mine and considering how something so simple can capture your imagination. "We're just going back in time," he said, pausing over a forkful.

"Our culture got so used to just using prime cuts, we didn't even see the oxtails and the shanks and the short ribs.

"Now people are more interested in quality, in things that taste more like beef, more like chicken, more like pork."

Oh, and my version? He admitted it was even better.

---- ∞ ----

Crisp Pork Belly on Cheddar Crackers

Makes 8 to 10 servings. From Joseph Bonaparte of the
Art Institute of Charlotte.

2 to 3 pounds fresh pork belly
4 tablespoons kosher salt
1 tablespoon sugar
1 tablespoon freshly cracked black pepper
1 tablespoon minced fresh gingerroot
1 tablespoon minced fresh garlic
1 tablespoon minced fresh rosemary
1 tablespoon fresh thyme leaves
1 tablespoon fresh sage leaves
1 onion, peeled and sliced
1 carrot, peeled and sliced
1 stalk celery, sliced
About 3 to 4 cups apple juice or fresh apple cider
1 to 2 cups chicken stock or water
Strawberry jam
Cheddar-mustard crackers (see recipe)

1. Mix the salt, sugar, pepper, ginger, garlic, rosemary, thyme and sage. Rub all over the pork belly, coating it well. Wrap tightly with plastic wrap and refrigerate for 1 to 3 days.

2. Preheat the oven to 250 degrees. Unwrap the pork and rinse off the seasoning mix, then dry with paper towels.

3. Place the sliced onions, carrots and celery in a roasting pan large enough to hold the pork. Add enough apple juice or cider to come halfway up the pork. Add enough stock or water to come 3/4 of the way up the meat. Cover the meat with parchment paper, then cover the pan tightly with heavy duty foil and a lid.

4. Place in the oven and cook about 6 hours, or until very tender. Line a jellyroll pan or cookie sheet with parchment paper. Carefully remove the pork belly from the cooking liq-

uid, lifting from the bottom with a couple of spatulas so it doesn't fall apart. Place it on the paper-lined pan, and place another sheet of parchment on top. Place another pan on top, then weigh it down with several pounds (such as heavy cans).

5. Refrigerate overnight. The cooking liquid can be strained and used for another recipe, such as soup. Remove from refrigerator, remove weights and peel off the paper. (Can be made to this point up to 4 days ahead. Refrigerate until ready to serve.)

6. Slice the firm pork belly into 1-by–2-inch cubes. Place in a skillet over medium-high heat and sear, turning carefully with tongs, until browned and crisped on all sides. Serve on a cheddar cracker with a dab of jam.

Cheddar-Mustard Crackers

Makes about 4 dozen. Adapted from Gourmet *magazine.*

Even if you don't top them with pork belly, these are tasty to keep on hand for entertaining. The dough can be made in advance and frozen. We used White Lily flour in testing.

2 sticks (1 cup) unsalted butter, softened
1 pound sharp cheddar, coarsely grated (preferably in a food processor; 5 cups)
1 large egg yolk
¼ teaspoon Dijon mustard
2 tablespoons dry mustard
¼ cup brown or yellow mustard seeds (we reduced to 2 table-spoons, which worked fine)
2 teaspoons salt
2 cups all-purpose flour, plus more for surface

1. Blend butter, cheese and egg yolk in a food processor until smooth. Add mustards, salt and flour and pulse just until combined. Transfer the soft dough to a bowl. Cover and chill 15 minutes.

2. Halve the dough and shape each half into a 12-inch log on a lightly floured surface. Wrap in wax paper and foil, chill until firm, at least 4 hours. (Dough can be frozen for several months. Defrost in the refrigerator before slicing.)

3. Place oven racks in upper and lower thirds of the oven and preheat to 350 degrees. Line 2 baking sheets with parchment paper (or nonstick baking mat, such as Silpat). Unwrap logs and cut into 1/8-inch-thick slices with a sharp knife. Place slices on baking sheet about 1 inch apart.

4. Bake until lightly brown around edges, switching position of pans halfway through baking, 12 to 15 minutes. Cool on a rack. Cool crackers and store in an airtight container.

Tangerine-Glazed Pork Belly

About 6 servings. Adapted from a recipe by Emeril Lagasse at www.foodtv.com.

Although Lagasse serves this on a salad of bitter greens, we served it as a main dish with sautéed mustard greens and roasted sweet potatoes.

4 to 5 pounds pork belly, cut into 5-by-3-inch portions
Salt and freshly ground pepper
1 large onion, coarsely chopped
2 carrots, peeled, halved and sliced
2 ribs celery, sliced
4 ¼ cups chicken stock
¾ cup sugar
4 cups tangerine juice, divided (8 to 10 tangerines, or use navel oranges, or a combination of oranges and tangerines)
¼ cup packed light brown sugar
4 sprigs fresh thyme
4 whole cloves
½ teaspoon whole allspice (or 1 teaspoon ground)

1. Heat broiler. Using a large knife, score the fat side of the belly diagonally, and season with salt and pepper on all sides. Place the onion, carrots and celery in the bottom of a large

roasting pan. Place the pork belly, scored side up, on top of the vegetables. Broil until golden brown, about 15 minutes. Turn meat-side up and broil 10 minutes.

2. Remove the pan from the oven and reduce the temperature to 300 degrees. Turn pork scored-side up and add chicken stock, 2 cups tangerine juice, brown sugar, thyme, cloves and allspice, stirring around the pan to combine. Cover the pan tightly with foil and bake 2 hours. Fold back the foil to create a vent and bake 2 hours longer, or until the meat is very tender.

3. Prepare the tangerine glaze while the meat is cooking: Using a fine wire-meshed sieve, strain pulp out of remaining 2 cups juice. Combine juice and sugar in a medium saucepan and bring to a boil. Reduce heat to a gentle boil and cook until the glaze is thick and syrupy, 30 to 40 minutes. (Watch carefully so it doesn't boil over. The glaze should be thick enough to coat the back of a spoon.)

4. Remove pan from the oven and cool pork slightly in the braising liquid. (Can be made to this point several hours in advance and refrigerated in the braising liquid. Rewarm it about 30 minutes before continuing.)

5. Heat broiler. Remove the pork belly from the braising liquid and pat dry. Brush on all sides with the tangerine blaze. Place on a baking sheet lined with foil and broil 4 to 5 minutes, or until crispy around the edges and golden brown. Drizzle with remaining glaze and serve.

BUTTER: A LOVE STORY

By Molly O'Neill

from *Saveur*

Molly O'Neill has slaved in hot restaurant kitchens, gone to
cooking school (La Varenne), written a best-selling cookbook
(*The New York Times Cookbook*), and published an affecting
memoir (*Mostly True*), yet somehow she still can rhapsodize
over something as simple as butter.

"Anything can be improved with a little *but*-tor," Julia
Child once told me, as we readied a chicken to roast
for dinner in her Cambridge, Massachusetts, home. She shoved a
handful of softened butter between the animal's raw flesh and its
skin and then, scooping up another lavish sufficiency of the stuff
with her fingers, massaged it over the entire exterior of the bird.

This was early on in the Gourmet Revolution—1979, if memory serves—and the butter we were using was your basic grocery
store brick, not the chic little paper-wrapped ingots many small
creameries are producing today. Still, I'd always believed that any
butter was better than no butter. It could gently baste and enrich
roasted foods and also snap and sizzle in a hot pan as it browned
ingredients to a flavorful crispness. It could be whipped into cake
frosting, give lift and crumb to pastries, and lend body and luster to
all sorts of sauces. Whether used as a cooking medium or as a flavoring, butter was the wonder fat: it made bridges between oppo-
sites, eased stark contrasts, and mellowed sharp flavors. Back then,
butter elevated ordinary life to epicurean adventure. Butter was
good.

And then butter was bad.

And now butter is back.

Of course, to some it remains an all but forbidden saturated fat. But as recent studies revealed the health risks posed by artificially produced trans fats—those partially hydrogenated plant oils that give many margarines and shortenings a solidity akin to butter's—butter rose again as an emblem of honest food. Indeed, what I want when I eat butter is the same thing I want when I hang a picture of a sun-dappled landscape on the wall: to be reminded of something real and enduring, a part of the world to which I can always return. Like a painting, the taste of butter takes you places.

BUTTER EXISTS AROUND THE GLOBE in wildly different guises, from the mild-tasting, soldierly supermarket sticks found in the States to the pungently flavored preserved versions stored in earthenware vessels across the Middle East. It's an ancient source of protein and fat: well before the modern era, many animal-herding cultures had independently developed methods for butter production that were tailored to their particular climate. In warm regions, for example, butter was often fermented or clarified to prevent the rapid onset of rancidity. Cow's milk is the most popular source of butter, but the milk of sheep, goats, buffalo, and yaks can also be churned and kneaded to make butter.

In every case, the science is the same: cream is agitated by whipping or churning until the fat globules within it are broken up, causing them to bond with other fats and congeal into a solid mass. In *On Food and Cooking* (Scribner, 1984), the food writer Harold McGee counsels, "[A]ll cooks should relax now and then and intentionally overwhip some cream! The coming of butter is an everyday miracle." If the cream has been allowed to sour, or "ripen," slightly before it's churned, the result is the tangy cultured butter favored across most of Europe. Britons and Americans tend to prefer sweet cream butter, made from fresh cream. And in agrarian communities, it is possible to find raw-cream butter (made from unpasteurized milk), which has a fresh, grassy, and—to most people who have sampled it—unforgettably delicious flavor.

History tells us that butter made on the farm almost always had very distinct, if not always distinctive, tastes. Before refrigeration, butter produced in coastal areas was sometimes stored in cold seawater and thus yielded flavors more reminiscent of surf than of turf. In Ireland, Scotland, and parts of Scandinavia, butter was packed in barrels and stored in peat bogs—a method whose fruits I've mercifully never sampled. In pre-industrial America, according to Richard Hooker's *Food and Drink in America: A History* (Bobbs-Merrill, 1981), butter frequently tasted of winter vegetables, like turnips and cabbage, because it was stored alongside them in cellars and winter barns.

By the middle part of the 19th century, the advent of refrigeration, coupled with advances in the technology of mass production and distribution, made fresh, sweet-tasting butter widely available in industrializing countries. It was a democratizing moment in the history of butter, but then, butters that are created equally tend to taste and look and cook the same. Accordingly, by the middle of the 20th century, most Americans didn't think of butter as an agricultural product anymore. Thus margarine—which cost less than butter, could be produced in a factory, and was, for a time, championed by the American Heart Association as a heart-healthy butter substitute—was primed to become America's fat du jour.

A food sleuth retracing the events of the past half century in the West need only follow butter to discover the culinary ethos of a given era. Though the sales of margarine in this country had eclipsed those of butter by 1960, a backlash was stirring. Butter, chefs hastened to remind us, is the very foundation of fine cooking; there were reasons why the people of Belle Époque France lusted for it. Leading the counterinsurgency in the early 1970s was Madeleine Kamman, the French-born culinary guru who taught classes to American chefs and home cooks throughout the Northeast and in France. She embarked on a butter-thickened-sauce campaign that was aimed at stamping out floury, dowdy old roux-thickened sauces.

Thickening with butter, or mounting—which entails the whisking of chips of very cold butter into a heated sauce—wasn't new, but it was a bedrock principle of nouvelle cuisine, which was being minted in France around that time by chefs like Michel Guérard and the Troisgros brothers. The theory was that butter added in this way lightened sauces and allowed the accompanying flavors to shine. Armed with Kamman's book *The Making of a Cook* (Atheneum, 1971), which promoted the technique, a generation of young American chefs laid the groundwork for an American version of nouvelle cuisine. (That said, many cooks of the day felt that the revolution's new butter theory went a little too far, and I won't contest the point: an old-fashioned roux can be a thing of buttery beauty, a quiet and understated presence down deep in the soul of a béchamel or a velouté.)

By the late 1970s, young warriors of taste were championing butter with a monomaniacal passion. Restaurant menus were slick with the stuff: compound butters, seasoned with everything from garlic to basil, were tucked into bread baskets and served atop steaks. Many pastry chefs insisted, for instance, that the crusts for all tarts and pies be made with butter—take that, Crisco!—even though, truth be told, the result was often too much heft and not enough flake.

By the 1990s, the pendulum had begun to swing back again. Riding a wave of dietary-health research on the benefits of the Mediterranean diet, olive oil began to replace butter as the fat of choice in the United States. Tasting oils from Morocco, Italy, California, and elsewhere, we began to understand how tiny variations in flavor bespeak place and climate and offer windows onto diverse worlds.

The food writer Waverley Root understood that nothing is more powerful than cooking fat in the defining of regional tastes. In *The Food of France* (Vintage, 1992), Root divided that country into three culinary kingdoms: the hilly regions of Alsace and the Dordogne were the lands of duck, goose, and pork fat; sunny Provence was the domain of oil, primarily from olives; and northern France was all about butter. In the United States, however, food preferences have been informed less by geography than by a calculus of cost, novelty, and health concerns. Heart-healthy olive oil made us feel virtuous if not invincible and, possibly, assured of eternal life. Butter, suddenly, seemed passé, even ordinary.

HANDMADE REGIONAL BUTTERS from small creameries arrived just in time. I had my first taste of American artisanal butter about ten years ago under the tutelage of Thomas Keller at his first restaurant, the French Laundry, in Yountville, California. There, several butters were presented with bread, and experiencing the differences between them—in color, texture, taste, and aroma—came as an awakening. Just like olive oil, I realized, butter evoked the environment it came from: the smell and salinity of the air, say, or the perfume of the local grass.

One of the butters Keller made famous is produced by Diane St. Claire at Animal Farm, a small dairy operation in Orwell, Vermont. In 1999, when St. Clair taught herself to make butter from the milk of her tiny herd of Jersey cows, she found that each batch of butter looked and tasted slightly different, depending on when it was made and when the cows had been grazing. "It's not a product that's homogenous; that's part of the adventure of eating it," St. Clair says. It's amazing the difference the human touch, too, can have on butter. St. Clair kneads hers by hand on a cold marble slab to extract as much moisture as possible and concentrate the flavorful butterfat, just as farmwives did for centuries before machines were designed to perform that task. The result is a creamy, high-fat butter with a pure, undiluted flavor.

Barbara Lynch, the chef at No. 9 Park in Boston, which uses St. Clair's butter, loves Animal Farm butter so much that she recently purchased a "cow-share" from the farm—which means that her customers can experience butter from a single cow, a Jersey named Hopi. "It's incredibly creamy and grassy at the same time, with a tang, like crème fraîche, at the end."

Like many causes célèbres of the Gourmet Revolution, butter that's this good is the pie in the eye of industrial food. And, to be sure, it's nice to be able to summon moral authority—look, no chemicals! No multinational corporate marketing!—to rationalize our indulgences, but that's not really necessary. For me, eating butter—whether in an unapologetically rich beurre blanc napping sautéed spring vegetables, in a creamy, parmesan-spiked risotto, or on a slice of crusty bread—is its own reward. We're lucky to be living in an age when good, handmade butters are popping up all around us, with their soft, mellow innocence and pure, honest character, like rabbits in the spring.

LOST FOODS RECLAIMED

By Rick Nichols

from the *Philadelphia Inquirer*

The hallmark of Rick Nichols's regular columns for the *Inquirer* is his ability to capture a slice of life as we know it and put a thoughtful big-picture spin on it. His eager appetite is matched only by his nostalgic passion for preserving local food cultures.

L arry Rossi's piece of Eden is situated in a crook of Neshaminy Creek, a floodplain off Bridgetown Pike in Langhorne, Bucks County, where after 10 hard years, his efforts, finally, are bearing fruit: This month he's picking his first crop of pawpaws.

It is tempting to regard him as a single-minded, perhaps quixotic figure—a Johnny Pawpawseed, say—obsessed with reviving the fortunes of America's largest native fruit, storied once for its creamy, aromatic, banana-mango flesh; all but forgotten today.

But in the bigger picture, he is one more foot soldier in a movement determined to bring back the taste of a paradise lost—the luxurious flavor of heritage pork before the fat was bred out, and Bourbon Red turkeys that fly; of heirloom cranberries (from a Pine Barrens bog called Paradise Hill); and, of course, the iconic buffalo (the heart-healthier red meat) that came close to extinction on the Great Plains.

They are distant memories, some, like the Bourbon Red, closer in flavor to America's original wildfowl; others—like imported European apple stock—so bred for uniform color and storage and spotlessness that they lost their inner cider-ness and pie-perfection.

Sometimes you don't know what you've got till it's gone. And getting it back requires untold time, patience, dead-ends and, well, Larry Rossi and his pawpaws stand as an object lesson.

Still, championed by the Slow Food Movement, by Alice Waters, the local-seasonal guru, and the flowering of farm markets, the lust for one more bite has created a market niche, and for the first time in years, the pioneering wholesaler—Heritage Foods USA—has realized a profit.

This is the frontier beyond—or maybe *adjoining*—the fence of "grass-fed," and "organic," and "humanely slaughtered." (Indeed, "field-harvested" is the new term of art for killing buffalo in their outdoor stomping grounds, sparing them the stress of the slaughterhouse.) It is not necessarily a cohesive movement, marching to a single drummer. It has put good intentions in tension, pitted "Eat Local" champions against ventures such as Heritage, a mail-order marketer of family-farmed, heirloom breeds of beef, bison, turkey and fruit.

"Eat local is fine if you live in Napa or Vermont," argues Patrick Martins, Heritage's president and the founder of Slow Food USA: "But what about the [purebred pork] farmer in Kansas with no local population? What about getting a taste of wild salmon?"

Until the breeds—the light, sweet Duroc pork, for instance—are reestablished, he maintains, eating locally shouldn't rule out the imperative to "ship nationally."

In that spirit, Heritage was offering this month about 12 pawpaws from a Maryland farmer for $107 (including overnight shipping). That gave Larry Rossi a chuckle: Locally, he sells his pawpaws for a third of that, mostly to chefs.

But he doesn't have many.

Which is the heritage-food dilemma in a nutshell. It's one thing to re-create the taste of Original-Recipe America. It's another to make enough of it to go around.

On a sparkling afternoon last week, Larry Rossi surveyed his pawpaw patch—750 trees, their beagle-ear leaves drooping, in rows running north-south (to catch the morning and afternoon sun) in the creekside silt loam.

He was the orchardist more than 10 years ago at Snipes Gardens and Nursery in Morrisville, Bucks County, when he became intrigued with the research of Neal Peterson, the godfather of the pawpaw.

Talk to pawpaw apostles and behold its mystical powers—as a cancer-fighter (compounds in the bark), vitamin pill, a link to noble history: Lewis and Clark credited it with saving them from starvation. Indians used its fiber to make cord. It was celebrated in folk song, and served in custard pies in inns across the 19th century.

It still grows in the wild. You can find it here and there along the Wissahickon, and along stretches of the Susquehanna, and in hidden groves beyond the reach of development. But it is difficult to forage, and a devil to cultivate, costing by some accounts seven times more than an apple tree to bring to harvest. Its shelf life is shorter than a peach's.

Certain varieties, though, can be incomparably, silkily sublime, their flesh a rich, natural custard akin to creamy banana, but infinitely more delicate and complex. Cut one in half and spoon it out, and you pick up whiffs of tropical vanilla, or mango, or pineapple, or coconut. (Pawpaw, by the way, is *not* short for papaya.)

Rossi almost gave up. He planted his first saplings 10 years ago on land donated by his day-job employer, a local contractor. Marauding bucks rubbed off the bark. Drought killed a third of his trees the first year. He put in drip-tubing irrigation. Then in 1999, Hurricane Floyd sent seven feet of water over the patch, flattening trees, tearing up the buried irrigation.

But he got stubborn; stuck it out.

Old, original flavors come and go, sometimes fading away as their habitats (like the pawpaw's) shrink: The soft, walnut-y flavor of the butternut is all but gone, and the wintergreen note of teaberry. Pollution wrote an end to the Delaware's shad, terrapin and oyster trade. Some flavors were consumed to death: In the 1880s, Inga Saffron writes in *Caviar*, the tiny port of Caviar, New Jersey, near current-day Greenwich, supplied more caviar than anywhere in the world. But within 29 years, sturgeon had been fished out of Delaware Bay.

The sturgeon haven't revived. But other species have fared better. Heritage breeds of turkeys—associated with America's most nostalgic food holiday—have become the profit center for Heritage USA. Now, Princeton's Griggstown Quail Farm has gotten into the act: Its slow-growing Bourbon Red turkeys ($7.25 a pound!) range free in outdoor pens, not far from the quail and pheasant.

But the most visible success story is the revival of America's original "cattle," the bison, once pushed to the edge of extinction. In *The Worst Hard Time*, his chronicle of the Dust Bowl, Timothy Egan notes that in 1872–73, seven million pounds of buffalo tongues alone were shipped out of Dodge City, Kansas Two years later, Texans were implored to exterminate every last buffalo in the Panhandle to deny Indians their chief foodstuff, and make the world safe for "speckled cattle."

Brave new buffalo ranchers have cropped up locally—at Hillside Farms near Telford, Montgomery County, and Backyard Bison in Coopersburg in upper Bucks County, among others, part of a trend that has restored 500,000 buffalo to the range. But as with other aspects of the heritage movement, major suppliers (such as Ted Turner, who backs Ted's Montana Grill at Broad and Spruce) don't always see eye-to-eye with small-time local yokels. Smaller operators favor grass-feeding, respecting the animal's natural biology. But former cattle ranchers who've come to dominate the industry favor finishing bison, like beef, on grain diets.

So it goes, the struggle between popularizing a newer breed of eco-gastronomy, and keeping it true and pure.

Near Union Mills, Maryland, an hour north of Baltimore, Jim Davis, the pawpaw farmer who wholesales to Heritage USA, straddles the two worlds. He has built his Deep Run Pawpaw Orchard up to an estimable 1,200 trees, supplying local farmstands. But he has had to make some un-green concessions to ship nationally: Fragile pawpaws require sturdy boxes, packing in multiple layers of bubble wrap, and individual foam sleeves. He's thinking of adding another wrinkle: wine grapes.

Larry Rossi? He has his own ideas. He sees a future in the bramble business; he's heard of a new way to grow blackberries.

Pawpaws: E-mail Larry Rossi at thepawpawguy@msn.com

Meats, produce, seafood and fruit: Heritage Foods USA, www.heritagefoodsusa.com; 212-980-6603

Heritage turkeys: www.griggstownquailfarm.com; 908-359-5218

Locally raised bison: www.hillsidefarms.biz; 215-723-8499 or www.backyardbison.com; 610-346-6640

Heirloom cranberries: Paradise Hill Farm, 64 Mill St., Vincentown, N.J., 609-234-9241

Ruling the Roost

By Jill Wendholt Silva

from the *Kansas City Star*

The *Star's* award-winning food editor and author of the cookbook *Eating For Life*, Silva explores many byways of Midwest food culture—including this poultry farm, where doing things the old-fashioned way is suddenly the latest thing.

On a bitterly cold February afternoon, a jaunty black-and-white striped Barred Plymouth Rock rooster with a brilliant red comb ruffles his chest feathers and struts across the barnyard to strains of classical music.

"Chopin?" Molly O'Neill asks as lush piano melodies float from a set of speakers in the nearby garage.

"Yes. The music soothes them, but it also keeps foxes and other critters away," replies Ryon Carey, a 34-year-old farmer who raises heritage poultry breeds.

As the brood pecks and preens, O'Neill removes a glove and shakes her pen to get the slow-moving ink to flow. The former *New York Times Sunday Magazine* food columnist and her research crew of three have traveled to the picturesque Swedish hamlet on the edge of the scenic Flint Hills to collect timeworn recipes for her next cookbook, *One Big Table: A Portrait of the Nation at the Table* (Simon & Schuster), due out in 2009.

As part of her research, O'Neill spent the morning in the kitchen at Messiah Lutheran Church interviewing a crew of local cooks who have volunteered to prepare such farmhouse standards as chicken and dumplings, chicken and noodles, pressed chicken sandwiches, chicken potpie, Huntington chicken, chicken salad and fried chicken. No ordinary chicken dinner, the four-course feast is designed to showcase heritage chickens—rare breeds dating to the 1800s with bucolic sounding names: Barred Rock, Jersey Giant and New Hampshire Red.

"People don't realize that the chicken was once one of the most diverse livestock in the world. There were once more than 200 distinct breeds," says Frank Reese Jr., the host of the church supper. Today, commercial breeders rely on just a handful of fast-growing hybrids.

As the owner and founder of Good Shepherd Turkey Ranch, Reese's campaign to maintain diversity of flavor in a world of dry, sawdusty turkey and bland boneless, skinless chicken breasts has rapidly turned him into a celebrity farmer. In 2001 *New York Times* food writer Marian Burros went in search of a Norman Rockwell turkey that tasted juicy and flavorful, like something grandmother might have served before the 1950s. Burros tracked down Reese and, after a taste test, wrote about the superior flavor of these heritage breeds.

Heritage Foods USA was the first organization to make heritage turkeys available to the public. As the sales and marketing arm of Slow Food USA, an international nonprofit organization dedicated to preserving endangered and artisan foods, it sold 800 heritage turkeys in 2002. In 2004 Heritage Foods USA was spun off as an independent company. Patrick Martins, former Slow Foods executive director, followed. As the company's co-founder, he brought Reese's turkeys to the attention of still more gourmet, natural and local food enthusiasts. Shortly before Thanksgiving 2007, Reese was featured as "Person of the Week" on ABC *Nightly News* and received a plug on *The Martha Stewart Show*, which generated thousands of hits to www.reese turkeys.com.

For Thanksgiving 2008, Reese is on target to raise 12,000 turkeys. "But," Reese admits, "turkey is a once-a-year investment."

"When I heard Frank was moving from turkey to chicken . . . I knew it was a really different ball game," O'Neill tells the 40 dinner guests. The group included representatives from Whole Foods, Dean & DeLuca, the Animal Welfare Institute and Slow Food.

Shelling out $200 with shipping for a holiday bird once a year is a luxury. But Reese is betting there is an even larger group of consumers out there willing to pay a more modest $4.99 per pound to serve a special chicken for Sunday dinner several times a year. Eventually Reese hopes to be selling 200 birds a week using a handpicked network of farmers. But his mission is actually more a labor of love than commerce. None of the farmers who supply Good Shepherd Turkey Ranch is making a living solely from heritage chicken. Even Reese must supplement his farm income by working as a nurse anesthetist.

So far, Good Shepherd Turkey Ranch heritage chickens are only trickling onto the local market. Area Hen House markets each have a half dozen heritage chickens available in the frozen meat section.

Time is of the essence, and Reese gets downright teary-eyed and his voice breaks when he thinks of the breeds that may still be lost. "My biggest fear is my death," the robust 59-year-old says. "If I die right now, it's pretty much over. I'm the one who keeps pushing this forward."

Cooking for a Cause

Steve Pope stands over a cutting board and chops carrot rounds destined for a simmering pot of *hühnersuppe mit butterkugeln für das brot*, a German-style chicken soup with tiny dumplings known as "butter balls." The Messiah Lutheran Church kitchen is abuzz with cooks preparing dishes for the Friday night supper. Pope, a childhood friend of Reese, has been drafted into service. Following his great-grandmother's recipe, he makes the butter balls from bread crumbs moistened with broth, eggs and cream and seasoned with allspice. They float in a rich, golden broth pooling up from a simmering young Buckeye rooster.

The Buckeye is an American breed that originated in Ohio and is the only breed developed by a woman. A deep chestnut colored bird, it has stout, muscular thighs and a broad and well-rounded breast. "The Buckeye gives that particular flavor, that very soup kind of taste to it, which makes it wonderful," Pope says.

No stranger to fowl, Pope grew up near Wichita where his parents owned a chicken processing plant and he spent summers stamping egg cartons. "I could pluck a chicken before you get to Colonel Sanders and back," he jokes. But as a board member of the

Standard Bred Poultry Institute, Pope can also preach the chicken gospel. "It's interesting how every bird has a history," he says. "And with its history, calling it a heritage bird helps us understand there are things to honor about it. It has certain genetic traits. It cooks a certain way. It lives its life a certain way."

To be marketed as "heritage," the American Poultry Association requires a breed with a genetic line that is traceable back multiple generations. The poultry also must be able to mate naturally, to live a long, vigorous life outdoors and to grow at a slow rate, reaching market weight in no less than 14 weeks.

As local Bethany College students wearing black pants and white shirts serve the four-course dinner, I have the opportunity to experience the flavor and texture of chicken that is, well, chicken-y in a way few supermarket hens can match. The Barred Rock in the chicken and noodles is meaty, chewy. The Cornish fried chicken is rich and juicy beneath a greaseless crust. The Dutch oven-roasted chicken, basted with olive oil, has a lovely, crackly skin and a moist, buttery interior.

The robust flavors are a revelation, but so is Reese's ability to draw a diverse crowd of home cooks, farmers, poultry experts, supermarket managers, chefs, restaurateurs, food journalists—even artists. Pope is not surprised by Reese's newfound celebrity. "He has been very sincere. He has a passion behind it," Pope says. "There's not a hidden agenda. I think people see that and want to be a part of it. People are climbing on board for the right reasons."

Portrait of a Chicken

Lindsborg is an artist's haven, and Lee Becker's portraits of chickens are perched on easels in the church's fellowship hall. But Becker steers clear of sentimental, country-kitchen images. Instead, she paints realistic portraits of chickens and other farm animals as a poetic protest against factory farming.

The standard industrial broiler is a larger bird bred to grow at a more rapid rate and produce more meaty breasts. The transition has affected flavor, genetic diversity and animal welfare. "With poultry it's become so industrialized that old line breeds are hard to find, and it's hard to find farmers who know how to raise them," says Diane Halverson, farm animal adviser for the Washington, D.C.–based

Animal Welfare Institute. Because he is one of only a handful of breeders who can pass on the knowledge of how to raise these chickens to the next generation, Reese is working with Halverson and others to turn his 160-acre farm into the Standard Bred Poultry Institute, a resource center for the preservation of heritage poultry genetics and animal husbandry skills.

"I don't want an emotional response. I just want people to think again, and truly be aware of what they're buying," Reese says after the dinner. "It makes no difference if it's organic, free-range, Amish-raised. It's the same rapid-growing bird. The regular chicken on the rack.

"Our chickens are different. It's a whole different genetic animal. To have people come up to me and say, 'I never thought of that' was the greatest compliment of the evening."

Heritage Chicken Breeds

Barred Plymouth Rock: A fowl with a striking black and white feather pattern, the Barred Rock is yellow skinned and lays brown eggs. It is the first breed to be exhibited in a poultry show. It was admitted to the first American Standard of Excellence in 1874 and remained one of the premier meat birds in America between 1880 and 1951.

Buckeye: An American breed that originated in the Buckeye State (Ohio), the bird's feathers are a deep chestnut color. The Buckeye is unique because it is the only breed created by a woman. The breed has stout, muscular thighs, a broad and well-rounded breast, and a comb that resembles the Cornish of the early 20th century. It was admitted as a breed in 1904. (To round out the heritage chicken dinner, a North Carolina breeder sent two Buckeye birds but the breed will not be available at Hen House.)

Jersey Giants: An all-purpose breed for meat and egg production, the Jersey Giants are known for their excellent roasting quality. They originated in New Jersey during the 1880s by crossing Black Java, Dark Brahmas and Black Langshans. As their name implies, Jersey Giants are a large, very heavy fowl and are usually black in color.

New Hampshire Reds: Starting in 1915, the breed was developed in New Hampshire from Rhode Island Red stock. They are known for early maturity, quick feathering and large brown eggs. They were recognized as a distinct breed in 1935.

Cornish: These birds originated in Cornwall, England. The breed descended from well-muscled fighting chickens native to India. But they had a huge appetite and poor egg laying habits, so the breed was mostly kept by the wealthy who favored its large portions of meat. Cornish are valuable for crossing with other breeds, including the current industrial broiler. Years ago, the breed was marketed when young and tender and labeled as Cornish game hens, which commanded a premium price.

Source: Frank Reese

For online orders, go to www.heritagefoodsusa.com or www.reeseturkeys.com.

Tenderloin's a Steal, but at What Moral Price?

By John Kessler

from the *Atlanta Journal-Constitution*

A pull-no-punches restaurant critic, a meticulous recipe writer, a musing philosopher of all things culinary, Atlantan John Kessler juggles it all, and with an unassuming eloquence that can sometimes—often—touch the heart.

As a rule, I want to know where the beef I purchase comes from, how it was raised and what grade the U.S. Department of Agriculture, in its infinite wisdom, bestowed upon it.

But then I find a bargain like the $34 tenderloin at Super H. Mart. Not $34 a pound—$34 for the whole, nearly 5-pound tenderloin. At Whole Foods, they're asking $27.99 per pound.

Surely this cow was an also-ran brought up on some vast feedlot—some federally subsidized bovine hell on earth set up for the sole purpose of supplying Americans with the inexpensive meat they consider their birthright. I turn this shrink-wrapped torpedo of blood-red Bessie in my hands and think: $34.

I could have a dinner party for $34. I would cut the tenderloin into thick filets and marinate them overnight with olive oil, garlic, shallots and cracked black pepper. I'd grill them over real charcoal in my Weber kettle and serve them with creamed leeks, a sharp arugula salad and those potato wedges I roast in chicken stock until the stock disappears and the potatoes transform into cream and crust. Everyone loves those potatoes.

But will they love this tenderloin? The packaging offers no clue to its provenance. I assume it to be USDA Select. Sure, I'd want a better grade for strip steaks or rib eyes. Choice or Prime steaks would have the marbling and flavor that come from the longer time the cow spent on a corn diet. But tenderloin is more about texture than flavor.

Of course, so much of our corn production goes into feeding these cows rather than feeding humans. Not only would we get more bang for the caloric buck if we just ate the corn, we'd be making a healthier food choice.

Good lord, here I am again, stuck in a morass of moral relativism over food choices. I've dead-ended here before, standing like a dim-bulb fool in the middle of the supermarket, holding a package of individually quick-frozen chicken breasts and wondering if they came from a bird that was de-beaked as a chick in order to keep it from pecking its neighbors.

But . . . $34. I could just stick this tenderloin in the freezer. Then, when we've got one day to prepare something for a school potluck, I could roast the whole thing, let it cool to room temperature, slice it on a platter and serve it with an easy mash-up of sour cream and horseradish. With a dish like this, I could go into catering. I would buy decorative kale, maraschino cherries and plastic platters covered in shiny metallic laminate, and I'd become a fixture at Atlanta weddings and bar mitzvahs. The guy with the cheap tenderloin.

OK, this is so stupid. Why am I standing here, not buying? Um . . . guilt, maybe? I've lived in Colorado, so I've seen feedlots. I've smelled feedlots on the distance, long before I've seen them. I remembered reading somewhere* that cattle production generates more greenhouse gases than transportation.

This tenderloin has me frozen in indecision, yet I don't think twice about getting my favorite beef salad at the little Thai restaurant near our house.

I wonder if they've alerted store security about me. Strange, immobile man in the beef department: proceed with caution.

---

*"Livestock's Long Shadow: Environmental Issues and Options." A 2006 report to the United Nations Food and Agriculture Organization, by H. Steinfeld, P. Gerber, T. Wassenaar, V. Castel, M. Rosales, C. de Haan.

Thirty-four dollars! I spent more on my pampered Thanksgiving turkey.

Here's another thought: retro party. Whiskey sours, space-age bachelor pad music and a Beef Wellington. It's actually easy to make: smear the tenderloin with food-processed mushrooms and shallots cooked down to a dry paste, wrap it in a sheet of store-bought puff pastry and bake it until it looks like 1958. That's a lot of swank for a slender price.

Besides, this cheap tenderloin isn't like cheap hamburger, right? You don't know what's in that. Well, if you've read "Fast Food Nation," you do. E. coli's favorite medium. This muscle, on the other hand, remains whole and untrimmed of the fat and silverskin on its surface. I don't know where it came from, but it looks wholesome.

So I slip it into my cart. Thirty-four dollars. I can't resist.

Which I know, of course, is the wrong moral choice. This piece of beef was so cheap because of the presumed factory farming that produced it and the federal subsidies that benefit the meat industry. I should only buy meat produced on small, environmentally responsible farms.

But not this time. I wish I could afford to buy a whole tenderloin at Whole Foods, but that's not going to happen anytime soon. I want to make the right food choices, but I also want to enjoy the amazing variety of foods we have available to us in this country.

That's my dilemma. And it's all of ours.

Mangoes, Memories—
and Motorcycles

By Sona Pai
from www.culinate.com

Freelance writer Sona Pai may be based now in foodie-centric
Portland, Oregon, but she's also a first-generation Indian-
American. The tug-of-war between those two cultures brings
a special piquancy to her writing.

A few months ago, when I heard that the U.S. government had lifted its 18-year ban on importing mangoes
from India, I felt a little giddy. I remember eating these mangoes—
these amazing mangoes—while visiting my grandparents, aunts,
uncles, and cousins in India. These mangoes weren't like the
stringy, pale yellow ones we ate back home in Missouri, the ones
that were often sour and so fibrous they made me feel like flossing.
These were deep orange inside, buttery soft, and sweet as honey.

They're the mangoes my dad—back when he was a naughty little boy in Gujarat—used to steal from his neighbor's tree. I've visited his old house during each of my four trips to India, and each
time I imagine him, skinny and barefoot, scrambling up for a treat.

They're the mangoes my grandfather would haggle for at the
bazaar. He'd ignore small talk from the fruit wallah as he scruti-
nized the rows of fragrant fruit, squeezing this one, smelling that
one, accepting a sample, pretending it was no good.

The king of fruits, now available in the United States from
India. When the fruit wallah finally caved (a special price, he said,
in honor of my visit from America), my grandfather would select
six or seven mangoes, which would last us maybe two days. Back at

their airy apartment, my grandfather, grandmother, and I would eat mangoes after every meal, the three of us slurping away in happy silence.

Indian mangoes are known as the world's finest because they have the competitive advantage of being the world's first. The mango tree, *Mangifera indica*, originated somewhere between India and Myanmar about 4,000 years ago. Indians have been cultivating them ever since, selecting and propagating the sweetest fruits with the least fiber, and planting more than two million acres of them.

Mangoes, a symbol of love, fertility, and good fortune, infuse Indian life and culture. On special occasions, like weddings, New Year's Day, and Diwali, mango leaves adorn the doorways of Indian homes and temples. The shape of the mango fruit inspired the distinctive Indian pattern, known in the West as paisley, that swoops and swirls across Indian fabrics, artwork, and the henna-inked hands and feet of a bride-to-be.

Indians eat mangoes ripe and unripe, raw and cooked, dried and pickled. They blend them with yogurt in a cool glass of mango lassi or serve them sprinkled with a little salt, lime, and chile powder. They simmer them down into mango chutney and preserve them in mustard oil with salt, lime, and spices like cumin, turmeric, fennel, and fenugreek. And they blend them into desserts such as the rich, milky ice cream known as *kulfi*.

Portuguese colonists brought mangoes to Africa and the Americas, where they now grow in the Caribbean, Latin America, Florida, California, and Hawaii. But commercial interests led growers in these parts to breed mangoes with more, not less, fiber; the stringy fiber gives mangoes a more shelf-stable structure and, unfortunately, the texture of a wool sweater. These mangoes are cheaper and easier for Americans to get their hands on, but as anyone who has ever tasted an Indian mango will tell you, there's no comparison. Period.

The Sweet, and Then the Sour

India first applied for permission to ship mangoes to the United States in 1989. But rather than choose between two agricultural evils—invasive pests or the high levels of pesticides required to eradicate them—the U.S. government barred the Indian fruits from American shores. Since then, the Indian population in United States has grown from just under 800,000 in 1990 to m than 2.2 million in 2004, and demand for Indian mangoes has increased along with it.

As these immigrants settled into their new homes, they got used to the compromises that came with assimilation. They seasoned Rice Krispies, Corn Flakes, and potato chips to replicate the spicy, salty snacks they used to buy for a few rupees on the street. They made sweet-and-sour chutney with apple butter instead of fresh dates and tamarind. They ate mangoes from Mexico with names like Tommy Atkins, Haden, Keitt, and Kent, instead of their beloved Alphonso, Kesar, Dussheri, and Khajri.

Some tried to stuff contraband mangoes into their suitcases on return trips from India, and U.S. customs officials grew accustomed to asking gray-haired aunties in saris if they were carrying any mangoes. Most learned to settle for the New World mangoes that Madhur Jaffrey has called "pleasantly hued but lifeless rocks," because that's all they could legally get.

Until now.

When news of the Indian mango's arrival hit, Indians all over America cheered. In news stories and on blogs, they recalled the mango memories of their youth and argued over which Indian variety was the best. American government officials held ceremonies to mark this significant step in U.S.-India economic relations. They ate mangoes and lauded the "King of Fruits" and "The World's Best Mangoes."

Forbes magazine reported that, upon tasting an Indian mango for the first time on his 2006 trip to India, George W. Bush turned to Indian Prime Minister Manmohan Singh and said, "This is a hell of a fruit."

The first Indian mangoes arrived in the States in May of this year. As I searched for information about when and where I could get them, I read as much as I could about their impending arrival. Steadily, with each bit of new information I found, the thought of eating Indian mangoes in America became a little less sweet.

First, there's the rub. To get from India to me, these mangoes would of course have to travel thousands of miles. How would that fit into my growing insistence on local produce?

Second, there's the trade-off. Magazines and newspapers widely reported that, in exchange for the mangoes, India would ease its emissions standards to make room for American Harley-Davidson motorcycles on its already choked roads. Do I really want to add to India's pollution problem just so I can eat some tropical fruit in America?

And third, there's the catch. Still worried about pests—particularly the mango seed weevil, which bores through a mango's flesh and then matures within its seed—the United States is accepting Indian mangoes on one condition: They must first be irradiated to destroy the weevils, which haven't yet made their way into North American crops. That means those delicious fruits—the ones that you can spoon like custard and that taste like sunshine—would have to be zapped with gamma rays before they reached my plate.

Currently, mangoes from Mexico and other countries must also be treated to eliminate pests like fruit flies. This is commonly done by fumigation or with hot-water baths. Indian mangoes are the first fruits to be irradiated overseas and approved for import into America.

While the U.S. Department of Agriculture's Animal and Plant Health Inspection Service (APHIS) assures us that irradiated fruit is perfectly safe, plenty of food-safety advocates have their doubts. Irradiation destroys the mango seed weevil and makes mangoes more shelf-stable so they can withstand their long journey overseas, but it's not clear what effect it has on their nutritional value or their taste. There's also scientific debate over whether irradiation is a safe technology or a harmful one.

Just Go to the Mango

All of this is, frankly, more than I want to deal with when it comes to mangoes. I don't want to think about carbon emissions and food miles or Harleys and gamma rays; I just want to eat my favorite fruit. I guess, like my parents did when they came to this country as immigrants more than 40 years ago, I'll simply have to make some compromises.

I'll continue to eat local, seasonal fruit whenever I can, which is no chore in Portland, Oregon, where I live. I'll do just fine with the amazing raspberries, blackberries, cherries, strawberries, peaches, nectarines, pears, apples, and grapes from my local farmers' market. Occasionally, I'll treat myself to a New World mango as a luxury. They may be stringy, but the ripe ones are still delicious. And I'll always keep a can of mango pulp from the Indian grocery store in the pantry. (Processed mangoes don't require irradiation.)

When I have children, I'll tuck paper towels into their shirts after dinner, like my mom did for me and my little brother. I'll cut a mango in slivers they can slurp right off of the peel, just like my mom did, and I'll watch them get sticky with mango juice all over their faces and arms. Like my mom, I'll stand over the sink, slurping the pulp from the mango's large, flat seed, until the day my kids figure out it's the best part.

When they're old enough, I'll take them to India during mango season, even though it's blistering hot. I'll show them where their grandfather used to climb a tree for stolen sweets. I'll take them to a bazaar and let them smell the mangoes and squeeze them, and I'll tell them how their great-grandfather used to haggle.

When we visit India, I'll feed them the mangoes their grandparents and great-grandparents grew up eating. I'll tell them how the hot, hot sun and the brutal monsoons give mangoes just what they need to grow soft and sweet and perfect, and I'll tell them they won't find mangoes like these anywhere else in the world.

Gimme Mangoes

The U.S. government's decision to import Indian mangoes came just as India's mango season hit full swing this year. Importers scrambled to get them here as soon as possible, and that meant by plane, which is expensive; as a result, this year's shipments have sold out quickly (mostly at Indian groceries) for the premium prices of $35 to $40 a case, or about $3 to $4 per mango. Keep an eye out for them late next spring, in more cities and at better prices.

In the meantime, mangoes from Central America, both conventional and organic, are widely available. Look for mangoes that smell like you want them to taste, and that give slightly when you squeeze them. At home, put them in a paper bag for a few days to ripen them.

When you've got a nice, ripe mango, this is the best way to eat it: Hold the mango with both hands and, turning it, squeeze gently, until the flesh inside softens into a pulp. (Don't let the skin break under the pressure.) When the mango starts to feel like a water balloon, pop off the little stem nub at the top and begin slurping. When you've slurped out all of the juice, pull out the seed and slurp some more.

Mango Lassi

From the Sona Pai *collection*
Yields 1 to 2 glasses
This might be the best beverage in the world, especially on a hot summer day. If your fresh mangoes are stringy, strain the pulp first to eliminate the fibers. You can also make this with canned mango pulp, which you can find at Indian grocery and specialty stores. To make more, just multiply the recipe. All measurements are to taste.

½ cup mango pulp
1 cup plain yogurt
¼–½ cup cold water
Sugar to taste (optional)
¼– ½ tsp. ground cardamom

1. In a blender, combine the mango pulp and yogurt. Add water until the mixture reaches the desired consistency. It should be thin enough to drink, but still a little thick, like a smoothie. Add sugar and cardamom to taste. Pour into glasses and serve.

The Meat of the Matter

I Melt with You

By Janet A. Zimmerman

from eGullet

One of the great things about the Web site eGullet is that it lets
foodies around the country, both amateur and professional—
like Atlanta-based Janet Zimmerman, a food writer and culinary instructor—wax eloquent on the food folks really eat.

My first real job after leaving graduate school was in the
Bank of America Center in downtown San Francisco.
Like most liberal-arts–educated, underemployed ex-academicians, I
made only enough money to get by. My lunches were leftovers or
tuna sandwiches brought from home. But once every couple of
weeks, I'd splurge and treat myself to a patty melt.

In the lowest level of the BofA building was a cafeteria of the
sort that I came to realize was ubiquitous in large office buildings
and hospitals: subsidized, with various stations—a grill, a hot line, a
sandwich station and a salad bar. The first time I ventured down
there (I'd forgotten to bring a lunch or had nothing to bring), I felt
a prick of shame and self-pity. No one in my department ate there,
despite the lunchtime stream of secretaries from my floor picking
up sandwiches for their bosses.

At the grill, though, they offered a patty melt, redemption for
countless cafeteria faults. It didn't take long for me to discover that
only if you ordered a rare burger did they cook it from scratch
(anything else was precooked and just finished on the grill), so although I prefer hamburgers cooked a little more, my unfailing order became a patty melt, rare. It took awhile to cook; I'd pull out a
book and catch up on a few pages while keeping an eye on the

progress—the patty grilling while the onions sizzled on the flattop, next to the rye bread that crisped while the Swiss cheese warmed and softened on top. The result was reliably perfect: a fresh, hot patty melt (even better, it was subsidized by my employer).

In time, I made friends at work and was promoted. The promotion came with a large enough raise to upgrade my lunch splurges; on most Fridays (after too many drinks and not enough sleep most Thursday nights) my friends and I would slouch off to the grill down the street, known for its Bloody Marys and burgers. The drinks were good; the burgers were . . . okay. They were fine, really, but they weren't patty melts.

The fact is inescapable: when compared with a burger, the patty melt is superior. Don't get me wrong; I like burgers when they're well made, with good toppings. But that's the thing: a burger is defined by what else is on it—a cheeseburger, a mushroom burger, a bacon burger—or by its ostensible origin—a French burger, a Southwestern burger. A burger is the sum of its parts, not an entity unto itself, as is the patty melt. The patty melt needs no condiments, no regional variations, no additions. It just is.

BOTH *The Food Lover's Companion* and *The Food Chronology* have plummeted in my estimation: neither includes a mention of the patty melt. (Both have entries for the hamburger, and *Food Lover's* also includes the Reuben sandwich.) Search the Internet for the history of the patty melt, and you come up empty. Apparently, no one cares when and how the patty melt came to be, who gave birth to this love child of the grilled cheese sandwich and the burger. Theories abound on who first put burger to bun and introduced the ancestor of today's hamburger. Hot debates rage about whether the Reuben was the invention of Arthur Reuben of New York's Reuben's Deli or of a poker-playing Omaha grocer named Reuben Kay. But the patty melt slipped into the repertoire of diner specials without notice, much less fanfare. No one writes conjectural histories about it; when it's mentioned at all, it's as a variation of the hamburger. This is misguided. If I had to imagine the origins of the melt, I'd lean toward this scenario:

A customer—a traveling salesman, let's say—walks into a diner sometime in the 40s. He sees the grillman flipping a griddled sandwich on rye bread. Intrigued, he asks what it is. "A Reuben sandwich," the cook answers. "It's the latest rage, from Reuben's Deli in New York." ("You're wrong—it's from Omaha," a woman's voice calls out from the back of the kitchen.)

"What's in it?" the salesman asks.

"Corned beef, Swiss cheese, sauerkraut." ("Russian dressing!" says the voice from the back.)

Maybe the salesman is a patriotic American who eschews all things German during the war years; maybe he just doesn't like sauerkraut. "Could you make one with some of those grilled onions on it instead?" he asks.

"I could," comes the laconic reply. "But I'm out of corned beef."

Undeterred, the salesman suggests, "How about you put one of those hamburger patties on it, then?"

The cook pauses, lifts an eyebrow. "Sure. You don't like it, though, you still have to pay for it."

"It's a deal," says the salesman. "Except," he adds in a whisper, "please don't put Russian dressing on it, okay?"

"Not a chance," says the cook. "She's crazy."

If the salesman had been a local and returned to order the sandwich again and again, history might have remembered him. If the cook had been more imaginative, perhaps he would have given the sandwich a catchy name and legends would have started to form. As it was, the cook made it for the salesman, and later tried it himself. He liked it enough to add to the Specials menu from time to time, especially when he had too many onions and not enough sauerkraut. His daughter—I've decided that's who it was in the back—kept trying to get him to add Russian dressing because she'd bought a case of gallon bottles by mistake, but he held firm. (Hey, it's my history. No Russian dressing.)

DESPITE THE LACK OF A TRADITION, an official history or an "authentic" recipe, the patty melt is remarkable for the stability of its preparation. Occasionally, a spiritual descendent of that daughter tries to force Russian dressing on it. Once in a while, you find a specious, non-Swiss cheese insinuating its way between the rye bread and onions. But when you order a patty melt, you mostly know what you're getting. The Reuben might come in for bastardization (turkey Reubens, pastrami Reubens), but it's rare to find a melt assaulted in such a way. Why tamper with perfection?

The Platonic ideal of the patty melt starts with a slice of rye bread topped with a thin layer of Swiss cheese. On top of that goes a hot hamburger patty, sautéed onions, and another thin layer of cheese. Ending, of course, with another slice of bread. The bread is buttered and the sandwich goes on a heated griddle so that the bread gets golden brown and the cheese melts. Crunchy bread, melty cheese, onions and beef. Simple, pure, perfect.

Which is not to say that every patty melt in the real world is a good one. Common faults include improperly cooked or insufficient onions or only one layer of cheese, which diminish the power of the patty melt but aren't fatal. But sometimes you get a patty melt so bad, you want to cry for the injustice of it.

My speculative history of the patty melt came to me after an unfortunate experience at a bar and grill, where I ordered a patty melt and my date ordered a Reuben. When we got our order, we realized that they'd switched the set-ups for the sandwiches; my hamburger patty ended up on the sandwich with sauerkraut and Russian dressing, and his corned beef ended up on my patty melt prep. He was content to keep them, and why not? He had corned beef, Swiss cheese and onions on rye. I had a burger with sauerkraut and Russian dressing. I insisted on sending them back to be corrected. (The relationship was doomed.)

And there was a popular burger chain in the San Francisco area whose "patty melt" came on plain, cold rye bread. Not grilled, not griddled, not even toasted. Inadequate onions, and one lone slice of barely melted cheese, which congealed as I tried to eat it.

But the good memories far outweigh the bad ones: early morning patty melts consumed after the bars closed; road trip patty melts when the only restaurant around was Denny's or one of its clones, making a patty melt the only rational dinner choice; the defining moment of grown-up-hood, when my mom let me order a patty melt for breakfast. I don't remember when I first tried one, but I do recall the first time I ever had a patty melt made at home.

I was in college; a fellow philosophy major (well, the only other philosophy major besides me) and I had a few hours to kill between classes. She lived close to campus, so we walked to her house for lunch. "Let's make patty melts" were words I'd never heard before. It had never occurred to me that one could make them at home. But we did, or, more precisely, she did. I sliced cheese.

I didn't begin making patty melts at home right away after that; in fact, it was years before I did. Grilled cheese, yes ("grilled cheese sandwich" is a misnomer, but "griddled cheese sandwich" just doesn't have the right cadence, so grilled it is)—grilled cheese sandwiches have seen me through lean times and heartbreaks. Tuna melts were a frequent weekend lunch or easy dinner. Even the occasional Reuben came out of my kitchen; despite the essential imbalance in that sandwich—too skewed toward salt and sour; not enough sweet—I do like it (hold the Russian dressing, please).

My family didn't make hamburgers at home, except for rare summertime outdoor dinners. Burgers were for restaurants, for special occasions. Cooking hamburger patties at home wasn't part of my repertoire, despite that singular college experience. My series of older, unventilated kitchens in San Francisco apartments discouraged me from starting. But the other week I was wandering through the grocery store, searching more for inspiration than ingredients, and I spied the guys in back packaging ground beef (I like to think they'd just ground it, but my imagination isn't that strong). I thought, "I'll make a burger." I compiled a mental list of necessities: tomatoes, pickles, buns. I picked up a small package of ground chuck and started toward the bread section when it struck me. I could make a patty melt. I had everything in my kitchen already—rye bread, onions, Gruyere. No other purchases necessary.

I could make a patty melt.

I sailed through the 10-items-or-fewer line (I love my grocery store for its grammatically correct signs) with my beef. I formed the patty and salted it. I sautéed onions, sliced cheese. Heated a cast iron skillet and a griddle. Cooked and assembled, and cooked again. Making a patty melt isn't difficult, but it is time-consuming. Timing is essential, and you can't rush it. As I bit into my sandwich, I felt a kinship with my imaginary salesman, admiration for every grill cook who'd ever made me a patty melt, and gratitude for every bite.

———

Patty Melt (makes one)

5 oz. ground chuck (more or less, depending on the size of
   your bread; if you have the time and equipment, grinding
   your own beef elevates the sandwich to a higher plane)
1 small onion
Two slices of rye bread
Swiss cheese (Gruyere or Emmenthaler are my recommendations, but even supermarket Swiss cheese works)—sliced
   thin or grated; you need enough for a thin layer on each
   slice of bread
Butter
Salt

1. Form the beef into an oval patty slightly larger than the bread slices. Place on a rack and salt both sides heavily. Let rest.

2. Meanwhile, slice the onion thin. Heat some butter in a small skillet and sauté the onion until it's very soft and beginning to brown. Set aside.

3. Heat a cast iron skillet (or your preferred burger cooking vessel).

4. Heat a griddle or large skillet over medium low heat. Butter one side of each slice of bread and lay the slices buttered side down on the griddle. Distribute the cheese evenly over the two pieces of bread. Spread the onions over the cheese on one piece of the bread—not both, or final assembly is a nightmare.

5. While the bread begins to brown and the cheese melts, cook the hamburger patty however you like it. I think medium-rare to medium works best, but the patty melt is forgiving.

6. When the meat is done, remove it to the rack and let it rest for a couple of minutes. Place the patty on the slice of bread with onions and top with the other slice. If you've timed it right, the sandwich should need just another minute or so on each side to turn deep golden brown and become the Platonic ideal of a patty melt.

7. Eat, enjoy. Thank the salesman.

Fat, Glorious Fat, Moves to the Center of the Plate

By Frank Bruni

from the *New York Times*

Previously a political reporter for the *Times*, Frank Bruni has
grown into his job as chief restaurant critic since he won that
powerful post in 2004. Though his opinions are often contro-
versial, he supports them with smart, confident, convincing
prose.

I'm not sure it's possible to behave with much dignity
around seven glistening pounds of pork butt, but on a recent night at Momofuku Ssäm Bar, five friends and I weren't even
encouraged to try.

Servers didn't bother to carve the mountain of meat. They
didn't give us any delicate way to do it, either. They just plopped it
in the center of the table, handed out sets of tongs, left us to our
own devices and let the pig scatter where it may.

It was an ugly scene, and it was a beautiful one. We lunged at the
flesh. Tore at it. Yanked it toward ourselves in dripping, jagged
hunks, sometimes ignoring the lettuce wraps on the side so we
could stuff it straight into our mouths. We looked, I realized, like
hyenas at an all-you-can-eat buffet on the veldt, and I wasn't surprised to notice other diners staring at us.

But what I saw on their faces wasn't disgust. It was envy. I'd venture that more than a few of them returned to Momofuku for
their own pig-outs. The restaurant, after all, sells about two whole
pork butts—a term that refers to part of the pig's shoulder, not to
its rump—every night.

These are times of bold temptation, as well as prompt surrender, for a carnivorous glutton in New York.

They're porky times, fatty times, which is to say very good times indeed. Any new logo for the city could justifiably place the Big Apple in the mouth of a spit-roasted pig, and if the health commissioner were really on his toes, he'd draw up a sizable list of restaurants required to hand out pills of Lipitor instead of after-dinner mints.

The list would encompass more than steak houses, which have multiplied exponentially over the last five years, because what's lumbered into particular favor with culinary tastemakers and the food-savvy set isn't just beef and isn't just any old piece of meat.

It's a piece of meat that's extra-messy, like one of the fat-ringed slabs of lamb at Trestle on Tenth, which opened last year. Sometimes it's a mammoth cut, sometimes just gooey nuggets of animal parts less conventionally appreciated or lyrically named than the tenderloin.

The menu at Momofuku, which also opened last year and seems to capture the culinary zeitgeist as well as any restaurant, has not only sweetbreads—the gateway offal—but also a veal head terrine that resembles a gelatinous amalgam of everything your mother ever told you to trim from a chop and shove to the side of your plate. That same description applies to a terrine of oxtail and pig's foot at Trestle on Tenth.

Trestle and Momofuku would be high on the health commissioner's list, but probably no higher than the new restaurant Resto, where some genius—and I am most certainly not being facetious—decided that deviled eggs aren't sufficiently rich on their own. No, they need amplification, and of course they need meat, so they're placed on rectangles of pork jowl. One more thing: these rectangles are deep-fried. At a certain point, I suppose, there's no turning back.

It's as if decades of proliferating sushi and shrinking plates, of clean California cuisine and exhortations to graze, have fostered a robust (or is that rotund?) counterculture of chefs and diners eager to cut against the nutritional grain and straight into the bellies of beasts. In fact, bellies (most often pork, more recently lamb) are this counterculture's LSD.

Its Timothy Leary might well be David Chang, the chef at Momofuku, where steamed buns are filled with strips of pork belly. Or maybe it's Zak Pelaccio, the chef at the tellingly named restaurant Fatty Crab. One of its best-selling dishes, called the fatty duck, takes strips of a bird not exactly known for its leanness, dusts them with cornstarch and deep-fries them.

The "crispy pork" with pickled watermelon in a dish that Fatty Crab mockingly labels a salad amounts to cubes of fried pork belly, and the rest of the menu (pork ribs, small burgers doused with mayonnaise and aptly named fatty sliders) works a similarly clogged vein. During a recent lunch there with a dauntless friend, I was touched by the way our server—let's call him Sisyphus—replenished the moist towelettes at our table over and over again. What we really needed him to do was put a dropcloth under us and, at meal's end, hose us down.

Mr. Pelaccio's appreciation of a fatty rib extends from pork to lamb, and at the restaurant 5 Ninth, from which he recently severed his ties, he occasionally served lamb ribs, the far reaches of which incorporated bits of lamb belly, he said.

He recalled in a recent telephone conversation that when 5 Ninth opened in the meatpacking district three years ago and he asked one of his suppliers about getting him this meat, he learned that the supplier *was selling his lamb ribs to a woman down the street to grind into dog food.*

Back then, Mr. Pelaccio said, no one much wanted them. "I could buy lamb ribs for a dollar a pound," he said. "Now it's $2.50." Lamb ribs are definitely on the rise.

They're a fixture at Resto, and that's no accident: Resto's executive chef, Ryan Skeen, worked for Mr. Pelaccio at 5 Ninth. And he's a fellow cholesterol enthusiast, that's for sure. In addition to putting pork jowl below deviled eggs, he grinds fatback into the restaurant' burgers and combines pigs' head meat with mayonnaise in sandwiches served on toasted brioche.

He told me on the phone recently that when he outlined his prospective menu for investors, they asked him if he might want to consider "some lighter dishes, like tuna tartare."

He nixed that idea. "It wouldn't be true to my nature," he said. Lamb ribs, on the other hand, are. "I think the fat of lamb is an amazing flavor."

So does the chef Seamus Mullen, who just put together a new menu for the Spanish restaurant Suba on the Lower East Side. One of the dishes on it is a lamb triptych including a square of fat-swaddled lamb belly that's seared on a plancha.

"Fat's great," said Mr. Mullen, whose Suba menu also has pork belly—in two dishes. He added that more chefs and diners were coming to that conclusion and realizing that "a well-marbled rib eye has a lot more flavor than a lean filet mignon."

Indeed they are, and the prevalence of rib eyes on menus around town demonstrates that even beyond Momofuku, Resto and the city's most committed champions of advanced gluttony, there's an embrace of less prissy, more vigorous eating.

There are other signs of this spirit as well. These days a New York restaurant is more likely to present an entree of Kobe or wagyu beef, which is synonymous with fattiness, than of bison, once touted and promoted for its relative leanness. If a fillet of fish isn't showered with pork, then it's wrapped in it, like the monkfish at Cafe Cluny or the sea bass "saltimbocca" at Insieme, both of which wear cloaks of prosciutto.

Meatballs are everywhere, sweetbreads are close behind, and I even detect inklings of a marrow surge, what with the continuing expansion of the Blue Ribbon family and the recent opening, in the Time Warner Center, of a new branch of Landmarc. The Blue Ribbon and Landmarc restaurants are big on marrow bones but don't go as far as Craftsteak, which serves an appetizer of fried cubes of marrow.

Some of the restaurants in the gluttony brigade have been around a while and helped point the way. Take Prune, which the chef Gabrielle Hamilton opened in 1999, charting a brave and beloved course of battered, deep-fried sweetbreads sauced with bacon and butter; of marrow bones with sea salt; and of house-made lamb sausages.

All of these dishes have been on Ms. Hamilton's menu from the start, when it was much more surprising for diners to encounter them and, she recalls, people struggled to describe the little restaurant's big fare.

"I think it got called a lot of things, like a macho-eating menu," she said, adding that she hastened to warn diners that "it could be gross if you have the sweetbreads and the bones and the chocolate cake. You eat one of those things."

A year before Prune came Babbo, where the chef Mario Batali scattered organ meat across the menu and presaged the lardo pizza he would serve at Otto with lardo bruschetta, though he didn't have the nerve to call it that. He told diners that the toasted bread was covered in prosciutto bianco, or white prosciutto, a nonsense term he coined to disguise the truth.

"I knew that they wouldn't eat it if I just said, 'This is the fat of a pig melted onto toast,'" Mr. Batali told me.

Now, however, "lardo is sought after, and it no longer raises people's hackles," he said in a recent phone conversation. "People finally realize that fat is truly delicious, particularly pork fat."

The unabashed names of the restaurants that feed that creed support his assertion. In addition to Fatty Crab there are, in the Williamsburg section of Brooklyn, Pies 'n' Thighs and Fette Sau, German for fat pig.

There's also the Spotted Pig, a Greenwich Village gastropub in which Mr. Batali is an investor. The British chef April Bloomfield guides its kitchen, which turns out roasted pork sandwiches, hamburgers dripping with melted Roquefort and toast slathered with chicken liver. Like Mr. Pelaccio and Mr. Chang, Ms. Bloomfield is among the city's most celebrated young chefs.

Fette Sau belongs to a posse of new barbecue joints, the spread of which, along with the growth in gastropubs, is yet another sign of these fleshy, flabby times. Even slightly older joints have raised the level of their game of late.

Last year Daisy May's BBQ U.S.A., which opened in 2003, began serving not only whole pork butts but also whole pigs. They weigh 30 to 35 pounds, are meant to feed a dozen or so people and cost $480. Adam Perry Lang, the chef and co-owner of Daisy May's, says that he sells at least two of them a night.

It's some ritual. Before the platter of pig appeared before the group I'd assembled, a server set up two perpendicular wood braces to support it. They formed a cross, a reminder—as if we would need one—that something died for the deadly sin dearest to us.

That something was pretty much intact: snout pointed straight toward me, two little ears, four little hooves and a profoundly bronzed hide. The server carved into that skin and peeled away flaps of it, exposing a lustrous layer of fat and a deep reservoir of meat. The rest was up to us, a few sets of plastic tongs and some dull plastic knives.

"This really puts you in touch with your barbaric self," said a woman in our group as she tugged at individual ribs along the pig's midsection. Her fingers were slick with grease.

A man in the group flashed back to his two previous dinners. "I had suckling pig in Boston on Saturday," he said. "I had a pork chop at Inoteca last night."

He paused for a beat, then added: "It's a lifestyle choice."

So it is, and there's a wicked, wonderful cluster of restaurants to support it.

A Glutton's Guide to New York

CRAFTSTEAK, 85 10th Avenue (15th Street); (212) 400-6699. Fried marrow.

DAISY MAY'S BBQ U.S.A., 623 11th Avenue (46th Street), (212) 977-1500. Whole pork butt, whole pig.

FATTY CRAB, 643 Hudson Street (Horatio Street); (212) 352-3590 or 3592. Fatty duck, pork belly and watermelon "salad," pork ribs, fatty sliders.

MOMOFUKU SSÄM BAR, 207 Second Avenue (13th Street); (212) 254-3500. Whole pork butt, steamed pork belly buns, sweetbreads, veal head terrine.

OTTO, 1 Fifth Avenue (Eighth Street); (212) 995-9559. Lardo pizza.

PRUNE, 54 East First Street (First Avenue); (212) 677-6221. Sweetbreads, marrow bones, lamb sausage.

RESTO, 111 East 29th Street; (212) 685-5585. Deviled eggs on pork jowl, burger with fatback, pig's head sandwiches, lamb ribs.

THE SPOTTED PIG, 314 West 11th Street (Greenwich Street); (212) 620-0393. Cubano pork sandwich, burger with Roquefort, chicken liver toast.

SUBA, 109 Ludlow Street (Delancey Street); (212) 982-5714. Lamb belly.

TRESTLE ON TENTH, 242 10th Avenue (24th Street); (212) 645-5659. Saddle of lamb, oxtail and pig's foot terrine.

RAISING THE STEAKS

By Barry Estabrook

from *Gourmet*

Ah, the legendary Kobe beef. Trust Barry Estabrook—who
raises his own poultry and produce on a farm in Vermont
when he's not writing incisive investigative food pieces for
Gourmet—to separate the hype from the reality.

I first tasted Kobe beef at the Kobe club, a sleek midtown
Manhattan temple to the legendary steak. Overhead, 2,000
samurai swords hung, business ends downward, from the ceiling,
while black-clad staff almost seemed to float through the darkness
like shadows. Just after Jude Law and Michael Caine sat down a
couple of tables over, a waiter materialized to my left and, with a
flourish, presented me with a sizzling ten-ounce rib eye. There was
a tiny paper Japanese flag jutting from a toothpick that had been
jabbed into the $175 entrée.

I put a morsel in my mouth, and my surroundings became
unimportant. A thin, salty sear on the outside crackled and then
released a warm gush of what seemed like beefy, buttery pudding,
as rich as foie gras. With that one bite, I understood why Kobe has
become the signature dish of the decade, with sales tripling during
the past five years, not only at urban trendsetters but also at virtually every self-respecting steak house in the country and even at
ambitious midrange grills, where Kobe burgers are the new lunch-
eon item du jour.

AS THE MEAT MELTED IN MY MOUTH, I marveled. The night before,
I'd grilled a grass-finished skirt steak. How could two cuts of beef

be so utterly different, the one pale pink and requiring neither knife nor teeth, the other—from an animal that had spent its life grazing on pasture as a cow is supposed to do—tangy, chewy, and bloody?

Like many people, I am familiar with Kobe lore: These supremely pampered bovines pass their days in almost Zen-like bliss, getting regular massages and subsisting on all the grain they can eat, washed down with cold Kirin beer. "Imagine a life completely free of stress, with as much tender-loving-care you could ever want" is how the Web site of an American importer of Kobe beef puts it. "Sound too good to be true?"

That was an interesting question, and I wondered why I'd never thought to ask it myself. Why the massages? Why the beer? Was this science or mystical malarkey?

Getting to see Kobe beef on the hoof is anything but easy. Raymond Blanc, co-owner of the *Michelin* two-star Le Manoir aux Quat' Saisons, outside Oxford, England, is one of the few Western chefs to have visited a Japanese Kobe farm. Blanc's knowledge of meat production has its roots back in the 1950s, in rural Besançon, France. "I have a deep understanding of country life and of feeding livestock," he said, pausing to sample a dish brought into his office by a sous-chef and issue orders for corrections. "On our farms, you have the kitchen on one side, and you just open the door and there's the stable."

While touring Japan in 1993, Blanc visited several major cities. As soon as he arrived in Kobe, he asked to see a beef farm. His request brought a surprisingly cool response from his hitherto accommodating Japanese hosts. "Yes, yes, yes," they said, but it never happened. So Blanc organized his own trip to the countryside— and was shocked by what he saw.

"The animals were kept in some kind of crate, so there could be very little movement. They were very dirty from their own manure—and I know a dirty cow from a clean cow. It was disgusting, such a contradiction from what I'd read."

Blanc's observations were confirmed for me by knowledgeable experts. David Blackmore, an Australian cattle rancher who has visited Japanese farms and agricultural centers a dozen times over the four decades he's been in the business, raises an internationally renowned herd of 2,000 full-blood Wagyu (pronounced "wah-gyu" or "way-gyu") cattle north of Melbourne. Wagyu, he explained, is the breed from which Kobe meat comes, but the meat can only properly be called Kobe if it comes from a pure strain of Wagyu raised in the Hyogo prefecture, which includes the city of Kobe.

Traditional Japanese producers, Blackmore said, raise their 1,600-pound cattle in highly confined areas. "From the time they are a week old until they are three and a half years old, these steers are commonly kept in a lean-to behind someone's house," said Blackmore, "where they get bored and go off their feed. Their gut stops working. The best way to start their gut working again is to give them a bottle of beer.

"The steers have been lying in their own manure," he continued. "The farmers are proud of their cattle, and the first thing they do is grab a bit of straw and rub the manure off. That could be seen as being massaged. Wagyu can also get a lot of joint swelling. I can imagine that the farmers would be massaging joints so they could get the animals off to market."

Charles Gaskins, a professor of animal science and a Wagyu expert at Washington State University—he's also one of the directors of the American Wagyu Association—puts it somewhat less diplomatically. "The steers grow so big and heavy, they get arthritic," he said. "It's a matter of keeping the animals going until they are ready to be harvested."

So MUCH FOR IMAGES of plump cattle grazing contentedly in a sea of waving grass, attended by devoted servants who massage them and pour them beer. (And where is all that pasture to begin with, given that Japan is so short of land?) It's hard not to draw a parallel to mass-produced veal calves—the main difference being that a veal calf's misery is over in five or six months, whereas Kobe cattle endure these conditions for three years. Japanese farmers, of course, don't see it this way. Attempts to reach an official with Japan's Kobe association failed. However, Kengo Kuba, an importer of Japanese meats into the United States, has spent time on farms in that country. He insists that the animals are well treated, "like family." The beer and massage, he contends, relax the animals and make their meat more tender.

"My impression is that the farmers think this individual treatment is actually a good thing for the animal," says Dr. Michael Appleby, animal-welfare adviser at the World Society for the Protection of Animals. "But cattle are herd animals—social animals—that require a certain amount of exercise and freedom of movement for their physical and emotional health."

Nature—in the form of genetics—rather than nurture plays the most important role in the ineffable tenderness of the famous beef. Because of Buddhist and Shinto tenets, beef was not consumed in Japan until the Meiji Restoration, the reign that began in 1868 and signified a turning toward the West. Before then, Japanese cattle were draft animals, raised for strength and endurance, and this probably led to the development of the Wagyu's signature trait—vast stores of intramuscular fat that could be called upon for bursts of energy and that also resulted in heavily marbled meat.

Blackmore's Wagyu, like the Wagyu raised in the United States, lead lives that are strikingly different from those in Japan. For one thing, his cows are allowed to raise their own calves for ten months on open pasture. After the calves are weaned, they remain on pasture for six more months before they go into open-sided barns for up to 600 days to slowly gain weight on a blend of grains. As for the quality of this more humanely raised meat, Blackmore lists Thomas Keller, of the French Laundry and Per Se, among his regular American customers.

That confinement isn't necessary to produce the holy grail of beef is clear when I visit a working Wagyu cattle farm owned by Henry Schmidek, a former professor of neurosurgery who has retired to 130 acres in Vermont. A herd of about 50 graze at the bottom of a field. Schmidek cups his hands, trilling, "Here, here, here," and the squat, black animals trot clumsily toward us. For centuries, their progenitors were bred as workmates for humans, he notes, and today's Wagyu are docile, even-tempered animals.

Like almost all American Wagyu, Schmidek's cattle are not full-bloods. They were originally the result of impregnating Black Angus cows with Wagyu semen, resulting in a 50–50 cross; now he

breeds each new generation to full-bloods, so the percentage of
Wagyu continues to increase in his herd. On average, the meat
costs less than half of what you'd pay for Japanese Kobe, but it still
gets ratings that exceed the USDA's top grade of "Prime," which
has a greater amount of marbling than cuts graded "Choice" and
"Select."

"American Wagyu is more appropriate to the eating style we
have here," said Shane Lindsay, the owner of Brand Advantage, a
wholesaler of Wagyu and other meats. "You're really not going to
want a big slab of Kobe slapped on your plate." And, it turns out,
you're not likely to get one, no matter how stratospheric the price
or what the menu claims. Very little, if any, real Kobe reaches the
United States. According to Lindsay, none of the slaughterhouses
permitted to export to this country is in Hyogo prefecture. The
high-ticket meat often marketed here as Kobe probably comes
from Wagyu cattle raised in other parts of Japan. But Lindsay, who
lived in Japan for four years, says that the difference is impercepti-
ble. "They are the same breed of cattle raised the same way."

The evening I sampled Japanese Kobe, I also tucked into a slice
of Wagyu from the States, garnished with, yes, a tiny paper facsim-
ile of the Stars and Stripes. It had the same over-the-top, beefy flavor but lacked the melt-in-your-mouth sensuality and tenderness
of Kobe. On the other hand, I could have polished off a nice, thick
American Wagyu steak without a richness overdose. For my
money, it was the better bargain. And anyway, after seeing
Schmidek's cattle moving freely across that pasture, Prime will do
just fine, thanks. I've lost my taste for beef raised in a crate, Kobe or
not Kobe.

Yes, Virginia,
They *Do* Eat Guinea Pigs

By Scott Gold

from *The Shameless Carnivore*

Scott Gold eats meat, and he's not afraid who knows it. He
even maintains a Web site (www.shamelesscarnivote.com)
about his carnivorous proclivities and parlayed his blog into
an entire book, stuffed with meat-centric information and
bursts of gonzo prose.

About halfway through the Month of Meat, I got an
e-mail from a friend alerting me to an Ecuadorian
restaurant in Brooklyn that specializes in serving guinea pig.

Yes, guinea pig.

Even more so than rabbit, the notion of eating guinea pigs elic-
its from most Americans a loathing and disgust they'd normally reserve for, say, devoted followers of the Church of Satan, or those
perverts nabbed red-handed by Chris Hansen on *Dateline*'s "To
Catch a Predator." They may not say it outright (well, some do),
but most people, when I tell them I've eaten guinea pig, are quick
to see me as some kind of sick deviant. They employ the cuteness
defense, which I rebut with enthusiasm, but it rarely does any
good. Rabbit they've seen on menus, even if they don't order it, so
at least they have an inkling that some people eat them, but guinea
pigs? Those . . . *pets*? The rodents used in scientific experiments?
Who would possibly want to eat such a thing?

Millions of people, as a matter of fact. Guinea pigs, also known
as *cuy* or *cuye*—are a prized delicacy in the mountainous regions of
Ecuador. It's a dish enjoyed with great passion and fervor at every

special occasion, from weddings to births, christenings, birthdays, and anniversaries. And in the Andes, it's less a celebratory treat than a dietary staple—Peruvians consume an estimated sixty-five million of the furry little guys every year. The eating of *cuy* is such an important aspect of their culture and heritage, there is even a cathedral in Cuzco in which you'll find a re-creation of da Vinci's *The Last Supper*, with one notable difference from the original: directly in the center of the painting, lying placidly on a serving platter directly in front of the Christ figure, you can clearly see the image of a roasted guinea pig. If meat could be so integral to a people's culture that they depict it as being enjoyed by the son of God on the evening before he sacrifices himself to save mankind from its sins, I just *had* to try it.

The popularity of *cuy* in that part of the world should come as no surprise when you consider the animal itself: guinea pigs are small but meaty, similar in size and nutritional value to rabbits, and just as easy to breed. If you're relatively poor, which many people in Peru, Ecuador, and Bolivia are, breeding guinea pigs is an economical source of consistently renewable protein, and it takes much less space and effort than keeping cattle, pigs, or poultry. It makes such perfect sense, and when you think about it, it's hard to believe that more people and cultures around the world aren't enjoying *cuy* as much as our Andean friends. True, some might get turned off by the cute factor, or the pet factor, or the rodent factor (guinea pigs, being members of the order Rodentia, are cousins to rats and squirrels as well as rabbits), but their popularity as a food source isn't solely based on economics. It's not just a poverty food—these people love their *cuy* with the same ardent passion with which we Louisianians love our crawfish and oysters, Italians from Parma adore their prosciutto, and Kansas City natives worship BBQ ribs. I was once in a cab on the way to the airport when I got to talking with the driver, who it turned out was originally from Ecuador. Naturally, it didn't take long for the conversation to turn to food, and then to *cuy*. The man immediately began to wax rhapsodic about his adoration for guinea pigs, rolling his head at the memories of feasts in his past (which, I admit, worried me a little, as we were on the Brooklyn-Queens Expressway, not known for the forgiving nature of its traffic). "Oh man," he told me, "I love the *cuy*. Love! And if you don't love the *cuy* . . . you are *not* from Ecuador!" With that, I was sold.

Even in New York City, where you can get just about anything if you look with a little effort, guinea pigs are hard to come by. At least as dinner. But luckily enough one of my carnivorous compatriots discovered an Ecuadorian restaurant in Brooklyn that claimed to serve *cuy*, hence that fateful e-mail. It was expensive, though (thirty bucks a pop, believe it or not), and you had to give the restaurant advance notice so they could get in touch with their supplier, but still, it seemed to be worth the trouble and expense, given the tales of untold taste sensations my Ecuadorian cabbie was eager to share with me. So I gave them a call.

"We no have them now," the restaurant man explained in heavily accented English. I asked if he could get some by Saturday. "Is maybe," he said. "I see . . . you call back Saturday, I tell you if we get the *cuy*." I agreed, and set about gathering a group of adventurous friends who might be eager to taste a storied South American delicacy. Some were revolted (naturally), others intrigued by the idea and willing to find out what the fuss was all about, though they had no desire to eat any *cuy* themselves, for which I declared them cowardly fuddy-duddies, but I was happy for the company. A few others, including my friends Brad and Katie, who'd shared yakitori, yak, and llama with me, were quick to join in, as was my friend Nina, who'd actually traveled to Peru but timidly passed on the *cuy* while there, which she felt in retrospect to be a real error. She was keen to redeem herself, though, and I was more than pleased to offer her the opportunity. By the weekend, I'd gathered a group of six, four of whom were excited to get our guinea pig on, including myself. The anticipation was killing me.

Problem was, I had no idea whether or not the restaurant would be able to get our *cuy* on the day we'd all planned to go, which, it turns out, they weren't. I was crestfallen. No guinea pigs? "Well," said Vegetarian Sarah (the one who'd tried my marinated kangaroo), "why don't you just go to the pet store?"

"You're kidding, right?"

"Well, why not?" she asked matter-of-factly. To her, it seemed perfectly sensible to go down to the local pet shop, pick out a nice, tender guinea pig, kill and clean it, then roast it up in my backyard.

I was genuinely shocked by this idea, mainly because it had been put forth by a vegetarian (what had that kangaroo *done* to her?), but I also had to ask myself—was it really that unreasonable? When you think about it, how different is that from what your basic Peruvian might do, and after all, I was supposed to be the Shameless Carnivore and everything. I considered the prospect for a moment, thoughtfully weighing the respective pros and cons. Then I decided against it, because doing so would be crazy, and I told Sarah as much.

"Those guinea pigs are for petting, not for eating," I explained. "Who knows, maybe they have all sorts of genetic deficiencies and health problems," a reasonable assumption, given the guinea pig's inclination toward inbreeding, even cannibalism. I thought back to my high school biology lab, which featured a terrarium filled with the most screwed-up guinea pigs I've ever seen in my life. They'd gone absolutely batshit from generations of incest. One day, our instructor, Dr. Leslie, couldn't find one of the young boars (male guinea pigs are "boars," females "sows"), until it turned up underneath the wood chips, rendered little more than a skeleton by its lunatic cannibal relatives. "Oh no!" I remember him exclaiming. "He went and ate his uncle-daddy!" This was not the type of creature I wanted on my supper plate.

We didn't have to wait long to get our *cuy* fix. I called the Ecuadorian place the following Monday, and it turns out that they had just gotten a fresh order of *cuy* from their supplier. I hastily reassembled our guinea pig crew and set off to Brooklyn's Park Slope neighborhood, eager and excited to finally try this prized South American dish.

I can't quite say what I expected from a restaurant that specializes in rodents, but as we entered we saw little more than a neighborhood joint: brightly lit, tile floors, inflatable Corona marketing decorations (an airplane, a giant beer bottle), jukebox in the corner filled with Latin music, which played softly over speakers as we took our seats. The only thing that hinted at the place's theme was a handwoven tapestry with an Inca design and the word *Ecuador* hanging above the bar. Well, that and the food. As with the yakitori restaurant, the menu here was both laminated and filled with meat dishes and English translations of their original names, many of which were comical: *bistec regular* translated as "regular steak" (we couldn't find "irregular steak" anywhere—maybe it would be a great deal, like buying an irregular shirt), and *bistec Ecuatoriano* became "steak in Ecudorian steak." Steak *in* steak? Could it really be? We surmised that it was a typo, that the restaurant's owners had intended to label it "steak in Ecuadorian *sauce*," though I couldn't help but daydream about the implications of stuffing one steak into another. God, that would be brilliant. Just to make sure, my friend Liz agreed to order it, as she'd already declared that she would be wimping out on the *patates con cuy*, or "potatoes with *cuy*," which four of us eagerly ordered up as soon as we could get our waitress's attention.

I'd done a little bit of research about how this *cuy* thing was supposed to go down, and I gathered two very important slices of information about what to expect: 1) the guinea pig is served whole, like a tiny suckling pig—minus most of the inner organs—and the entire animal is there waiting to be devoured, head, claws, you name it; 2) speaking of devouring, you're actually supposed to eat everything, so that by the time you've finished, there should be nothing left on the plate but bones. I knew all of this, and I thought I'd fully warmed to the idea of eating a whole guinea pig—I'd made sure to bring a healthy attitude and appetite, both of which were enhanced by the first couple of beers I sucked down as we anxiously waited for the main course to arrive—but nothing, I mean nothing, can prepare you for the moment of truth, when a smiling server sets a bright-orange animal down on a plate in front of you.

We burst into laughter, because that's what terrified people do in situations like this—it would probably be seen as impolite to start hollering your head off right there at the table. It's a horrifying thing, seeing a roasted rodent for the first time like this, placed simply on a serving dish over a bed of potatoes, a thick tomato slice, and a halved hard-boiled egg. It wasn't just that lying belly-down like that, it looked like it had been actively trying to run away at the time of its demise, much like those poor Pompeiian people immortalized in volcanic ash two thousand years ago, nor was it that I could plainly see its little claws, teeth, whiskers (yes, whiskers!), and the tongue hanging out of its mouth. No—what alarmed me most was the expression on the creatures' faces:

It looked *pissed*.

It had every right to be, of course: you'd be more than a little miffed if some cheery Ecuadorian turned you into a meal, and this guinea pig showed it, displaying every ounce of fury and disdain for its untimely fate. With its jaws agape and empty eye sockets squinting like Clint Eastwood's unnamed cowboy just before a gunfight,* my *cuy*'s face seemed locked in an anguished, permanent, silent scream. It's not an easy thing to confront your meal's accusatory facial expression as you stick a fork in him—Vegetarian Sarah, who for God knows what reason had decided to join us, found herself needing to place a napkin over the head of Katie's guinea pig, which she claimed as staring at her—but I was hungry, and he was dinner. So we dug in.

When you get past the initial shock and focus on the taste, *cuy* turns out to be intriguingly delicious. The animal has been slow-cooked in toto and, like a suckling pig, should emerge from the oven with a deep orange, crackly skin on the outside and tender, succulent meat within. In this case, the skin was more chewy than crispy, so I mostly forwent it in favor of picking hot scraps of meat from the delicate bones. Gourmands often compare *cuy* to quail, even though the two animals have little in common biologically, because both have darkly colored meat and a fine bone structure; however, the meat from my guinea pig was on the oily side, most likely from subcutaneous fat that had been rendered during the roasting, leaving my fingers covered in flavorful grease, which I naturally licked off. After about forty-five minutes of working our way through the entire animal, some interesting options presented themselves.

"Hey," said Nina, clearly pleased by her decision to make up for her past *cuy* cowardice. "Why don't you eat one of the ears?" That's right, I thought, you *are* supposed to eat everything . . . so I picked up the animal's head, now barely attached to the body by a thin sheaf of skin, placed the cranium to my mouth and tore away one

---

*Well, not entirely empty—the eyeballs liquefy inside the orbits during the cooking process, which *cuy* enthusiasts make sure to cherish, sucking the boiled ocular fluid right out of the head. Yum!

of the little triangular ears with my teeth, then thoughtfully chewed away. It was crunchy and little meaty; remarkably similar to a tiny pork cracklin. "It's good," I declared. "You should try it!" Then came the kidneys, the liver, the bits of flesh in the cheeks and jowls, the neck, the tongue . . . I lost myself a little then, going into a wordless, rhythmic trance state as I enthusiastically disposed of each new morsel until all that remained was a pile of bones and a little skin. By the time I'd finished and was downing the rest of my beer, it dawned on me why *cuy* has been considered such a special, prized meal by South Americans for centuries. It's a ritual as much as a food, with each part of the whole animal bringing a different texture, taste, and pleasure. Yes, it's safe to say that devouring a whole animal in this way is about as joyfully barbaric as carnivorism gets.

It was marvelous.

Personal Tastes

Losing My Carnivirginity: The Diary of a Lapsed Vegetarian

By Khyber Oser

from *Gastronomica*

Though Khyber Oser generally writes about baseball and col-
lectibles, this autobiographical essay reveals how he, a lifelong
vegetarian, fell off the veggie wagon—and with good reason.

I was born vegetarian—the same way some kids are born
Baptist. It wasn't my choice, but I embraced it. I still do.
At twenty-five, I've never had a steak, a burger, even turkey on
Thanksgiving.

I'm also a Francophile, though not from the womb. I started
taking *français* in seventh grade, went to Aix-en-Provence on a
high-school exchange program, and studied in Paris as a college
junior. I shamelessly love the language, country, arts, people—
everything except the cuisine.

It's sacrilege, I know. To be a lover of all things French is, by definition, to bow down before filet mignon and foie gras. Yet here I
am, a lifelong veggie for whom foie gras conjures images of animal
torture. Both times I've been to France, my vegetarian force field
was fully engaged. It seemed natural that my host families would
make separate meals for me; all my life I've asked people to accommodate my way of eating.

That's what vegetarians do. Or, in my case, *did*.

I've just arrived in France for the third time, and along with my
usual things I've packed a life-altering decision: I'm temporarily

converting from vegetarian to carnivore. For the next two weeks, as I visit my French friends and host families, I plan to eat whatever is served, make amends for past slights, broaden my horizons, and expand my palate. I don't want to be a high-needs guest this time around, an isolationist who fulfills stereotypes about Americans. I'm ready to consume French culture to the fullest when my hosts and I break bread together. And if that means foie gras, then (gulp) so be it.

Well Done

My gastronomic journey began in the South of France, with Vincent. He and I have been friends since Penn State, when my ears perked up on campus one day as a group of French students conversed in their native tongue. *J'adore la France*, I told them proudly. Could we get together sometime? Hang out? Speak French? Talk socialism?

They thought me strange, as Americans or Frenchmen go, but came to embrace me despite my overzealous love for their country and my perplexing vegetarianism. Vincent and I have remained close ever since. He seems downright giddy about my quest to be a surrogate meathead. His motto, he told me, is "Food is for enjoying."

We went to his parents' house in Ardéche tonight for my deflowering dinner. Vincent's mother, Martine, knowing nothing of my carnivirginity, ensured that my first experience would be a memorable one. She seduced me with steak. It landed on my plate looking nothing like the huge, gravy-laden American ones I've seen. It was thin and oblong, with crisp, wild edges. *So this is the Moment of Truth,* I sighed to myself. *A quarter-century of animal abstention ends here, without pomp or pageantry. No retirement party. No gold watch. No one from PETA playing "Taps" on a bugle.* I took a giant swig of wine and brought the first bite to my mouth. Slowly but surely, I managed to finish the whole tender steak. Vincent smiled, nodding his proud approval.

Burger's Remorse

I always assumed meat would make me violently ill since my body wasn't used to it. But I felt fine going to sleep, and I even woke up hungry. Eleven of us sat down to lunch on this summer

Saturday: Vincent, his parents, two uncles, an aunt, a cousin, three kids, and me. We started by noshing on the regional specialty of cured sausage, *saucisson Ardéchois*. Feeling bold after clearing my first hurdle last night, I unwrapped one of the dense, bite-sized links, stared at its crimson meat and pearly white fat kernels, then chomped down. It was sinewy, yet shockingly juicy. I don't think any other food could possibly have made me feel so aware by its taste and texture that I was eating flesh. *Blech!* I lunged for a slice of baguette as a chaser.

Our first course was creamed spinach with real bacon bits. As the wine flowed, the men sang songs by Georges Brassens, and everyone reveled in food and togetherness, a merry maelstrom of French culture. For a brief, shining moment, I couldn't even imagine trying to be vegetarian. Then came Martine's Moroccan patties. It was surreal—and sad—to eat my first-ever hamburger. I enjoyed the taste, but it left me feeling more empty than full. I've always watched people scarf down burgers and seen eyebrows raise at the discovery that I've never had one. It was part of my identity, my uniqueness. No longer.

Sardines Sans Can

Vincent and I picked up his girlfriend, Sophie, that morning at the Avignon train station, then headed toward his house in Istres. Apparently, Sophie likes to push the envelope with me. She wants me to enjoy French culture as much as she does—and if that means introducing me to the most challenging foods she knows, all the better.

When she said we were having sardines for dinner, I pictured the ones crammed in a tin. But these were much bigger, probably eight inches long. Sophie cut out the organs (a disemboweling for which she called me into the kitchen so I could have the *complete* experience), dipped the fish in flour, fried them up, and doled out three to each of us. By avoiding direct eye contact with mine, I was able to filet them myself, separating the bones, head, and tail. I even ate the skin. But nothing could prepare me for the fact that each fish had two sacs, just below the meat, of thousands of eggs stuck together. Double *blech!* Enough challenges, I decided. I finished all six egg pockets by cheating; I smothered each bite in *tapenade*.

Guilty Gourmet

Foie gras. I'd heard so much about it, the cruelty and the singularly exquisite taste both, but hoped I wouldn't have to try it—this trip or ever. Sophie left no doubt. She not only wanted me to sample it, she wanted me to have the lion's share. In the end, my willingness to please and my curiosity outweighed my trepidation.

It was shock at first sight. The glass-jarred specimen contained duck liver in the center surrounded by fat that looked like creamy, bright-yellow canuba wax. Spreading it on toasted baguette, the fat tasted like soft butter but richer and—I'm guessing here—ducky in flavor. The liver had a delicate, smooth consistency. It all gave me a rush of energy, and I must admit—with my deepest apologies to force-fed fowl the world over—foie gras *is* amazing. May the vegetarian gods strike me down.

Chickenhearted

Finally, a reprieve! On a 1-to-10 scale of difficulty, with sardine caviar and foie gras ranking 10, chicken has to be a mere 5 or 6, right? No big deal.

Or so I thought. Sophie prepared a whole chicken with chestnut stuffing, and I ate a leg and thigh right off the bone. *So far, so good*, I thought . . . until Sophie bestowed upon me the guest's honor of the chicken's heart. *Merde.* I could see coagulated blood resting up against a protruding valve. She also showed me the inner pathway where the blood pumped through. *Mmm, thanks for pointing that out.* I couldn't eat the bloody valve, but I did nibble the organ. It tasted like meat. Sophie did me the favor of finishing off the delicacy on her plate with no hesitation at all.

BBQ

I left Vincent's this morning—though not because of the Chicken Heart Incident. My high-school exchange student, Magali, had asked me if I wanted to come to a pool party at her parents' house in Aix-en-Provence. *Bien sûr!* Now I'm staying in the same guest room as I did nearly a decade ago, the first time I ever left the States, smoked a cigarette, or got drunk. When I greeted her parents, they immediately asked if I'm still a vegetarian.

My reputation precedes me.

Magali's ten friends showed up around dinnertime for a barbecue: chicken and sausages. The smell of meat cooking on a grill has always made my mouth water. Now I know what it tastes like—absolutely incredible.

Making Up for Lost Meals

Hemingway called Paris a "moveable feast," saying that for those who visit in their youth, the city stays with them forever. Tonight, after five years away, I returned to Paree for a feast of a more literal sort with Martine and Jean-Claude, my study-abroad host family in whose apartment I had lived for four months without eating one iota of meat.

This was my true redemption meal—and it came on the final full day of my trip. Martine served chicken, and I had seconds. It felt wonderful to graciously partake in one of her specialties that I hadn't been able to (didn't want to) eat the first time around, and to not set myself apart on a night of such memories and warmth.

Homeward Bound

My French food odyssey, *c'est fini*. I'm flying over the Atlantic now, and the flight attendant has just handed me my dinner—a vegetarian dish that looks vaguely like tofu but tastes like a damp sponge. I made the special request months ago, but now I'm second-guessing myself. The airline's Chicken Marsala looks tempting.

The burning question is: What am I?

A vegetarian again? Or a carnivorous convert?

It was all so easy when the boundaries were clear. For twenty-five years I resolutely drew the line at meat. For the past two weeks, my threshold was to eat whatever my French hosts were kind enough to offer—a clean dividing line in its own right. Now I'm at a crossroads. If I retreat to my comfort zone, the strict vegetarianism I know so well, I risk alienating meat eaters and missing out on new experiences. If I press forward as a *lapsed* vegetarian, consciously choosing to eat meat when nonmeat alternatives are available, I can expect my meals to come with a heaping side dish of guilt.

One thing I know for sure is that my days of rigidity are over. Food is culture, and culture should be shared—in another country or at a neighbor's house. It's one thing to eat a certain way within the four walls of my own kitchen, another to impose them on the rest of the world. For now, I'll start by being a flexible vegetarian—a *flexitarian*. As for the future, I think I'll chew on it for a while.

FAT'S WHAT I'M TALKING ABOUT

By Tim Carman

from *Washington City Paper*

Tim Carman has hopped around the country, honing his skills as a food editor at the *Houston Press* and *Kansas City Star* before landing in Washington, D.C. His irreverent Young & Hungry food column for this alt weekly explores D.C. eateries with refreshing wit.

My wife admits to being a cookie snob. Carrie has, on occasion, sampled a chocolate chip cookie enthusiastically endorsed by some kindly fool, only to throw the offending treat into the wastebasket after a single courtesy bite. For years, I've been telling her about the cookies I used to eat as a child, these gooey snacks made with rolled oats and semisweet chocolate chips, and for years, I never made them. I think I was secretly afraid the cookies would suck.

Well, I recently phoned my mom in Kansas City for the recipe, and I have to say I was indeed horrified. Not by the story she told me about the recipe's creator (who died in 1972 when her husband apparently pushed her down the stairs, or so says Mom, who has a thing for intrigue), but by one of the featured ingredients: a full cup of Crisco. Could this hydrogenated headhunter actually be the reason these cookies taste so great?

I'm afraid so. The first batch I pulled from the oven was as crunchy and wickedly luxuriant as I remembered; these things had body, like no cookie should. Even Carrie agreed. We spent the rest of the evening sneaking into the kitchen to nibble cookies in the dark.

The episode got me thinking about how many other crappy foods—or foods made with crappy ingredients—I privately enjoy. (And just for the record, I used the Crisco that's fully hydrogenated, which apparently doesn't cause a coronary right there at the table.) This is not an easy subject to broach. We're bombarded from all directions about what foods to avoid. It's as if the Catholic Church has infiltrated the culinary world, telling us we're all going to hell if we chow down on a Whopper.

Food writers, in particular, act like the high priests of gustatory wisdom. On one hand, you have Michael Pollan and Nina Planck issuing fiats on what's food and what isn't. Here's a sample quote from Pollan's new manifesto, *In Defense of Food*: "Don't eat anything your great grandmother wouldn't recognize as food. Why your great grandmother? Because at this point your mother and possibly your grandmother is as confused as the rest of us; to be safe we need to go back at least a couple of generations, to a time before the advent of most modern foods."

On the other hand, you have food writers like me dishing out stars and accolades to restaurants that buy cured hams from Spanish pigs that dine on acorns or raw beef from Japanese cows that drink beer and—seriously—get massages. We've become a nation of snobs and food-a-phobes. When a moderator at a Smithsonian panel discussion in 2006 asked Anthony Bourdain to pick a favorite between Burger King and McDonald's, the celebrity nonchef shot back: "That's like [choosing between] herpes or chlamydia."

For his part, Pollan has been doing fine work in trying to unravel the mysteries of food science and marketing in his effort to steer us back to a saner diet. But I worry he's off-base. His advice on eating seems neo-Luddite to me. We can't force people to stop consuming fatty, sweet, processed foodstuffs any more than we can force them to ditch their iPods and retreat back to 3-foot-wide boomboxes propped on their shoulders. Commercial foods are here to stay.

I have a better idea: Let's stop obsessing about nutrition, fat counts, carbohydrates, and scientific studies about which food or drink will let us live long enough to watch the Social Security system go bankrupt. Personally, I'm tired of all the fear and guilt tied to food in America (not to mention the books about how to overcome the fear and guilt tied to food in America).

I'd really like to take the guilt out of my guilty pleasures. I mean, will one sweet, salty McDonald's cheeseburger kill you? Of course not. Five thousand of them might, but so would 5,000 plates of crispy sweetbreads at your favorite four-star restaurant. And if you'd really like to swear off some highly processed ambrosia that'll kill you over time, stop drinking those designer cocktails and pricey bottles of wine. Talk about something you can't grow in your garden (as much as I wish I could plant a nice crop of single-malt scotches).

Ever since that Crisco cookie, I've reconnected with some of the foods, or some of the places, I used to like before I felt the need to squirrel away my pedestrian eating habits. You know what? I still really like the Burrito Supreme at Taco Bell, particularly when the pimply kid pumps the sour cream evenly across the beans, shredded lettuce, cheddar cheese, ground beef, and diced tomatoes. I also can't believe how much I drool over the crumbly biscuits at Popeyes; they're even tastier after you slather them with strawberry jam squeezed from a packet. And I swear that some days the cracker-crust pizza at Stained Glass Pub in Silver Spring tastes better than any of those boutique pies—especially when you can play Buzztime trivia while eating.

But I think the real eye-opener came when Carrie and I visited the Olive Garden in Hyattsville. We arrived around 9 p.m. on a Monday—and had to wait for a table. The diners here were not conducting some suburban eating experiment, as we were. People at two different tables were actually celebrating birthdays, clearly without a critic's recommendation or even the promise of house-made pasta. This is the way America eats, and I can understand why. Olive Garden is our corporate red-sauce house; its lasagna and fettuccini Alfredo are as flavorful as anything I ever ate at A.V. Ristortante Italiano.

Which brings me to a final thought: Some places I enjoy really do serve their share of crappy food, like the late, lamented A.V. I was reminded of this while sitting at the Tastee Diner in Silver Spring, wolfing down the greasiest patty melt this side of Friendly's. Despite this, I was content. I was content to dine with people who felt like my neighbors, not like the food cognoscenti test-driving the trendiest new restaurant. The woman by the window at Tastee was reading a Sue Grafton mystery. The man across the aisle occupied a four-top booth all by himself, with only his dishes and his thoughts to keep him company. And me? I had dropped 50 cents into the tabletop jukebox to hear Marvin Gaye and Tammi Terrell sing "Ain't Nothing Like the Real Thing."

Two with the Flu

By John Thorne

from *Mouth Wide Open: A Cook and His Appetite*

It's always a good year when there's a new collection of writings by John Thorne, garnered from his newsletter *Simple Cooking* as well as other publications. Thorne is a culinary radical, intently cutting through hype to get back to the essentials: Classic recipes and comfort foods.

A fever of 103 degrees, night shivers, a dry harsh cough, aching muscles, stuffy nose, giddy head . . . and then, just as I managed to stagger onto the road to recovery, Matt succumbed to the same virus herself. As I lay in bed, sweaty, querulous, bored by and stiff from my confinement there but with no inclination to get up, I began to think about what we might have for supper. Neither of us had much appetite, but, even so, we both hungered for something soothing and warm that would slide effortlessly down our gullets, stroking our taste buds, comforting the rawness in our throats, and calming our queasy stomachs as it went.

I mentally pawed through the contents of our cupboards, searching for something with sufficient potency to lure me out from under the covers. Not that I was in the mood to attempt anything in the way of creative cookery. In fact, what I really wanted was chicken noodle soup . . . but without the tedium of downing spoonful after spoonful of broth. In other words, I craved chicken noodle soup without the soup. Let's call it . . . noodle chicken.

As an intellectual exercise, concocting the ideal restorative is no simple matter. But instinct, given free rein, can make it seem that way. I had recently bought, on pure speculation, a package of the thin Japanese wheat noodles called *somen*. I was drawn to them not because I had any idea of how I would use them but because they were divided—within the cellophane package itself—into neat little bundles, each bound with a blue ribbon. Now the residue of my fever made the thought of these silky strands slithering down my throat so compelling that it began to pull everything else together along behind it.

Despite my state of convalescence, I wanted potency, not blandness—but potency sheathed in a velvet glove. The noodles, being Japanese, naturally suggested soy sauce, minced ginger and garlic, slivered scallions. I also wanted an intensely flavored chicken broth and tender chunks of chicken meat—which, thanks to our cook-ahead method (see below), I already had on hand. This seemed a good starting point, quite sufficient in itself . . . and yet I still wasn't out of bed. That, it seemed, required something de luxe, a simple but persuasive touch of pampering—on the order of poached quail eggs or miniature shiitake mushroom caps, neither of which, of course, were lying around, or tender little dumplings, which would require too much effort. But there was a bright red pepper. If I could only face the task of peeling it. . . .

Surprisingly, I could. In fact, I was already shuffling in the direction of the kitchen, a gleam in my eye.

The result was something so delicious that it has been a regular presence at our table ever since. I say this not to boast but to express a feeling only a little short of astonishment. I almost never work up a recipe out of whole cloth—such cooking talents as I have are usually directed at coming up with a special understanding of a familiar and typically very ordinary dish. I do occasionally whip up something to eat from whatever happens to be in the kitchen, but the whole point of such hunger-driven cooking lies in its unabashed immediacy—me hungry, me eat—which all but rules out any notion of reproducibility.

In this instance, however, hunger had little to do with what was going on. I was sick a lot when I was a child; in fact, for several years I had made a deal with God. When things got too much for me, I would tell Him so in my prayers that night—and the next morning

I would wake up with a fever. My memories of the resulting times in bed are not of being lovingly cosseted but of total immersion in comforting solitude. For me, being sick was a way of securing the right to be left alone. The comforter's task, then, was not so much to soothe what hurt as to tempt me back into everyday life.

Until a tonsillectomy permanently exorcised this ability, my mother found the best way to treat these mysterious bouts of fever was to let boredom work the cure—a remedy that remains effective for most things that ail me today. But if tedium is the stick, the carrot has never been as easy to find. Consequently, this stratagem of my own inner comforter—to lure me into the kitchen and then succeed in making me supremely happy there— seems all the more impressive. I'd be the last one to know if these dishes have any true medicinal qualities; what I can testify to is their powers of enticement—for cook and eater alike.

Introduction

As you will see, the following two recipes are identical in spirit and all but identical in their ingredients. I have chosen to present them separately because neither is a variation of the other but is rather a separate orchestration of the same inspirational force. Each requires two easily obtained and inexpensive items—a cooking thermometer that can be immersed in simmering water and a quart-size microwavable ziplock bag (a Ziploc "double zipper" bag by preference), which we use for poaching meat. The method described below has three unique advantages: (1) the meat's juices and flavor are neither diluted nor lost during the cooking process; (2) the scum produced in the cooking clings to the sides of the bag, eliminating the need for skimming; and (3) the meat can be cooked in a small amount of liquid with no worry that it will overcook or dry out. This method also makes it possible to cook two or three cuts of meat simultaneously in the same pot—removing each bag at the end of its ideal cooking time. The meat, removed from its bag and refrigerated in its own juices, keeps for several days until needed. Note that the addition of water—called for in the following instructions—is necessary only when additional meat broth is wanted.

Meat–Cooking Method

Fill a large pot about half full of hot tap water and set it on the stove. Turn the flame to high. Meanwhile, put the pieces of meat into a quart-size microwavable ziplock bag. Dissolve 1 teaspoon of kosher salt in 1 cup of water. Pour this over the meat. Tie the bag shut after forcing out as much air as possible. Lower this into the water on the stove. Insert a thermometer into the water (we use an instant-read and hold it in place with the pot's cover). Bring the temperature up to 170°F and then adjust the heat to keep it there (a 5°F fluctuation in either direction is of no concern). Once this temperature has been reached, if you are preparing chicken, cook it for 3 hours; if beef, cook it for 8 hours.

When the meat is ready, grasp the knot of the bag with a pair of kitchen tongs. Lift the bag out and set it into a shallow bowl. Gingerly untie the knot and open the bag. Let its contents cool for 20 minutes. Remove the meat and shred it, discarding any bone, pieces of fat, or cartilage. Put the shredded meat into a bowl. Fold the top of the cooking bag over until it reaches about halfway down the bag's side. Now close one hand tightly around the top of the bag and hold the bottom firmly with the other. Invert it over the bowl of meat and loosen your fingers enough to allow the broth to stream into the bowl, closing off the flow when it reaches the fat. Reserve about a tablespoon of the fat separately (if desired) and discard the rest. Refrigerate the bowl of meat and broth and cover when cool. As noted above, this can be done a couple of days before proceeding with the rest of the recipe.

—∞—

Noodle Chicken

[Serves 2 with the flu]

kosher salt
1 tablespoon each chicken fat and peanut oil or 2 tablespoons
    peanut oil
1 tablespoon soy sauce
¼ tablespoon sugar (optional)
6 large leaves Napa or Chinese cabbage
6 scallions, including green tops, trimmed

1 large garlic clove, minced

1 large red bell pepper, cored, seeded, and peeled (see note)

4 chicken thighs, cooked and shredded as directed above,
   with accompanying broth (see note)

1-inch chunk ginger, peeled and grated or minced (see note)

1 teaspoon fresh chile paste (see note) or hot sauce to taste

¼ pound Japanese somen noodles (see note)

1. Fill a pasta pot with 4 quarts of water and bring this to a boil. Stir in 1 to 2 tablespoons of salt. Put into a separate medium-size pot the chicken fat and/or peanut oil, 1 teaspoon of salt, the soy sauce, and the sugar (if using) and begin to heat this over a medium-low flame.

2. Cut the thick white stems of the cabbage into ½-inch strips. When you reach the green leaves, cut these in half from top to bottom, then cut these into ½-inch strips also. Keep the stems and leaves separate.

3. Slice the scallions into 2-inch lengths, then cut these in half vertically (all but the narrowest green ends, which can be used whole). When the oil in the pot is hot and the soy sauce has begun to release its odor, add the cabbage stem pieces, the scallion strips, and the minced clove of garlic. Stir all this occasionally for several minutes, until the scallions are wilted and soft and the cabbage stem pieces tender.

4. Cut the peeled red bell pepper pieces into ½-inch strips. When the scallions and cabbage stems have softened, add the pepper pieces and the strips of cabbage leaf to the pot. Mix well and cook another 2 or 3 minutes, stirring occasionally, until the leaves have wilted. Then add the chicken meat and the jellied broth. Turn the heat up to medium.

5. When the chicken jelly has melted, stir in the minced ginger and the fresh chile paste. Continue cooking until the chicken meat is heated through. Taste the broth for seasoning, adjusting as necessary.

6. Strew the noodles into the roiling salted water in the other pot. Cook until tender—about 3 minutes—and pour out into a colander or large sieve. Shake out any excess water and divide the noodles between two large soup bowls. Then

ladle over the contents of the medium pot and serve at once. Chopsticks are optional.

Cook's Notes:

Bell Pepper: Use a vegetable peeler or very sharp paring knife to remove the skin from the pepper. (Doing this makes a real difference to the finished dish, so don't skip this step.)

Chicken Thighs: Matt and I both prefer dark meat to light. We suspect that a chicken breast would be an acceptable replacement, but we've never been able to bring ourselves to find out.

Ginger: I almost never use a garlic press to crush garlic, but crushing ginger in one makes sense, since gingerroot is full of coarse fibers that add nothing to a dish. Cutting the peeled ginger into garlic-size chunks and squeezing them through a garlic press produces a flavor-intensive purée. Otherwise, use a porcelain ginger grater or mince the ginger with a cleaver.

Fresh Chile Paste: Sometimes called sambal oelek, *this can be found in Asian grocery stores and some supermarkets. Look for the gold label with a red rooster on it and a simple list of ingredients—fresh chile paste, vinegar, salt, and preservatives. To temper the fire, we sieve out all the seeds when we start a new jar.*

Somen Noodles: These thin white noodles, made of wheat, are related to udon noodles but are noticeably thinner—a delicate wisp of a noodle that still manages to retain a distinct texture and delicious taste. Most of the packages available at our Asian grocery come from Korea, where the noodle is called somyun *and is also very popular. Typically, the Japanese eat somen cold and the Koreans eat them hot, tossed in fiery sauces. These noodles cook very quickly; don't let them get mushy.*

Noodle Beef

[Serves 2 with the flu]

kosher salt
2 tablespoons peanut oil

1 tablespoon soy sauce
¼ tablespoon sugar (optional)
2 medium to large carrots, peeled
1 small to medium head bok choy
6 scallions, including green tops, trimmed
1 garlic clove, minced
1 pound boneless beef short ribs, cooked and shredded as di-
    rected on page 72, with accompanying broth (see note)
1-inch chunk ginger, peeled and grated or minced (see above)
1 teaspoon fresh chile paste (see above) or hot sauce to taste
¼ pound Japanese somen noodles (see above)

1. Fill a pasta pot with 4 quarts of water and bring this to a boil. Stir in 1 to 2 tablespoons of salt. Into a separate medium-size pot put the peanut oil, 1 teaspoon of salt, the soy sauce, and the sugar (if using) and begin to heat this over a medium-low flame.

2. Cut the carrots into thirds. Turn the resulting cylinders on end and slice each vertically into wide thin strips. Add these together to the pot with the hot oil and flavorings, tossing the mixture with a spatula as you do. Cook these for 5 minutes before adding any other ingredients.

3. Cut both the thick white stems and the green leaves of the bok choy into ½-inch strips but keep them separate. Slice the scallions into 2-inch lengths, then cut these in half vertically (all but the narrowest green ends, which can be used whole).

4. Stir the bok choy stem pieces, the scallion strips, and the minced clove of garlic in with the carrot slices. Cook, stirring occasionally, for several minutes, until the scallions are wilted and soft and the cabbage stem pieces are tender. Taste a piece of carrot—at this point it should be soft but still slightly crisp. If so, add the shredded beef and its jellied broth. Turn the heat up to medium.

5. When the beef jelly has melted, stir in the minced ginger and the fresh chile paste. Continue cooking until the beef is heated through. Taste the broth for seasoning, adjusting as necessary.

6. Strew the noodles into the roiling salted water in the other pot. Cook until tender—about 3 minutes—and pour

out into a colander or large sieve. Shake out any excess water and divide the noodles between two large soup bowls. Then ladle over the contents of the medium pot and serve at once. Chopsticks are optional.

Variations:
A good handful of fresh bean sprouts or snow peas makes a delicious addition to either version of this dish.
Cook's Note:
Beef: Boneless beef short ribs are our particular favorite for this dish. If these are only available with the bone in, buy about 1½ pounds to account for the waste. Thick-cut blade steak is a good second choice.

Further Reading: *A Soothing Broth*

Treating food as if it were a subspecies of medicine is depressingly common these days, and those who embrace that notion as an answer to all their health concerns must have a hard time organizing the daily menus, with this to be eaten to strengthen the immune system, that to ward off cancer, the other to keep the arteries flowing cleanly, the bones from crumbling, the brain's synapses firing smoothly, and unwanted fat cells on the run. "Regimen" is the word for this sort of disciplined eating, where pleasure is always subsumed to the needs of the rigorously healthy life.

There is, however, another, very different tradition of food-as-medicine writing, directed to those who find that the consequences of their not-so-ordered lives have put them in need of a restorative or calmative or analeptic—something, in other words, that will gently coax back to terra firma what excess has driven up into a tree.

This is the subject of a valuable and very appealing little volume by Pat Willard called *A Soothing Broth*, an extended meditation on the role of the cook as comforter, with a widely gathered collection of "tonics, custards, soups, and other cure-alls for colds, coughs, upset tummies, and out-of-sort days." Most such books are directed to the fellow sufferer, a sharing of what the author has found palliative when under the weather. But for Willard, it is the role of soother, not sufferer, that strikes a chord of deep emotional resonance, and that makes her book all the richer: its subject is really the act of feeding as a form of reconnection to those we care about as well as for.

Illness and other acute forms of bodily discomfort shove the sufferer off into a separate world of pain. The bowl of steaming broth or the shimmering spoonful of custard is a rescue line tossed across that abyss; any tug at the other end means a diminution of feelings of helplessness and isolation at both ends of the rope. And this is equally true when the patient needing succor lies within ourselves.

Willard's writing, consequently, is always as suggestive about and sensitive to the needs of the caregiver as it is to those of the cared-for, a balance that carries over into the collection of old-fashioned recipes and remedies (often, of course, the two are the same) that she has gathered from amateur and professional comforters alike. (Tending the sick at home was, until very recently, almost as regular—and as exhausting—a task as doing the weekly laundry.)

She includes concoctions for specific ailments—apple soup for constipation; velvet cream for insomnia; *lait de poule* (hen's milk, a frothy mixture of orange flower water, sugar, and egg yolks, blended into boiling water) for a sore throat—as well as those that are universally solace-giving, like junket eggnog and stewed macaroni (about which she writes: "The macaroni is melting soft, surrounded by a thin sauce of milk; it has the effect of making your stomach feel as if it is wrapped up in a comforting quilt").

I also enjoyed her recipes for various restoratives and invigorating tonics, some repellent (the family fled the house when her grandmother set about preparing her seaweed-based winter tonic), others quite inviting (who could refuse a morning dose of "good quality" bourbon infused with sage blossoms and lemon peel?). *A Soothing Broth* is, in short, a treat as well as a treatment—and a replacement for half the stuff in your medicine cabinet.

Road Trip to Chinatown: Tasting Your Heritage, One Bite at a Time

By Eve M. Tai

from *Gastronomica*

This excellent quarterly journal explores the meeting of food and culture—a fascinating intersection indeed, perfectly exemplified in this memoir by Seattle-based freelance writer Eve M. Tai about her Asian-American childhood's perplexing food rituals.

All Chinatowns smells the same. The year is 1975; I am fourteen years old; and I could be in Los Angeles, Chicago, or New York. It doesn't matter. The smell is the same—a mix of ginger, shiitake mushrooms, durian husks, tofu, fish, and rice. It is earthy, palpable, and old country-ish. Cabbage leaves glued flat to wet sidewalks, overripe papaya, deep-fried pork. The smell greets you as soon as you cross the border into Chinatown, informing you of your arrival.

I don't like Chinatowns. They are a world away from our suburban house in Detroit with its clipped and coddled lawn, living room furniture from New England, and cars tucked tidily in a double garage. My parents, both professors, drag my sister, brother, and me to Chinatowns across the country the way a fishing boat scours its net across the ocean floor, missing nothing. We dread plunging into these strange worlds where we hear little English and barely any Mandarin, which we speak. In Chinatown, traffic follows no logic, men spit on sidewalks, and restaurant bathrooms harbor broken towel dispensers and toilets that smell like sweat. The streets never rest; crowds swallow up my family and spit us out again. Everyone talks at once, their Cantonese tones twanging like notes from slide guitars. The old ladies especially, with their flashing gold teeth, jade pendants, and skin dotted with liver spots, aggravate me. They cackle in Cantonese and flap their skinny arms up and down. I am never sure if they are cursing me or commenting on the world at large.

Our parents embarrass us by randomly approaching strangers, as though any Chinese person qualifies to be our personal friend. My siblings and I not so secretly call all Chinese *peng you*, "friend," our American-inflected tone deadly with disdain. Our ventures into Chinatown remind me of roots that I prefer to keep hidden. Whenever I walk those streets, navigating the rivulets of water, the garbage, the spit, I can't avoid confronting the truth of my origins. I reassure myself that people in Chinatowns are a different kind of Chinese than me, less American. They can't speak English; they practice dirty habits; they hang their underwear outside to dry.

I want to be American. Whitebread. Plain vanilla. I see no point in standing out with our strange language, our blackened wok, our mirror glued to the front door to ward off bad spirits. It is one thing to act Chinese in the privacy of our home, quite another to act Chinese in public. That just shows my parents' ignorance, their resistance to new ways, and their attachments to obsolete old-world values that carry no relevance in America. The fact that my parents' journey to America resulted from tragedies—the brutal Japanese occupation of China during the 1930s and 1940s, followed by a civil war—is lost on me.

Chinatowns are messy, dirty, and *foreign*. They can never seem to contain themselves properly, spilling their lives out into the streets and sidewalks from spindly weird crates overflowing with bok choy and food carts with barbecued ducks skewered onto hooks. This is America. Why can't Chinatowns display sparkling clean counters and neat rows of newspapers and canned goods? Most of all, why do they have to smell?

We visit Chinatowns everywhere: my native Detroit, Windsor, Chicago, Los Angeles, Philadelphia, Washington, D.C., and, of course, the meccas—San Francisco, New York, and Toronto.

Toronto. The very word sinks my already moody adolescent constitution. Not again! We kids groan. Why can't we just eat pizza like normal families? My family power-pilgrimages at least twice a year to Toronto, a five-hour drive from Detroit. The goal? To eat at as many Chinese restaurants as possible within forty-eight hours. And when we aren't eating, we are stuffing the trunk of our silver Buick LeSabre until it sags with cans of pickled cucumbers, jars of bamboo shoots, and boxes of one-thousand-year-old eggs, cured until the whites resemble opaque black marble.

The customs agent at the border crossing in Canada asks, "What will you be doing in Canada?" And my father, his brow furrowed above his horn-rimmed glasses, his hands resting on the steering wheel, replies, simply, "Eating."

The agent raises his eyebrows, looks at my father again, then hearing no additional explanation, scans the rest of us—my mother in the front seat, her eyes dreamy at the thought of roasted chestnuts, my sister and brother in the backseat, poking each other's ribs, and me, passive in a way that suggests that my father's answer is all too true. "Can you believe it?" I want to say, and thereby disassociate myself from my parents. It seems to me absurd to drive five hours to another country, cooped up with my siblings who alternate between arm wrestling and giggling, merely to visit a Chinatown. They are all the same. What difference does it make?

The difference, of course, is that Toronto's Chinatown is the real deal. It makes Detroit's small enclave, anchored by the Golden Dragon restaurant, a place for amateurs. Toronto is for the serious foodie. Toronto is the epicenter. If you can't be in China, you can be in Toronto on Yonge Street with its double-parked cars, shouting vendors, and streams of pedestrians flowing from sidewalk to street to sidewalk again, oblivious to the traffic, which, in any case, hardly budges. Stores blare sticky sweet Chinese pop music. Theater marquees blink and dance, featuring the latest action movie with Hong Kong's hottest star (who, I later learned, was none other than Jackie Chan).

All the signs are in Chinese: the advertisements, the store awnings, the store windows, the street signs, the public notices, the stenciled shipping crates, and the newspapers. English words don't help, for they are merely sounded-out approximations of the Chinese words.

Why bother writing Fung Wong Lau? It's still Chinese. I pick out the simplest of characters—*person, big, dragon*. I find the character for my name, *hua*, everywhere, and I can't decide if this cheapens my name or lends it more importance.

My parents seek out restaurants that don't cater to *wai guo ren*, foreigners. By foreigner, they don't mean themselves. Banks of aquariums greet us at the entrance, bubbling away with crab, lobster, grouper, and prawns. Inside the dining room the noise level soars ten notches. Chinese consider this the perfect ambience, the more *ruh nao*—lively or animated, literally "warm noisy"—the better. Each time the kitchen doors fly open, the hum of overhead fans and the click-clack of the cooks stir-frying in giant woks rush out. Platters clatter, patrons shout and laugh, waiters holler. The waiters wear black vests, crooked bow ties, and white shirts rolled up at the sleeves, as though they were attending a formal dinner and got drafted into helping in the kitchen. On the round table, a tilting stack of ceramic teacups and a metal teapot that slaps shut and open. A lazy susan. My father pours tea for each of us, wheeling the cups around. I order Coke and set the can to my left. My little teacup on my right. East meets West.

Dishes arrive in an endless parade from the kitchen—green pepper and squid, spicy fried-pork lettuce wraps, seafood noodles, marinated pork hock, and anise beef. They pile on the lazy susan, threatening to slide off. We spin the lazy susan in the same way that a filling machine rotates in a factory, each of us heaping our bowls before the dishes rotate to the next station. We grasp porcelain bowls of rice in our left hands and a pair of slippery plastic chopsticks in the right. As we gulp down pork dumplings, chicken velvet soup, and Chinese broccoli in oyster sauce, I forget that I don't like Chinatowns. My sister Helen, aged eleven, remains true to our American ways and stages her resistance by eating peanut butter and jelly sandwiches. (These days, Helen, now forty, still regrets this misguided rebellion. "I lost two whole years of Chinese food!")

Dessert? Who has room for dessert? Orange slices, almond cookies, thick wedges of watermelon. My mother is already discussing the next restaurant with my father.

One time we arrive in Toronto long after the city has gone to bed. Despite the late hour, my parents show no interest in finding our hotel. Instead, my mother twists and turns a street map around, trying to navigate while my father stretches his neck to study the street signs. I fall asleep. When I wake up, we are parked in front of a dark, shuttered storefront on a dark, shadowed street. To my astonishment, my parents hop out of the car, abandoning the usual caution they exercise in similarly darkened streets at similarly late hours in downtown Detroit. Their voices are pointed, excited, like teenagers discovering a new mall. "This is the place!" they exclaim over and over.

They knock on the storefront's glass door. My father steps backward, places his hands on the small of his back, and arches his chest, scanning the windows above. My mother raps again. And again. Then the two gather and conference in loud whispers, as though they haven't already woken up everyone within a block.

Finally, the flicker of gray fluorescent lights. A Chinese couple materializes in the back of the store and shuffles to the front door. The man is skinny, and his thin cotton robe hangs open at the chest, exposing his ribbed undershirt. The woman's hair poofs out on the left side, nestling a single pink sponge curler. Both of them rub their eyes, squinting at the door.

My parents' faces light up and they shout in Chinese. "You're here. You're here!" as though the Pope himself has arrived to give an off-the-record blessing. More rapping on the glass, even though by now the shopkeepers are clearly awake. Back at home, inconveniencing someone even slightly—say, interrupting the mailman's delivery by saying hello—draws sharp reprimands to mind our manners. And here are my parents, excited about pulling strangers out of bed.

My parents announce that we have driven all the way from Detroit just to visit this bakery. This is only half true. With two days to go, we will also fit in five full meals, three snacks, and two shopping expeditions. But the owners are clearly pleased to hear this compliment. Or perhaps they see the look on my father's face and know that this is not a man who will be denied his Chinese baked goods.

My mother extracts me from the car, my body sleepy and limp. She nudges me toward the display case and points to the rows of *bao* and *bing*, pastries and buns stuffed with lotus-seed paste, black sesame seeds, and red bean paste. My favorite is there, egg custard tarts, yellow as sunlight and gently sweet. I can barely prop my eyes open. My mother flicks the back of her hand on my shoulder. "Wake up, *sa gua*—silly," she says, "Look at these goodies!"

A clock hangs on the pale green wall behind the counter, its wire cord dangling like a tail. It is 12:25 in the morning.

When I am thirty years old, I "return home" to China (as my parents would see it) for the first time. The plane glides over wet emerald fields, the dark water shining like mirrors into the sky. I land in Shanghai, my mother's hometown. A few hours later I am walking on a Shanghai street, a canopy of chartreuse sycamore leaves above. People. Everywhere, people. Walking, bicycling, driving, chatting, eating. Cooking, sitting, marketing, brushing teeth. These are lives lived inside out. The street swarms with neighbors in a dance as choreographed and invisible as that of honeybees. I see woven bamboo baskets piled high with turnips and lotus roots and eggplants. Plastic buckets swimming with eels. Piles of sesame-crusted pancakes. Little cooking carts with portable gas burners. On the ground, thong slippers, silk-embroidered slippers, soft cloth slippers, all displayed on worn cotton sheets.

I have never set foot in Shanghai, or in China, or even in Asia. Yet this market feels familiar, as though my thirty-year-old bones have been carrying around a seed that, with the right conditions, now germinates. I sniff. Of course. It's that smell. Why wouldn't China, the mothership of all Chinatowns, smell like Chinatown?

A woman in a floral blouse squats behind an oil drum and a wok alive with boiling oil. Beside her, a green plastic tub contains something foul. I gag. I begin to push away through the crowds, away from the woman, when I see her smile faintly at me, a Chinese Mona Lisa. Her smile catches me. I stop and turn around. The woman leans over the green tub and scoops out a few squares of something soft and spongy, textured. She drops the squares into the wok; the hot oil swallows them eagerly.

And then I know. I know what's in the wok because the smell tells me. The woman is cooking "stinky tofu." I have only heard about stinky tofu. My mother used to talk about it whenever she reminisced about her girlhood in Shanghai. Stinky tofu, so delicious, she would say, her eyes closed. You have no idea how delicious. Stinky tofu made you forget all the badness in the world—the Japanese hunting your parents, the bombs dropping on Shanghai, the gunboats cruising the waters, the slow, heart-breaking collapse of the world you love.

The woman fishes out the tofu squares with a flat wired spoon. What my mother never told me is that stinky tofu doesn't stay that way. Before me now, the row of tofu squares sits on a wire rack, golden and crisp. What my mother never told me is that once you fry stinky tofu, it becomes as fragrant and delicate as spring. The woman scoops three squares onto a plate, sprinkles chopped scallions on top, and slaps a dab of red chile sauce on the side. I bite into the first square; I bite into China.

Though I have never lived in Chinatown, Chinatown is where I was raised. From the outside, my life in Seattle resembles that of my neighbors—I drink chai lattes at Starbucks, play the latest Norah Jones CD, wear fleece jackets, and participate in that most American of activities, psychotherapy. But it is in Chinatown where my roots tug at me the most.

If Chinatown feels that way to me, then I can only imagine how it feels for my parents. In 1949 my parents fled their war-ravaged home, losing family members in the chaos before landing almost ten years later—alone and foreign—in graduate school at the University of Illinois. Three of my grandparents were buried in China by the time I was born at the dawn of the space age. From 1949 to the time that President Nixon called on Beijing in 1972, a period of over twenty years, China sequestered itself, cut off from the world. My parents' sisters, brothers, aunts, uncles, cousins, second cousins, great-aunts, great-uncles were all left behind "back there," cloaked in a strange land where no one could visit and no one could leave. At the core of it, my parents' eating frenzies in Chinatown, those road trips to Toronto, were about feeding the heart, about filling themselves up with reminders of a home they could no longer return to. With every jar of pickled radishes, every package of rice noodles, every can of straw mushrooms, my parents could literally take China home with them.

If you were to propose this idea to my parents, they would shrug it off. Reading too much into it, they would say. It's simple—Chinatown is where you get the best food for cheap. Practicality ranks high with my parents' generation, simply because it had to once. So perhaps the idea that Chinatown connects me to my roots is a luxury affordable only by my generation—the one born here in clean hospitals, educated in American schools, and raised without ever worrying that our doors might be smashed in the middle of the night by Japanese soldiers or Red Guards.

And what of the next generation? The one my parents refer to as "you Americans," as though my siblings and I are foreigners in our own family? The answer is this: our bellies and therefore our identities are fundamentally Chinese. Over Christmas last year, I visit the Getty Museum in Los Angeles with my parents, my brother, Mike, and his wife, Linda. My mother mentions having dinner that night at a Chinese restaurant in Irvine whose specialty is fried salt and pepper squid. Minutes later we are lined up at the shuttle to return to the parking lot. There's no time to waste.

Today when I visit Seattle's Chinatown (now renamed the more politically correct "International District"), I do so without the benefit of my parents' expert tutelage. My Mandarin slips away with every passing year, and many of the foods remain mysterious to me. But even if I can't remember the name of a certain dish, a certain dim sum, a certain fruit, there is always that smell. The smell of generations before me extending back across the Pacific Ocean. The smell that beckoned my family five hours from Detroit to Toronto. The smell of home.

RED BEANS AND RICE: RISING TO THE OCCASION

By Sara Roahen
from *Gumbo Tales*

Former food critic for New Orleans's *Gambit Weekly*,
Wisconsin-born Sara Roahen has since moved to Philadelphia, but this ode to her adopted city and its rich food
culture—both pre- and post-Katrina—is the sort of book only
an enthusiastic transplant could have written.

Like savvy politicians, food is equally powerful as a di-
vider and a uniter. North Carolina, for instance, would
be a more peaceful place if the state could just officially sever
down the middle, with whole-hog barbecue eaters on one side
and those who prefer pork shoulder on the other. Fingernails are
sharpened for family reunions in Louisiana, where the shade of
one's roux gumbo is noted and discussed and sometimes battled
over. Matt and I stood divided on the po-boy, unable to share one
until I finally agreed that mayonnaise is not the devil's condiment.

Unlike politicians, however, food unites with complete sincer-
ity. It harbors no ulterior motives; its power is irreversible. Red
beans and rice is my best example.

COMPARED WITH ITS COOKING TIME, which according to lore ought
to take an entire Monday, red beans and rice, the consummate
New Orleans dish, requires virtually no prep work. You rinse the
beans following an overnight soak (an optional though recommended step); you chop some vegetables and any combination of
sausage, tasso, ham, pickle meat, and pig tails; you add water, fire,

and possibly a cracked ham bone; and then you walk away to fold laundry, work the crossword, crawl under the covers, or begin whatever other activity consumes your usual Monday. Any New Orleanian who cooks by tradition could produce a pot of red beans while also tending to a gumbo and smothering a chicken, which made it all the more embarrassing one Monday when, along with the brown smudge on a stalk of celery that had aged in my refrigerator since the last pot of beans, I cut off the tip of my thumb.

"How much? Does it look like a fish scale or a pencil eraser?" Matt asked over the phone.

During the nearly six years I had worked as a professional cook, I had cut and burned myself so often that I no longer recall which incident caused which scar, divot, and speck of permanent numbness that now plot the landscape of my arms and hands. But I had never before foraged through a pile of diced vegetables to find a former piece of myself of a size that could be compared to a No. 2 pencil eraser.

"I'll be there in ten minutes," Matt said.

It was six o'clock in the evening, too late to be starting a pot of red beans anyway, but it was Monday and my friend Pableaux hadn't called. After swaddling my estranged flesh in plastic wrap and setting it on ice inside a Mason jar for portability (a move that later won me laughs, if not a single painkiller, from the emergency room staff), I kept my mind off the throbbing by calling and berating him: "From now on, I'm *always* invited to red beans!"

If there was a first pot of red beans in New Orleans, documentation of it hasn't been found. Everyone here knows, though, that whether true or myth, red beans and rice became a Monday staple for two reasons: it made good use of the ham bone from Sunday dinner, and cooks could stir the low-maintenance dish infrequently while tending to housework back when Monday was laundry day and people still set their washtubs over charcoal furnaces in the backyard.

Some sources point to African slaves, who survived on beans and rice, a protein-rich combination, during their nightmarish trips to this country and who later, when they began cooking in plantation kitchens, used the same ingredients as a canvas for expressing the heritage of their homeland. (The African American cultural transference helps explain other regional food preparations, like okra gumbos, rice fritters called *calas*, and smoking techniques.) Other sources credit the French Canadians ousted from Canada for introducing the red bean when they relocated to southwestern Louisiana, though the Monday red beans ritual is weaker in other parts of the state today, which suggests that it's always been more of a city dish.

The origin of red beans and rice means little to most modern New Orleanians, who care only that no Monday passes without at least one helping. I count myself in that number, and I blame and thank my friend and neighbor Pableaux Johnson for what became a Monday habit on good weeks and a desperation on others.

A native of New Iberia, a pretty town that idles along Bayou Teche in Cajun country, Pableaux (né Paul) moved to New Orleans roughly a year after Matt and I did. I met him through a mutual friend, though if she hadn't introduced us we would have met through another friend, or in a café, or at the dentist's. It's virtually impossible *not* to meet Pableaux, a magnetic extrovert, and once you're in, you're in. "Wanna come over for red beans on Monday?" he asks, and you agree at once, so convinced by his enthusiasm that you neglect to run his name through Google first.

Five years after my first taste of his red beans, I thought to ask why he began cooking for strangers when he moved to town. "Because I knew they would come. And this table needs to be fed once a week," he said, resting his palm on the long, homely oval slab of laminated wood around which he and his grandmother's other twenty-three grandchildren grew up eating. They were the second generation to do so. It's not happenstance that Pableaux is the one member of his sprawling clan who wanted the table, given the fitting way he describes himself: "a Cajun grandmother with a beard." On red bean Mondays, during deadline crises, and for the duration of hurricane evacuations, during which he corrals friends inside a one-room church he domesticated in St. Martinville, Pableaux displays the herding instincts of a border collie and the cooking abilities of a woman who knits between shots of hot sauce. I've met no finer onion smotherer, no more ardent devotee of the andouille link, no better tamer of the red bean.

To begin a batch, Pableaux eyeballs a measure of red beans, dumps them into a pot, and covers them with water for a quickie couple-hour soak. By observing the contents of other shoppers' grocery carts, I learned early that the only beans suitable for making New Orleans red beans and rice are the ones packaged in chunky, cellophane-wrapped rolls and marked with the classic Camellia-brand red rose. While Camellia's packaging calls the legumes within "red kidney beans," Camellia red beans are unlike any other kidney beans I've ever cooked. For one thing, they exhibit a dusky dark pink color, a lighter shade of pink than regular kidney beans, which have a more maroonish hue; also, they're squatter, more compact, not so kidney-shaped. Camellia's red beans have thinner skins than other kidneys, which is not to call them weak; on the contrary, they bloat with hot pepper and pork fat like a blistered ballerina on opening night, with stoicism and delicacy.

When I once mentioned my Camellia preference to Pableaux, never imagining that there was another side to the argument, he balked. "What? Red beans, kidney beans—they're all the same. I use whatever I got, whatever kind is cheapest that week." And then he accused me of being a red bean brandist.

To settle the score, I phone up Camellia's packaging plant in Harahan. The receptionist, unwilling to weigh in herself, transferred me to a woman who apparently thought I was issuing a quiz when I posed the question "What's the difference between a Camellia red bean and an ordinary kidney bean?"

"Is it that we only use Grade A beans?" she asked.

I tried to clarify, explaining that I wasn't looking for secret formulas, just for confirmation that Camellia beans were somehow special—their genes grafted from some long-lost beanstalk, their waterings dictated by some obscure lunar chart, their growing soil fertilized with fairy dust, anything. The woman assured me that no, Camellia beans are just ordinary kidneys. When I pressed further, she excused herself. "We're really busy. Maybe if you can call back in a few days. . . . "

It was so odd. An informal survey of other New Orleanians assured me that I wasn't the only red bean brand partisan. Willie Mae

Seaton, the nonagenarian who served red beans every weekday at her Scotch House restaurant before it flooded (the restaurant reopened, but Willie Mae has retired) sided with me over a cup of coffee and chicory one morning. "No red beans taste like the Camellia beans," she confirmed. When I told Willie Mae about Pableaux and the woman at the packing plant, she commiserated. "That's all right, because you know the difference, don't you?"

Other ingredients are not so arbitrary at Pableaux's house, which until recently he shared with his wife, Ariana French, a subtler though equally generous personality. There, red beans are always made with Louisiana andouille, a hard, heavily smoked and seasoned pork sausage—except when there's a small side pot of vegetarian beans, which the rare guest requires. (The vegetarians must know that Pableaux's pots are too well seasoned with lard ever to cook meatless honestly.) It's always a banner Monday when pork lust has driven Pableaux thirty miles northwest to Laplace, known locally as the Andouille Capital of the World, where the *charcutiers* at Jacob's World Famous Andouille smoke their mighty, garlic-powered links so hardily over pecan wood they turn almost black.

Even on regular Mondays, when the andouille comes from Langenstein's or Zara's, neighborhood markets partial to local products, Pableaux's beans might get an extra concentrated kick of red pepper and warm spices from tasso, a seasoned and smoked pork shoulder product that's difficult to find outside Louisiana. Tasso is leaner and more like jerky than sausage, tangy and primarily used as a flavoring agent, like salt pork or pancetta; sometimes it's made with turkey instead. Pableaux might also throw in some hot sausage or bacon fat. He's not of the ham bone school, whose marrow fetish produces the creamiest beans in town, but some weeks his red beans are so meaty you do wonder whether there's still a pig living in the state.

I could pick Pableaux's red beans from a lineup according to other signatures: dried sweet basil, bay leaves, and acid (lemon juice, vinegar, Tabasco) zinging across the surface of the pork-swollen richness. You smell all these things before you cross the threshold of his second-floor apartment; I've caught whiffs of the aromatic simmering from the driveway. Rendered pork fat, weeping garlic, collapsing beans. This is the smell of a Monday in New

Orleans, the all-day reminder of what you want to be eating. The aromas thicken as you wind up Pableaux's staircase, cringing past a Nordik Trak, stomach groaning. By the time you descend those same stairs a few hours later, the smells are braided into our hair, woven among the fibers of your clothing, clinging to your skin.

Most red bean recipes call for all or some combination of the local holy trinity of vegetables: onion, celery, and green bell pepper. Also garlic, which may not have a place in the trinity but is no less hallowed. New Orleanians call these starter vegetables their seasoning, as in "I save some of my seasoning to add at the end of cooking for more flavor." So many regional staple dishes build upon an identical seasoning base that you can cheat and buy the vegetables prechopped by the pint in the produce section of any supermarket here. Before moving to New Orleans, I defined *seasoning* as the dried herbs and spices sold in small over-priced bottles in the baking goods aisle. It took me years to embrace the local usage of the word, and it wasn't until I whacked off the tip of my thumb that I worked this advanced New Orleans–speak into conversation. The injury turned out to be superficial, but I kept the outsized white dressing on my hand for five days anyway, as bait for sympathetic questions, to which I couldn't wait to replay, "Oh, the knife slipped while I was chopping my seasoning."

Whereas some cooks don't even bother sautéing their vegetables, opting simply to boil them with the beans, Pableaux sweats his to a sweet golden jam. Then he adds them to his chopped pork products, which have been similarly cooked on the stovetop, rendered of their fat, and singed with a dark caramely varnish on all sides. At this point he calls anyone in the vicinity to the stove. "Look at this!" he yells, by which he means, Stick your nose inside this pot and take a whiff. "Is there anything better?" Not much.

The final essential components of a proper pot of red beans, and of an infinite number of other traditional Louisiana dishes, are chopped green onion tops and parsley—"the green stuff," as Matt calls them. At Pableaux's, these are added at the end of cooking and also passed around the table for garnishing, and they are the only fresh vegetables you will eat during Monday dinner if he's in charge. Crystal hot sauce counts as a side dish. In deference to the ways of his Cajun people (the Creoles do it, too), there's always butter and hot French bread on the table.

And then there's rice, without which the dish wouldn't be complete and Mondays wouldn't smell quite right. Rice is one of Louisiana's most important agricultural products, after sugarcane and cotton. At first I found Louisiana table rice to be comparable to the parboiled rice I grew up eating with pepper steak and in tuna fish casseroles in Wisconsin. I snubbed it, driving to an imports store in Metairie for basmati by the bushel, but eventually I came to agree with diehard locals who argue that the discrete grains and muted flavor of Louisiana rice make it a perfect foil for the state's heavy and heavily seasoned beans, étouffées, jambalayas, and gumbos. (In some parts of the state, the preference is for stickier rice.) A rice cooker in the corner of Pableaux's kitchen chugs steam clouds aromatic with a twiggy, popcornlike perfume. When the sensor clicks, indicating that the rice is ready, you grab a porcelain bowl, marry rice from the cooker with beans from the stove in a proportion that has become your own Monday signature, then head for a seat at the long oval table. That is, providing you've been invited.

IN HIS BOOK *The Great Good Place: Cafés, Coffee Shops, Bookstores, Bars, Hair Salons, and Other Hangouts at the Heart of a Community*, the author Ray Oldenburg discusses the importance and disappearance of the "third place" in modern America. A third place, he writes, is an informal gathering spot that helps create a sense of community, a place where neighbors can unwind, meet, perhaps eat or drink, and momentarily break from their first and second places, which are home and work, respectively. While the author correctly laments that third places have steadily faded from the American landscape since World War II, the abundance of timeworn neighborhood restaurants in New Orleans, all of which serve roughly the same food, including red beans and rice every Monday, ensures that third places aren't obsolete here.

Then again, since a favorite neighborhood restaurant is something passed down through New Orleans families like cemetery crypts, many of them seem to cultivate a sort of members-only air. This social phenomenon is fascinating to observe, but it's not so welcoming for a newcomer. Simply frequenting a third place doesn't make it your own, as Matt and I learned after doing time in every bar, café, and restaurant within walking distance of our home when we moved here. Though my restaurant reviewing job sent us to restaurants all over town, we didn't establish a third place in New Orleans until we met Pableaux.

We never knew whom we would meet around the rice cooker. Pableaux's red bean guest list on any given Monday could include his sister and two nephews visiting from Baton Rouge, a screenwriter he met at the coffee shop, a couple who I always suspected invited him to their wedding to secure future red bean invitations, married sociology professors, a female Protestant minister, his college roommate, Ariana, and whoever he had met that afternoon. His grandmother's table thus became Oldenburg's "social condenser," a place where we developed friendships, discussed social and political issues, and debated the superiority of local hot sauce brands. Like Matt and me, in the beginning the majority of Pableaux's red bean invitees were transplants to the city, often fresh from the U-Haul. Because his ritual was identical to what New Orleans natives also do on Mondays, including those who open cans of Blue Runner red beans, for many of us the first red bean Monday at Pableaux's marked the first time we felt like active, meaningful participants in the local culture of domestic eating. I don't think it's exaggerating to say that through the humble red bean, Pableaux single-handedly helped countless people begin to love living in this city.

Matt and I were not unique in finding our third place in his dining room, and therein lies a sticking point, a flaw in the third-place ideal. As Pableaux's grandmotherly qualities aren't limited by biology, over time his red bean black book exceeded his own grandmother's brood and continued to grow. As the table seats only ten comfortably, no matter how tight you are with Pableaux, he can't feed you every week.

Whereas mythology would have New Orleans red beans simmering from dawn to dusk, a sputtering pressure cooker allows Pableaux to make last-minute plans. An invitation might come as late as four o'clock on Monday afternoon—or not—just late enough to mess you up if you haven't formulated a backup dinner plan. I've run into other red bean semiregulars on Mondays at the supermarket, wondering what to cook. "You didn't get a call either, huh? Who do you think is there?" we ask each other, admitting that it makes us feel better about ourselves to see others who haven't made the cut. One friend who was never invited as often as she would have liked asked me once, "What did I ever do to Pableaux? I even ate seconds last time. Should I buy him sausage or something?" I suggested that she try calling him on Monday afternoons, to trigger his memory of her. Not that I ever stooped so low, letting red bean paranoia get the better of me.

One Monday, Pableaux called early with an invitation, and I paged Matt at work to deliver the good news. Then, late in the afternoon, he called back to cancel: "The stove broke." I'm sure it says more about my character than his that I didn't believe him. I heard kitchen noises in the background, and he sounded excited and happy, which is not the same as disappointed and apologetic. I irrationally concluded that he must have made alternate plans without including us. A small part of me worried that he'd found someone better to take our seats. Forever.

Pableaux and Ariana lived five blocks from us, which was too close to resist for someone who once spent an entire summer successfully stalking her wayward boyfriend. As the sun set that Monday, I commissioned Stephanie, another red bean semiregular and an obedient younger sibling, to creep past their house with me. We looked for lights in the kitchen and sniffed the air outside for that telltale aroma. We detected neither, which was only mildly comforting, because we thought we could hear voices coming from the second-story patio. I never found out what really happened that night, and I've never told Pableaux about the lapse of composure his red beans triggered. I trust that he'll take it as a compliment. His little joke turned out to be a prophecy: he has become like a grandmother. No one else's red beans taste quite right.

THE ORDINARINESS OF RED BEANS and the unfussy process of preparing them to local tastes do not prohibit chefs from building entire careers on the dish. Buster Holmes, whose Buster Holmes Restaurant on Burgundy Street in the French Quarter closed before my time, cooked red beans for the first-ever Jazz Fest and became known internationally for his reportedly top-notch version. According to his cookbook, he used only seven ingredients, one of them being half a stick of margarine, which his recipe instructs should be melted into the beans five minutes before serving.

"I know better not to put a pot on the stove unless I have red beans," Willie Mae Seaton, whose favorite red bean seasoning meat is pickle tips with the gristle bone, told me once. While Miss Willie Mae is perhaps more lauded for the chicken that she butchered herself and then fried so thoroughly that even the bones crackled in your teeth, red beans are closer to her heart. "I just love me some red beans," she said. "This is a red bean city here. If you don't have no red beans, you just *out*."

On August 29, 2005, none of the reliable, necessary red beans and rice preparations that New Orleanians had known for entire lifetimes were available. Not the ones I liked at Crabby Jack's, thick and creamy as softened butter. Not the ones crowned with a behemoth ham shank at Smilie's. Not the free ones at Donna's Bar and Grill, where the New Orleans jazzman Bob French had a standing Monday night gig. Not the gravylike ones in Mandich's red bean soup, shot through with rice and sausage. Not Tom Fitzmorris's favorite at Dunbar's. Not the ones at Mandina's, or Franky & Johnny's, or Praline Connection, or Joey K's. . . .

It was Katrina Monday. New Orleans was just *out*.

PABLEAUX AND I COVER THE SAME BEAT, New Orleans food, only he's better at it. A superior byline for the job does not exist, and he applies the same quality that has so many of us dying to crowd around his table on Monday nights to connecting with editors, which makes him a darling—or a disturbance, depending on your position—of the freelance food writing world.

While I'd like to think it's my solid sense of self-worth that quells my envy, it's more likely Pableaux's bigheartedness, and his red beans, that have kept us friends. It's true, that cliché that cookbook writers, old-timer head-shakers, and pushers of family values preach: dinner matters. Cooking for one another and gathering around a table together to eat brings people eye to eye, literally and figuratively. It forges alliances, it eases conversation, and it can be the only palliative during desperate times.

It's not unusual in New Orleans to eat three meals a day composed of native foods and combinations that are unknown, or at least unattainable, in the rest of the world. Katrina drove that home even while she drove us away. During the days immediately following the storm—first when no one remaining could get out of the city, and then when everyone was forced to leave—it was spirit-crushing to think of losing the city's rich food culture, but it was infinitely worse to imagine everyone there who just needed to eat. Morally correct or not, I did think about red beans on Katrina Monday; by the following Monday, I was longing for them. In monitoring the Internet for news of the city and its displaced, I found I wasn't alone.

In September 2005, the *Times-Picayune* ran a story by Michael Perlstein about hurricane refugees who had been flown, not by choice, to shelters in Milwaukee, Wisconsin. For some of them it had been a first-ever plane flight, and probably for many a first-ever week without red beans. "It's a nice town and all, but I don't think I could live here. I'm hungry for some red beans and rice real bad," one woman said. In closing the article with her quote, the New Orleans reporter, also displaced in Milwaukee, betrayed how much he also missed home.

In Hawaii, another reporter interviewed a manager from Popeye's, the fried chicken chain founded in New Orleans, which serves startlingly tasty red beans (moles say the secret is lard). The manager had been transferred in the wake of the storm, and he remained flabbergasted, not by Hawaii's beauty or its beaches but by its sticky rice. "I can't eat this rice with nothing on it," he told the reporter, Jarvis DeBerry. "I just can't seem to eat rice without beans, green beans, or gumbo on it. I just can't." He said he had broken in the kitchen of his new Hawaiian apartment by making a pot of red beans, but he hadn't been able to locate Camellia beans or Louisiana smoked sausage on the island. "They were good, but they're just not the same."

In the meantime, Pableaux and Ariana had holed up in their church-turned-country-house in St. Martinville, forming their own hurricane shelter and acting as a triage station for friends—some homeless, some just hungry. Red beans became everyday food for the same reason that the dish has remained a New Orleans staple for so long: one pound of beans plus sausage and some rice can stretch to feed and console an extended family, a neighborhood, a congregation. I received reports from their hurricane commune while cozied into my in-laws' New York apartment, where I had developed a raging case of homesickness and a throbbing, impossible hunger for red beans and rice, even though I was eating shamefully well.

Unlike the hundreds of thousands of other New Orleanians who had lost their homes, their jobs, and their lives, I soon moved back to New Orleans, where Pableaux had resumed his Monday ritual. For a couple of months he cooked them in our house, as my roommate. He and Ariana had split—amicably, as they say in Hollywood, only this time for real. She remained a regular at his red beans table.

Inevitably, the one-year anniversary of Katrina rolled around, and with it, for many of us, the impossible task of deciding how to spend the day. Gospel concerts had been scheduled, second lines, memorials, prayer services, vigils, relief dinners, television specials. But the difficult post-Katrina era was not over, wouldn't be over for years—ever?—and so commemoration felt premature—not inappropriate, but not settling either. Too much had changed and too much hadn't. What, we wondered, could possibly feel meaningful? Even the prospect of eating, the most common means of both celebrating and mourning in this city, sounded indulgent. And yet wouldn't it be missing the point to spend the day alone? Being here and being together were two of the few things New Orleanians who had been able to return still had in their favor.

And then someone remembered that most of us had missed eating red beans and rice on Katrina Monday the previous year. We had been in hotel rooms or cars or shelters or foreign states or hospitals or attics or pain. Many New Orleanians had been hungry that day; others had lost their appetite. Realizing this, Pableaux decided to observe the sad turning of a year by making Tuesday, August 29, 2006, an honorary Monday. He cooked a triple batch of red beans with andouille from Laplace and invited everyone he saw, table space be damned.

PANACEA

By Dorothy Allison

from the *New York Times Magazine*

Anyone who's read Dorothy Allison's semi-autobiographical
novel *Bastard Out of Carolina* knows the travails of her childhood, growing up dirt-poor in the Deep South. The hunger
she writes about in this poignant essay will never go away.

Gravy is the simplest, tastiest, most memory-laden dish I
know how to make: a little flour, salt and pepper, crispy
bits of whatever meat anchored the meal, a couple of cups of water
or milk and slow stirring to break up lumps. That's it. It smells of
home, the door locked against the night and a stillness made safe
by the sound of a spoon going round in a pan. It is anticipation,
the last thing prepared before the meal comes to the table, the
bowl in Mama's hand closing the day out peacefully, no matter
what came before.

My mother's gravy was a savory country gravy, heavy on the
black pepper. Best of all was steak—cube steak. People call it
country-fried steak, but Mama always called it cube steak. She began with odd, indented slabs of cheap meat carried home from the
diner where she was on her feet all day. My sisters and I would
pound the "steak" while she rested. The little round mouth of the
Coke bottle thudded into the meat over and over until each piece
was not only dimpled but flattened out half again as wide as it had
been. By the time Mama stopped us, the steaks would be tender-
ized almost to pieces. Then she would shoo us out of the way,
make up the biscuits and sift some of the flour onto a plate.
Dredged in flour, the steaks went into a hot cast-iron skillet with a

good covering of bacon fat. So long as we set the table and were useful, we were allowed to watch Mama cook the steaks and then set them aside on a brown paper bag. Then she took the plate of leftover flour and sprinkled it in the pan, stirring it as it browned and the pan filled with little brown flour pebbles and charred bits of meat. A lot of water and a little milk made steam rise up in a sweet cloud. Mama worked the gravy with a fork until all was smooth and silky. She might pour the gravy over the steaks or she might serve it in a bowl. It was not until I was grown that I understood that gravy poured over the meat before it came to the table meant there was not much meat.

In one tract house or another, first in South Carolina and then Florida, where we moved when I was a teenager, Mama made magic with cheap meat, flour and determination—hiding from us how desperate things might be. She did such a good job of it that we came to believe cube steak a luxury, better than the rare T-bone our uncles might bring around as a surprise.

My son, Wolf, was born when I was past 40 and the author of a best-selling novel. That means he has grown up a middle-class child—one who sometimes asks me for stories of my childhood but knows nothing of what it means to grow up poor and afraid. I have worked to make sure of that. His favorite foods are all dishes I never even knew existed until I was a voting adult: spinach soufflés, steamed mussels and sautéed brussels sprouts. He has almost never eaten an egg yolk and never took an interest in gravy, not even on Thanksgiving turkey.

"No, thank you," he said, very politely.

My feelings were hurt. How could my child not like my gravy? Maybe it was the giblets I chopped and added? Next time I made a smooth, pristine gravy with no bits of anything. Wolf didn't touch it.

This time I sighed. I had to face the truth. My gravy was nowhere near as good as my mother's had been, and my son was not me. He had never gone to bed hungry and had no idea how important a locked door could be. I could not be unhappy about that.

Then there was the duck.

It was three years ago, and I wanted to do something special for the holidays to celebrate our aunt Mary moving up from Arizona. At the grocery, there was a big sale sign—ducks and geese at discount. A duck, a goose, a British Christmas dinner. I had read the novels. I had a brand-new roasting pan. So just because I could, I bought one of each—the goose for Christmas and the duck for New Year's.

Christmas was wonderful, but the goose was not a success. It came out pretty but dry. I stripped the leftovers for the dogs and worried. What was I going to do with that duck? I thought about giving up and making a ham. But my pride got in my way. I could cook. I was my mother's daughter.

It was clear to me that what was going to be necessary was a gravy—a good gravy. I read up on ducks and followed directions. I hung the bird over the sink in the warm kitchen and watched the fat drip off. After a while the bird looked greasy but lean. I shooed everyone out and went back to basics. There was no bacon fat in my fridge, but there was bacon. I wrapped the duck in bacon, threw an obscuring layer of aluminum foil over the top and put it in the roasting pan.

You could smell the bacon in the steam coming out the top of the oven, but maybe I was the only one who noticed. It was New Year's after all, with family and friends and lots of dishes. There were greens and black-eyed peas and sweet potatoes with marshmallows. There were pies and loud music—lots of things to distract everyone away from the oven.

When the duck was done, I set it on a platter and disappeared the bacon slices. Then I poured off almost all the grease and took a spoon after the blackened bits in the bottom of the pan. Maybe the duck would be dry as the goose had been. But the bits in the bottom of the pan looked like great cracklings. I scraped and dredged and turned on the heat, then sprinkled flour and pepper across the oily surface. It cooked into the familiar brown pebbles. I squeezed a bite between my fingers and tasted salty, rich flavor. Uh-huh. A cup of skim milk brought up steam through which I stirred steadily. Another cup went after the first, then a cup of water. I used a fork to squash the lumps and kept stirring. Every now and then I would taste the gravy again and then go searching in my cupboard. Yes, more black pepper and a little bottled magic from K-Paul's Louisiana Kitchen. At the last minute I reached over and spooned in some of the creamy liquid off the black-eyed peas. It made me laugh—but the gravy smelled wonderful.

Soon there were offers to help carry in the dishes. My son was standing by me at the stove. He was staring at the gravy I was still stirring. He leaned forward over the pan.

"Mmm."

I looked at him. His big green eyes were wide and hungry. I used a wooden spoon. Blew on the gravy to cool it, then let him lick a taste.

"Oh, that's wonderful!" he said.

After that everyone was quick to the table. The duck was perfect, everyone said so. I felt as if I had passed some ancient rite or earned some essential vindication. There was no gravy left when the meal was done.

Every now and then, I make duck again. But more often, I do what I know. I roast a chicken or pan-fry a steak and make pan gravy to go with it. Sometimes my boy comes to watch me cook. I watch him. He is getting so tall, now four inches taller than I and growing fast, while the world looms ever larger and more uncertain. I try not to worry. I try to make him feel he is home and safe and will always be so, no matter what comes to the door.

—∞∞∞—

Roast Duck

Serves 4 to 6. Adapted from Dorothy Allison.

1 4- to 6-pound duck
¼ cup peeled and halved baby onions
¼ cup chopped carrots
2 tablespoons butter, cut into cubes
¼ teaspoon dried savory, sage or thyme
Salt and pepper
6 thick slices bacon
¼ cup flour
¾ cups whole milk

1. Preheat the oven to 350 degrees. Remove the duck giblets. If you choose, chop and sauté the giblets and set them aside to toss into the gravy later.

2. Prick the duck's skin with a fork. Rinse and pat dry with paper towels. Twist the wing tips under the back and place the duck, breast side up, on a rack set in a roasting pan. Stuff onions, carrots and butter into the cavity. Sprinkle the duck all over with the dried herbs and ½ teaspoon each of salt and pepper. Lay bacon slices crosswise over the breast. Roast duck in the oven until the internal temperature reaches 180 degrees, 1 ½ to 2 hours.

3. Place duck on a serving platter and tent with foil. Remove vegetables from cavity. (Check to see if the vegetables are edible. If still raw, microwave until tender and feed to the dogs.)

4. Prepare the gravy by pouring off all but 3 tablespoons of the fat from the pan. Place the pan over medium heat. Using a wooden spoon, scrape up the burned bits stuck to the bottom and then sprinkle with the flour. Cook, stirring, to toast the flour, about 3 minutes. Add the milk and ½ cup water. Bring to a boil, then reduce the heat and simmer. If too thick, loosen with water. Season with salt and pepper to taste.

RECIPE INDEX

❧

EDITOR'S ACKNOWLEDGMENTS

Thanks to all the food writers and editors who shared with me their own favorite pieces of the year, even when written by others—what a remarkably generous group of professionals you are. Thanks also to the good folks at New York City's Kitchen Arts and Letters bookstore, who helped get worthy books into my hands. Matthew, Cisca, and Nat deserve thanks, too, for their unfailing editorial support. Most of all, my gratitude goes out to Bob, Hugh, Tom, and Grace, who put up with leftovers and last-minute pizza orders when deadlines loomed. I owe you more than you'll ever know.

PERMISSIONS ACKNOWLEDGMENTS

About the Editor

Holly Hughes is a writer, the former executive editor of Fodor's Travel Publications and author of *Frommer's 500 Places to Take the Kids Before They Grow Up.*

Submissions for *Best Food Writing 2009*

Submissions and nominations for *Best Food Writing 2009* should be forwarded no later than June 1, 2009, to Holly Hughes at Best Food Writing 2009, c/o Da Capo Press, 387 Park Avenue South, Penthouse, New York, NY 10016, or e-mailed to best.food@perseusbooks.com. We Regret that, due to volume, we cannot acknowledge receipt of all submissions.